Hammaming in the Sham

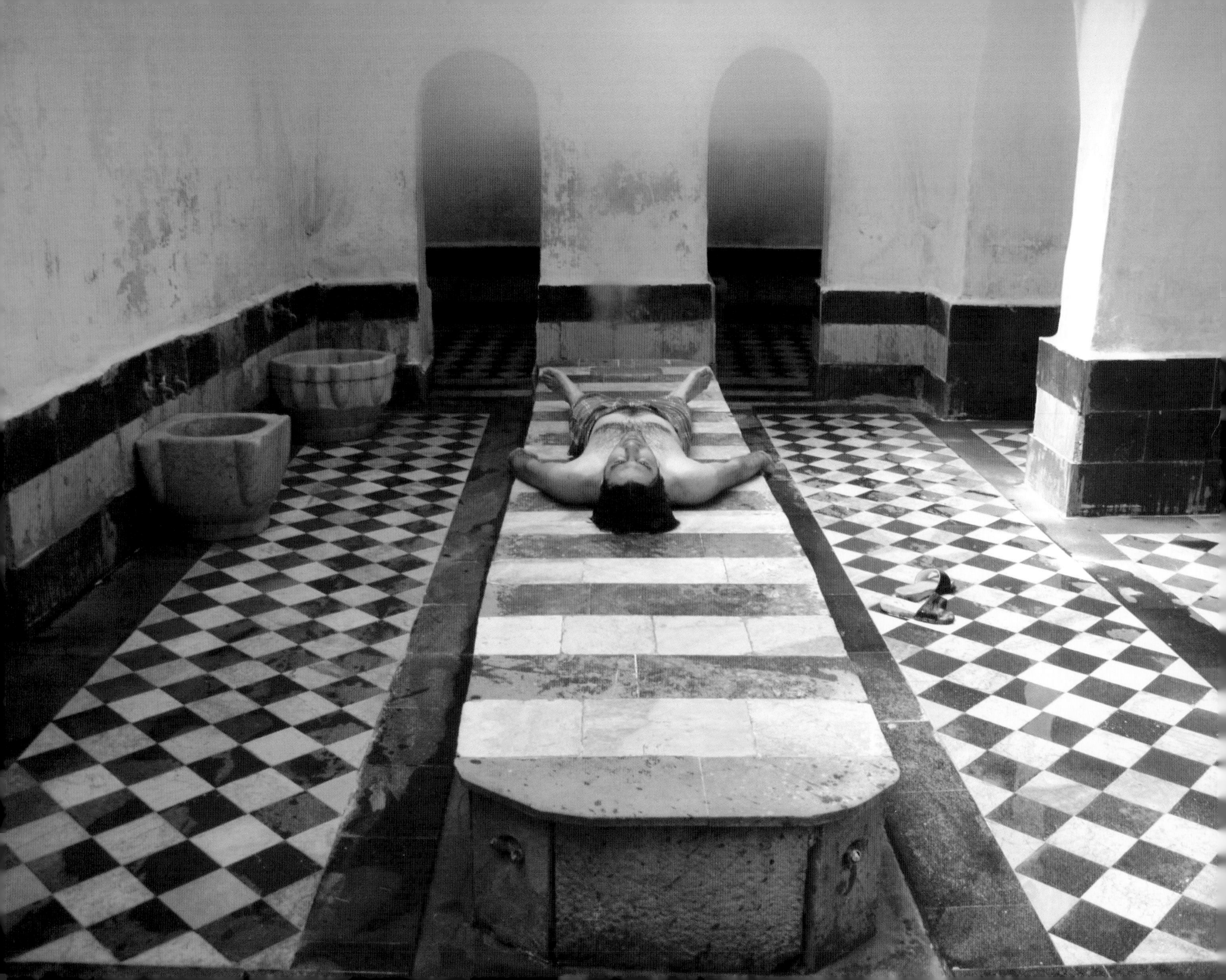

Hammaming in the Sham

A Journey through the Turkish Baths of Damascus, Aleppo and Beyond

Richard Boggs

Garnet
PUBLISHING

Hammaming in the Sham
A Journey Through the Turkish Baths of Damascus, Aleppo and Beyond

Published by
Garnet Publishing Limited
8 Southern Court
South Street
Reading
RG1 4QS
UK

www.garnetpublishing.co.uk
www.twitter.com/Garnetpub
www.facebook.com/Garnetpub
garnetpub.wordpress.com

First Paperback Edition, 2012

ISBN: 978-1-85964-284-9

British Library Cataloguing-in-Publication Data
A catalogue record for this book is available from the British Library

Typeset by Samantha Barden
Jacket design by David Rose

Printed and bound in Lebanon by International Press:
interpress@int-press.com

To my father,
and in memory of my mother

Contents

Acknowledgements viii

Glossary ix

Introduction 1

1 Hammaming in Bilad al-Sham 3

2 Cathedrals of the Flesh 63

3 Aleppo and Beyond 115

4 Revival 155

Epilogue 173

Index 177

Acknowledgements

I would like to thank the managers and workers in the hammams of Syria for allowing me to enter their world.

Thanks also to Alan Cockburn, Laurence Bardout, Omar Berakdar and my sister Diane for reading the text. Any mistakes are my own!

My thanks to my brother Jonathan and his wife Karen for time by the sea in Cloughey.

Finally, I would like to thank Dan Nunn and Samantha Barden at Garnet. I wrote the text and took the photographs, but they have created this book.

Glossary

The meaning of words given below is for how they are used in this text.

Ablaq
Banding of contrasting stone

Bab
Gateway, door or city gate

Badieh
The wilderness

Barakah
Blessing or spiritual power believed to reside in holy places and persons

Barrani
The first of the hammam's three bathing rooms where temperatures are not very hot; the first main room of the hammam

Beit al-nar
The hot part of the floor in the *jouwani* over the heating duct

Bilad al-Sham
The region bordering the eastern Mediterranean that is roughly equivalent to the modern states of Syria and Lebanon and part of Palestine

Derwish
Sufi mystic; poor person

Finjan
A small cup with no handle, for coffee

Foul
Brown fava beans

Futa
A long piece of cloth like a light towel that is worn when bathing

Hadith
Saying attributed to the Prophet Mohammed

Hajj
The pilgrimage to Mecca

Halal
Lawful or permitted in Islamic law

Hamam
Variant spelling of *hammam*, used to refer to public baths in Turkey

Hammam
Public bathing house, often called a Turkish bath in English; rooms for bathing in a private house

Haram
Forbidden in Islam. Informally, you might show disapproval of someone's actions by saying *Haram!*

Haramlek
The private family area of an Ottoman house

Hijama
A traditional kind of blood letting in which 'bad blood' is removed through the use of suction cups

Hijri
The Islamic calendar, the first year of which dates from the Prophet Mohammed's migration from Mecca to Medina

Imam
The leader of a mosque's congregation

Jelabiyah
A tunic-like garment that usually reaches the ankles

Jinn
Spirits believed by Muslims to have free will and to influence humanity

Jouwani
The hottest room in the hammam (apart from the steam room) where bathers sweat it out

Kibbeh
A traditional Syrian food of fried bulgur and minced beef

Leef
A circular sisal scrub that is used to clean the bather's skin

Madrassah
School; school for religious studies

Maqqam
A shrine

Maqsurah
Smaller, more private room off the main rooms in a hammam

Maristan
A hospital (often attached to a mosque)

Mashrabīyah
Latticed window overlooking a street

Mi'allim
The manager, the one in charge

Minbar
Pulpit

Miraj
The Prophet Mohammed's ascent into the heavens

Mukeyyis
The person whose job is to exfoliate the bather's skin in the hammam

Muqarnas
Decoration that gives a 'stalactite' effect to a dome or entrance

Nargileh
Pipe for smoking, the smoke being cooled through water

Naoura
Water wheel used to raise water from a river

Ramadan
The Islamic month of fasting

Sebil
A drinking fountain

Selamlek
The public quarters of an Ottoman home

Shebab
Youths; the lads

Sheikh
An elderly leader of the community

Silsileh
Chain

Sirwal
Loose-fitting trousers traditionally worn in the Arab world

Suq
Market; market place

Tasai
Bowl used for pouring water over the body when washing

Wali
A saintly person; governor

Waqf
Endowment or trust

Wasta
Someone who acts as an intermediary

Wastani
The moderately warm room in the hammam which connects the *barrani* with the *jouwani*

Ziyārah
Pilgrimage to, or worshipping at, a holy person's tomb or holy site

Introduction

The *Ecclesiastical History of Socrates* talks of Bishop Sisinnios, who 'was accustomed to indulge himself by wearing smart new garments, and by bathing twice a day in the public baths. When someone asked him why he, a bishop, bathed himself twice a day, he replied: "Because you do not give me time for a third."'

William Dalrymple[1]

With the First Lieutenant

It was in a restaurant in Damascus that I announced my intention. I would often go to eat with the first lieutenant when he had officially finished his duties, and we would dip together into the usual dishes of *foul* beans and hummus as the waiters served us with affable ease.

Despite his position, the lieutenant had a mischievous approach to life, and we sometimes discussed topics that were not normally broached in Syria. (I never knew whether his work extended into the evenings when we ate out or drank arak together on the balcony of my flat, or whether it was just his enquiring mind that led the lieutenant to seek out the company of foreigners.)

Eventually I confided in the first lieutenant my project. But the announcement wasn't met with the lieutenant's usual laughter (like when he raised his glass of arak on the balcony and called out an irreverent toast). Indeed, on hearing my plans the lieutenant was genuinely shocked:

– You can't do that! You must have permission!

I would write a book about the hammams of Syria, recording their traditions even as they disappeared. Strangely enough, although he disapproved of the project, and knew some things about hammams, the first lieutenant had never actually been to one. His explanation for this was clear enough:

– We are a simple people in Lattakia, and we bathe in the sea.

I laughed it off, the first lieutenant's disapproval, for this was where our outlooks would never match. I was a man with a mission, but not the kind of assignment that most foreigners are suspected of entertaining in this region of the world. Like in that film *The Swimmer* where Burt Lancaster strips bare and dives into American society, crossing swimming pool after suburban pool across Connecticut, so, with only a towel wrapped around my waist (a waist that is somewhat expanding with Syrian cuisine and middle age), and with a bar of Aleppo soap scented of bay and myrtle in my hand, I would hammam my way across Syria, from Damascus right up to Aleppo, if not beyond.

Notes

1 Dalrymple, William, *From the Holy Mountain* (Harper Collins, 1997), p. 37.

1

Hammaming in Bilad al-Sham

'The hamam, after all, was an Islamic
interpretation of the Roman bath.'[1]

A History Lesson in a Hammam

Damascus is not without its history.

In the mountains above Damascus Cain is said to have killed Abel, the very mountain-side opening in horror at the deed. But then Adam himself is said to have been formed from the clay of the River Barada[2] that rises in the snowy mountains of the ante-Lebanon and waters the desert plain, creating a green girdle of orchards around the city, 'like a halo around the moon'.

If you climb up the illegal settlements above the Friday Market you can still visit the shrine on Mount Qassioun that marks the first spilling of human blood. The guide to the shrine will genially point out where a hand is imprinted in the rock, with the word 'Allah' in the rock alongside it, above where the rock surface is dabbed with a splash of red paint, just for effect. Fashionable young women cover themselves and earnestly pray at the shrine, or light a candle perhaps, for in Syria such holy places are often common to both Christians and Muslims.

From the mountaintop Damascus can be seen spreading out in the oasis below, the dull brown of the city shaped like a comet's tail[3] in the surrounding vegetation, before the greenness yields to desert. From the line of cafés cut across the mountain, parts of the city are quite distinct below: the jumble of flat roofs of those who have just settled beneath; the cupolas of the line of mosques and tombs that is Salihiye; the boulevard of Abu Roumaneh stretching through the posh suburbs where I taught. Through the haze you might just make out the maze of alleys that is the old city, and even the minarets and dome of the Umayyad Mosque, the landmark towards which everything is orientated.

My interest, however, lies not so much in the mosque as in the hammams near its doors. Two of the best hammams in Syria are just outside the walls of the Umayyad Mosque, and in one of these, Hammam al-Malek al-Zaher, I had perhaps my simplest lesson in Syrian history.

The hammam is named after the Mamluk sovereign who drove the Crusaders out of Syria, but in fact predates al-Malek al-Zaher's rule, for the baths were once part of a tenth-century house. One corner of the hammam has a Roman pillar incorporated into its structure, no doubt borrowed from the site of the nearby temple and, maybe a millennium later, still not returned.

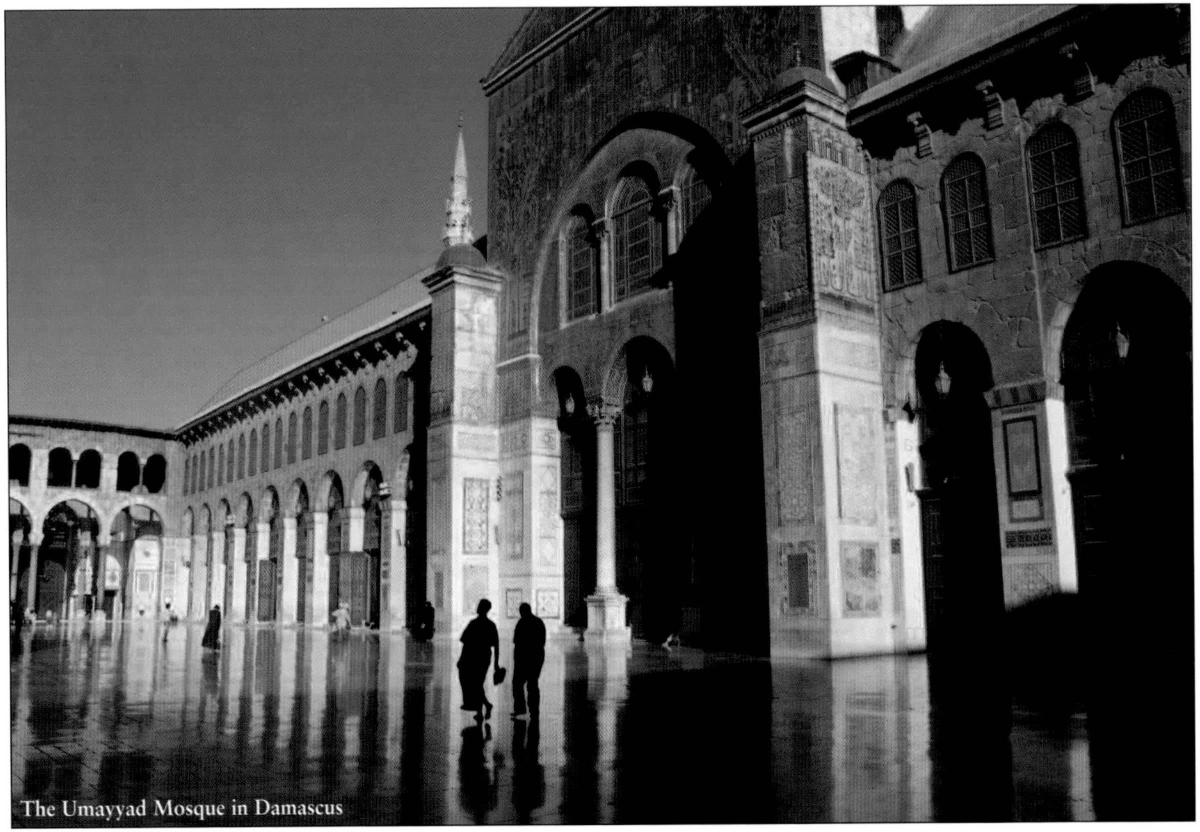

The Umayyad Mosque in Damascus

I knew the hammam from the days when it was plastered over in tiles of dubious effect. If the beauty of the east is veiled, hidden so that it is not exposed to the public eye, this has certainly been true of the hammams of Syria: hammams going back seven or eight hundred years have been covered in the kind of tiles that might have graced your auntie's bathroom in the 1970s.

As I crossed the hammam one day in my wooden clogs (clogs are the traditional footwear of the hammam, to avoid contact with the impurities of another's bath water) I had my usual banter with the attendants:

– *Ya, Irlandi!* I called to one of the workers.

He laughed, and one of the other attendants joined in:

– And why do you call him Irish?
– Well, look at his red hair!
– And what would you call me?
– You? You're absolutely Damascene.
– Not me! I'm Caucasian.

And indeed, although the country is officially called the Syrian Arab Republic, there is a wealth of non-Arab minorities within its borders. On closer examination the attendant's looks did support his claim.

– I'm Caucasian. My family were from Turkey.

My geography of the region wasn't good enough to challenge the equation of the Caucasus with Turkey, but I concurred:

– Ah! Like the hammam itself! We are after all in a Turkish bath.

At this point I was most decidely corrected by the 'Caucasian' attendant:

– Not at all. This bath isn't Turkish; it's Roman.

And here there is a linguistic problem, for the word used in Arabic for the public baths – *hammam* – can most easily be translated into English as 'Turkish bath', a term which is probably inappropriate for the hammams I explore, and a phrase this attendant objected to. I conceded:

– Okay. It's not Turkish. It's probably Mamluk.

We were standing in a hammam named after a great Mamluk leader, and the Mamluks were, after the Romans, bathers *sans pareil*. The attendant, however, would not compromise:

– No, the hammam is Roman. Even this arch in front of you is Roman.

I wasn't convinced by the arch, for the interiors of hammams are often much modified, and this hammam underwent a makeover or two even during my time in Syria. I had to admit, however, that the other great hammam just down the way, Hammam Silsileh, did advertise itself as a 'Roman Bath'. But here in Hammam al-Malek al-Zaher, as we stood by the stacks of green Aleppan soap made from laurel and olives, and the piled circles of saisal with which the next bathers would scrub themselves down in their communal wash, I received the simplest explanation of the development of the hammams in Syria.

The attendant gave me my history lesson in colloquial Arabic, for if he had little classical Arabic, I had none:

– Here we are just by the Umayyad Mosque. The mosque was once the Roman Temple of Jupiter.

I agreed with the obvious. And before it had been Jupiter's it had been a site of worship for Haddad, an Aramean god. Haddad had not so much been ousted in a religious coup as absorbed into the civilisation which followed, just as in Lebanon the Virgin Mary has been absorbed into traditions of Rome's Diana, and has been traditionally pictured with the moon beneath her feet.[4]

The attendant went on:

– So the Romans would have bathed here before going to the Temple.

I concurred:

– And the hammam is built according to the classic Roman structure of three rooms. And after the Romans came the

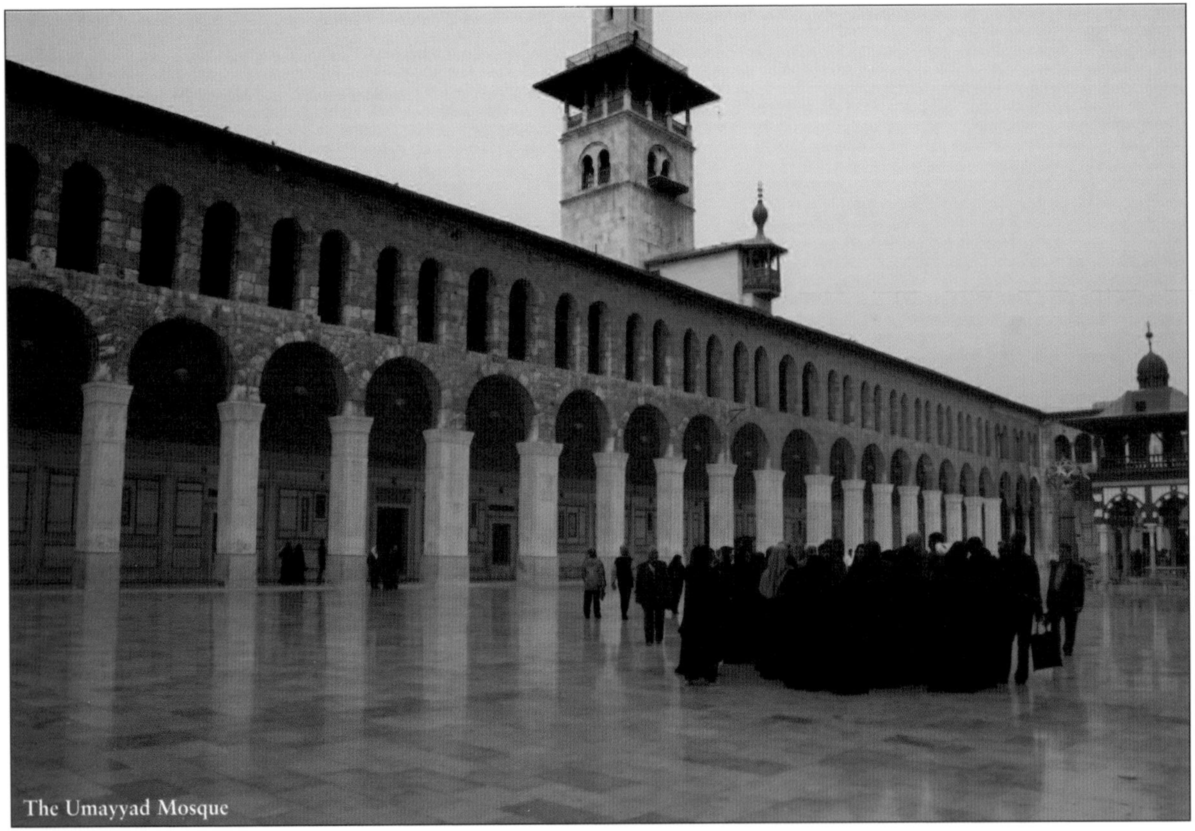
The Umayyad Mosque

Christians. And they made the temple into a church.

– Okay.

– And they would have bathed before they went to church.

– Maybe.

(I had my doubts about this one, for there were people who claimed that those who were baptised in Christ had no need of further washing.)

– And after Christianity came Islam.

– And Muslims bathe here in this hammam before Friday prayers.

It all made sense: civilisation after civilisation had taken the city, adapting the site that was once a temple to the god Haddad for their religious needs. But the conquerors must have claimed not just the holy site but the neighbouring hammams, for some kind of ritual cleansing is generally part and parcel of religious duties.

I doubted whether this hammam had ever been Roman, although archaeologists are excavating a Roman hammam at the Umayyad Mosque's south gate. But the first principle of hammaming was clear: Syria's hammaming traditions were inherited from the Romans.

Aphamea

A friend had told me of a hammam in Aphamea, the ruins of a city of the Seleucid Empire, famed for the cavalry horses bred among its rich pastures.[5] My stated goal was the hammam, but who could come to Syria and not visit Aphamea? Antony and Cleopatra had once passed through its colonnades.

In pursuit of this hammam, I got off the bus after the Arab castle of Shayzar, beyond which the Orontes River flows by ancient water wheels. An unhurried throng of motorbikes at an intersection was functioning as a taxi fleet. Soon I was passing through rolling countryside with Mohammed, not unhandsome in the red-checked keffiyeh wrapped around his head *à la Arafat*. The great plain of the Orontes below us was all neatly cultivated squares, and I savoured a landscape of cornfields and olives.

We drove through wheat fields that seemed to stretch as far as the distant haze of the Ansariye Mountains, until at a T-junction two men in seriously grey suits stopped us. They seemed a little out of place in the cornfields around us; guarding an embassy in Damascus might have been more their milieu. They asked

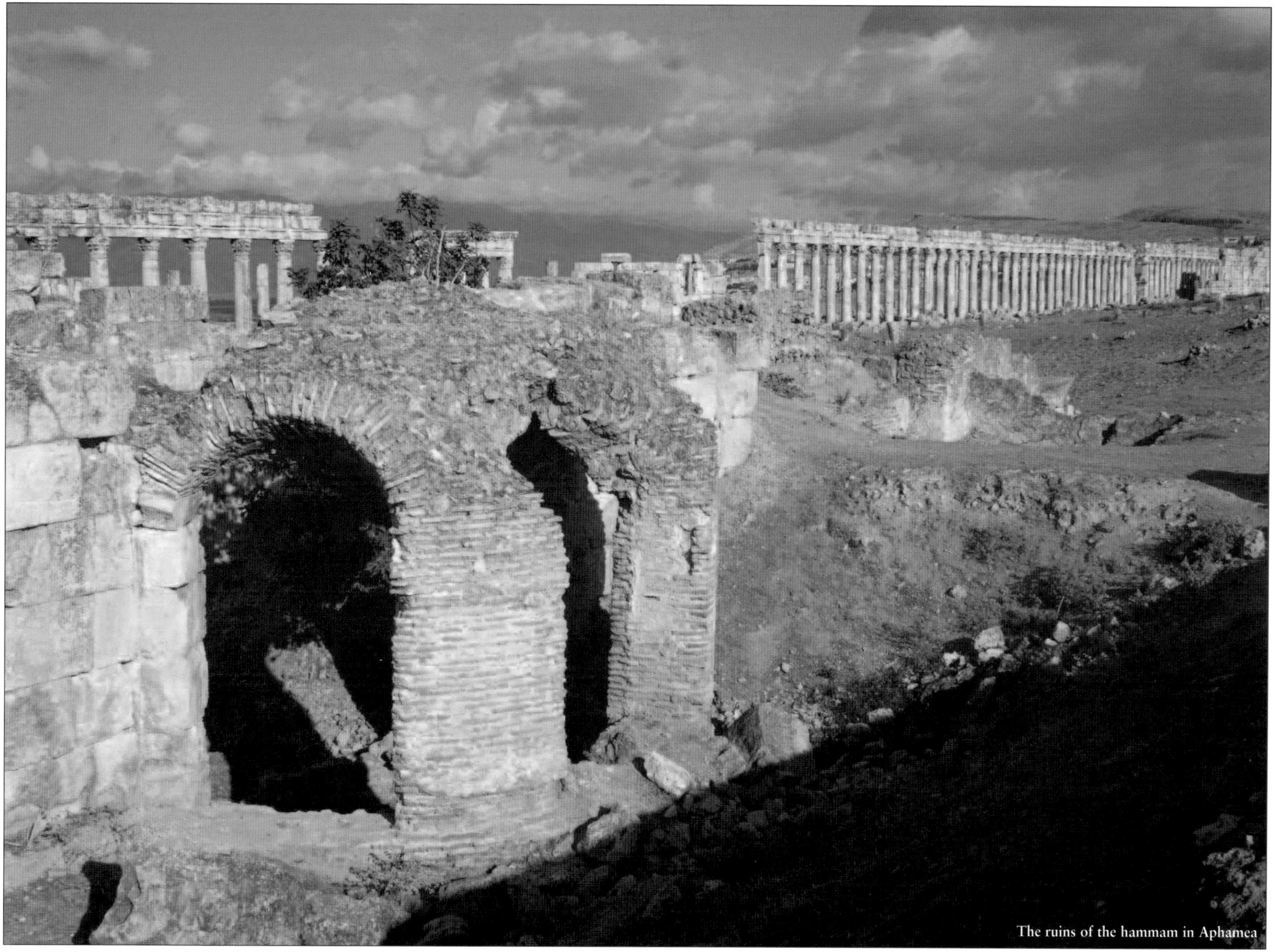

The ruins of the hammam in Aphamea

Mohammed where he was taking me. Surely we weren't trying to avoid the ticket office?

They seemed to know Mohammed, and I relaxed a bit. I could even buy a ticket at the Syrian not the foreigners' rate, they suggested. Or even better, why didn't we enter the ruins by the far side and avoid the ticket office altogether? Or, best of all (and here, for some reason, there was a bit of a chuckle), Mohammed himself could take me directly to the hammam! I must admit I was a little surprised to think of the hammam as still functioning – it must have been some kind of natural spring that the locals still used. And so we set off again over the gentle undulations, a breeze almost caressing us through the wheat as we travelled.

Suddenly the colonnades of Aphamea rose up from among the corn. That is all there was: two clean lines of limestone colonnades stretching for a mile above the swirling patterns of corn, with the harvesters making their way through the wheat.

True to his promise, Mohammed avoided the golden splendour of the pillars and took me directly to the hammam. The locals certainly were not bathing, for here there was neither fountain nor pool; my destination was a dried-out ruin part way along the colonnade. Two fairly spacious rooms formed the ruined Roman hammam: a curved inner room that sported a fig tree growing out of the rubble, and another room with a central arch that framed part of the colonnade. I had to admit that although the hammam itself was a bit of a let-down, it had a prime site by the *cardo maximus* and one of the best views in Syria.

After Mohammed and I had argued over the fare, for he had refused to let me pay anything, my driver disappeared, and a local 'guide' arrived, offering both information ('the colonnade has 1,200 columns...') and local antiquities. The antique coins offered – one Byzantine, one from the time of Queen Zenobia in Palmyra, and one 'Arab' – were rather tempting, and they could have been bought with an easy conscience, for they had probably just been manufactured up the road in Homs.

When the guide went off, I sat in the shade of the votive column near the baths. The fields were half-harvested, the reapers were resting in the shade of a lorry, and sheep were munching as gleaners among the stubble. My only companions were now the birds: kites flew overhead, swallows chirped among imperial glory, and an owl perched on the colonnade looked down on everything, even though it was midday. Where else in the world could you arrive at such a site and be the only visitor?

I sat in the stillness of the afternoon and read from a book of poems that I had picked up in a tired old Mamluk hammam in Homs that functioned not just as a place for the poor to wash, but as a second-hand bookshop for undergraduates. A hammam in Homs might seem a rather unlikely place to buy the *Penguin Book of English Verse*, but there has been an interesting relationship between books and hammams. Wasn't a library an essential part of the Roman hammam? Bathers may once have reclined to read in the hammam I had just visited.

The corn grew right up to the columns, and spilled onto the paving stones where the ruts made by the cartwheels of travellers on their way to Antioch maybe two millennia ago could still be seen. I settled down to some pre-Elizabethan poetry:

They flee from me that
sometime did me seek

With naked fote stalking
within my chamber.

This is how it would be at almost any site I visited in Syria. In the oasis city of Palmyra, below the towers of the dead, I found hammam ruins scattered by the desert colonnade. At Serjilla, one of the many 'Dead Cities' between Hama and Aleppo, the hammam was so grand I at first mistook it for a Byzantine church. This civilisation – once rich in olives and wine and wheat – had fallen into stony oblivion, perhaps as the Byzantines and Umayyads fought it out. The hammam, however, survives as the greatest monument of town life; bathing was civilisation.

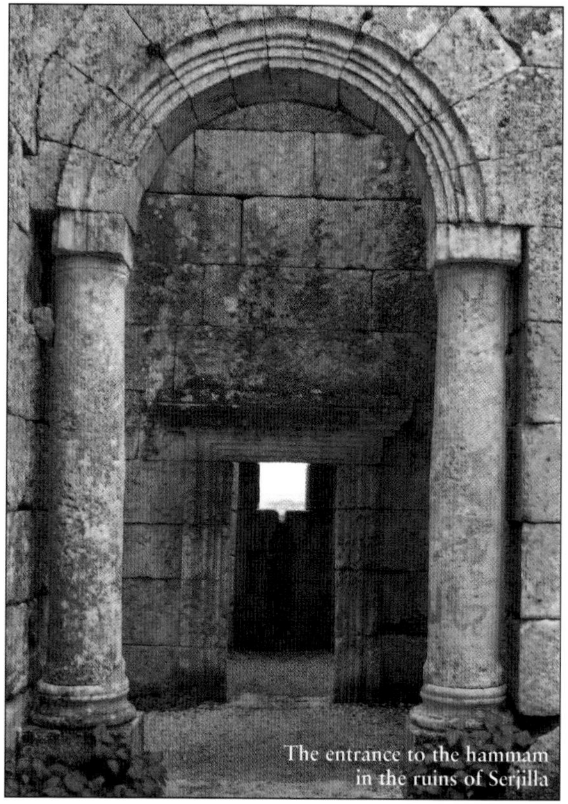

The entrance to the hammam in the ruins of Serjilla

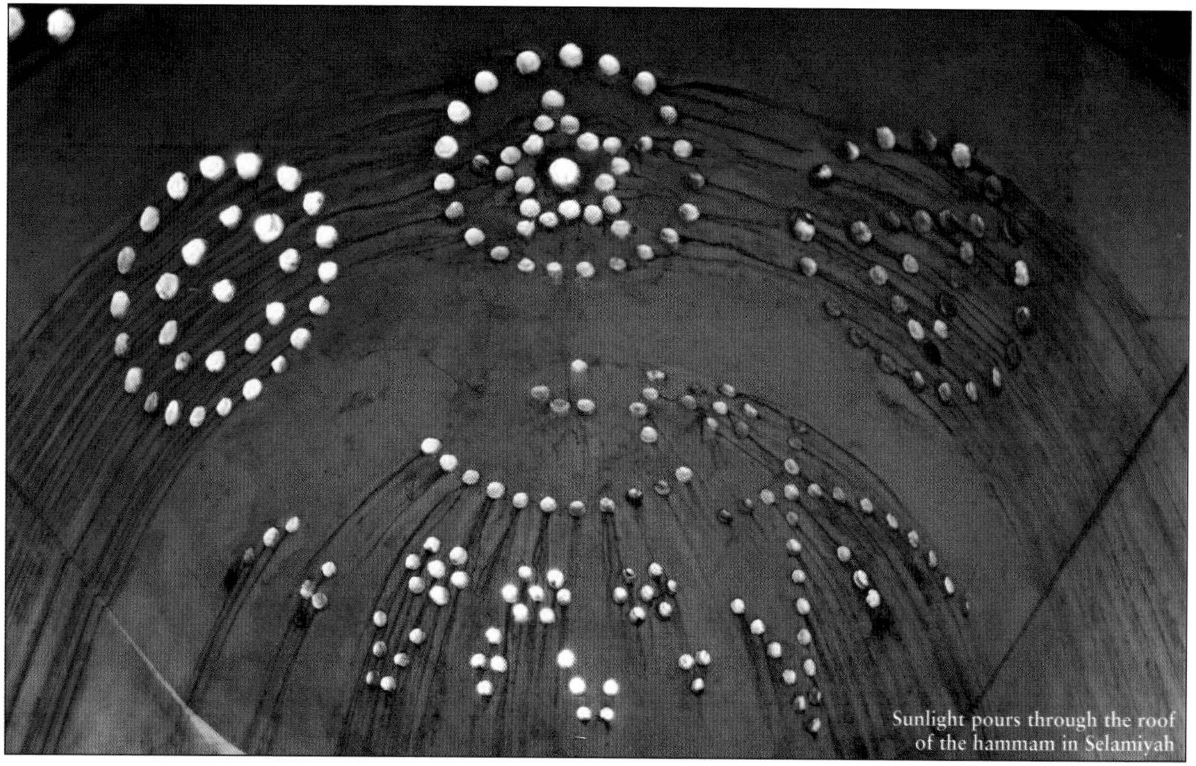

Sunlight pours through the roof of the hammam in Selamiyah

A Roman Tradition

It is perhaps in Bosra that the Roman baths of Syria are most evident, but even in the Ismaili town of Selamiyah the Roman origins of its hammam are evident. It wasn't really by design that I went to Bosra; on my way to Dera'a (where T. E. Lawrence lived out his fantasies with the Turks) a Palestinian passenger on the bus invited me to visit Bosra instead. It is a foolish traveller who doesn't forgo the set itinerary in response to a spontaneous invitation, and I accepted.

After travelling through barren, basalt landscapes, I found myself taking in the ruins of Bosra's South Baths, a massive structure with a columned porch, as impressive as Bosra's Byzantine cathedral to the east. Through the porch was a domed vestibule where the bather would have undressed in spacious splendour. The hammam's architecture reflected the stages through which the bather would have progressed. The vestibule led to the cold room, which in turn led to the warm room, which had a hot room on either side where bathers would have sweated it out.

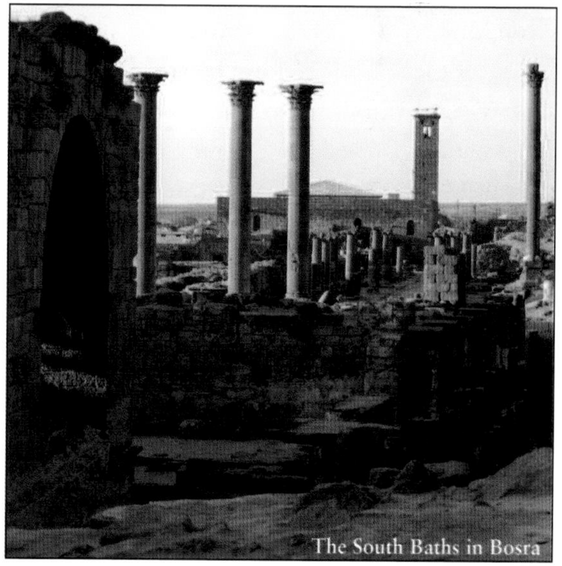

The South Baths in Bosra

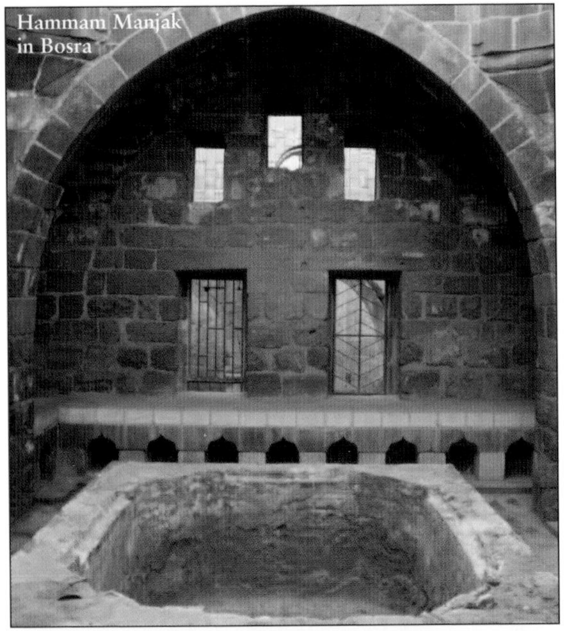

Hammam Manjak in Bosra

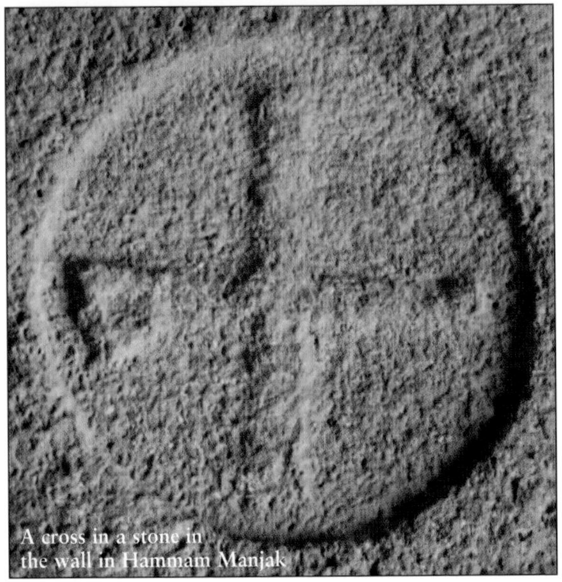

A cross in a stone in the wall in Hammam Manjak

But the South Baths is not the only hammam in Bosra. Opposite the Mosque of the Caliph Omar I found Hammam Manjak. This hammam is not Roman but was constructed in the fourteenth century by those great builders of hammams, the Mamluks. Although it does not have the T-shape of Bosra's Roman hammam, the Mamluk hammam essentially mirrors the Roman hammam's structure.

Built opposite a mosque rather than near a temple, (a mosque with Byzantine pillars absorbed into its walls), its entrance rooms led to a reception room where a raised pool filled the central floor. From here a corridor led to the hammam proper. But I had problems checking the hammam within; the building was locked. One of the great travel quests in the Arab world is to find the man with the key to the public monument, but I jumped up on to one of the walls to view the maze of piped cubicles beneath.

Here pilgrims who had left Damascus to travel to Mecca on the *hajj* would have cleansed themselves before setting out again on their desert crossing. Clearly the Mamluks were into recycling, for stones with crosses from some nearby church and symbols that were precursors of the swastika from a place of worship were incorporated into the walls of the hammam's outer rooms.

Bosra had appeal: the ruins were not just at the heart of a community, but incorporated into the homes, the stones of the great monuments having been carried off to build the local houses. (It is the same all over Syria: the citadel in Aleppo was stripped of the casing that covered its slopes to furnish the buildings beneath, just as in Cairo the limestone that once covered the pyramids was recycled to furnish the mosques.)

Near the local bakery citizens set circles of unleavened bread to cool on the remains of ancient pillars. That for me was the charm of the place: these were living ruins – and I had the place to myself. But unfortunately, in order to conform to the perceived tastes of Westerners doing tours of the Levant, many of the local people had been moved out of their homes and their basalt-built houses were now blocked up. Sanitisation in the name of tourism – the authentic local culture replaced with something artificial – was already underway.

In terms of size, Bosra's Roman hammam could have competed with the local Byzantine cathedral, but not with its amphitheatre. I thought of the Swiss explorer John Lewis Burckhardt, who had travelled through the basalt landscapes of the Houran two centuries earlier, but missed Bosra's greatest monument: one of the biggest amphitheatres outside Rome then lay beneath the sands. Further down the road in what is now Jordan, Burckhardt did receive his consolation prize; pursuing rumours of a hidden city, he stumbled across Petra and its Nabatean sepulchres, the mountains carved out to house the dead in monumental splendour.

I could live with Bosra without its amphitheatre, for I never felt that Syria for me should be a reverent perusal of historical sites. When I think back on Bosra it is not just its basalt monuments that I remember; there was the Palestinian home with its begonias in pots and Islamic texts and photographs of the brothers on the walls and a supper of cheese and olives. In the evening, my host's brother, a student at the technical school, sat next to me in his khakis, his arm slung over my shoulder. Even when travelling there is no escape from the role of English teacher, and I was given his course book to explain:

> The good tradesman always takes a pride in his work... Even when his boss is absent he continues to work, for it is his work that he loves...

It was further along that bleak basalt landscape, in the Druze area near Suweida, that I sat with friends by the ruins of a Byzantine church with vine leaves carved on its entrance, and sarcophagi scattered in its depths. In vain we scanned the landscape for the grove of oaks mentioned in the guide book. Finally we realized that the grove that evaded us was in fact the single surviving oak right above our heads.

I suppose that was the day that put Roman pillars and Byzantine ruins in perspective for me. In that basalt plateau of the Druze there is hardly a roundabout or a garden wall that doesn't exhibit a sculpted lion or a Roman pillar, or some unread Greek inscription across the lintel of a doorway.

Syria for me was not going to be a diligent exploration of dead ruins. I would study a more living architecture – the hammams, and the world that they contained.

A Tradition Absorbed

At the end of the eighteenth century two British doctors living in Aleppo wrote their *Natural History of Aleppo*. (A European presence in Aleppo was nothing new, for there had been a Venetian consulate in the Coppersmiths' Khan opposite a hammam in the *suq* since the days of Shakespeare.)

True to the spirit of the Enlightenment, and precursing Napoleon's documenting of Egyptian life, the doctors took out their thermometers and recorded not the fevers of their patients but the temperatures of a hammam in Aleppo, moving from room to room:

> In the month of February, when the mercury in Farhenheit's thermometer stood at fifty-four, in the open air, it rose in the burany to sixty-four... From this chamber a door opens into a narrow passage, leading to the wustany or middle chamber... The thermometer in the passage rose to seventy-five, and in this chamber to ninety. From the middle chamber a door opens immediately into the inner chamber, or juany, which is much larger than the wustany, and considerably hotter, the mercury rising here to one hundred.[6]

What the Russells were documenting was the quintessential structure of the Roman hammam, reflected in the South Baths I had seen in Bosra. The first Islamic baths would have been modelled on the Roman structure, with the three-room composition typical of a Roman bath (*frigidarium*, *tepidarium* and *calidarium*) imitated in the Islamic bath. Bathing involved three rooms, with temperatures coolish in the *barrani*, moderately warm in the *wastani* (the room which connects the outer and inner rooms) and intensely hot in the *jouwani*, where the bather would have really sweated it out. In addition, hammams developed a spacious dressing room where bathers would undress and later relax after their hammam. It seemed to my amateur eye, however (scholars of Islamic architecture might see things differently!), that in many hammams the *barrani* and dressing room were one and the same.

What has changed in the structure of hammams since Mark Antony gave Syria to Cleopatra as a wedding gift, is the heating system. The Romans had a system beneath the floors of raised pillars through which heat circulated. Right in the centre of Beirut the Roman hammam system can still be seen, and at Umm Quais in the far north of Jordan, with the Sea of Galilee a haze in the distance,

I came across the heating system of a Roman hammam which still retained its essential components. In Syria, however, a system evolved in which heat and smoke from a furnace passed along a duct under the floor of the *jouwani* to a chimney.[7] Nowadays though it is steam from diesel boilers that heats the hammams.

The Arabs absorbed the Roman hammam structure, but renamed the rooms. It's simple: the outer room, the coolest, is called the *barrani*. The middle room, with a moderate heat, is called the *wastani*. The innermost room – the hottest where you experience the hammam proper – is called the *jouwani*. These three words for the main rooms of the hammam – *barrani*, *wastani* and *jouwani* – are the essential Arabic for this book.

The aesthetics of each room can be quite different. Surprisingly, one of the most beautiful Ottoman hammams in Syria can be found in the heart of the fairly characterless city of Homs; even the great documenter of Syrian monuments, Ross Burns, found little of interest in this 'rather drab city'.[8] The Ottoman hammam in the *suq* however is a wonder. The first room where you undress on raised platforms is not unlike the interior of a Methodist chapel with a rickety balcony. The *wastani* rooms connect to the innermost hammam – these are spacious and moderately

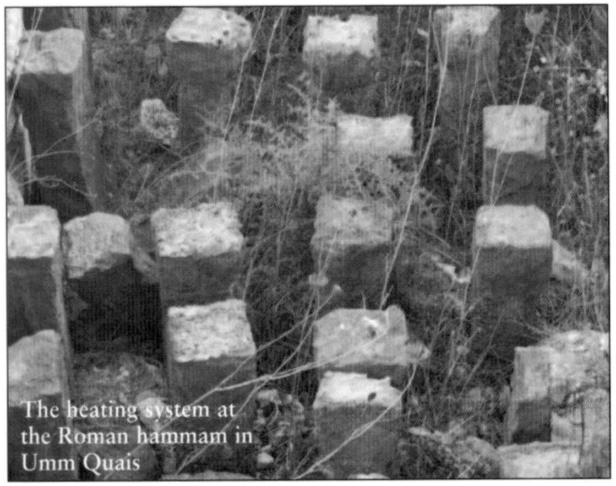

The heating system at the Roman hammam in Umm Quais

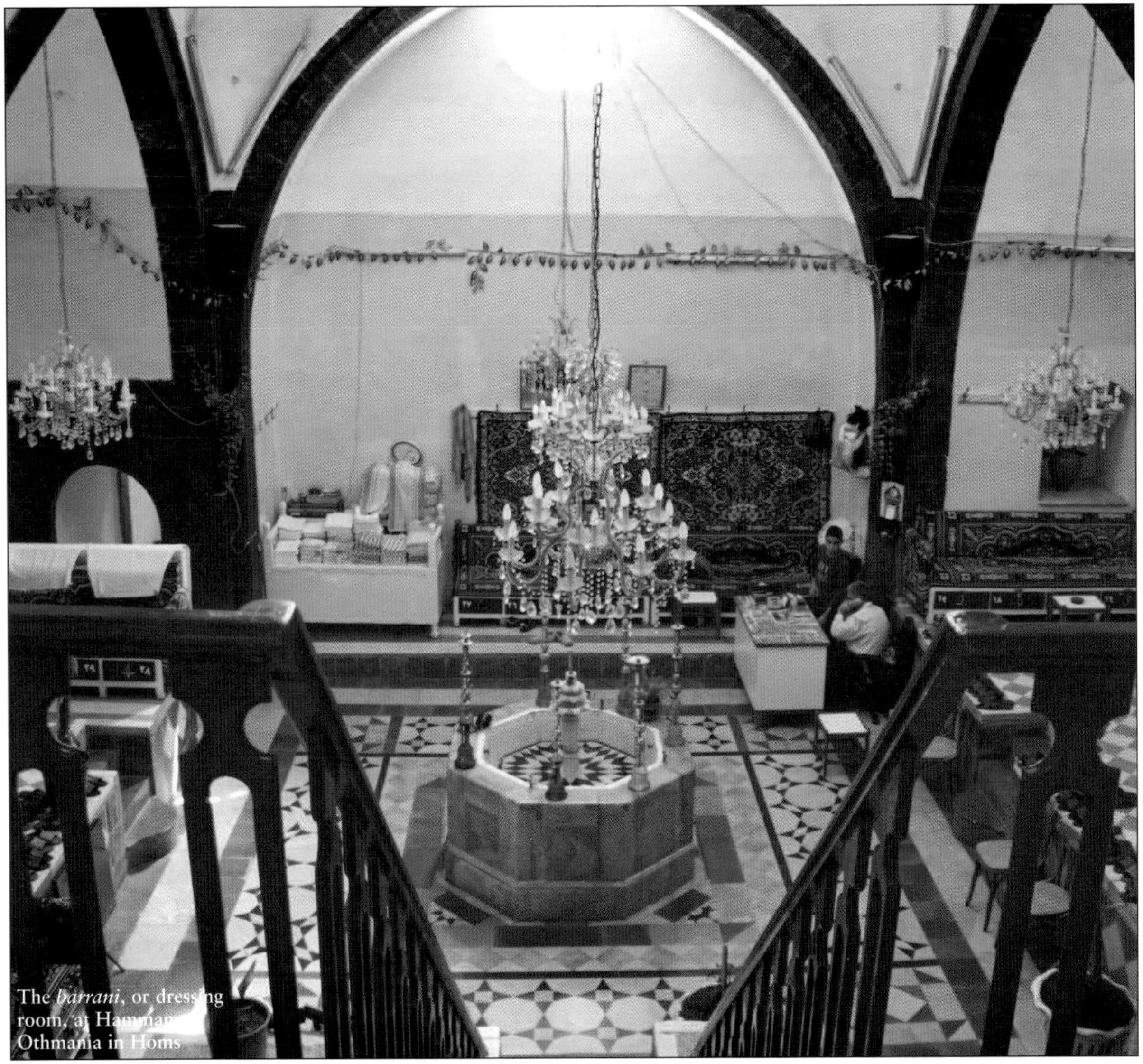

The *barrani*, or dressing room, at Hammam Othmania in Homs

cool and are really just a transitional area where you might change out of your wet towel beneath exquisite roofs or wash alone in moderate warmth. The *jouwani*, the hottest room, is the most atmospheric with its algaed walls and daylight sifting through lingering steam.

Since the Russells documented Aleppan life, many hammaming traditions have survived, but the number of bathers has certainly decreased. And I suspect that if the Russells were alive today their thermometers might not record quite the same temperatures; with the price of heating oil nowadays some hammams no longer maintain their intense heat.

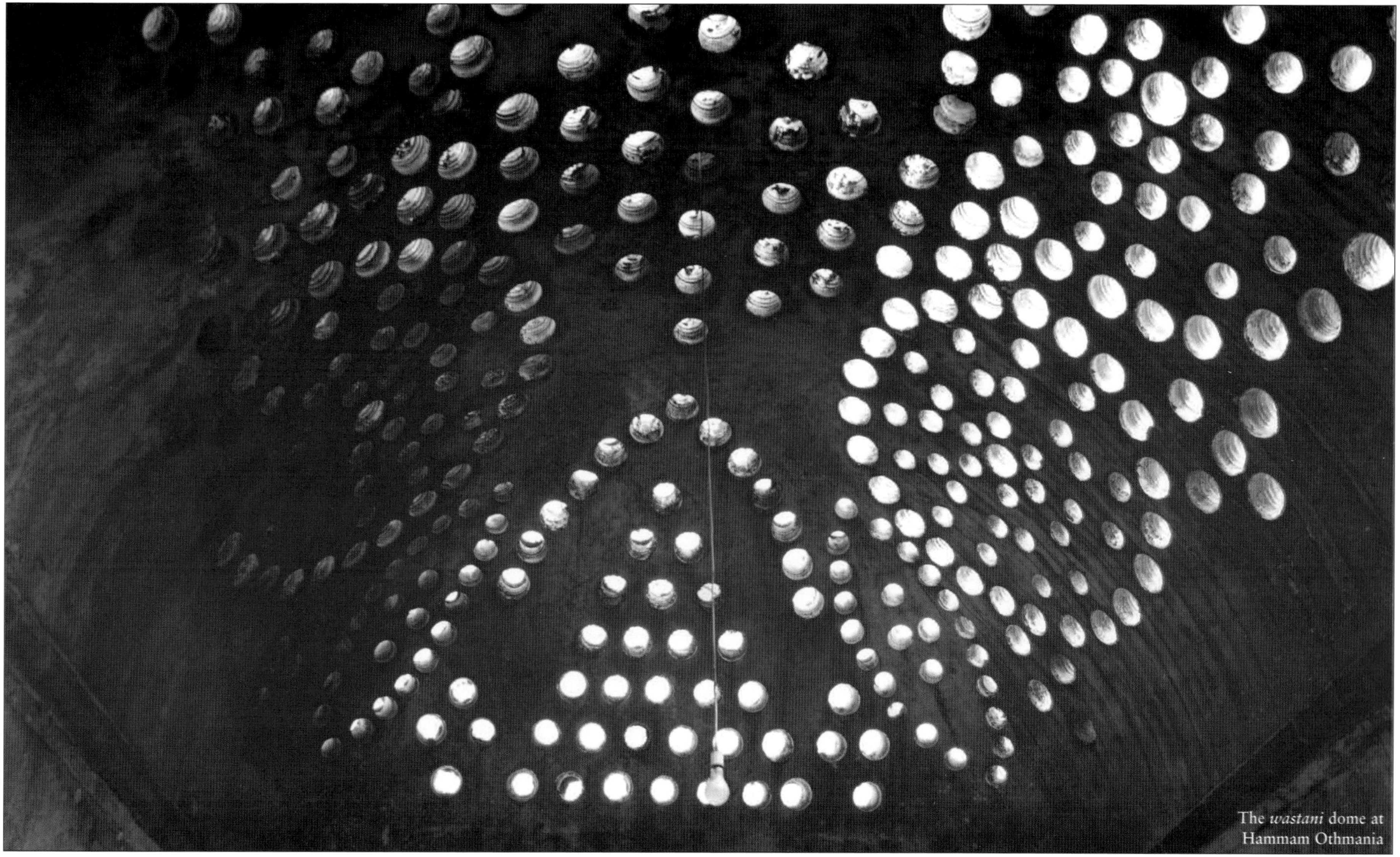
The *wastani* dome at Hammam Othmania

The atmosphere too will have changed; the candles or oil lamps that would have lit the hammams from some niche in the wall have been replaced by the harsh glare of fluorescent lights. Who could document the Arab love affair with the fluorescent tube, not to mention the loudspeaker! With one flick of a switch the dreamy afternoon light in the hammam is shattered, and the fluorescent tubes hanging like a trapeze artist's bars from the dome fix all and sundry with their unforgiving glare.

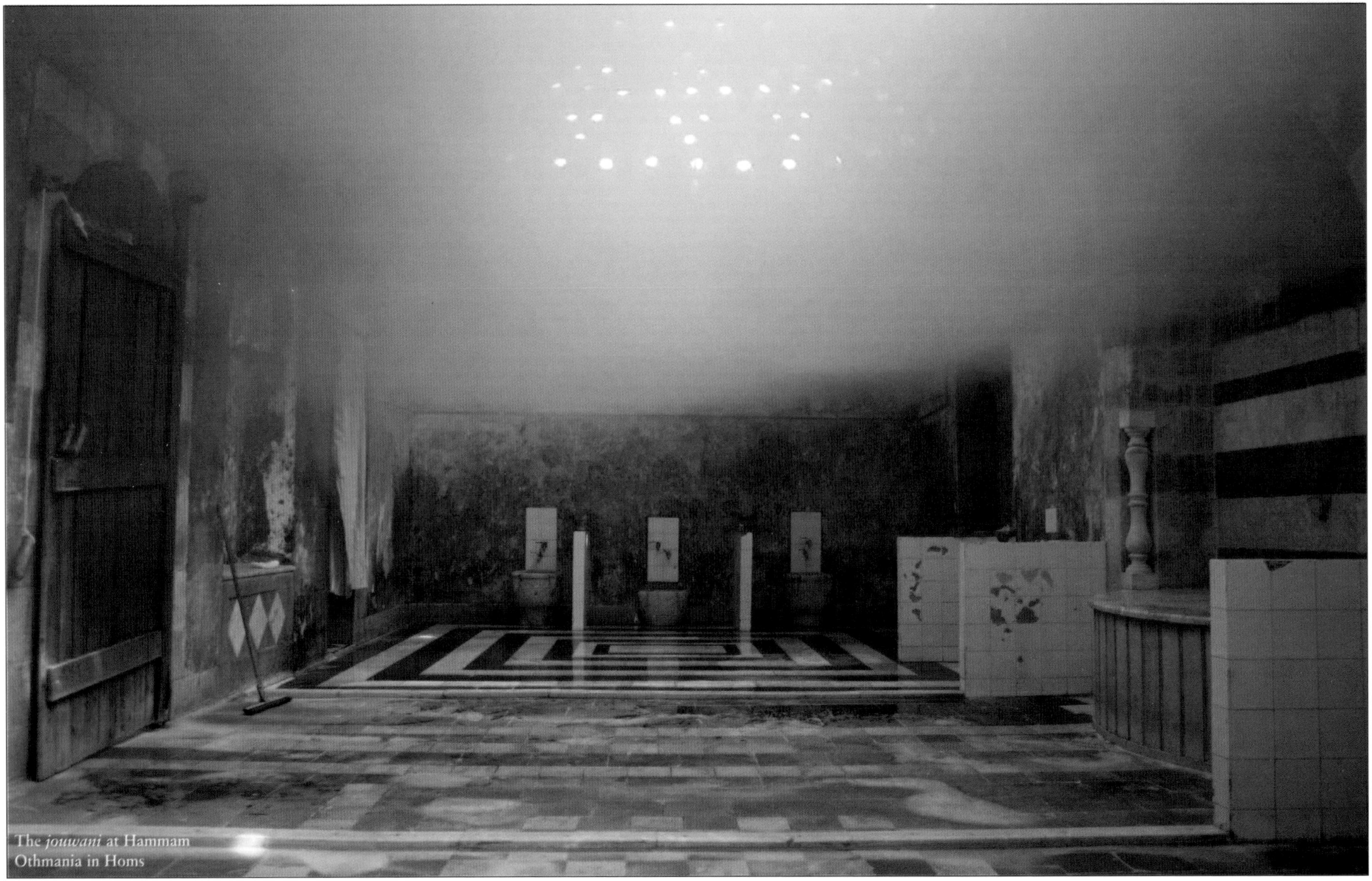

The *jouwani* at Hammam Othmania in Homs

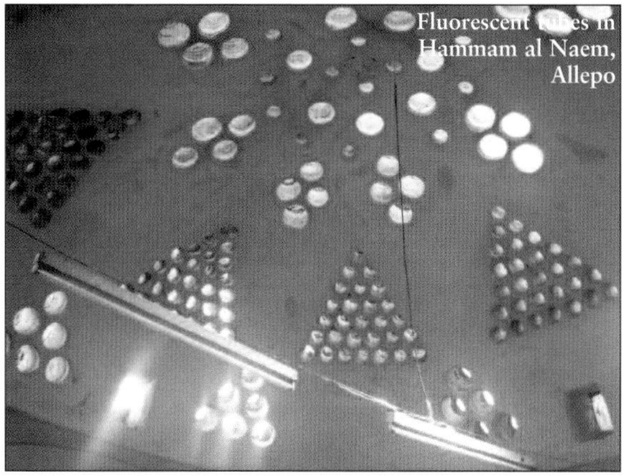

Fluorescent tubes in Hammam al Naem, Allepo

The thick electric cables falling over some intricately honeycombed doorway, the minarets of Mamluk mosques culminating in fluorescent strips, the flyover carved through an Ottoman area of Damascus – there is a general indifference to the concept of cultural heritage. In *The Street Philosopher and the Holy Fool*, Marius Kociejowski rails against the desecration of the architecture around him in Aleppo:

> Everywhere one looks there are electrical cables, makeshift repairs, advertising posters and fluorescent tubes. Who first brought in the fluorescent tube?[9]

It takes a foreigner to notice such things; for the indigeneous these unfortunate imports have become the norm.

Despite the fluorescent lighting, the basic structure of the hammam remains intact. To put it simply, a Roman tradition became an Islamic one. However, the libraries which were an integral part of the Roman bath – for the reclining citizen might have refreshed the mind as well as the body – were not brought into the Islamic bathing tradition. Indeed, it is said that with the Arab conquest of Roman Egypt the works in the great library of Alexandria were used to fuel the hammams, but this might best be taken with a pinch of salt. Given that the Arab general Amr ibn al-As reported back to the Caliph Omar that he had taken a city with 4,000 palaces, 4,000 baths and 400 theatres, it seems that the Alexandrians were not just conversant with the art of bathing.[10]

Whatever the reason, the functions of the baths were somewhat reduced; hammams serve the body, not the intellect.

Islamisation

When other cultures were conquered during the spread of Arab civilisation they were said to have 'opened to Islam', just as people are 'invited' to become Muslims – an invitation I have received more times than I care to count.

Ibn Battuta's account of the 'opening' of Damascus to Islam centres on what was then the Byzantine Church of Saint John, built on the site of the temple of Haddad in the heart of the city. (Today the pillars of the Roman temple still lead to the mosque from the *suq*, sheltering the sellers of religious books and tamarind drinks beneath.) It seems that initially there was some kind of

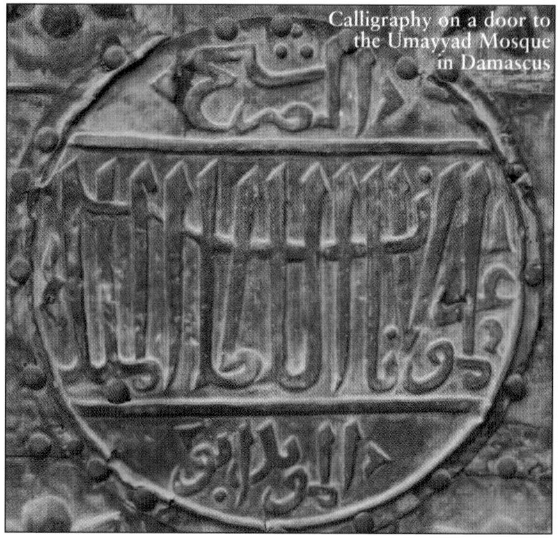

Calligraphy on a door to the Umayyad Mosque in Damascus

agreement between the local Christians and the invading Arabs; only half of the church site was appropriated as a mosque, the other half remained for Christian worship.

If we are to believe the account given by Ibn Battuta, a fourteenth-century traveller from Tangiers who spent time as a poor scholar in Damascus, the conquering forces showed exemplary tolerance:

> The site of the mosque was a church, and when the Muslims captured Damascus, one of their commanders entered from one side by the sword and reached as far as the middle of the church, while the other entered peaceably from the eastern side and reached the middle also. So the Muslims made the half of the church which they had entered by force into a mosque and the half which they had

> entered by peaceful agreement remained as a church.[11]

Indeed, in Jerusalem the Caliph Omar refused to pray in the Church of the Holy Sepulchre so that the local Christians could retain their church. Such tolerance was not unusual, with Greek-speaking Christians retaining key posts in the Umayyad Empire. The compromise concerning the Church of St John did not last, however. The Caliph Waleed, not content with half a church, laid claim to the entire site, and set about demolishing the Cathedral of Saint John with his own hands.

The Caliph Waleed sent for 12,000 artisans from the Byzantine Emperor to build the greatest wonder of Damascus, the Umayyad Mosque, all green and gold in its mosaics of pavilions and palaces, rivers and orchards, so that even today the worshipper doesn't know whether it is Damascus portrayed on the dazzling walls or paradise itself as described in the Qur'an:

> Such is the paradise promised to the righteous, streams run through it, its fruits never fail; it never lacks shade.[12]

For that world traveller of the fourteenth century, no mosque in the world could match that of Damascus for its beauty – and Ibn Battuta had prayed in many a mosque. When he left Tangiers to go on the *hajj*, it took many years for him to complete his journey; somewhat distracted, his travels took him not just to Mecca but to China. With the authority of a traveller who had covered some 13,000 miles, Ibn Battuta could finally state that the Umayyad Mosque was:

> The most magnificent mosque in the world, the finest in construction and noblest in beauty, grace and perfection; it is matchless and unequalled.[13]

What with earthquakes and fires and attempts at restoration, the mosque is not quite the marvel it was; over a century ago a workman's pipe set the roof on fire as it was being repaired with pitch, and the marvellous mosaics 'perished in incandescent showers', with the marble panelling 'crumbling into heaps of lime'.[14]

But it is still a marvel. The mosaicked courtyard is now a marbled floor, shimmering like a pool in the morning light – like that palace floor of Solomon, where the Queen of Sheba, the visiting Bilquis, thinking the floor a reflecting pool, bared her legs before the dumbfounded king to step through its waters.

The Other Wonders of Damascus

It seems that before Caliph Waleed graced the city with his mosque, the citizens of Damascus had other marvels to enjoy.

The first marvel in those days was the air – a little difficult to imagine now, with the minibuses ferrying their passengers throughout Damascus, choking the streets with diesel fumes. But even today, evening breezes blowing in from the desert still refresh the city, and it is those winds that for Gertrude Bell made Damascus a city of the desert.

A century ago this scholar of Persian poetry saw in Damascus a desert purity. For her, more than twelve hundred years after the Islamic conquest, Damascus still had the purity of the early caliphs who, although ruling an empire, still milked their goats. Damascus was the last Muslim capital to be ruled by bedouin traditions, and the desert permeated the city:

> The desert stretches up to its walls, the breath of it is blown in by every wind, the spirit of it comes through the eastern gates with every camel driver.[15]

Today the evening breezes bear the scent of the jasmine that cascades over suburban walls, intoxicating the streets with its sweetness. It is the heady scent of jasmine that I will forever associate with Damascus, the starry flowers in the half-light of a summer evening with all their perfumed excess.

The second wonder was the water of Damascus – indeed there are people who still say it:

> – Aleppo for its food, Homs for its girls, and Damascus for its water.

It is the waters of the River Barada seeping into the desert that gave birth to this city on the Silk Route. Students still learn of the beauty of the River Barada as recorded by the poets, although it is hard to reconcile the rivers of Damascus (are they not the Abana and the Pharpar of the Bible?[16]) with the sad trickle nowadays passing underground through Martyrs' Square.

The third wonder of Damascus was its fruit. It is the Fiji spring that supplies Damascus with water, and today the hillsides of Ein el Fiji still bloom briefly with almond and apple blossom when the short, sharp winter ends. Spring-time is a shock of blossom beneath barren hills, with families picnicking in the orchards. Summer is a succession of local fruit: apricots yield to the bloom of peaches; then baskets of bursting figs fill the markets until, announcing the approach of autumn, pears and plums give way to wine-dark pomegranates.

The fourth wonder for Waleed was the city's hammams, and they for me are still a marvel of the city. Until very recently any quarter would have had its hammam, along with its place of worship and the baker's and a barber perhaps, for these were the essentials of life. When European royalty were bathing once a year, in dire need of 'all the perfumes of the east', the men of Damascus could have nipped into a hammam at the end of a day's work.

Legend has it that at one time Damascus had a hammam for every day of the year. Even after the Ottoman Empire collapsed and the French occupied Damascus (those Syrians who had rebelled against Ottoman rule were thus betrayed, the French occupying Syria while the British claimed Mesopotamia), the architect Sauvaget recorded some fifty hammams still in use. Then, what with the building of modern flats with bathrooms, the decline rapidly set in, and of those legendary 365 hammams, maybe 18 or so are still in use today.

Some hammams still stand in a state of decay, closed up and semi-derelict, the rubbish dumped beneath their walls like Hammam Asakakri, a hammam built by a sheikh, and described as small and elegant by M. Kayall in 1989.[17] Others function as a warehouse or a carpenters' workshop or the like, the décor of their domes flaking where sparrows fly through – like the Tailors' Hammam in the heart of the *suq*, now used as an underwear shop. Others are entirely lost, not just in Damascus but in Aleppo as well, their destruction sanctioned by the authorities in

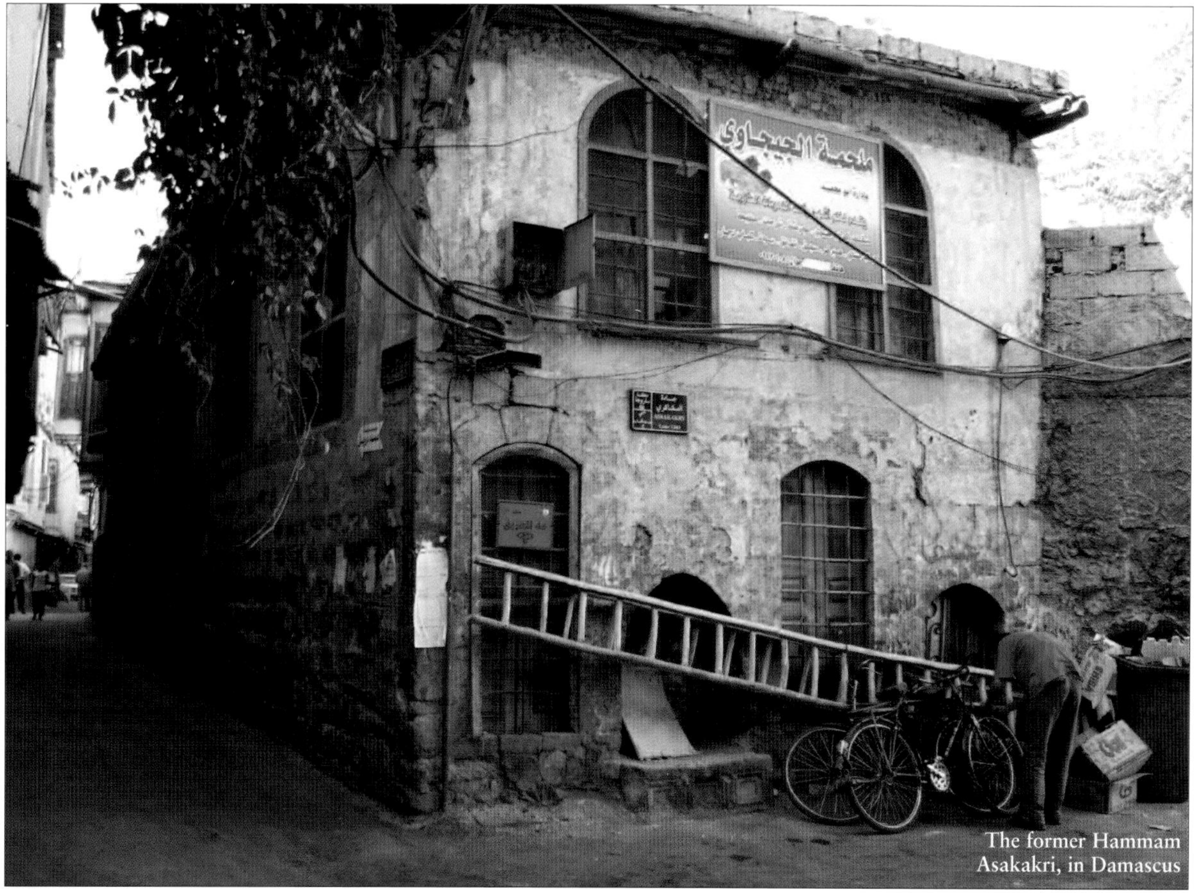

The former Hammam Asakakri, in Damascus

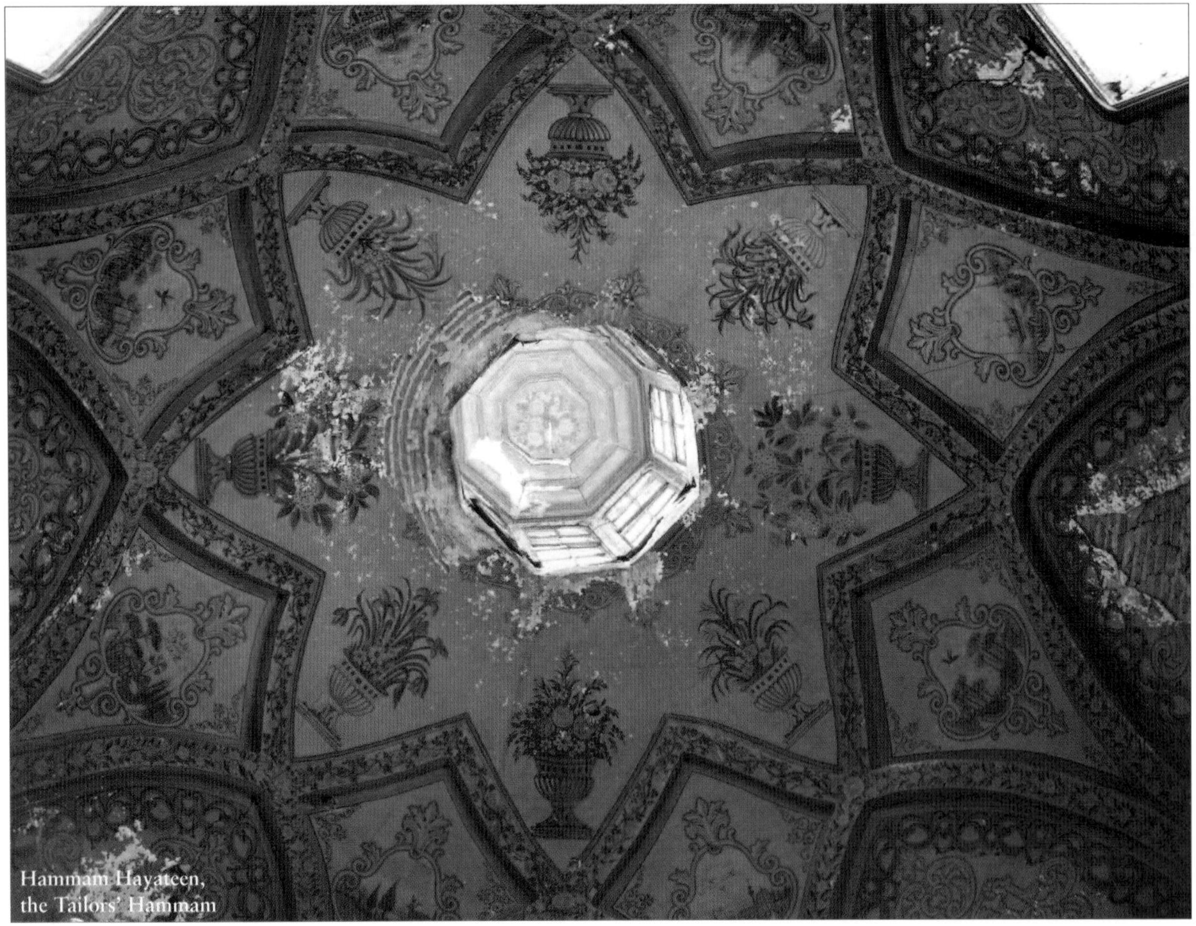

Hammam Hayateen,
the Tailors' Hammam

order to widen some road or other, their loss recorded by some lover of domes and dying traditions.

Holy Ground

Damascus is a holy city. Jews have built a synagogue in Jobar commemorating where the prophet Elijah is said to have lived; for Christians it is from Damascus that Saint Paul escaped over city walls in a basket, and for Muslims, companions of the Prophet are buried in its graveyards.

According to Damascene tradition, the Prophet passed so close to Damascus that there is still a village called Qaddam commemorating the place where he stood (in Arabic *qaddam* means foot) and surveyed the Byzantine city. Damascenes say that on viewing the distant city surrounded by orchards, the Prophet refused to enter – shunning the earthly paradise for that of the hereafter, saying that a man could enter paradise only once.

And it is to Damascus that Muslims claim Jesus will finally return, and (or so the Damascene Islamic version goes) give the call to prayer from the south-eastern minaret of the Umayyad Mosque.

It is a city sanctified by saints and prophets. In the prayer hall of the Umayyad Mosque, Christians and Muslims alike visit the shrine of John the Baptist, the sexes carefully segregated near the gilded memorial. In a nearby hall, Shi'a pilgrims come to revere the shrine of Hussein who met a fate similar to St John, his head delivered to the Umayyad ruler of the day, and so a rival to the caliphate was disposed of, and divisions confirmed that split the Islamic world even now. Escorted by their tour guide, Iranian pilgrims beat their breasts in grief, wail with sorrow as if Hussein had been killed just yesterday, and have their photographs taken in his domed shrine.

The Umayyads, rather than govern their Islamic world from Medina or Mecca, made Damascus the centre of their rule. And when they lost the Arab world, they continued their rule in Andalusia, the *mihrab* of the great mosque of Cordoba with its horseshoe arches oriented not towards Mecca but south, as if they had never left Damascus for exile in Europe.

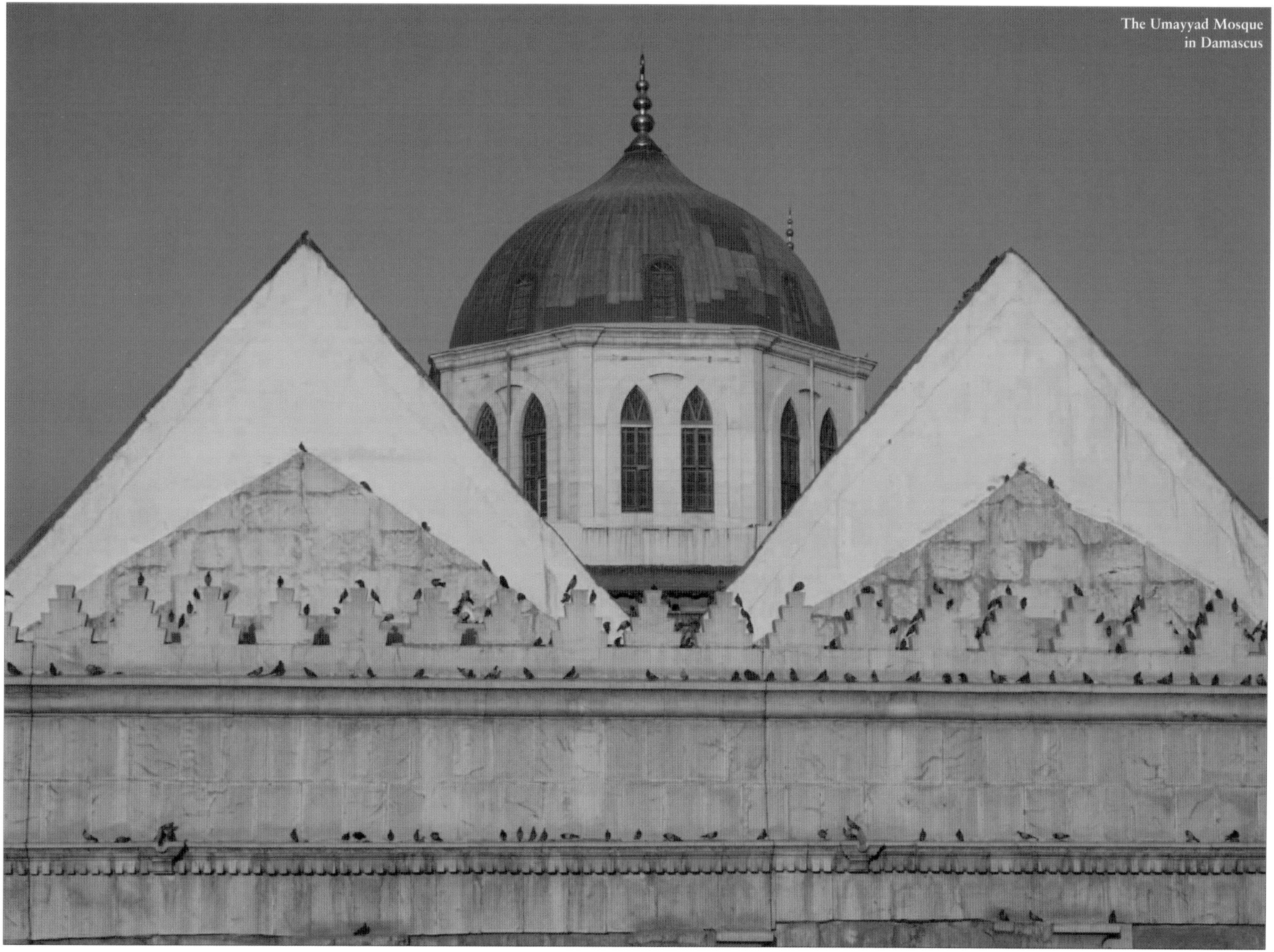
The Umayyad Mosque in Damascus

In Damascus lie the giants of Islamic history. Nur al-Din, the wager of jihad against the Crusaders, is buried here. His tomb lies

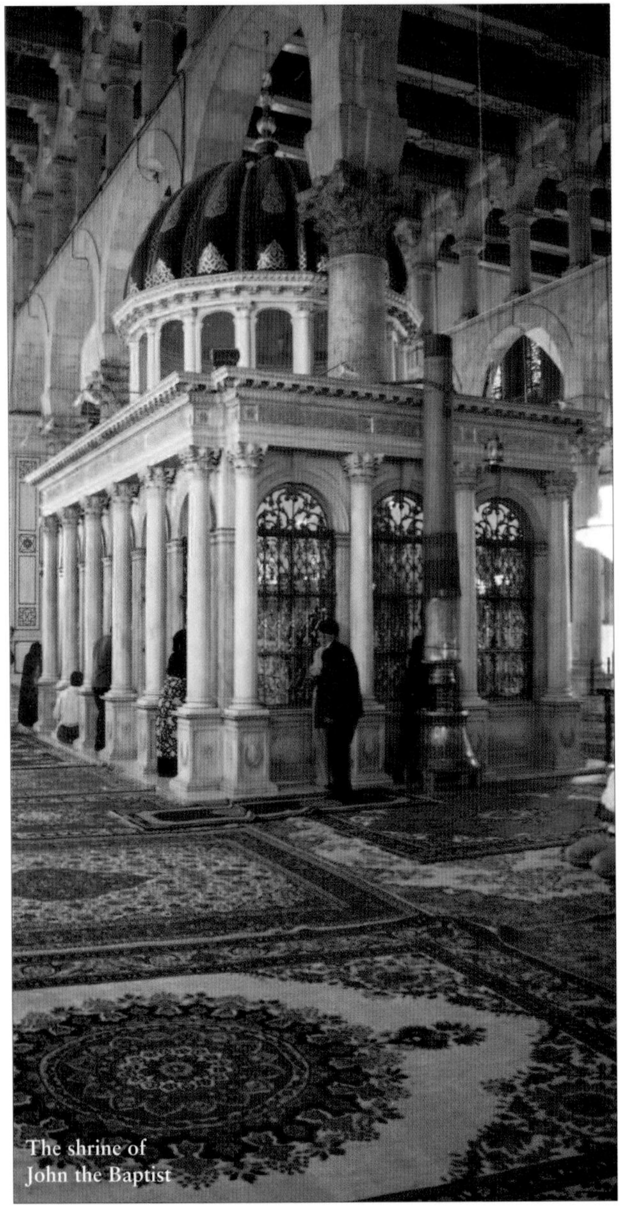
The shrine of John the Baptist

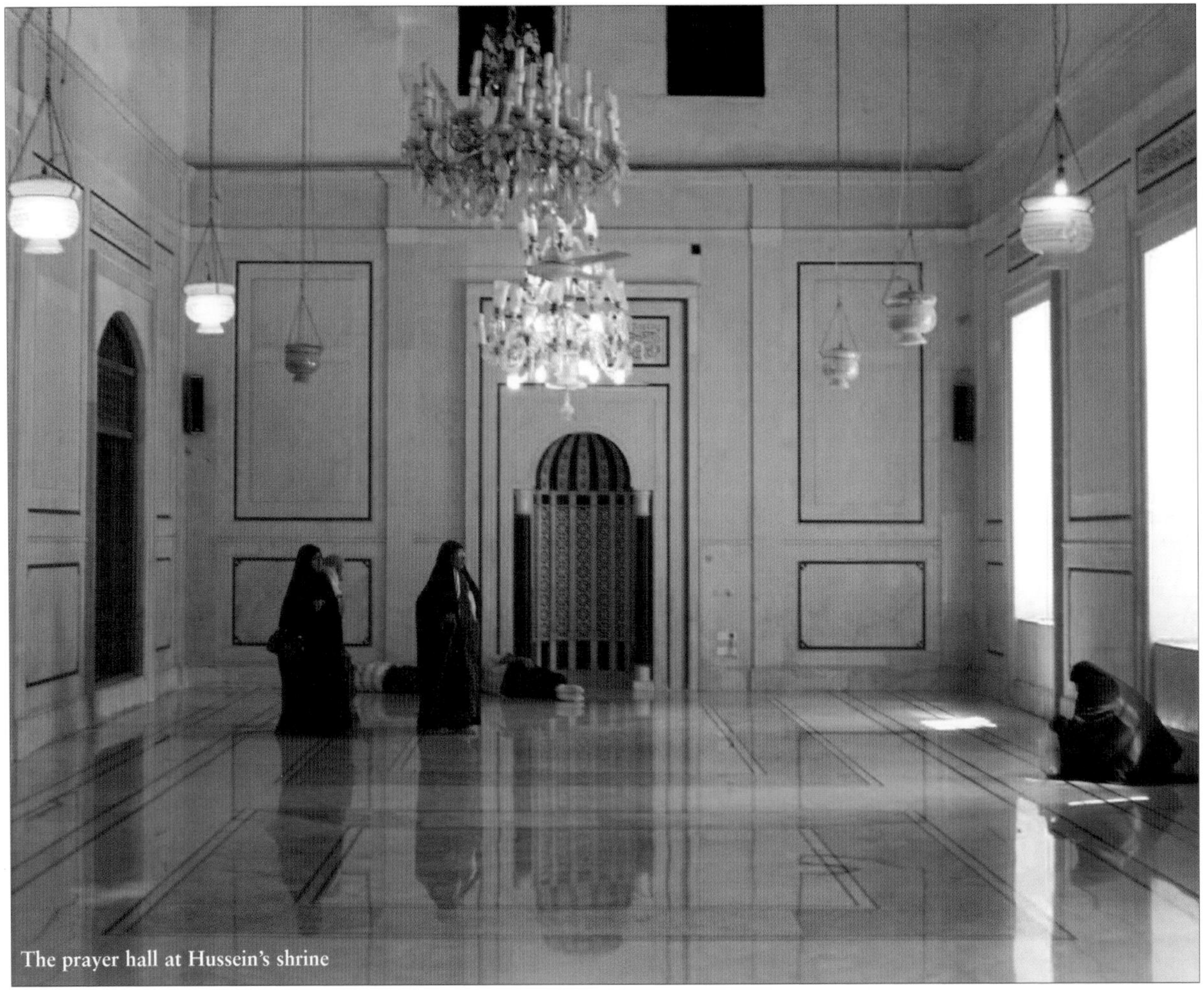
The prayer hall at Hussein's shrine

largely ignored in the *suq* – the square walls rising delicately to a pointed dome, all honeycombed *muqarnas* layered in dust – but the hammam he built to fund the *madrassah* or religious school where he is buried is much frequented today.

The very skyline of the city is one of minarets and mausoleums. The Kurdish liberator of Jerusalem, Saladeen, is buried near the Umayyad Mosque, a sign in Arabic announcing his resting place as a shrine. Modern-day visitors wishing to pay their respects are confronted by two different caskets: one suitably austere, and one less appropriately ornate, his tomb renovated after the wishes of a visiting Kaiser. T. E.

Lawrence, having taken Damascus with Prince Faisal, is said to have paid homage at his hero's tomb.

The rusty-red cupolas of mausoleums define the skyline – monuments built by rulers who knew their days were numbered and had their deeds inscribed in stone before their successor held sway. Both mystics and Arab nationalists have their place, and sometimes even lie buried together. The great Sufi, Mohi al-Din ibn 'Arabi, is buried below Qassioun Mountain in Salihiye.

For some time the mystic Mohi al-Din ibn 'Arabi shared his tomb with the Algerian 'Abd al-Qadir who fought the French in Algeria, and gave refuge to the Christians of Damascus during the city's sectarian massacres of 1880. Observing mystic and nationalist resting beneath one dome, Colin Thubron writes in his homage to the city, *Mirror to Damascus*, 'two men were never coupled more strangely in one tomb'.[18]

The Algerian's body has been returned to his native soil, but women still come to touch the tomb of Mohi al-Din ibn 'Arabi, imploring him to intercede with God to grant them children. However, it is not just by his domed tomb that Ibn 'Arabi is remembered. Nearby, just below the market, are the domes of the Hammam Muqaddam, opposite which a forgotten tomb, its dome collapsed on the grave beneath, half recalls some knight who fought with Saladeen to re-take Jerusalem. There, in the depths of the hammam, a basalt bathing font is remembered as the one used by the thirteenth-century mystic.

The font remains in the hammam, surrounded by bathroom tiles. Seeing its solid shape, the basalt rock devoid of any ornamentation, I at first imagined ibn 'Arabi to have been some miserable fundamentalist, as dour and sour as his dark font in the hammam.

In that I was quite mistaken.

The Islamic Hammam

The discerning passerby in Damascus may still catch sight today of a Greek inscription referring to the return of the Messiah, not in the Christian quarter of the city, but built into the main wall of the Umayyad Mosque. Just as the traditions of others were built upon, so Roman bathing traditions were incorporated into Islamic life.

Initially, however, Islam showed resistance to the baths of Christendom and the pagan world, and they were not immediately absorbed into Islam. The Mother of the Faithful, Aisha, a wife of the Prophet, is reported as saying:

> The Apostle of Allah (peace be upon him) forbade to enter the hot baths. He then permitted men to enter them in lower garments.[19]

It seems that over the years some kind of process of accommodation took place. The hammams in the conquered world were perhaps rather raunchy affairs, at odds with the Islamic taboo on nudity. It is reported that Aisha rebuked certain women she met from Syria over this issue:

> She said: Perhaps you belong to the place where women enter hot baths (for washing). They said: Yes. She said: I heard the Apostle of Allah (peace be upon him) say: If a woman puts off her clothes in a place other than her house, she tears the veil between her and Allah, the Exalted.[20]

Public bathing Roman-fashion was incompatible with Arab concepts of modesty.

Hammaming was not fully embraced by some religious authorities. In the fourteenth century Ibn Battuta financed his travels by working as a travelling *qadi*, a kind of itinerant religious-legal authority. Like many a traveller today, his travels did not go without sexual pleasures. Travelling in order to do the *hajj* did not stop him from marrying a Damascene woman during Ramadan, only to continue on his journey a couple of weeks later, leaving his wife behind.

Our serial polygamist later enjoyed the immodest beauty of the women of the Maldives, but closer to home in Egypt Ibn Battuta was quite upset by the hammams, where he found men bathing in the buff. The travelling judge immediately contacted the authorities to enforce modesty among male bathers:

> I went to the governor and informed him of it. He told me not to leave and ordered the lessees of all the bath-houses to be brought before him. Articles were formally drawn up there and then making them subject to penalties if any person should enter a bath without a waist-wrapper, and the governor behaved to them with the greatest severity, after which I took leave of him.[21]

I wonder if the neglect of Cairo's last hammams today is not a yielding to similar, contemporary forces?

In contrast, Ibn Battuta much approved of hammaming in Basra, for in Iraq the bather was appropriately given three towels, a towel for each stage of the bathing – a towel for each room perhaps.

Today's hammams follow a system similar to that observed by Ibn Battuta in Iraq: the bather undresses and puts on a *futa* or wrap-round for bathing, then, when the bathing is over the attendant dries him down and wraps him in fresh (or sometimes not-so-fresh!) towels to wear briefly as he walks to the *barrani*. There he is wrapped again in clean towels in order to relax after his bath. The *futa* worn when bathing is quite different from the towels used for drying; while the towels worn in the *barrani* are usually white and may be hand-woven locally, the *futa* has all the brightness of a chequered tea towel.

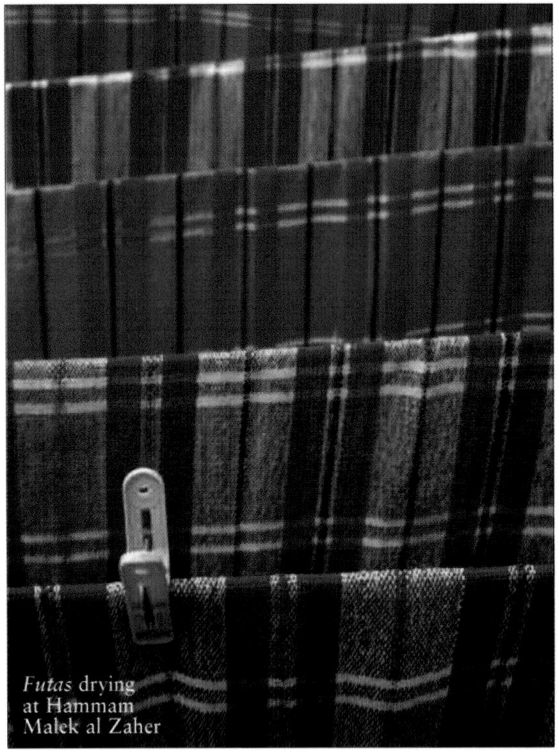
Futas drying at Hammam Malek al Zaher

If Ibn Battuta were to tour hammams today he would mostly approve of how bathers are dressed. Everyone will be wearing a *futa*. The word cannot really be translated as loin-cloth for it usually covers much more than the loins, and given that it is one metre long it would conform to even Ibn Battuta's criteria for modesty.

A male visitor to Syria is likely to find most bathers still following Islamic guidelines about covering the body from the waist down to the knees. The exception is the Iraqis (Syria gave refuge to over a million Iraqis following the invasion of their country) who seem not to share the average Damascene bather's prudishness. Our fourteenth-century itinerant judge would have had a fit to see a bather standing stark naked by the font in a Damascene hammam; ironically, however, such a bather is probably from Iraq, and is likely to be rebuked by the Syrian attendant for his lack of prissiness.

I am told that covering up is much less of an issue when women are hammaming. Lane, documenting Egyptian life in *The Manners and Customs of the Modern Egyptians*, devotes a whole chapter to hammam life (Cairo had between sixty and seventy hammams in Lane's day), painstakingly recording the four 'napkins' which men might wear in an Egyptian hammam. However, he says of the women bathing:

> Many women of the lower orders wear no covering whatever in the bath.[22]

The honour of women bathers, however, is much protected; in Syria a few hammams are reserved for women only, while others like Hammam Bakri are open to women during the day, and men at night for, as I have had it explained to me, what woman would be seen leaving a hammam in darkness? (Men, by the way, can bathe in Hammam Bakri all day on Friday, but given that false ceilings now block out the light that once sifted through patterned domes, something of the art of bathing has been lost.)

At the times of women's bathing the hammam windows looking out onto the street are firmly shuttered and a curtain is drawn over the outside door to signal the exclusion of men. Only once when I was new in Syria did I breach this forbidden zone. Not realising the significance of the curtain, I pulled it aside, pushed the door open and stepped into the hammam, to confront a woman in her nylon petticoat. It would be hard to say who was the more horrified – the intruder or the intruded upon.

That faux-pas of mine would not have happened in Turkey, for its hammams are divided into male and female sections. The one half of the hammam that is given for the use of men gracefully mirrors the half devoted to women. Although the great architect of Ottoman hammams, Sinan, has graced the Damascus skyline with the pencil minarets of his Tekkiye Mosque, and a soup kitchen opposite Ibn 'Arabi's shrine that is still in use today, he unfortunately did not extend his hammam building to Syria.

The existence of hammams in the Arab world is bound up with Islamic teachings about cleanliness, and the need for ritual purification before prayer. And so the owner of a hammam in Medan, on generously giving me a tour of the hammam, pointed to two areas where water could be poured and said in his urbane well-travelled way:

> These are for when a man hasn't got time for the full hammam, but needs to go through the cleansing ritual – say, he has had sex and now needs to do his prayers – these will suffice.

It was in this light that I came to understand the comment that a couple of bathers visiting Damascus made as they left Hammam Nur al-Din. They jokingly complained that they had partaken of *hammam nashif* – a dry hammam. They had washed in such a way that they were 'pure' in religious terms, but had not enjoyed the pleasures that might precede the act of purification.

A Stately Pleasure Dome

Hammams have always been an urban tradition, but I had heard of a hammam to be found in the Jordanian desert. Here, I might seem to be stepping beyond appopriate limits, but Bilad al-Sham has traditionally refered to an area far beyond the borders of the modern Syrian state. And so, in search of such a wonder, I travelled from Damascus down to Amman, with its Byzantine cathedral incorporated into the Umayyad Citadel above the city. From there I took a bus towards the dried-up oasis town of Azarak (where T. E.

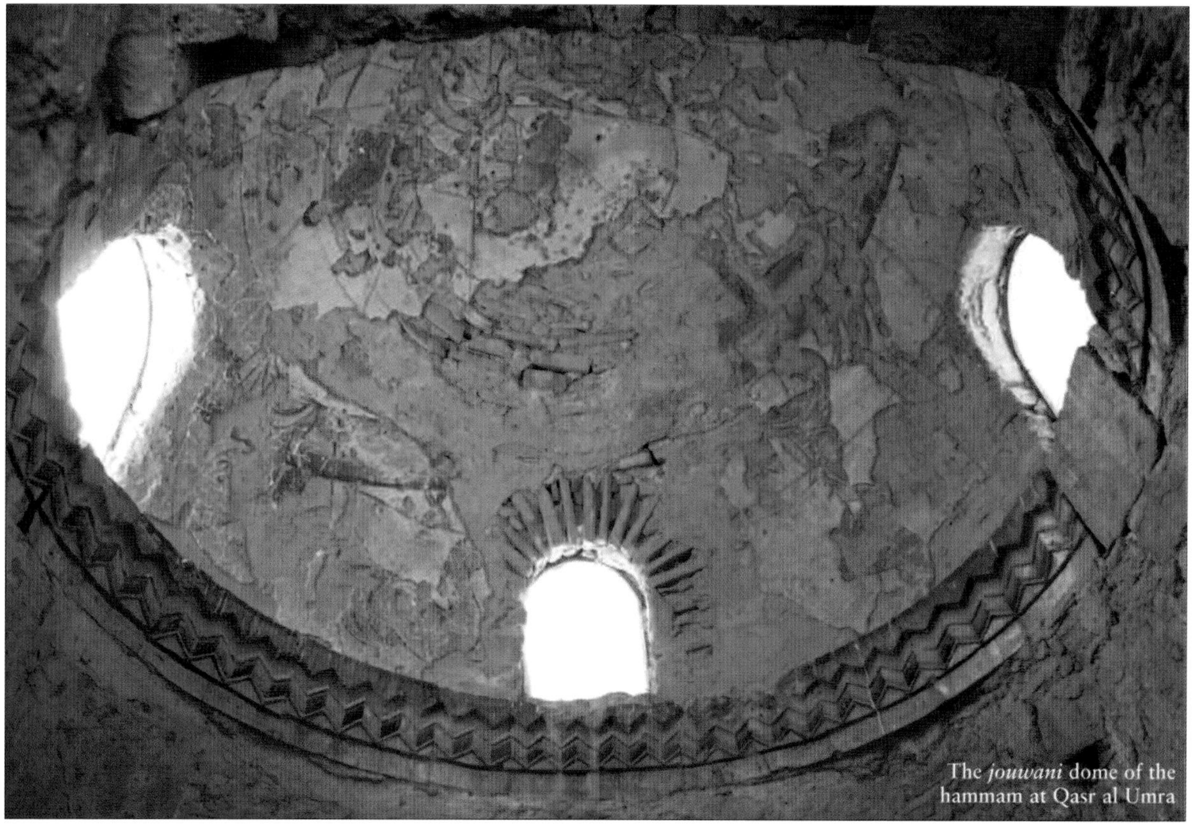

The *jouwani* dome of the hammam at Qasr al Umra

Lawrence had once shacked up with his troops in the fortress) and hitched a lift with a lorry driver across the steppe. Soon he dropped me at my destination: a rather stark building of three parallel vaults and a dome rising abruptly from the steppe, scarcely softened by the wild pistachio trees that dot the wadi there.

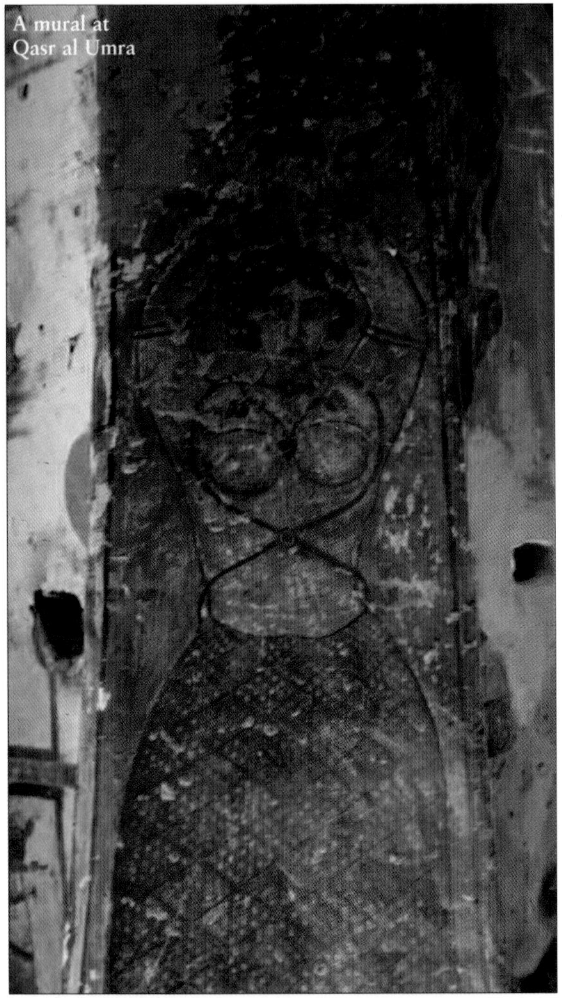
A mural at Qasr al Umra

I had arrived at Qasr al Umra. The Umayyads built not only their great mosques in Damascus and Aleppo but also retreats, pleasure palaces or hunting lodges perhaps, far from city life. Here another side to those who built the Umayyad Mosque was revealed, just as some will see a different side to the Kingdom of Saudi Arabia in the nightclubs of Lebanon and Damascus.

On entering the reception room I was greeted by a nymph-like woman bearing a cup above her head – a fresco on the arch. Beyond her was the throne room of the Umayyads, wine-red. Hunters and dancers and bathers competed on the reception hall walls; androgynous athletes wearing the Umayyad equivalent of thongs sported under trees. A solitary woman bathed semi-nude in an open pool, gazed on by male voyeurs.

This, one of the first examples of Islamic art, did not seem to me to be very Islamic. Unlike the Umayyad Mosque where there is no representation of the human form, the palace rooms were richly frescoed. Portrayed on the walls were the rulers of the world, from the Byzantine Emperor to the kings from Persia and Abyssinia and Spain, submitting to the Umayyads, the work itself undoubtedly undertaken by Byzantine artisans.

But my interest lay not so much in the reception room as what lay under the dome to which it led, for the Umayyads had taken to their country retreat the urban tradition of the hammam. An integral part of the palace, the hammam had the traditional three-room structure. From the ceiling of the first room a smoke-blackened face looked down on the would-be bather as Christ might have looked down from the roof of a Byzantine chapel.

How could a hammam have such a religious feel? But the sanctity of such ruins had not been much revered; graffiti was chiselled into the frescoes. The old bedouin guard told me it was *haram* (forbidden) so I assumed he was referring to the nudity of the females portrayed on the walls rather than the ignorant defacing of the murals.

There is a long tradition of graffiti in hammams: the sexual exploits of Roman bathers are recorded in hammam graffiti that has survived to this day. And my own name is carved in the *jouwani* of my favourite hammam in Damascus, where the soldiers from Derazor have chiselled theirs. The sadness of it – for a fresco to survive from the eighth century, only to be defaced by 'Ahmed was here'.

The middle room featured a Madonna and child, but this Madonna was more like some Venus sporting a generous backside. No doubt when T. E. Lawrence's bedouin companions took shelter in Qasr al Umra they had all had a good snigger.

The innermost room was the glory of it all, although the surface of the ochre-coloured cupola was disintegrating. The dome of this last room, the *jouwani*, was decorated with the zodiac (but then those Umayyads were great consulters of astrologers). It was on the dome of this hammam that the heavens were first represented not just on a flat surface but on a semi-hemisphere.

Not long after the death of the Prophet, an Umayyad prince would have lain on the marbled floor of the hammam and considered his future under the zodiac-emblazoned dome above him – Sagittarius shooting back at Scorpio, the Great Bear and the Little Bear at the dome's centre, Hydra stretched between the north and west. What part was that Umayyad prince destined to play in an empire that stretched from Spain to China?

I had come across the Umayyads' Bahrain. But in the visitors' centre outside, considerable white-washing was taking place. Denying any hints of pornographic titillation, the frescos were claimed to show Umayyad family values:

> ...thematic overtones are those of symbolising the empire, its riches in the arts and worldly goods, and the intimacy of family life.

I suspect those Umayyad princes did not bring their wives to bathe.

The Abbasids too had their hammams, also decorated with images, but even more opulent. Traditionally what has been seen as the spartan puritanism of the Umayyads has been contrasted with the perceived decadence of Baghdad. If desert traditions maintained the Spartan purity of the Umayyads for Gertrude Bell, she saw the armies of Islam as tied hand and foot with silk and gold in Baghdad.

The decadence of the times could be seen in the palace of Sharaf ad-Din in the 13th century. In the home of this 'poet and patron of poets', the very taps in the hammam appeared to sing:

> ...the water came out of pipes of silver or of silver-gilt, some of them in the shape of birds, so fashioned that as the water poured forth it produced the special note of the particular bird represented.[23]

Clearly the combination of wealth and kitsch much displayed in Middle East bathrooms goes back quite some time.

The Eternal Paradise

The other great hammam near the Umayyad Mosque in Damascus is Hammam Silsileh, situated between the columned northern entrance to the mosque and the Sitt Ruqaye Mosque. *Silsileh* in Arabic means 'chain' and it is said that a chain by the site separated the emir on his way to prayers from the populace. M. Kayall in his descriptions of Damascene baths explains, however, that a chain once hung from a *qantarrah* (bridge or arch) by the hammam, and after a dispute claimants would come and swear on the chain; if their word was true, the chain would not move.[24]

A few yards from the hammam is the shrine to a grand-daughter of the Prophet

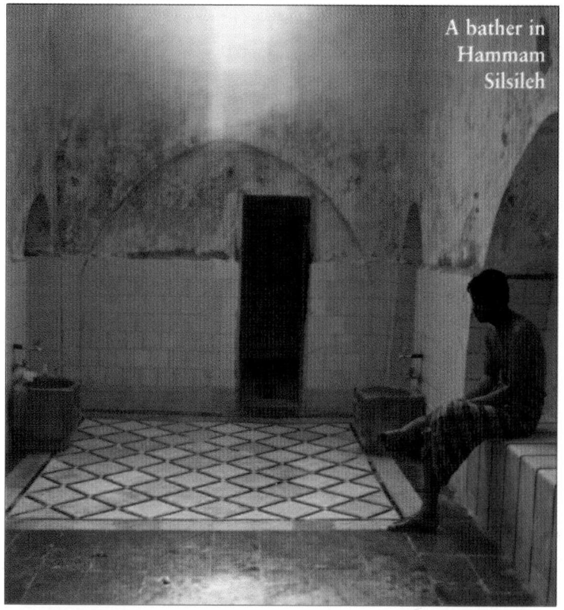
A bather in Hammam Silsileh

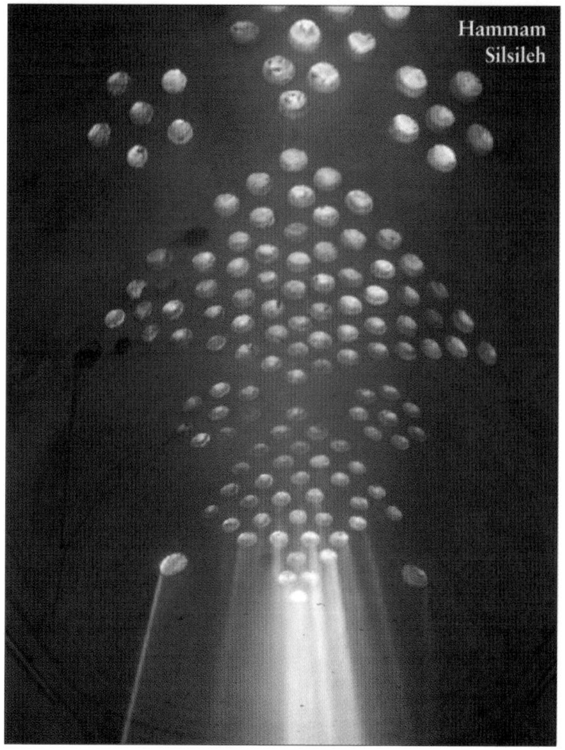
Hammam Silsileh

who was brought in triumph to Damascus after the civil conflict over the caliphate. Some pilgrims still throw dolls on to her gilded shrine, as if a little girl who died of grief over thirteen centuries ago might still need the comfort of a plaything. Unlike the more sober Sunni mosques, this Shi'a shrine has been built to dazzle; its interior is all reflecting mirrors and gilt, a place of mirrored glory.

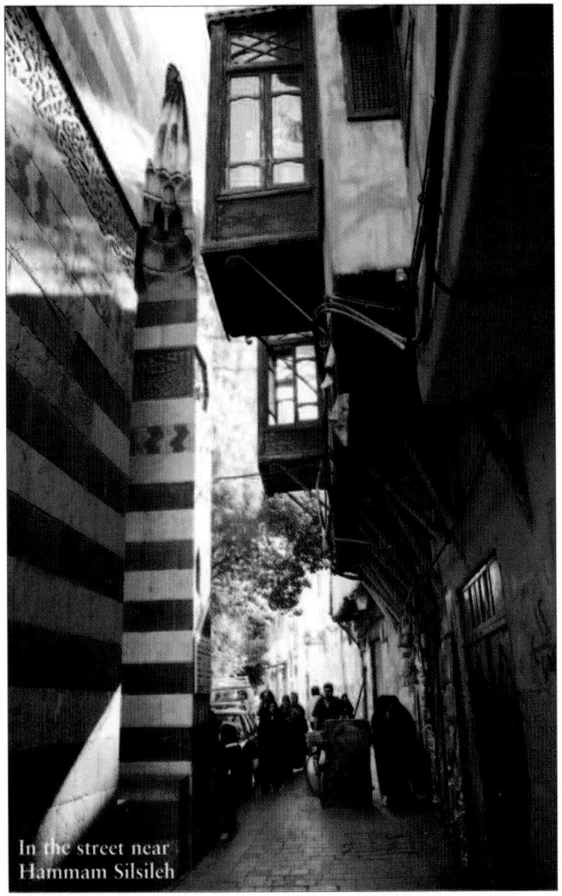

In the street near Hammam Silsileh

In contrast, the décor of the hammam is relatively subdued; it is rather tastefully decked out in red 'bedouin' rugs over the seats, with a circle of *nargilehs* for smoking arranged on the fountain. Bathing in Hammam Silsileh is a bit like taking part in a lucky dip: you never know who you might encounter within its walls. The hammam has a clientele that ranges from Iraqi refugees to visiting *shebab* from Aleppo, or lads from the coast doing their military service. (*Shebab* is a key word in Syrian society; it might best be translated as 'the lads' and has connotations of youth and affability.)

One day, however, when I popped in for a hammam, the scene was a dozen elderly men wearing pyjama-like trousers, made out of the same chequered green cloth. They were remembering an activity of their youth:

– And do you hammam here every week or so? I asked.
– The last time I came to a hammam was thirty years ago.
– And don't you miss the experience?
– I have a bathroom at home.

I don't know how often I have heard someone rebuke me with 'I've got a bathroom at home.' The private bathroom in the modern flat has contributed more than anything else to the demise of the hammams. (One writer, I cannot remember whom, dates the demise of Cairo's hammams to the revolution of Gamal Abdel Nasser, when electricity and piped water to homes became the norm.) It is foreigners who dream of the jasmine-scented courtyard in the old city; Damascenes know only too well the piercing drafts of winter and the bathroom across the freezing yard, and abandon the traditional Damascene home for a non-descript flat above the dual carriageway.

When I asked one of the bathers where he was from, he replied:

– *Min Damasc al feha'a w'all khalida.*

I got his drift, for one of them went on to talk about the trees of the Ghouta Oasis surrounding the city, but I suspected he was remembering a time before the orchards were surrounded by breeze-block walls and the olive trees were cut down.

Days later I made a few lexical enquiries, as I sat round a table with friends in the beautifully restored Ottoman house that is now called the Journalists' Club, our table under the yellowing winter leaves of a weeping tree, the wall inscribed with the family name of the merchant who had built the house some centuries ago.

– And how would you translate the word *feha'a*? I asked Yussuf.

Yussuf would have been puffing on his *narghile* at the time, or calling on the Kurdish lad with the charcoal to bring a fresh coal. Yussuf's family had been expelled in the forties from Palestine, and had settled in the Saruja quarter of Damascus. Such was the beauty of the area before modernity and developers savaged the Ottoman homes, the area had been called Little Istanbul.

At that time Yussuf would have been contemplating whether or not to go to the Gulf and pay the couple of thousand dollars required in order to escape two and a half years of military service. It was hard to say which would be worse – the tedium of military service or the sterility of the Gulf. (After enduring life in the Gulf for a year, Yussuf opted for military service. Near the Assassin castle of Massiaf he came to a happy arrangement with his commanding officer, pursuing a career in computers with the military downtown.) Even the scholarly Yussuf, however, was thrown by *feha'a*:

> – I couldn't. I couldn't even tell you in Arabic what the word means. But it has something to do with a woman's beauty. About her eyes. Something between brown and green.

This was a plausible explanation, but the urbane Omar was not convinced, for who could say that they have mastered the Arabic language? Omar's grandfather had been honoured with the title of *Basha* and he spoke of how his parents' conversation had been sprinkled with Turkish words. The exquisite houses in the heart of Damascus were often those of local Syrians who made good under Ottoman rule.

Perhaps this Ottoman perspective on things Syrian gave Omar a healthy scepticism and – true Damascene as he is – he instinctively made for his mobile phone, although it was near midnight. A minute or two later he came back to us:

> – I phoned a friend whose wife is called Feha'a. I told him not to misunderstand the nature of my inquiry, but I wanted to know the meaning of his wife's name. 'She's lying right beside me', he said. 'I'll ask her.'

We all laughed at the sensitivity of the situation, for an Arab wife is jealously guarded – his honour depends on hers. I could not imagine a Yemeni friend making a similar call, unless he wished to initiate tribal conflict. Nonplussed, Omar's friend had come back:

> – Paradise! I'm lying here next to Paradise!
> – Well, I hope I didn't disturb you from anything!
> – Don't worry about that. That all stopped a long time ago!

This left me with just the word *khalida*. I felt I half knew what that word meant, and I thought back to a speech I had heard when a naval admiral had referred to eternal guidance. However, I had not understood the reference, for the speech had been in classical Arabic. *Khalida* means 'eternal'. So now I had it: those old men in the hammam thought of themselves as living in Damascus the eternal paradise.

Paradise has taken a knock or two in the last fifty years. But despite the onslaught of modernity and the destruction of what should have been sacred, it is not just in the patchy mosaics of the Umayyad Mosque that hints of paradise remain.

Hammams and Castles

Some centuries after the Umayyads took Damascus, the Crusaders took Jerusalem, slaughtering the Muslim and Jewish inhabitants of the holy city. The Crusaders then settled down to rule Palestine, but such were the standards of hygiene and levels of infant mortality even among the aristocracy, the 'royal' line of the Frankish kingdom was in danger of dying out.

The 'royal' line was saved by absorbing some of the habits of the indigenous population. The Crusaders became somewhat civilised by the East; they even learnt to wash. Not everyone approved of these acquired habits, however, and some saw a softening of their military forces. Some diehards observed the new tendencies towards cleanliness with disgust:

> These children of noble ancestors are called *pullani*, soft and effeminate people reared in luxury, more used to baths than battles.[25]

A bit like Mark Antony perhaps – his Roman discipline melting before the soft beds of the East. Or like the Italian executive in the film *Hamam* who comes to Istanbul to sell the hammam inherited from his aunt, but instead yields to the rhythms of the city and discovers a softer, more sensual side to himself. Instead of selling the disused hammam he restores it.

A contemporary of Saladeen, Usama ibn Munqidh, who had grown up below the castle of Shayzar, recalls a Muslim bath attendant's impressions of his Crusader clients (or at least he has an attendant from Maarrat al Numan tell a story which might be Usama's own invention). Like many a tourist today in Istanbul, the Crusading knights would pop in for a hammam but fail to notice the etiquette of hammaming. Expressing Arab amusement at the Western failure to observe Arab norms about nudity and body hair, the attendant recalls the services he offered a Crusading knight:

> One day a Frankish knight came in. They do not follow our custom of wearing a cloth around the waist at the baths, and this fellow snatched off my loin-cloth and saw that I had just shaved my pubic hair. 'Salim,' he cried, 'it's magnificent! You shall certainly do the same for me.' He lay down and I shaved his hair there, which was as long as a beard...[26]

The knight's schoolboyish enthusiasm for Arab hygiene was such that he needed to share the experience with his wife. And so we have the first record of European mixed bathing in the hammam, with the attendant amused rather than affronted by the behaviour of foreigners:

> ...when he felt the place so agreeably smooth he said, 'Salim, you shall do the same for my Dama.' Then his valet fetched his wife, and she lay down on her back and the knight said, 'Now do to her as you did to me.' So I shaved her pubic hair, and all the time her husband was watching. Then he thanked me and paid me.[27]

At least the knight had the good sense to stay with his wife and the attendant. Nowadays not much has changed in terms of the Arab world and the perceived moral laxity of the West.

To what extent did the Crusaders absorb local customs? It seems to me that every Crusader castle on the Syrian coast has its hammam, but I suspect they were built not by Europeans but by those who expelled them. The belief that 'those who had been washed in Christ had no further need of washing' might underlie whether hammams featured or not in the castles of the Crusaders. I'll leave that matter to historians, but I imagine the new occupiers redesigned castle interiors to meet their own tastes.

Even with their hammams as later additions, Crusader castles are the architectural wonders of the coastal belt: Chastel Blanc with its stark tower housing both church and garrison; Marqab Castle brooding darkly above the Mediterranean; and, further inland, the massive stronghold of Krak des Chevaliers, 'buffeted by the wind, rid(ing) above the extended landscape with the confidence and mastery of a ship'.[28] Even Saladeen besieged the Krak for just a day and then marched on.

The Crusader castle later to be re-named in his honour as Saladeen's Castle was to be his prize. It was a *mukeyyis* in a two-roomed hammam in Lattakia (the Municipality had demolished the *barrani* in order to widen the road) who told me of a hammam in the castle in the mountains above the town. And so I found myself travelling on the back of a taxi-motorbike through scented pines and slopes decked with asphodel and cyclamen, which they call Mary's flower in the mountains, such is their devotion to the Virgin, breaking into flower. (In carrying an image of the Virgin Mary on his person, the first lieutenant – a Muslim of the Alawi sect – was closer to mainstream Irish traditions than myself.)

Suddenly we turned a bend and saw Saladeen's Castle rise above the ravine, its walls extending far along the edge of the outcrop. Given the wildness of the place, it was easy to see how this had been Lawrence's favourite castle when he had trekked around Syria as a student, writing letters to his mother about the holes in his socks after walking a thousand miles. It was

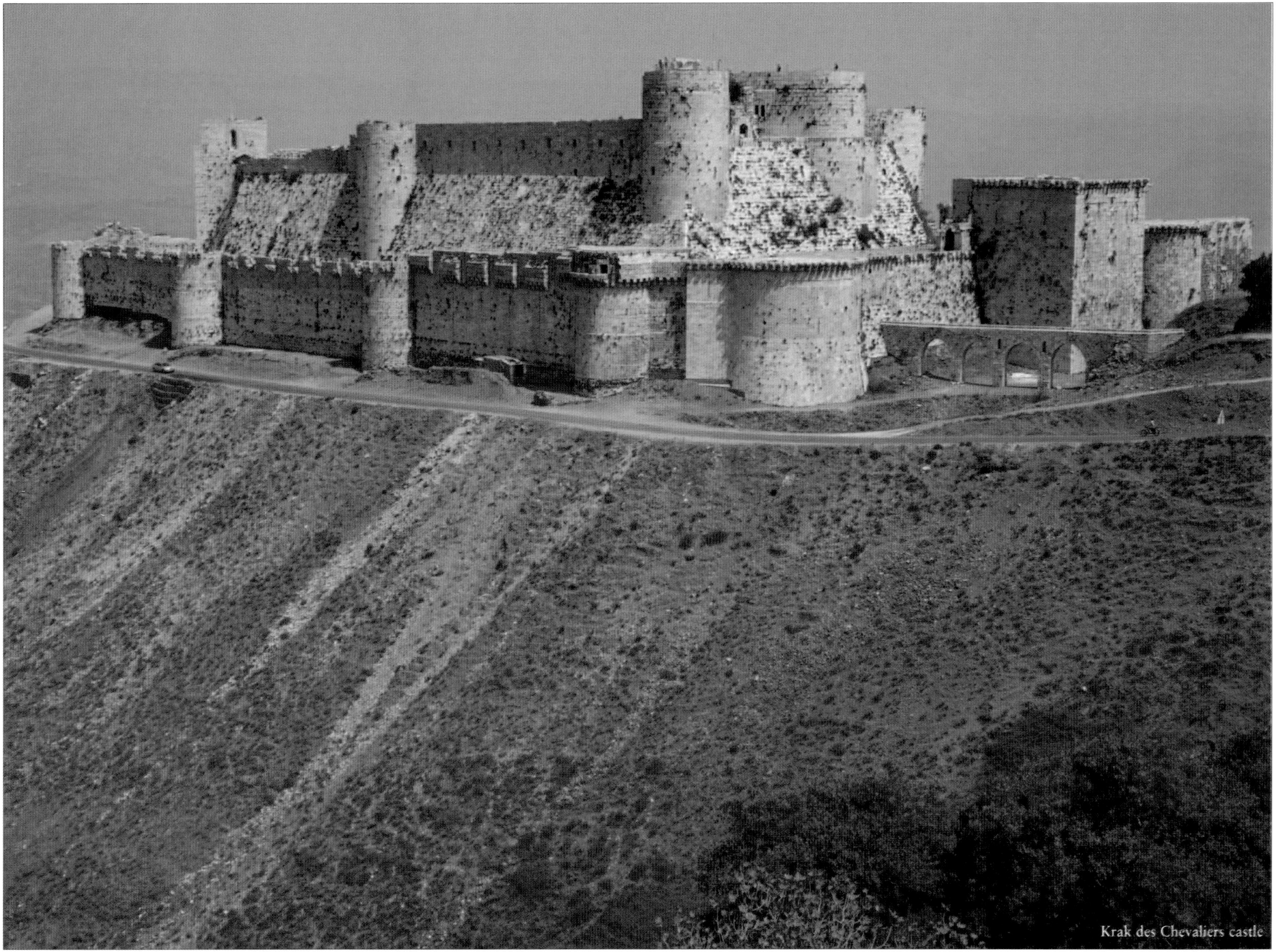

Krak des Chevaliers castle

hard to imagine how anyone could have carved out such a moat from the rock, or the pinnacle that once supported a drawbridge.

In tune with the current obsession with the glorious Arab past (what better way to escape the dreary present?), an historical drama was being filmed within the castle. When I stepped through the impressive doorway that led to the hammam, I found myself not alone: the actor playing the part of a long-haired warrior, Tareq bin Zead, was having a pee. It was Tareq who 'opened' Spain for the Arabs, presenting his own forces with a *fait accompli* when he landed in Europe, for he literally burned his boats:

> *Before you is the enemy*
> *And behind you is the sea.*

The Mamluk hammam itself was a strange one: there were the remnants of the water system that must once have been part of the central fountain, cut into the rock like some mysterious religious symbol. The doorway had all the height of Mamluk aspirations, with stalactite ornamentation to boot. But hammams that are museum-pieces are not my interest, and I followed in T. E. Lawrence's footsteps to visit the massive donjon, where Lawrence had recoiled from snakes.

For the romantic, nothing could match Saladeen's Castle. But the most evocative hammam I have ever visited lies in the ruins of the Assassins' castle of al-Kahf, a castle Ibn Battuta claims to have seen. Ibn Battuta comments on the Assassins setting out with poisoned daggers, but it was Marco Polo who mythologized the Assassins forever. He portrayed them as jumping off the battlements at the order of their commander in the hope of regaining the *hasheesh*-induced paradise they had lost; a fine piece of Orientalism indeed.

The hammam of al-Kahf lies outside the castle walls, and there's a headstone inscribed in telltale Mamluk fashion. Not much remains of the castle; its destruction was brought about by the outraged Lady Hester Stanhope after a French captain was held hostage within its walls.[29] Today nature has reclaimed what remains of the hammam, although fonts still lie in the *wastani*, and the massive reservoirs for water storage remain in the hillside. The dome of the *jouwani* has collapsed, and shrubs and creepers form a ring around the empty dome.

Wordsworth could have commemorated the sublime nature of such a place. For me there is nowhere more romantic in all Syria than this hammam, there in the remotest mountains where wild boars still roam in search of fallen acorns. May no tourist bus ever make it near that Assassin castle, desecrating the woodlands dotted with Alawi shrines! And may the hammam dome never be restored, but stay in its state of collapse, its wreath of greenery framing the sky!

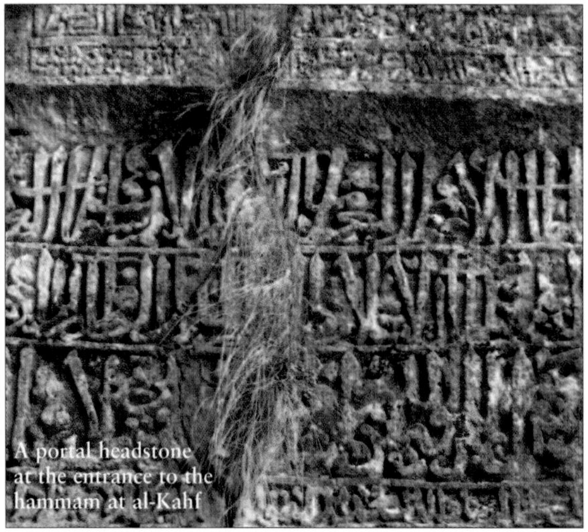

A portal headstone at the entrance to the hammam at al-Kahf

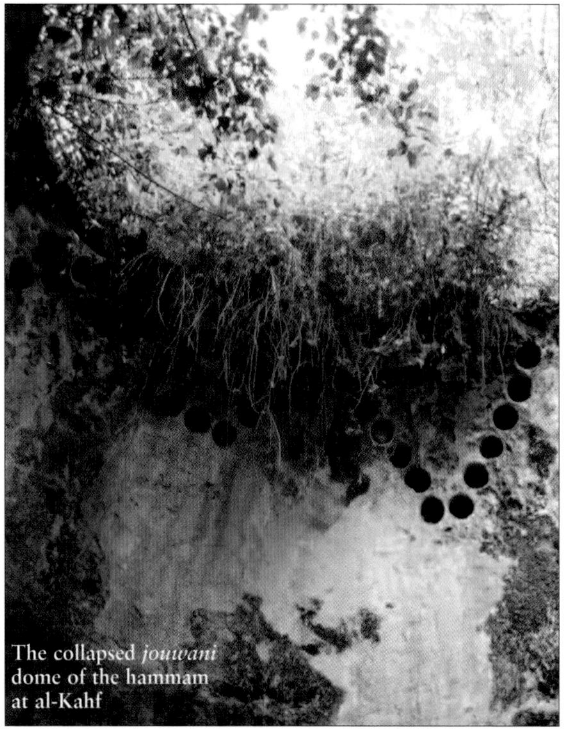

The collapsed *jouwani* dome of the hammam at al-Kahf

Soldiers Bathing

The rulers of Syria were often neither Arabs nor native speakers of Arabic but foreigners – whether the Kurdish Saladeen or Mamluks descended from Caucasian slaves, or Turkish rulers with little Arabic.

Mindful of the need for cleanliness among their soldiers, some built hammams, but also, conscious of their own mortality, those in power built mausoleums and *madrassahs* that would prolong their memory. Hammams, however, were also built by local Syrians as private enterprises, compatible with Islamic principles. And so the city of Damascus today is still graced with multi-domed hammams and the honeycombed portals of mausoleums and *madrassahs*.

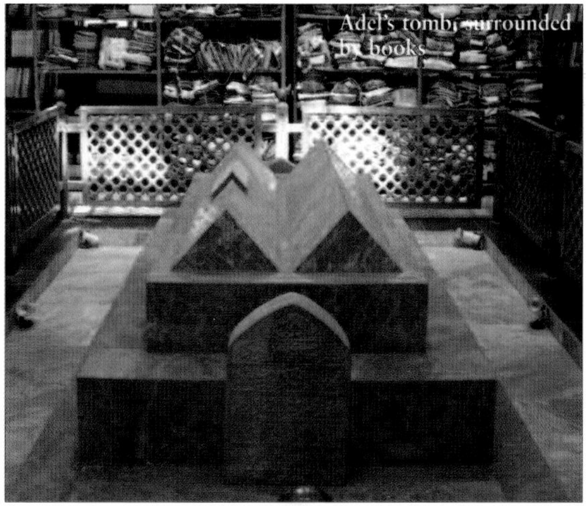
Adel's tomb, surrounded by books

Malek al-Zaher fought against the Crusader occupation of Syria. He is commemorated by a domed mausoleum near the hammam named after him (across the way his brother Adel is buried among stacks of books). Along the Orontes in Antioch (a city which is still within Syrian borders on contemporary Syrian maps), another hammam also commemorates al-Zaher: the Cundi Hammam, 'Cundi' being the Turkish rendering of the Arabic *jundi* or soldier. Malek al-Zaher drew up an endowment regulating how his hammam should be administered. I popped in there once, to a hammam all scented with thyme.

The issue of fighting Western occupiers of the region is of course not just a matter of Malek al-Zaher. I know of one hammam attendant who went to fight in Iraq soon after its occupation, leaving behind him his name carved on the wall of a hammam in Tripoli, Lebanon. On his safe return from Iraq I heard he kissed the floor of the Damascene hammam where he had worked (and ever been affable to me), grateful for his safe homecoming.

The tradition of rulers building hammams for their soldiers continued late into Ottoman times, and hints of soldiers having access to public baths have survived. I have heard of a hammam in the Turkish-governed part of Cyprus that has a sign advertising two soldiers for the price of one – a discount that might attract others than soldiers to bathe.

Even today, for one evening of the week, Hammam al Werd in the Saruja quarter of Damascus is dedicated to those doing their military service in a certain section of the forces. They are entitled to a free bath, and the Ministry I am told foots the bill. And so one evening a week the hammam fills with the laughter and pranks of Aleppan youth, the ageing hammam attendant keeping an eye on things like a headmistress at a sixth form dance.

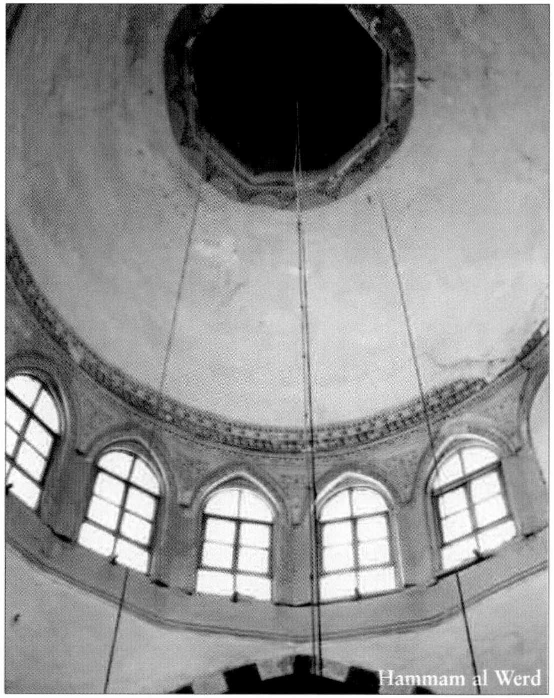
Hammam al Werd

Hammaming in Aleppo

Up in Aleppo, I was given a different viewpoint about hammaming traditions from that of the attendant who had given me the history lesson in the hammam in Damascus.

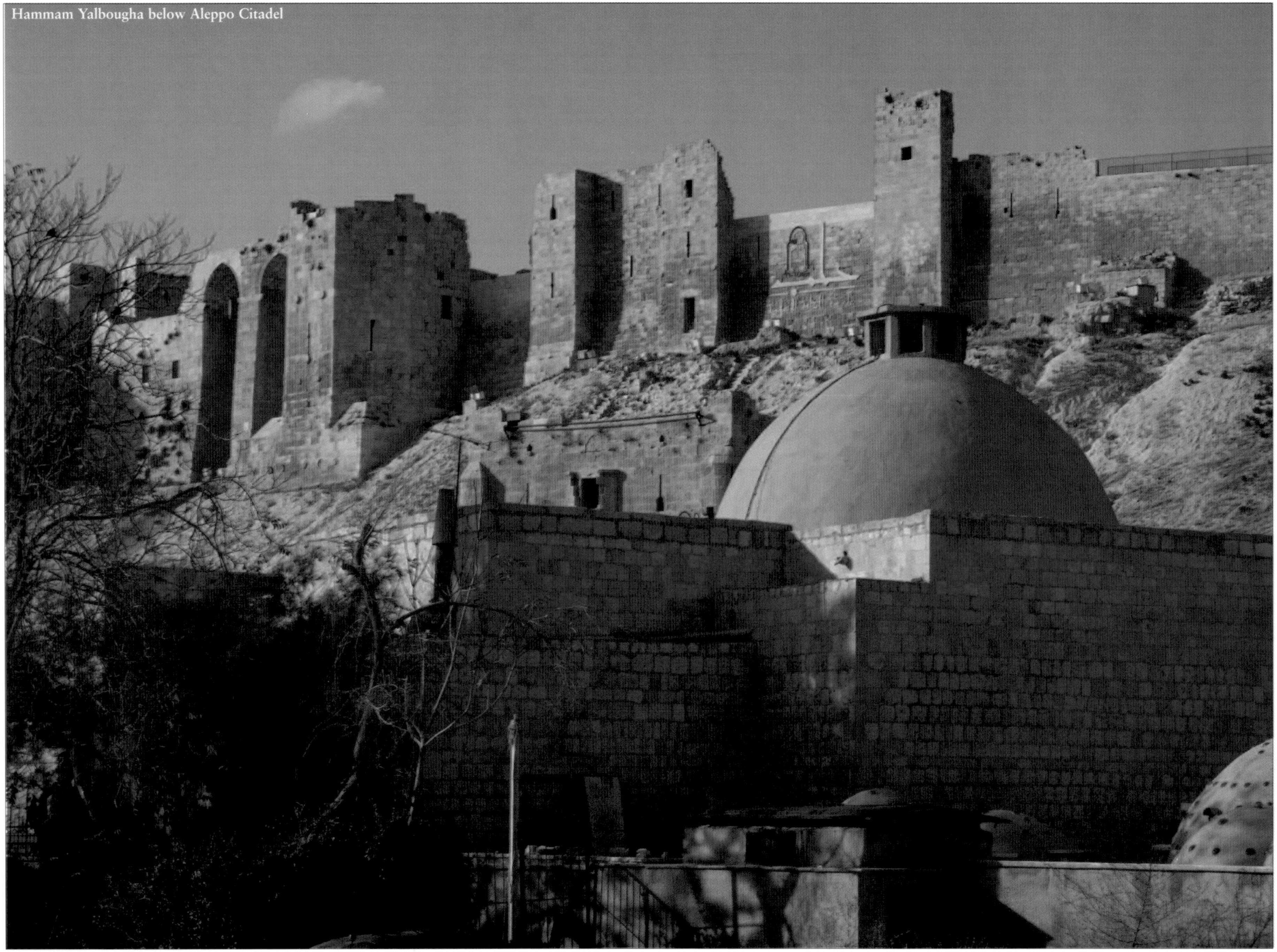

Hammam Yalbougha below Aleppo Citadel

If the best hammams of Damascus are by the Umayyad Mosque or in the *suqs* that surround it, the best hammams of Aleppo are orientated towards the Citadel or found in the *suq* or the streets beneath it. Many quarters, however, have had their own local hammam.

I had heard of a hammam in an area called 'The Dust of the Strangers', and so I walked up through the din of the Coppersmiths' Suq, up unknown lanes in search of a hammam that I thought might still be in use. In one of the narrow lanes some residents explained the origins of the name of the quarter; some foreigners had come to the area, died, and been buried on the spot. An ill fate indeed I thought, for I could probably relate to such a fate better than the speaker, but I continued my quest:

- And isn't there an old hammam somewhere around here?
- Hammam Almajeh.

I declined the invitation for tea, followed the cobbled street, took the appropriate turning, and finally reached a square. It looked as if the usual destruction had taken place, the neighbourhood demolished to make room for some shrine to modernity – an inexorable edifice in concrete rose near the swirling minaret of an ancient mosque. Already it had the air of something half-abandoned.

A couple of men were sitting outside a grocer's, and there was the usual invitation:

- Have a cola or something.
- No thanks, I just want to find out about the hammam here. I suppose it's closed.
- For the summer.
- And have you ever hammamed there?
- Of course. My mother used to take me when I was a kid. And I used to have a good look at...

There was no need for him to complete the sentence; it seems that mothers used to bring their sons to bathe with them beyond what might be called the years of innocence, the son enjoying the ambience of female nakedness in the hammam and retaining the memory for years to come. One Turkish writer records a male colleague reminiscing about the time his mother was told off for still bringing her son to the hammam:

> I recall a male colleague recording how the bath house attendant chided his mother saying 'next time why don't you bring his father as well?'[30]

I walked down towards the hammam, which had shrubs growing among the stones of its walls; this hammam was not just closed for the summer. A couple of elderly men sat on low stools, chatting under a vine. One of them wanted to enlighten me:

- The hammams, you see, the hammams are not an Arab tradition. They are from the Turks. In our own Islamic tradition washing is a private act, done in the home.
- So Hammam Almajeh is a Turkish hammam?
- The Hammam of the Apple Orchard.

The Hammam of the Apple-seller perhaps. Near the door was the remains of a kind of drinking fountain, something frequently incorporated into the exterior of the hammam, for the water that fed the hammam would also have served the community for drinking. There is many a water fountain or *sebil* near a hammam with a plaque commemorating the benefactor, its text encouraging the drinker to remember the soul of the departed. This *sebil*, however, had been cemented over.

- People used to bring their camels and horses here to drink, you know. Aleppo had a canal system built, with the water all from the one source, that used to feed every street of this city.

He was right: the development of an intricate water distribution system brought about a flourishing of hammams in the city of Aleppo.

The old man continued to reminisce:

- Aleppo was such a beautiful place fifty years ago. But then they put up those buildings of blocks and cement.

The changes had not just been in architecture:

- All that matters to people nowadays is dancing.

(Here he said the word 'dancing' with considerable distaste, and I am sure it was not the traditional *dhibki* of the countryside of which he disapproved.)

So for these Aleppans, hammams were an alien tradition, brought to Aleppo by the Turks. I never got the chance to see the sad decay of this hammam within however:

> – The owner of the hammam lives in Belgium. He was here yesterday. It's a pity you missed him!

Turkish Bath

Just off the Roman line between the city gate at Bab Antakia to where the *suq* disgorges below the citadel, is one of my favourite hammams in Aleppo: Hammam Nahesseen, the Coppersmiths' Hammam.

After hearing of the hammams as a tradition alien to things Arab, I downed the steps of the hammam, stripped off in the incredibly spacious *barrani*, and headed for the inner rooms. There I found the hammam's manager.

> – What are you doing here, Ibrahim? Don't you know the Arab proverb? The one about the carpenter's door?
> – The carpenter's door is always broken.
> – So what are you doing bathing in your own hammam?

Ibrahim, who manages one of the greatest hammams in Syria, is not one for pretensions, and we sat back and chatted:

> – I heard a strange thing. Someone claimed that the hammams are foreign to Syria, and were brought here by the Turks.

Ibrahim is not without a colloquial Arabic that can match any young man's street slang, but he surprised me with his confident assertion of an opposing view:

> – The hammams of Syria go back much further than the hammams of Istanbul. When it comes to the system of the hammams, the Turks learned it from us.
> – And you mean to tell me that words like *hammam* and *mukeyyis* are Arabic, not Turkish?
> – Of course.

Who could argue with Ibrahim on that score? The very word 'hammam' is rooted in the Arabic verb *hamma* to heat. I was well used to conspiracy theories in this region of the world, but this was a new one: it wasn't that the Arabs had got the Turkish bath from the Turks; the Turks had got the Turkish bath from the Syrians.

Ibrahim went off to have a shave. Not far from the hammam he has his own barber shop, decked out like his hammam in the latest wooden décor like a Finnish sauna. I suppose to a foreigner it is bizarre – to take

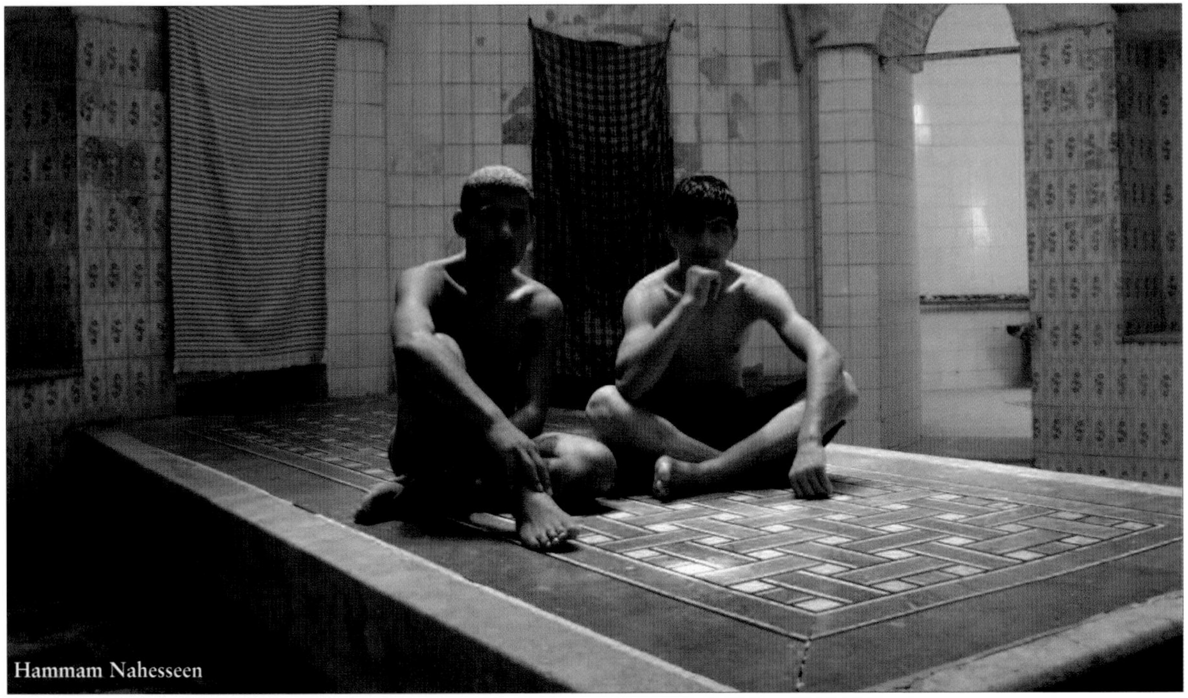

Hammam Nahesseen

an ancient hammam and strive to give it a contemporary Scandinavian feel, but I suppose this is what attracts local custom.

Ibrahim was off to his barber shop, but he normally preferred to have a chair set out in the hammam, and sit there with his comfortable belly exuding wealth and well-being as he was given a shave. There is a long tradition of the hammam as barber shop.

I suspect there is, however, many a Turk who would disagree with Ibrahim's assertion that the Turks learnt hammaming from the Arabs! Indeed, in Istanbul, in one of the magnificent hammams built by the greatest architect of the Ottoman Empire, Sinan, the manager told me how when the Turks had come from the East to settle in the area, they had brought with them their tradition of sweating it out on hot coals within their nomadic tents. A nomadic tradition developed into hammaming.

Despite what they might say in Istanbul, however, or what some Aleppans might have said outside the Apple Seller's Hammam, Ibrahim had given me the second principle of hammaming in Syria: it wasn't that the Turks gave hammams to the Arabs; it was from the Syrians that the Turks learnt how to bathe.

Hammams and Mosques

Despite its dubious 'pagan' origins and associations with nakedness, with time the hammams became inextricably linked to the mosque. Through a *wakf* or endowment benefactors would provide the means to fund the maintenance of the mosque they were building, and stipulate how things might continue long after their death. The advantage of the *wakf* system was that the property remained secure from any avaricious governor who might wish to add to the coffers of the state or to his personal wealth.

Indeed one thing that impressed Ibn Battuta, who was a poor scholar in need of funding when he travelled through Damascus, was the great number and variety of *wakfs* in the city. There was even an endowment – today we would just call it a charity – to assist those servants who had broken a plate in the house where they were working. Up in Aleppo I have heard of a benefactor who made the feeding of the neighbourhood cats a condition of the building of his mosque.

The endowment system explains why mosques and hammams are in such close proximity: the maintenance of the mosque has depended on the successful running of the hammam, for the profits from the hammam would fund the upkeep of the mosque. And given Islamic emphasis on ritual cleansing before worship, the two monuments have gone quite naturally together.

This relationship between mosque and hammam can clearly be seen in Hammam Tawrizi in Damascus and the mosque which it adjoins. I had heard from some hammam attendants that Tawrizi – a women's hammam – was the most beautiful hammam in all Damascus, but its location remained somewhat vague.

In search of this hammam I travelled to an area beyond Bab al-Jabiye and walked through a neighbourhood where there was no traffic, only bicycles. Someone stopped to drink from a fountain carved in the Ottoman style. Here there was the smell of goat's head soup, there the smell of fresh herbs. The old men had a certain courtesy, and would mention some other half-remembered hammam:

> – You're looking for a hammam? Hammam al Derb? But where is it? Just let me deliver this milk, and we'll go together.

If he thought he could direct me to Hammam al Derb he was much mistaken; it had long been demolished. It was an attendant in Hammam Ezeddin who finally pointed me in the right direction. Walking past fruit sellers and butchers I came across the hammam at the corner of an alley. The door was padlocked, and the whole building had the air of a place abandoned. Leaving aside the issue of it being a women's hammam, I was not going to gain entry. I was told that someone had undertaken the running of the hammam, but hadn't got the custom; they had locked up and gone off.

It wasn't just the hammam that was in a state of disrepair. At street level it was the usual scene of an 'office' with a couple of chairs or a carpenters' workshop or the like, but on the first floor the rooms seemed to be semi-derelict – the houses still jutted out over the street, but with just rotting frames in the windows, without glass. The mosque however was undergoing renovation but, unusually for Syria, they wouldn't let me in for a peek. Hopefully they would do something about the industrial gloss paint – much regretted by Burns – that nicely reflected the glare of the flourescent tubes within.

This was the first mosque in Damascus to be built not according to the usual courtyard plan, but with a prayer hall on one side of the lane and a square minaret on the other. The mosque and the hammam were built not long after Tamurlane sacked the city (but even Tamurlane savoured the beauty of Damascus before he destroyed it, and deported the city's craftsmen to build Samarkand.)[31] Standing in

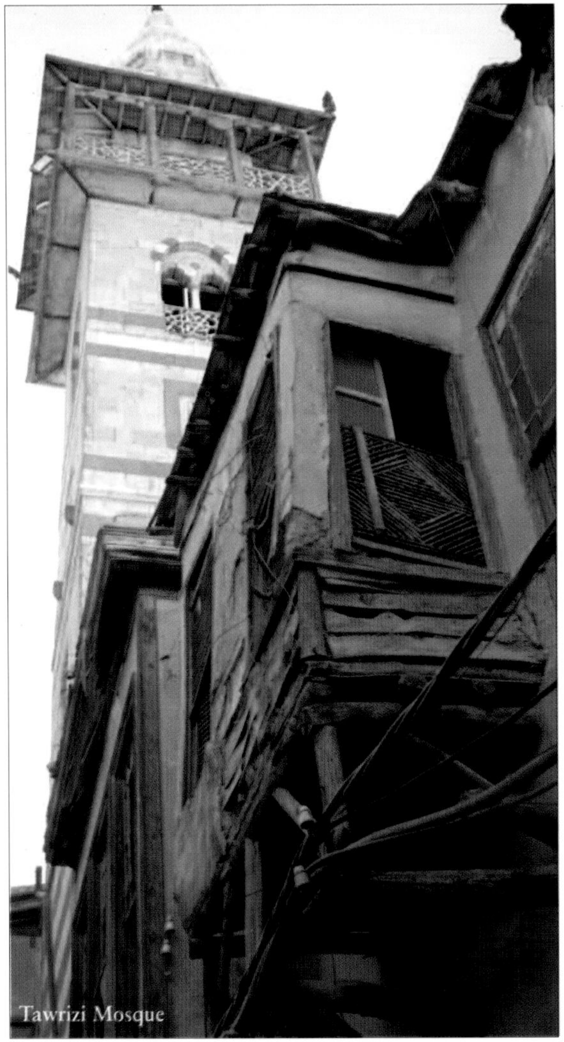
Tawrizi Mosque

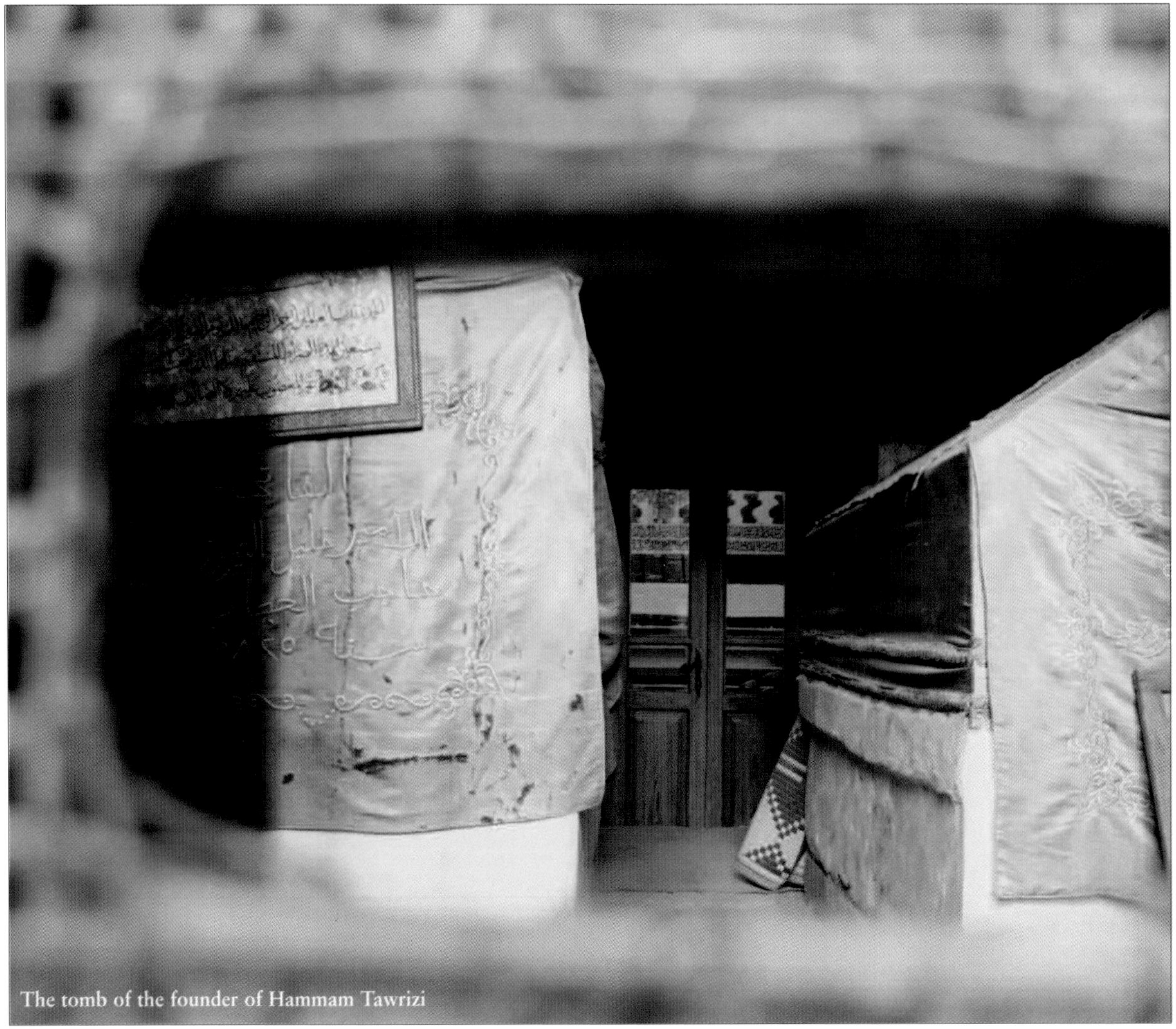
The tomb of the founder of Hammam Tawrizi

the laneway I could peep through the grill to where the holy man who had built both hammam and mosque was buried in the mosque he had never seen completed, the green pall of Islam over twin tombs. Who occupied the other tomb I wondered, surely not his wife?

Looking at the decayed beauty of the street, the area was again much in need of craftsmen to return it to its former glory. 'The most beautiful hammam in Damascus' now stood utterly neglected. But it was not just the hammam; the whole street was in a state of magnificent decay.

Hama

Hammam Tawrizi and its neighbouring mosque show the third principle of the hammams of Syria: the sheikh who built the mosque also built the hammam.

But hammams, although an urban tradition, are not found in Damascus and Aleppo alone. The other cities of Syria, Hama and Homs (cities described by T. E. Lawrence as 'fighting twins'), also have their hammams. Up in the once lovely Hama by the Orontes, behind the prison with its numbered stones awaiting restoration, down a lovely quarter where wool is still spun in the traditional way, I found Hammam al-Obeisi.

An Australian cavalry officer who was briefly stationed in Hama as World War I came to an end described the architecture of the town as one of 'enamelled beauty', for Hama is surrounded by the green of fields before they yield to the desert. The contrasting stones of the city, for Hama was built of soft sandstone and unyielding basalt, are described by Captain Dinning as having 'a fine mosaic effect'.[32] Similarly, for Gertrude Bell, Hama was the most picturesque town in Syria:

> The broad river with its water wheels is a constant element of beauty, the black and white striped towers of the mosques an exquisite architectural feature, the narrow, partly vaulted streets are traps to hold unrivalled effects of sun and shadow.[33]

This quarter still retained that beauty, and the little hammam at the end of the way certainly had its charm. The simple *barrani* was perfect for lounging in, and the attendants were affability itself. I started to bluff my way:

- And how old is the hammam? It looks Ottoman...

I was caught out:

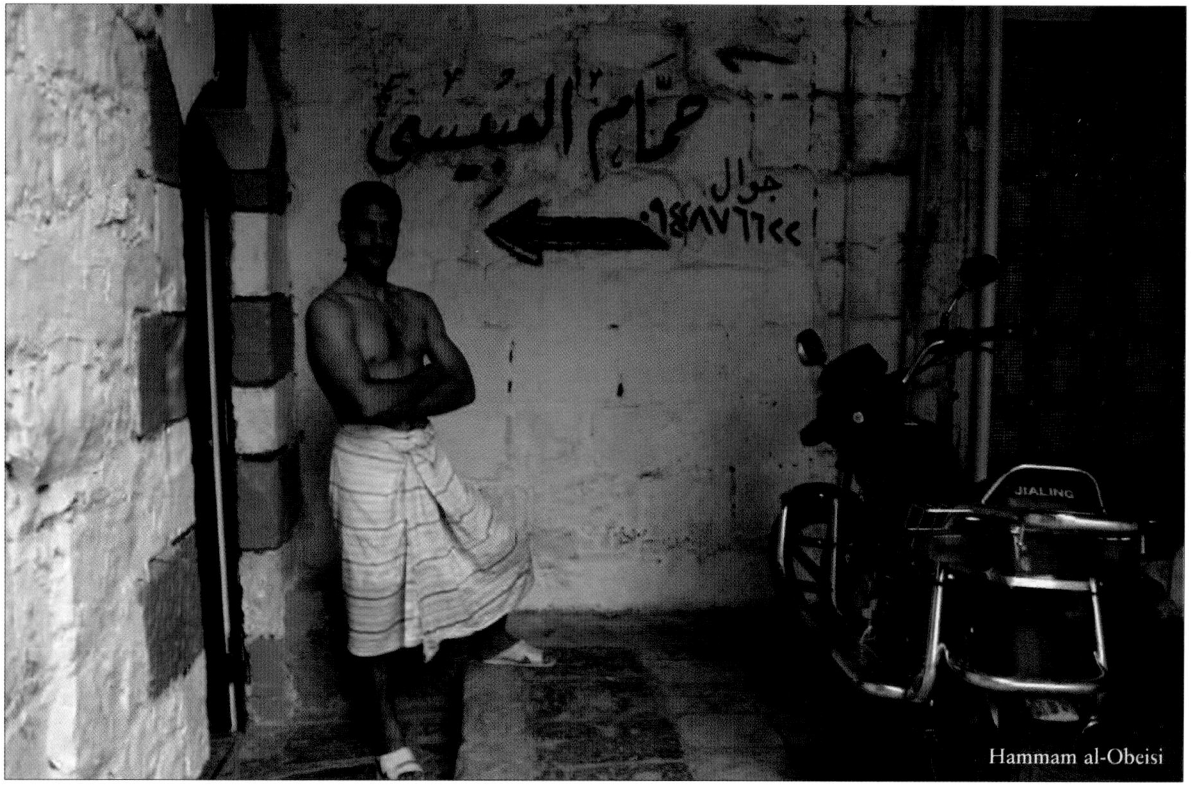

Hammam al-Obeisi

– Ottoman? This hammam's one thousand and twenty years old!

Severely reprimanded, I challenged the local expert:

– And how can you be so exact?
– It's written inside the mosque.

The hammam actually joined the mosque next door, so I nipped across to where a sheikh was sitting with a few boys. Hama has a reputation for religious extremism, but this sheikh couldn't have been more welcoming. He directed me to a notice supplied by the Ministry of Tourism dating the mosque as 479 *Hijri*. It seems the founder was a certain Sheikh Mohammed, son of Omar Obeisi. The sheikh went on to tell me the founder of the mosque was a Hashemite from the Hejaz, who married an Abbasid princess, daughter of the ruler of the region.

– And did the builder of the mosque also build the hammam?
– Yes, and he built the *naouras* as well.

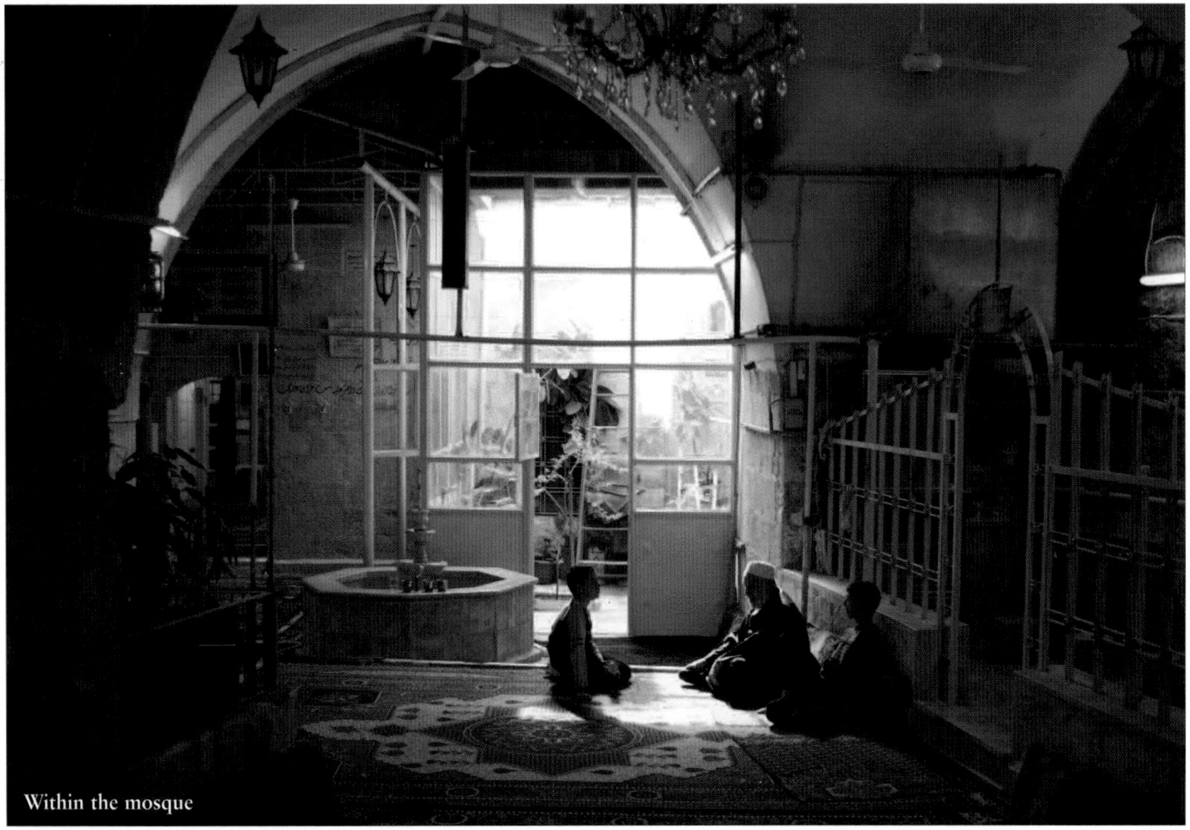
Within the mosque

Everything was interconnected. The same benefactor had built the mosque, the hammam next to it, and at least one of the iconic waterwheels of Hama.

The *naouras* or water wheels were rotating when Ibn Battuta stopped in Hama, raising water to the aqueducts that bring water to irrigate the fields. He compared them to turning spheres, as if seeing the metaphysical in those wooden circles. Six hundred years later Captain Dinning found the wheels still turning, and describes them in his memoirs:

> The small wheels hum like gnats. Of the great wheels one sounds like a giant oboe; it traverses a gamut of tones in a revolution; it moves so slowly that a revolution lasts many seconds. Another groans incessantly, as though labouring in extreme old age under the intolerable weight of its water and its years.[34]

One traveller has even documented the music of different wheels as musical score, contrasting the 'persistent and plaintive' melodies of individual wheels.[35]

Day and night the town fills with the groaning of the *naouras,* as if they were burdened with history. Since those days the weight of the years has increased; the town of Hama was much destroyed during the civil conflict of the 1980s.

I don't know if I have ever heard a more mournful sound than the water wheels of Hama. But despite the religious conservatism of the town (or perhaps because of its conservatism), Hama is a great place to hammam.

Hammams as Islamic Endowments

Much that was lovely in Hama has now gone, but it remains one of the best places in Syria to bathe, with three working hammams surviving. There's a simple rule – I'll call it another principle of hammaming: the more religiously conservative the area, the better the hammams.

In Aleppo this rule holds true and the hammams themselves have often been built as Islamic endowments. The monumental hammam of Bahram Pasha in the lovely area of Jedaidah is a perfect example, built as a *wakf* to the Bahramiya Mosque.

When I went in search of the hammam I found myself caught between the hammam and the coffee house opposite; despite the hammam's alternating bands of limestone and basalt, the façade of the seventeenth-century café was even more lovely. The coffee-house was like some of the old Christian merchant houses of the area, where the designs seem not so much cut from the stone, as woven from it, as a baker might weave a pattern from the dough before baking. The Russells described not just Aleppo's hammams but its coffee-houses, where the powers of the day might have found themselves victims of a satirical puppet show; there is a long tradition of cafés as places of intrigue and rebellion.

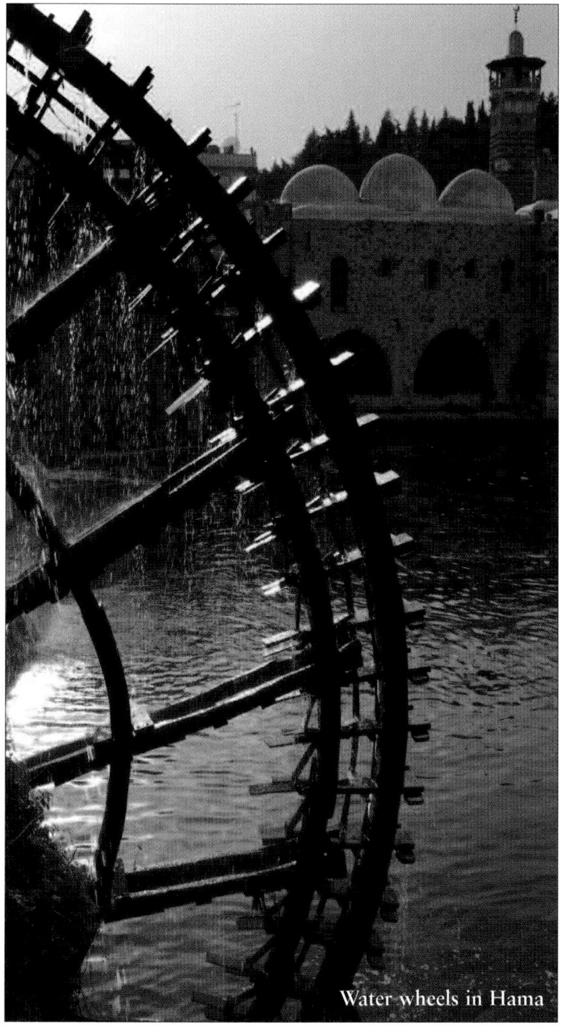
Water-wheels in Hama

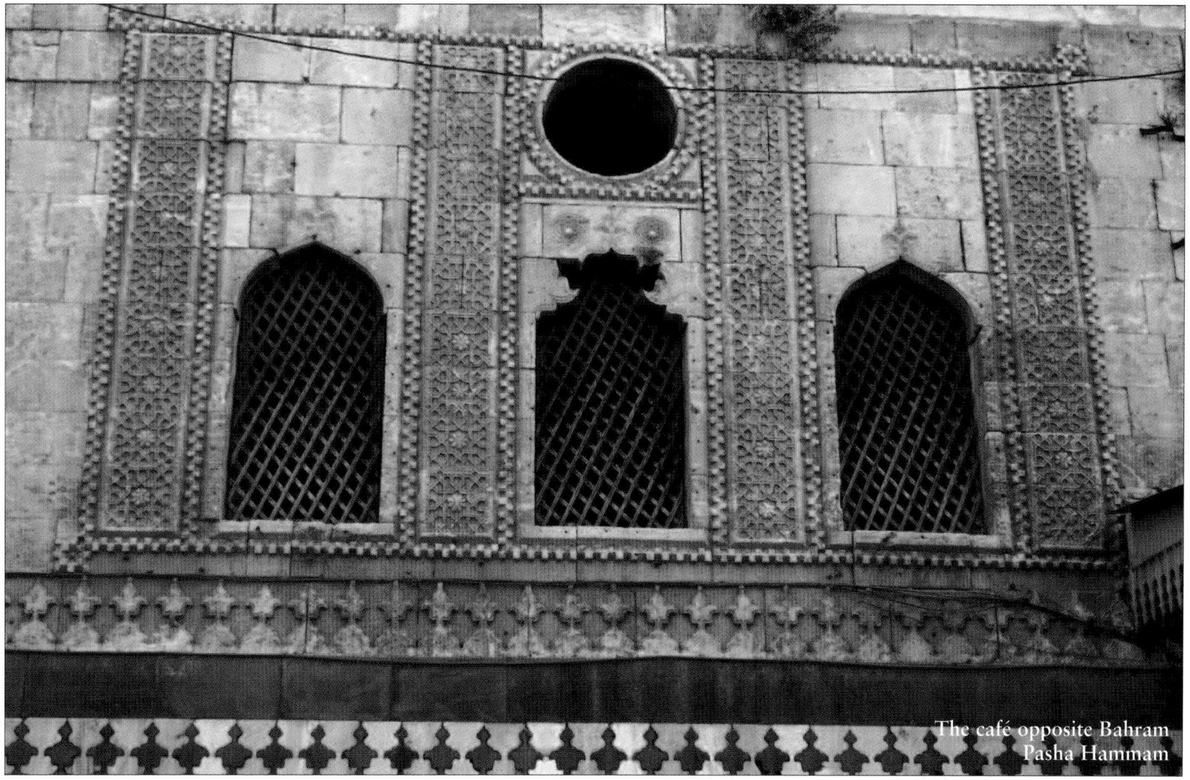
The café opposite Bahram Pasha Hammam

It was not enough just to find the hammam. It was most definitely closed, if not abandoned, and I found myself on the usual quest: I needed to find the man with the key. I was in luck, however, and the shopkeeper across the way opened for me a hammam with incredible spaciousness, a rush of cats, and cobwebbed aspidistras yellowing on a fountain. The size of the balcony suggested that this had once been a king of hammams. He turned to me:

– The owner doesn't want the hammam!

Without a thought I replied:

– Tell him, I'll buy it!

How I wished I could have bought it, this first Ottoman monument in the area outside the walls.[36] Back in the street a local man was called over as my guide. It seemed that much of the street had been part of another endowment.

– Here we have the hammam. And opposite was the café. And these shops you see now were once stables for the horses.

At that end of the street, tastefully renewed, there were chicken shops with butchers in wellington boots, a bakery, and a mosque where local people spread out their bread on the pavement to cool. Around the corner were the blacksmiths and the gas-seller who was also the *muezzin* of a nearby mosque – for a man who has a menial job might also be the one who calls the entire community to prayer.

In 'the great republic of Islam' (to quote Gertrude Bell) there is neither race nor class. Visiting the Umayyad Mosque in Damascus, Bell observed the faithful line up together for afternoon prayers:

> All sorts and grades of men stood side by side, from the learned doctor in a fur-lined coat and silken robes to the raggedest camel driver from the desert, for Islam is the only republic in the world and recognises no distinctions of wealth or rank.[37]

The only republic in the world! That at least is how it is in the mosque; a Pakistani labourer working in Saudi nowadays might find the reality a little different – I suspect he would find a well stratified pecking order.

It was not just the hammam that had been built to support the Bahramiya Mosque, the café too would have been a source of income for the later foundation. And the endowment deed not only provided for sweepers and lavatory attendants for those attending the mosque, it even laid down conditions for its imams: in a nice balancing act one would be of the Hanafi school and one Shafi'i.[38]

My guide continued in his matter-of-fact way in colloquial Arabic:

– The top floor was the barracks for the Ottoman troops...

As he continued he looked at me to see my reaction:

– ...the barracks where they slept and... [and here he used a very colloquial Arabic verb for intercourse]

He watched to see if a Westerner might be offended by such talk, or not know such Arabic words. I looked back at him, as if astonished that anyone could say such a thing:

– *Haram!* I said. *Haram!*

I was using the Arabic word used to respond to something that is found morally offensive. I pretended to be aghast:

– You're not telling me that those Ottoman soldiers had a hammam and only washed in it?

An Ottoman Hammam

On an island between Ireland and Scotland there is still the remains of a 'sweat house', a place of stones where the islanders used to sweat themselves out of a fever or clean before a fair day. The first time an Englishman admitted publicly to the shameful act of a daily wash, however, was in the eighteenth century. For his efforts to achieve personal cleanliness, Lord Harvey was satirized in Alexander Pope's verse as Lady Fanny. And when public baths did become the norm, the English class system imposed itself on even the act of swimming: at least one city had a two-pool system, with the water of the middle-class pool emptied into the workers' pool every week or so for the masses to swim in.

In contrast, in the Orient, personal cleanliness was held in high regard. In the mid-eighteenth century, just a few years after the death of Pope, the Ottoman governor of Damascus was building his Azem Palace in the heart of the city. This palace doesn't just have extensive courtyards but also a stylish three-roomed hammam which would have been not just a place to wash but to entertain. I suspect that it was after a hammam that many a business deal was clinched.

Perhaps I should not over-emphasise oriental bodily hygiene. The memoirs of a notable Damascene, Basheer Al Azemi, recall a childhood of genteel poverty when a visit to the public bath was a memorable occasion, what with the cost of the bath and the soap. He also provides an insight into family relations when he recalls one of the rare moments of intimacy with his mother when she sat and squeezed the lice from his hair. His memoir also hints about a taboo aspect of Ottoman life in Damascus; it was not just the 'honour' of the girls that needed to be protected.[39]

After the Mamluks, the Ottomans were the great hammamers. In Ottoman times the area around Medan expanded, for it was from here that the pilgrimage, a great source of revenue, departed and it was here that the chief financial official, Fathi al-Daftari, built one of the most elegant of Damascene hammams.

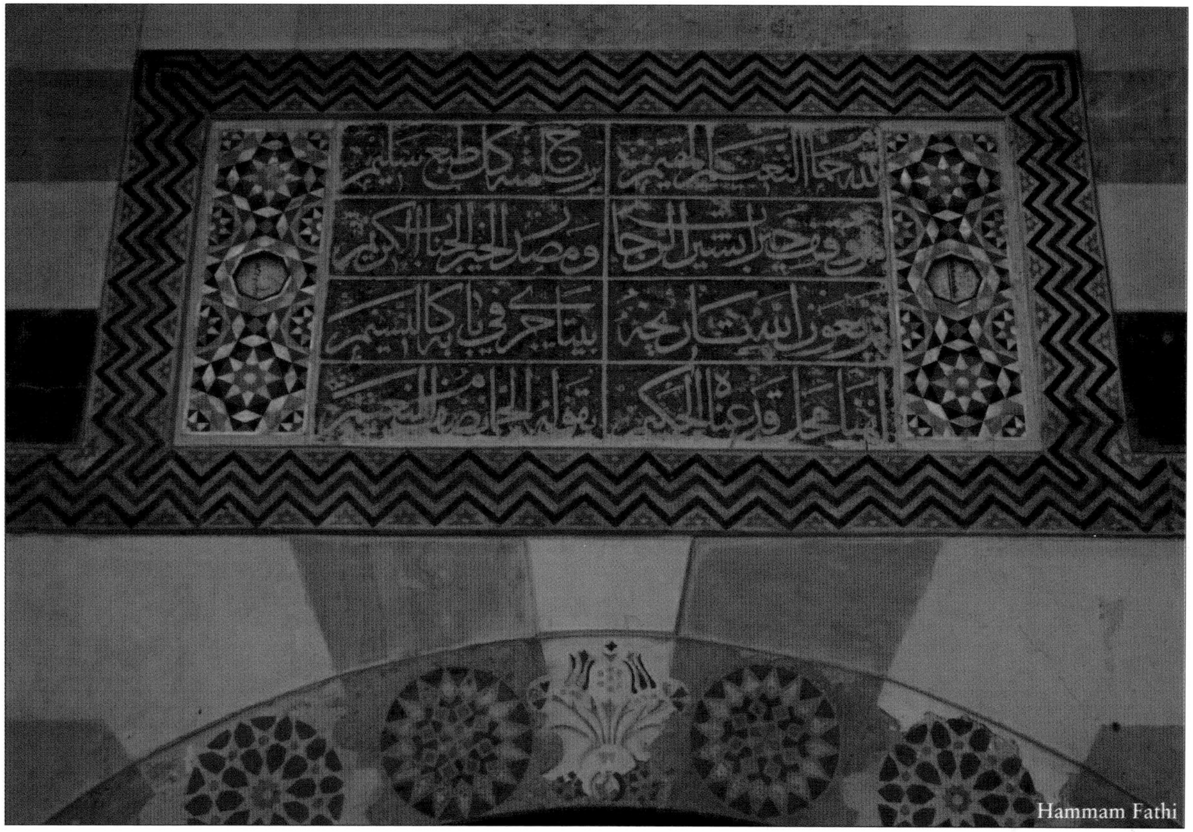

Hammam Fathi

When I went to Medan I was not much surprised, given the general rundown nature of the street, to find Hammam Fathi well and truly closed, if not semi-derelict. Even the lovely *sebil* in its wall had an abandoned air. But there were men working in the yard, and one leapt at the copy of M. Kayall's *Les Bains Damascains* which I was carrying with me. '*Ya hamak Allah*!', he pronounced affectionately, recognising someone smiling out from one of the photographs. And then from the departed soul to a lost hammam: 'Ah! Hammam Miliki! The most beautiful hammam, not in Damascus, but in all Syria!'

Needless to say 'the most beautiful hammam in Syria' was no more, and the fate of Hammam Fathi too looked uncertain. Fathi had been a local man made good, rising to great power, challenging the Azems who governed Damascus under Ottoman rule at that time. Fathi had built not only his hammam but the Qaimariye Mosque in a quarter of Damascus near the Umayyad Mosque – for me perhaps one of the loveliest buildings in Damascus, not far from one of the city's oldest hammams, the Qamariah – with a graceful courtyard of banded stone and citrus trees. Vines trail down the inscription above the doorway of the mosque, which parallels the inscription above the closed doorway of Fathi's hammam: 'This is the place the wise man meant when he said "A hammam is half a paradise".'

The tranquility of the citrus-greened courtyard belies the turbulence of the times. Fathi was executed (apparently he threw a better party than the Azems). I was told that all that he had built in Damascus, apart from these two monuments, was destroyed, but this is hearsay; written records might prove different. It was a mistake to challenge authority, even if you were the governor: The Azem governor, too, was perceived as getting too powerful and was called back by the Sultan in Istanbul. His career came to an end in a hammam in Ankara, for hammams were a traditional venue for dispatching rough justice.

I suppose disposing of a rival in the hammam saved getting blood on the carpets. One of the most notorious hammam assassinations was by the 'Queen of Egypt', Queen Shajarat al-Durr. With the death of her first husband she took power, consolidating her rule by marrying the Caliph's general, and in the mosques of Cairo the *khutba* of Friday prayers was said in her name and in her husband's. Perhaps the marriage was not just political expediency on Shajarat's part, however, for when Izz al-Din Aybak wanted to take a princess as his second wife, he was dispatched in the hammam. Shajarat too met a sticky end; this 'Egyptian Bilquis' was beaten to death with the clogs traditionally worn in the hammam, her body tossed half naked into the castle moat. Today her remains are honoured by a gilded shrine.[40]

The men continued flicking through M. Kayall's *Les Bains Damascains*:

– He was my grandfather. *Ya hamak allah!*

One read out an inscription that had not quite disappeared with a hammam's destruction, for M. Kayall had recorded it in his book as I have documented a passing way of life in mine:

– Why, that was my cousin – my cousin wrote that!

The hammams of Damascus had reached a sad state of decline. What I was told M. Kayall had said about another Damascene hammam could equally have been said about the decayed splendour of this Ottoman hammam in Medan:

> The people here could no more care about the ruin of this hammam than if they saw two goats butt each other in the road.[41]

Hammam al Werd

It was one of the first days of summer. The traffic policemen were out in their half-sleeved shirts and the canaries were singing in their cages outside the cafés when I went to Hammam al Werd.

In summer Damascenes tend to favour the fresh-water pools of the suburbs to the hammams, so there was just myself, the elderly attendant and two bathers – one in synthetic swimming trunks and another a Syrian in comfortable middle age. Given the idleness of the afternoon I sat in the *jouwani*. It was that lovely time of day when the late afternoon light comes through the honey-combed glass of the roof, and gives the hammam an almost sacred air.

It was a good opportunity to pump the attendant for information and I asked him how many working hammams there now were in Damascus. He said about fifteen. Together we went through the familiar litany of hammams I had visited, but he spoke of one or two that were unknown to me. My quest was in itself becoming like a chain – a visit to one hammam would lead to a casual reference to another hammam.

I asked which was the oldest hammam in the city.

– Hammam Nur al-Din. It is one thousand one hundred years old.

By those calculations the labourers of Damascus were enjoying a palatial hammam

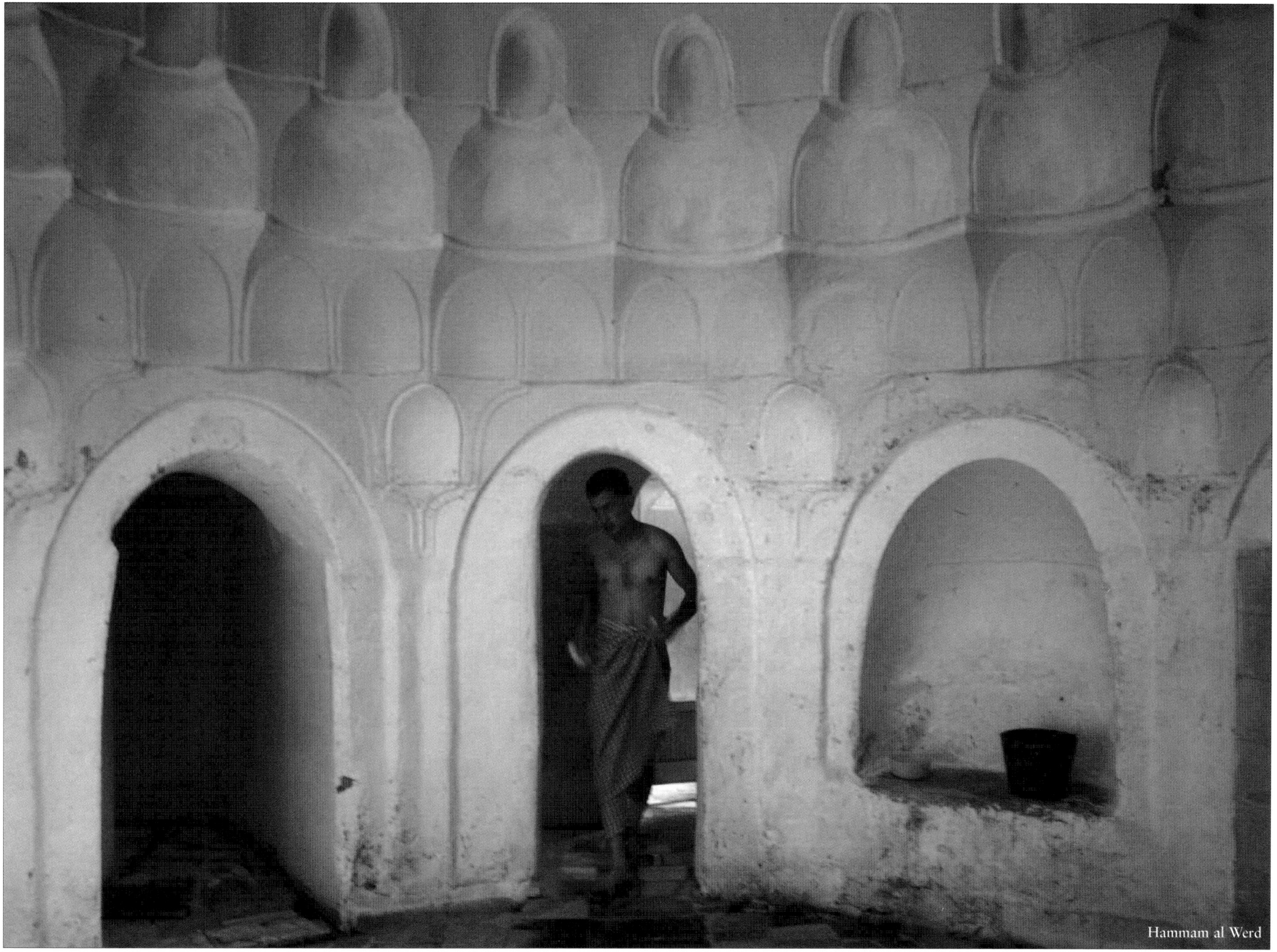
Hammam al Werd

when the royalty of England were bathing once or twice a year. (Even when Victoria came to the throne, Windsor Castle still did not have a single bathroom.) But the middle-aged bather was having none of this:

– Nur al-Din was the brother of Saladeen, he said scathingly.

Even I, with my scant knowledge of history, could figure out that we were going back about seven or eight hundred years not a thousand, although I wasn't convinced about the brotherly relations. Inheriting Damascus, Saladeen looked to master all Syria but Aleppo had its own prince, a son of Nur al-Din. Fortunately the young Al-Salih took ill, 'I Claudius' style, but refused the wine offered by doctors as medicine:

> Al-Salih asked: 'And do you really think that if God has decided to end my life he will change his mind if he sees me drinking wine?' The men of religion had to answer, No. 'Then', the dying man concluded, 'I do not want to meet my maker with a forbidden drink in my stomach.'[42]

Our informed bather continued:

– There were once hundreds of hammams in Damascus. Every area had its own hammam, for the essentials of life were there in every quarter: the mosque, the hammam, the baker and the barber.

This was certainly true of the Werd area even today, for outside the hammam was the barber's, and a few doors away was the mosque, and the bakery with its chocolate croissants. A scholar put it thus:

> During the 19th century the Saruja Quarter contained three hammams, four furns (oven-bakery), a Friday mosque (Jami' al Ward) with minaret, fifteen masjids (mosques) and a tahun (flour-mill) in the main street.[43]

I asked about the name al Werd. The attendant had the knack of putting things very simply:

– This is Hammam al Werd, named after Sheikh al-Werd. Every hammam has its sheikh.

Our scholar seemed to disagree. He went on to talk about the pilgrimage to Mecca, and those who died on the way, and their commemoration with holy tombs – but I couldn't quite catch his drift, for his Arabic was too classical for me, and I had to distance myself from the garlic of his breath, and I preferred the attendant's gentle explanation of things.

And so another principle of Syrian hammams was voiced for me: every hammam has its sheikh.

After Hammam al Werd

In the past, Saruja had been the most desirable area of Damascus, with the Ottoman rulers creating their own Little Istanbul outside the city walls:

> ... at the end of the 19th century the three wealthiest families, the Abid family of ... grain merchants, the Yusuf family of the amir of pilgrimage (al-hajj) and the politically powerful Azm family all lived in the Saruja quarter.[44]

Today's Saruja is one of decay, and deliberate neglect. Over the wall of some abandoned house orange trees still bear fruit, the family long moved out of the area. Gracious houses are broken up as tenements for the rural poor who have moved in. There are the ghostly timbers of houses that unfortunately caught fire some Friday afternoon...

This is how it is in Damascus – there will be the TV cameras nostalgically creating a bygone way of life using a few carefully preserved buildings as a set, while just a few hundred metres away yet another Ottoman building is being demolished. A kind of virtual Damascus is being created for TV (no one in the Arab world makes historical dramas like the Syrians do!) but as *Bab al Hara* is viewed by millions throughout the Arab world each Ramadan, almost no one notices the destruction of the real Damascus. Hammam al Werd will feature in a soap opera, but the hammams of Damascus are forgotten.

It was one Friday afternoon in Hammam al Werd that another bather told me he lived in the neighbourhood, just a few streets away

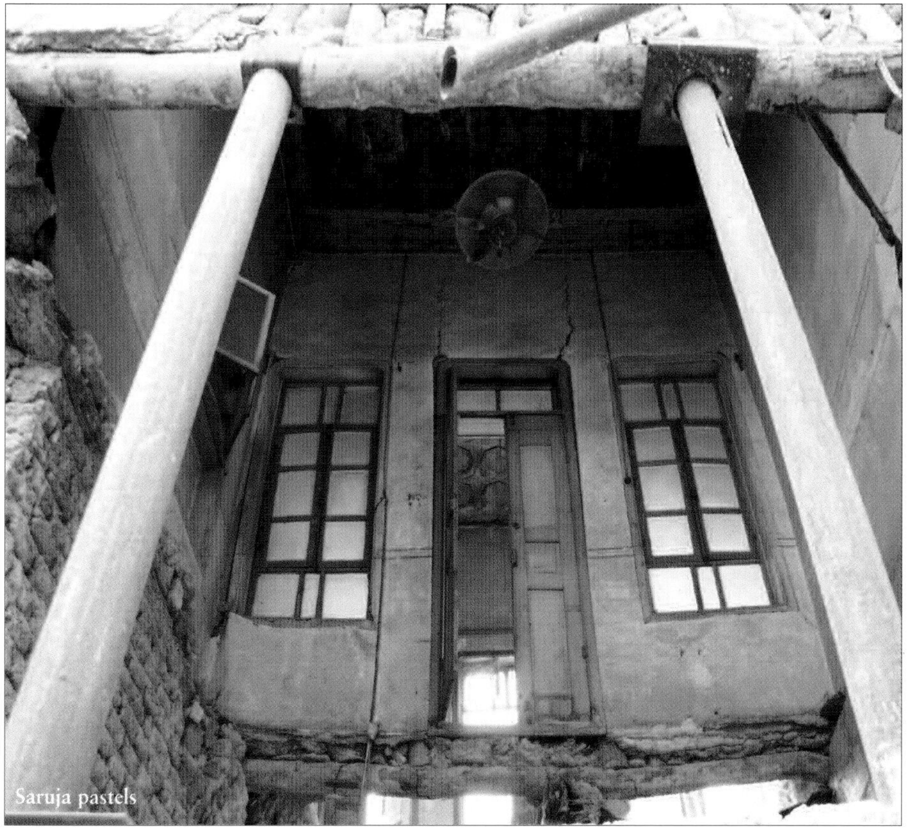

Saruja pastels

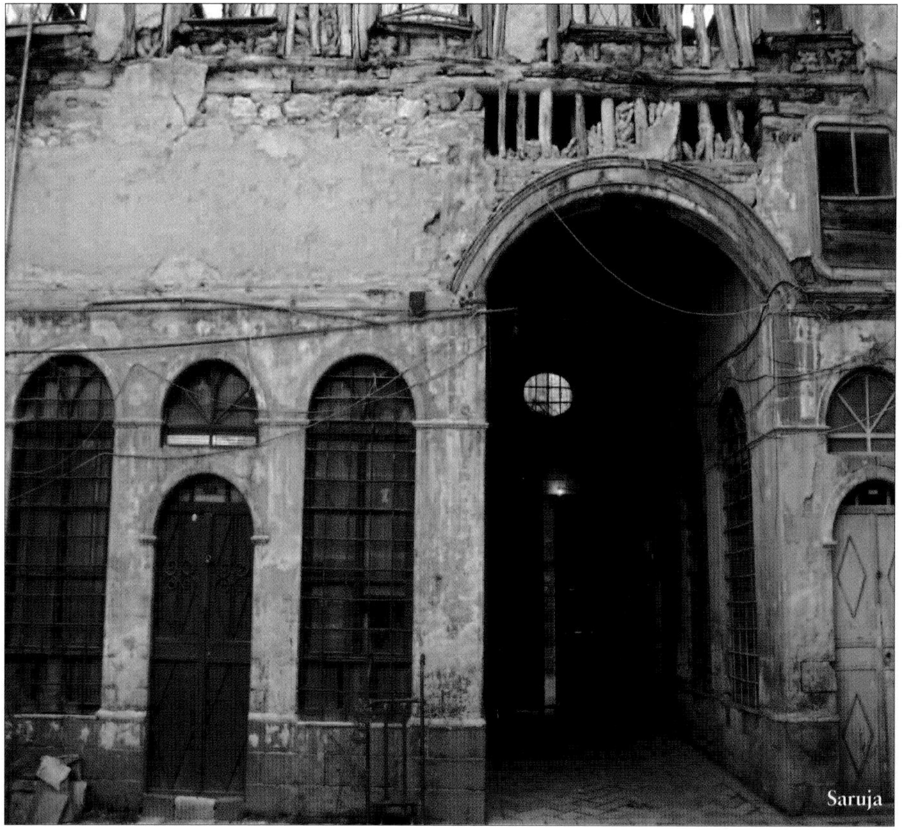

Saruja

in one of the old houses. I asked if I could visit, for I imagined a courtyard, and maybe orange trees and jasmine.

Ahmed affably agreed. Swathed in towels we sat in the foyer afterwards, under the carpeted walls of the hammam (yes, it is the walls that are covered in factory rugs) with the suspended wires of trailing plants hanging from the central dome. I turned to Ahmed:

– How old would you say the hammam is?

He surveyed the foyer:

– Maybe a hundred years?
– Some say seven hundred.

As we left, a cold wind blowing despite it being April, Ahmed explained that he lived with his mother and family. I had been pushy, so I invited him for tea in the café instead. However he insisted, and we went down a spotless lane. Ahmed went in first to warn the family of a stranger's presence. I knew the score; I waited, then followed.

We sat at the top of the stairs, on a kind of sofa overlooking a rickety banister and the washing. Like many a Georgian house in Dublin in the past, this house had been split up and partitioned off to accommodate several families. Rough sacking provided a kind of privacy.

– Here in Damascus you have to really cut yourself off from your neighbours. We don't live that way at all in Lattakia; there, we have normal relations.

Ahmed's mother brought coffee, then bananas and oranges. Ahmed had said his home was

Slenfai near Lattakia. I knew the place; it was home to my favourite castle:

– So you'll have been to Saladeen's Castle then?

The reply was to the point:

– We haven't the time or the money for that kind of thing.

I suppose it's the same all over the world; people leave the poverty of rural areas for the bright city lights, and set about the daily grind. I took in this family's surroundings and thought of the spaciousness of my own flat: the long salon with its furniture tastefully inlaid with mother-of-pearl; my study, all light and graced with plants. The balcony was perfect for drinks, with its geraniums and hibiscus in pots, and the neighbours' orange grove below.

Ahmed's mother invited us into the main room, but I had already broken the bounds of etiquette, and thought I should at least leave the women to their part of the house. Our cultural exchange continued:

– That house opposite us here (Ahmed pointed to the mud and straw wall across the street) ... how old would you say that is?
– I've no idea. Why?
– What we want, you know, is not this old kind of thing, but a modern house. In this part of the world we don't much care for the old; we want to knock it down and put up something new.

How true that was, and it was not just Syria. When I had lived in Yemen I had admired a painting of a mosque in the Taj Hotel, for the architecture of the little Sana'ani mosque suited the delicacy of a water colour. When I finally got round to taking my camera to try and capture its loveliness (when you live in a place there is no rush, those monuments will be there long after you are gone) I found not a 700-year-old mosque but a vacant lot. Dumbfounded, I asked the neighbours in the street what had happened. They gave a very simple explanation of things:

– It was old, so we knocked it down.

The logic of it was clear. And in place of a delightfully delicate mosque, in a city said to have been founded by a son of Noah, they put up a thing of breeze blocks that would not have been out of place next to a supermarket car park.

Ahmed laughed affably.

– I suppose you have a different way of looking at things. You are all educated over there in Europe. And you've been everywhere here. Me, I just know Lattakia and Damascus.
– But you drive a taxi! You must know Damascus better than me! And where do you go when you're not working?
– I'm always working. You mustn't think that I usually take a Friday off.
– But when you're not working, where do you go? I usually go out to the restaurants with friends.
– I have my relatives here. Married. You know I have one in New York, no, New Jersey. He's well-off, but he has forgotten us.

We exchanged telephone numbers. Maybe we would hammam the following Friday; he had never been to Hammam Nur al-Din. We went through the rituals: I said the usual *Daemi* (Always!) to thank them for the coffee, they wished me health and I left.

Sheikh Werd

Werd means 'rose' in English, and it was from the *mi'allim* of Hammam al Werd that I heard how the sheikh and the mosque and the hammam got their name.

It was one of those evenings when no-one seemed to be actually hammaming, but the *barrani* was packed with men in fawn-coloured gowns, sitting around and chatting. Hammam al Werd was functioning as a community centre.

The manager (the hammam is family run, but it has only been in their hands now for a couple of generations) went on to affably tell me of Sheikh Werd. Apparently the shiekh had not always had the name *Werd*. The story it seems began when the sheikh was summoned to a certain home in the neighbourhood. Finding herself alone with the sheikh, the woman of the house started to make advances.

In response the sheikh excused himself, saying he needed to use the bathroom. There,

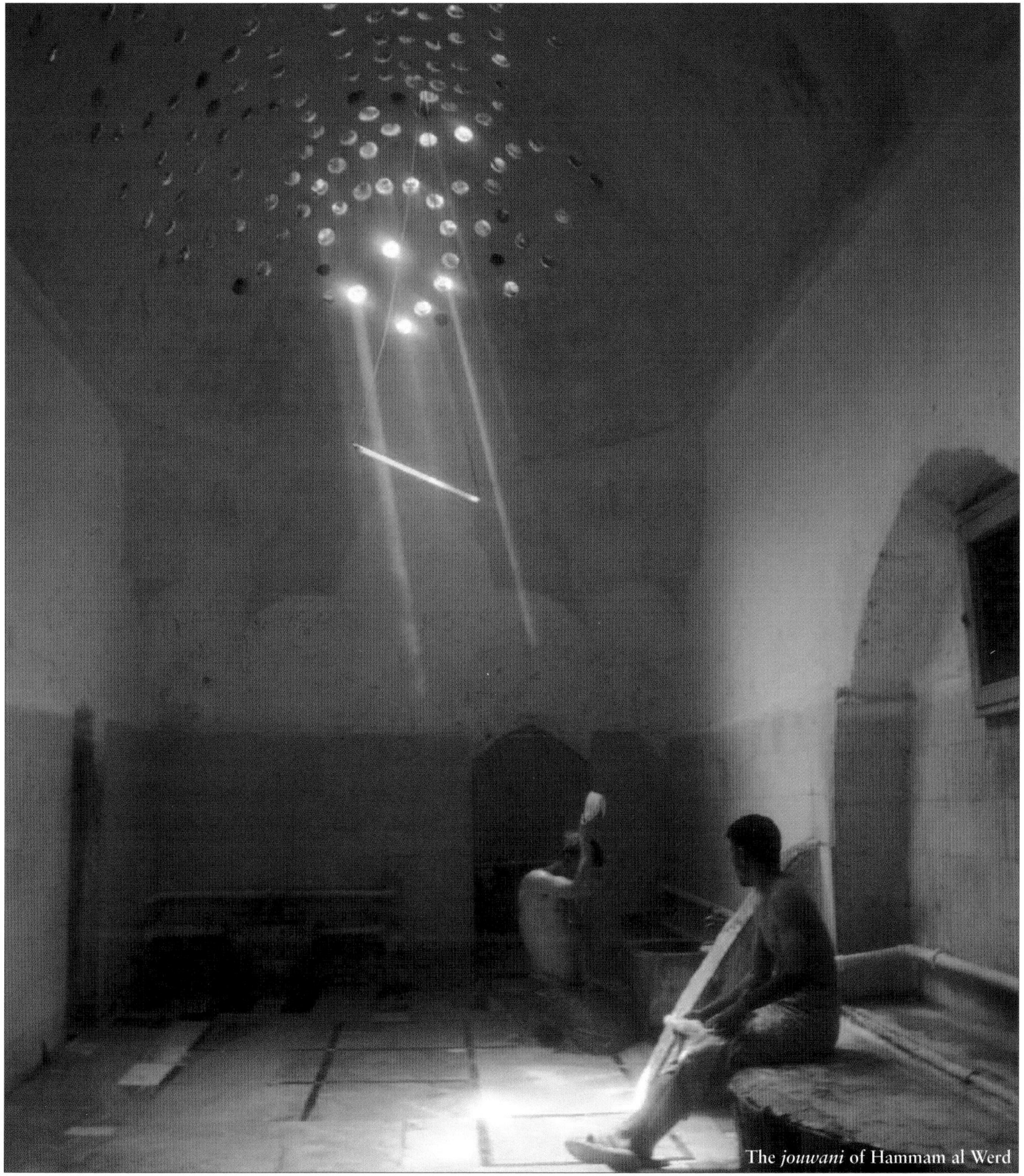
The *jouwani* of Hammam al Werd

he took the excrement from the toilet and smeared it all over his body. The woman of course was repulsed by the shiekh's new appearance, and he was able to leave the house, his virtue intact. (Over six centuries earlier Ibn Battuta had told a similar story in which an Egyptian sheikh, in order to repel a woman's advances, shaved off his moustache and eyebrows, and had a cult following of young men with shaven moustache and eyebrows as a result.)

On the shiekh's going out into the street, the people gathered round, and asked the sheikh about his lovely scent, for the sheikh (Genet-like, that same Genet who had served as a soldier in Damascus, and transformed the spit that had been showered on him elsewhere into the rose petals of his imagination) had undergone a transformation. He smelled not of excrement but of roses, and hence the sheikh, the mosque and the hammam all now have the name of *Werd*.

One evening a week they still light candles on the font that is said to be the sheikh's. I was told that the imam of the Werd Mosque encouraged those who manage the hammam to do this, so that the sheikh, centuries after his death, would not have to bathe in darkness.

Hammams and Sheiks

It is not just Hammam al Werd that has its sheikh. Among the dereliction of Saruja, just a minute or two from Hammam al Werd, is Hammam al Joseh. Even in a city like Damascus this had been an area of unparalled loveliness, and the hammam must have got its name from neighbouring giant walnut trees.

The hammam is closed now, and I was told the key was with the Municipality and that they were responsible for this hammam. (In fact it is the Ministry of *Awqaf* (Endowments) that is responsible for most of Syria's hammams.) Once, however, I managed to talk to the man who has the shop of canaries nearby into letting me have a tour, for he had the key then.

Colin Thubron had bathed here in the sixties, surprising the pipe smokers who were relaxing in the *barrani*. At the sight of a foreigner in a hammam one exclaimed, 'God is merciful! An infidel in a towel!' – but whether it was the foreigner's act of washing or his modest covering of the body that so surprised the natives of Damascus, Thubron does not say.

He then savoured the greenish light falling from glass-stoppered holes in the dome of the *wastani*, before being seized by 'a substantially muscled Turk' who put him through 'an organised purgatory' of scouring 'which may have lasted five or fifty minutes'.[45] After the ordeal with the *mukeyyis* Thubron dressed 'tenderly', feeling that it was not just the grime on his skin but his very pores that had disappeared. On leaving Hammam al Joseh he found the outside world 'wonderfully dirty'.

The sound of the *kabkabs* which Thubron relished – the wooden clogs clacking on marble floors – is heard no more in the hammam he calls the second oldest in Damascus, for it is now closed. Kayall writes that in the 1960s it had been one of the cleanest and most frequented of Damascene hammams, but had to be closed when people lost interest in bathing and the income wasn't enough to pay the workers' salaries or the heating.

Kayall had been afraid Hammam al Joseh would suffer the same fate as other hammams in his day – Hammam Fathi, Hammam Rufai, Hammam Sultan – and fall into a state of total disrepair. Hammam al Joseh is not just disused but collapsing in on itself; after some seven centuries the very dome of the *barrani* has fallen onto the floor, to the utter indifference of everyone around.

The building is permanently locked, but through the grid next to its door you can see a sheikh's tomb draped in green. On the iron grid over the window, devotees to the saint have left padlocks: tokens (the equivalent perhaps of a small ad in an Irish newspaper, a promise to St Jude) requesting the granting of a prayer, asking the saint to intervene with the Almighty.

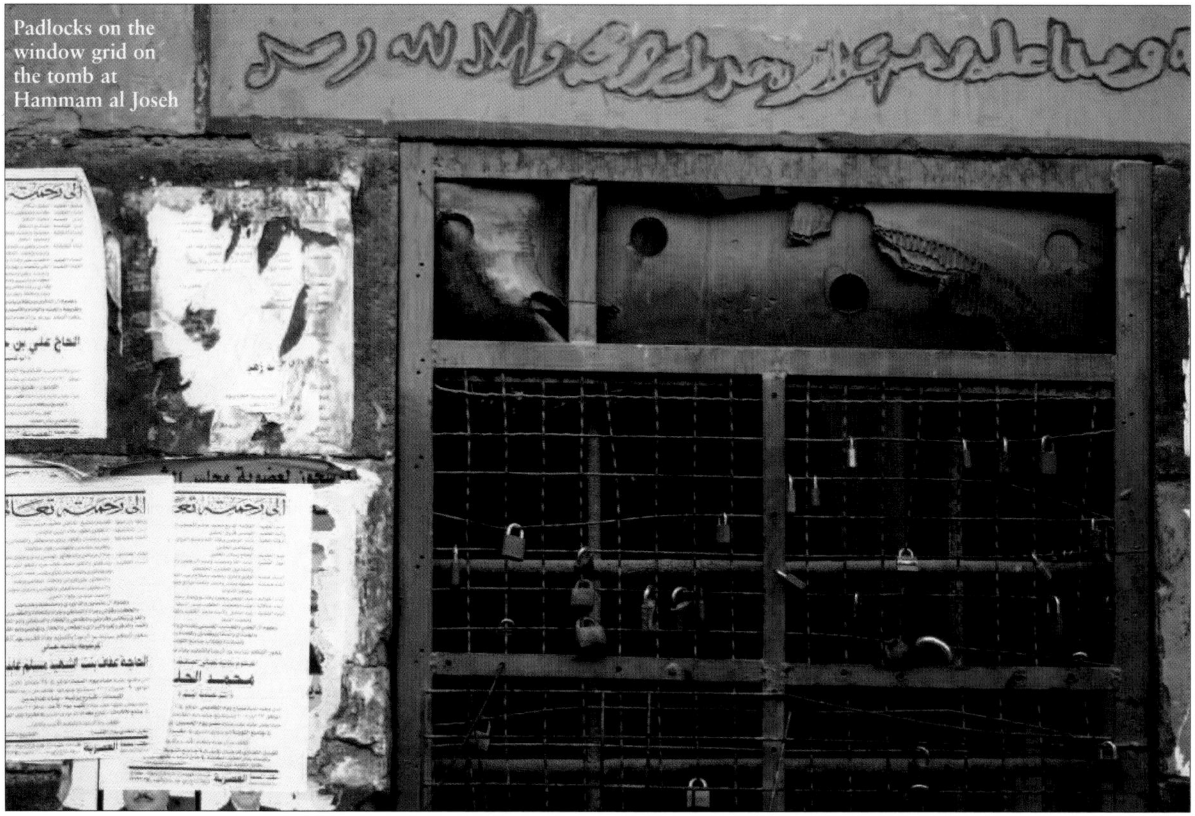
Padlocks on the window grid on the tomb at Hammam al Joseh

This is the saint of Saruja. I heard from Youssef who lives there that the area gets its name from the prince who built the courtyarded palaces outside the city walls. The local people however have a different slant on the origins of the name.

As Youssef heard the story, it goes something like this. There was a slave whose master had departed on the *hajj*. The woman of the house cooked some *kibbeh* (this is a staple of Damascene cuisine: balls of burghul, fried in fat, that meet your day's calorie requirement in just one bite). On tasting the *kibbeh* the house-slave said that he would like to take some to his master, for they were a favourite of his. Thinking the slave must be hungry, the woman of the house indulged the slave and gave him some. Seeing him again later that day she knew that she had been right, for the slave was still in Damascus.

However when the master of the house eventually returned, he thanked his wife for the *kibbeh* she had sent him. And so the area gets its name from the Arabic verb to return – '*rejah*' – after the slave who went after his master on the *hajj* to present him with his wife's *kibbeh* and returned.

The spiritual journey is a key concept for Islamic mystics. Youssef pointed to the journey of the Prophet on a winged steed to the heavens – *the miraj* – as an example of this. Every mystic will have his journey: for Mohi al-Din ibn 'Arabi there was not just the physical journey from Andalusia to Damascus, but the soul's journey towards God.

I would be travelling from hammam to hammam, something more to do with the flesh than the soul. It seems, however, that next to those hammams are the remains of holy men who, if you believe such things, in their journeying were transported beyond the limits of the material world, and still, centuries after their death, can intercede with the Almighty so that the prayer of a devout woman (it is more likely to be a woman than a man asking for intercession) might be granted.

When I was told about Sheikh Werd it was not presented as a story for my entertainment but historical fact. Similarly, when I mentioned a certain mosque to a hammam attendant, the mosque with the emerald-green minaret near Bab al-Jabiye, he told me how the Ottoman ruler Sinan had funded the building of this mosque through magic: Sinan had made a deal with a wizard.

According to the attendant, Sinan had been shown two boxes of treasure: on entering into a pact with the wizard the box on the left would be Sinan's, the one on the right, the magician's. Sinan did not fall for the magician's ploy however, and shifted the boxes; the wizard, not Sinan, got the box of *jinn*. Sinan's casket revealed golden oxen and a peasant farmer, and wherever they ploughed they dug up gold. And so, if the hammam attendant's view of history is to be believed, an Ottoman ruler funded one of the most beautiful mosques in Syria by deceiving a magician.

There is a whole system of beliefs in Syria at a grass-roots level that gives an interpretation of events very different from the historian's. I suspect Sinan would have funded his mosque by building a hammam like everyone else, but what I am following here is often what is said at a popular level,

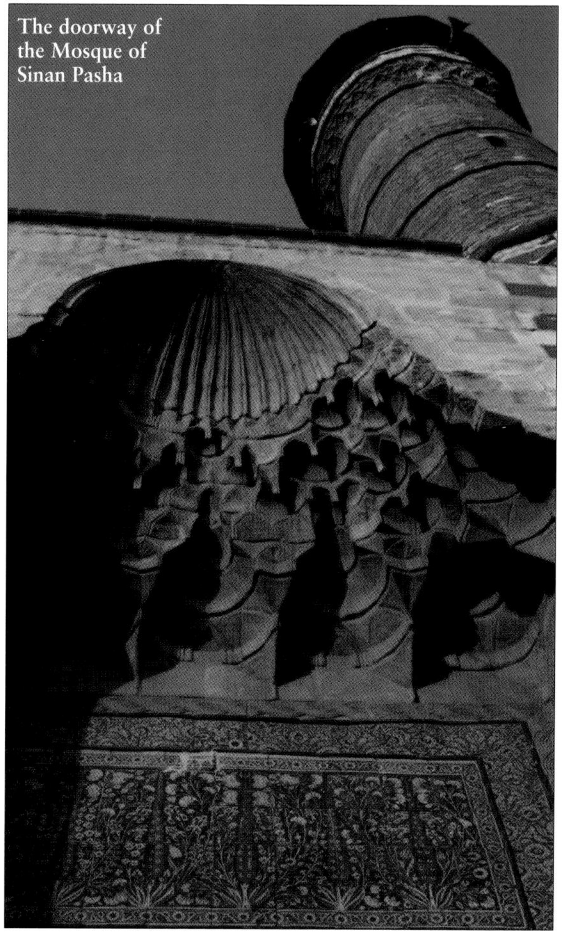
The doorway of the Mosque of Sinan Pasha

rather than what is recorded in official documents.

Beneath the mosque's enamelled minaret there is even today a kind of hiring fair where labourers wait in the hope of a day's work as the traffic grinds through Suq Sinaniye. One labourer told me he was from Marat al Numan, a place where Crusaders had literally devoured the inhabitants as part of their holy war. It was also the home of the tenth-century blind poet Abu al-Ala al-Ma'aari – a vegan and religious sceptic. The labourer quoted a few of al-Ma'aari's words and challenged me to explain them:

– I will do to no other what my father did to me.

I knew the story there; the poet had refused to reproduce and inflict life on another. I replied by attempting to quote a few words:

– In the world there are two types of people: those who have religion and no brains, and those who have brains and no religion.

The labourer was amused:

– That's us. We're the ones with religion and no brains!
– If that's the case you have something in common with us in Ireland!

A millenium after the poet's death, some Syrian labourers and a teacher of English had a good laugh at that observation worthy of Dublin's Dean Swift.

The Need to be Modern

One of my favourite hammams in all Syria is the Hammam Qaramaneh, right in the heart of Martyrs' Square. It was not just in the hammam but in the cafés nearby that I used to idle away my days. The fruit and vegetable market went right up to the door of the hammam, and on the other side there was the *suq al tibbin* where pigeon fanciers gathered under the wattled walls, pulling a salmon-coloured pigeon from a sack, bargaining to exchange it for another that took their fancy.

As the light softened in the late afternoon I would often see pigeons swirl in circles above the city, the light catching their wings as they dipped, and I would sometimes hear a pigeon-fancier coaxing their return. If another's bird should join his circling group the keeper of pigeons will claim it as his own. Given such dubious morals, and their tendency to hang out on roof tops with a view of the neighbours beneath, the owners of pigeons are not allowed to give testimony in a Syrian court of law. It is not only the law courts; pigeon fanciers are also not the most popular suitors in marriage, for who would want to marry their daughter to a man more likely to put turquoise bracelets on the leg of his favourite pigeon than on the wrist of his betrothed?

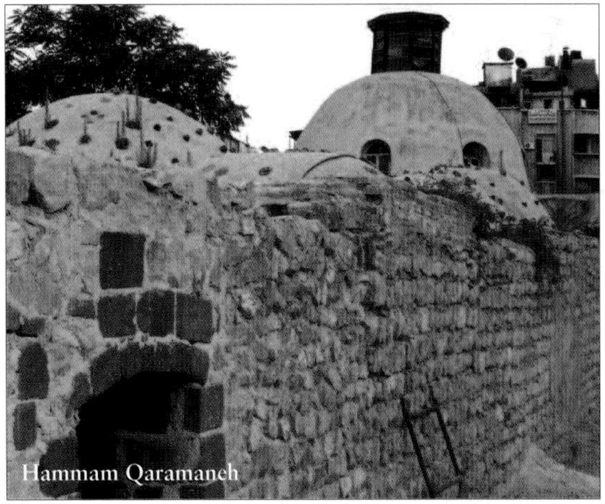
Hammam Qaramaneh

The notorious pigeon fanciers were not the only *shebab* to gather not far from the hammam. Lads from Derazor used to hang about in the cafés: from the banks of the Euphrates they were as much orientated towards Iraqi culture as Damascus, their accents setting them apart from the soft accent of the Damascenes – in this part of the world they sing their Arabic.

Suddenly it was all demolished – the fruit stalls, the Bride of the Desert café, the stalls of denim jackets and jeans – in some scheme to modernise the centre of the city. Now of all those buildings only the hammam survives, like one last tree in a clearing after a wood has been felled. The *suq* is now a public park, the plastic bags outnumbering the plants. And my favourite hammam stands sadly disused, awaiting restoration. It was not just the *suq* with its cafés and stalls that was laid low; unfortunately a wall of the hammam was taken away as the area was demolished – but sometimes a hammam is difficult to spot, even when it is one of the biggest in Damascus.

Fortunately the tomb by the hammam has also been spared. It used to be part of the

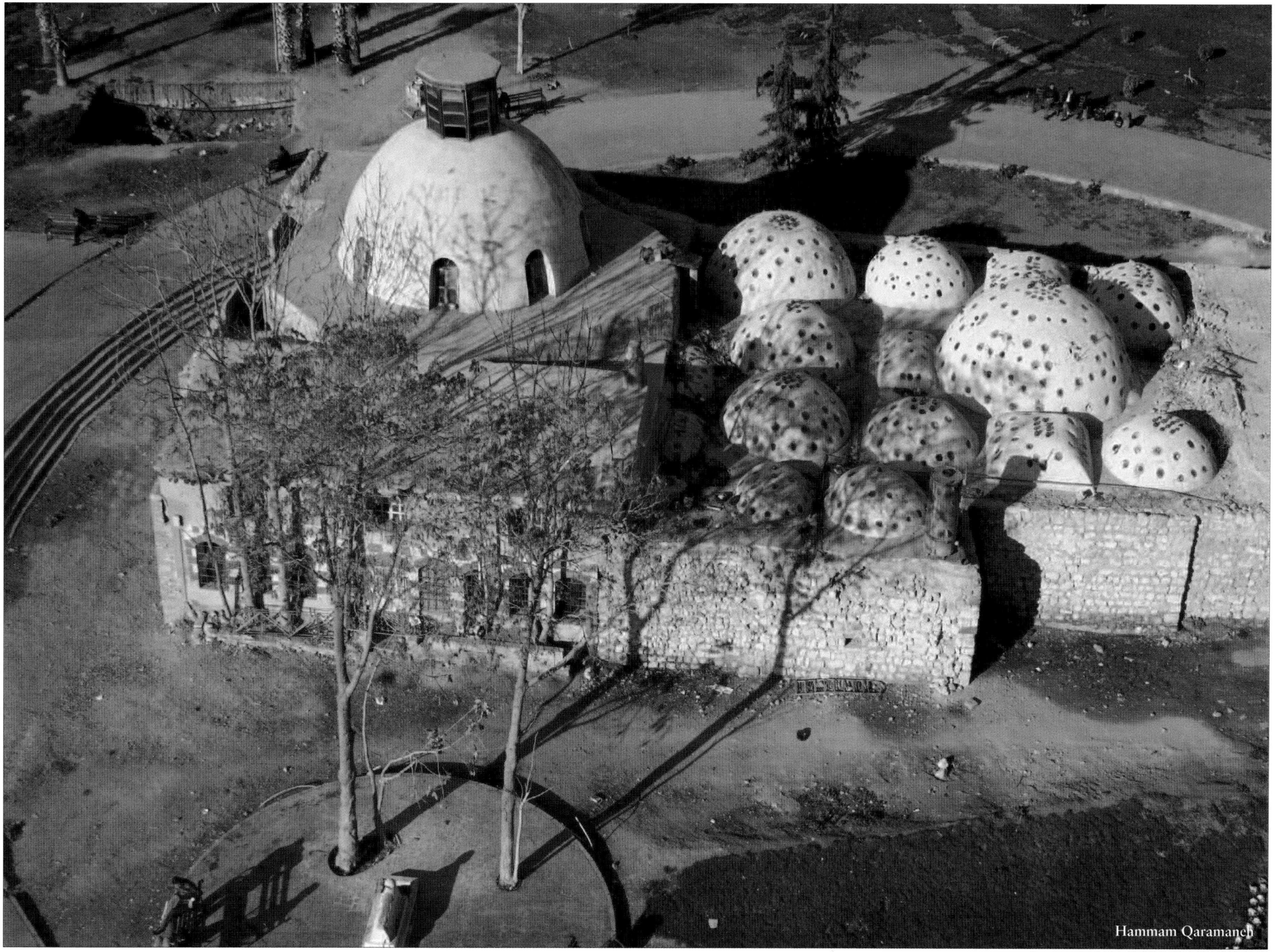

Hammam Qaramaneh

hammam's courtyard where the attendants hung out the towels to dry, and in the evenings a woman would come in – walking right through the *barrani* where the men dressed – to feed the cats by the tomb. On Thursday evenings one of the hammam attendants would light incense at the head of the tomb, sweetening the air in the sheikh's nameless memory.

How lovely – to be buried by a hammam, and to be its patron saint, and for your presence, centuries after your death, to be seen as bringing a blessing to the hammam.

The Judge's Hammam

While I was looking at Ecochard and Le Coeur's *Les Bains de Damas* in the French Institute for Arab Studies, someone heard of my interest and told me about Hammam al Gadi. Like anthropologists documenting a way of life that the coming of their civilisation would wipe out, so Ecochard recorded the hammams of his day, before they were destroyed in the modernisation of Syrian cities.

One sentence in Abdalla Hadjar's *Historical Monuments of Aleppo* – almost an aside as he writes about a mosque – reflects the fate of many of Syria's hammams:

> There was also a bath dating at least from the early Mamluk period, and probably earlier, but this was destroyed as a result of the highway construction.[46]

Hammams have been victims of not just electricity and bathrooms but the perceived need for wider roads. Hammam Sitti Adra (the Hammam of the Virgin) was demolished for a road-widening scheme after Ecochard documented it. What has been lost in the course of modernisation! And what a culture was contained within hammam walls! Sauvaget wrote that Emir Usama al-Halabi had bought marble and sculptures brought from Constantinople after its sacking in the fourth Crusade to embellish his hammam.[47] And how have hammams fallen! As the citizens of Damascus frequented hammams less and less, Hammam Sami became used as a laundry and then a printing press.

One of Damascus' ancient hammams mentioned in Ibn Assakir's documentation of Damascus was Hammam al Gadi, the Judge's Hammam. It seems that a judge used to stop and bathe before attending hearings in the nearby court; as other hammams had a sheikh, so this one had a judge. (I wonder what effect the presence of a judge, if he was in the Ibn Battuta tradition, would have had on those bathing within.)

My fellow reader urged me to go to Hammam al Gadi straight away, and seemed to approve of what I was doing – recording a way of life that was passing fast. Where the long tunnel of Suq Madhat Pasha intersects with the chaos of another street, I asked for the hammam, but they looked at me uncomprehendingly. I had failed to drop the

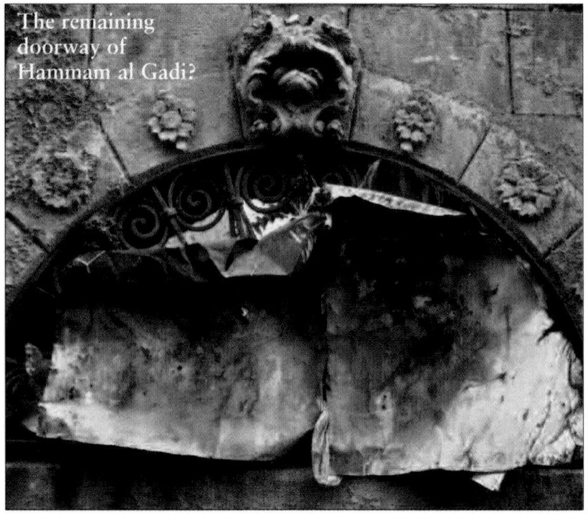
The remaining doorway of Hammam al Gadi?

'G' at the beginning of the word as they do in Damascene dialect. Finally a man revving up his car engine took me to a shop and asked the *shebab* to read the address.

> – Ah the Hammam al 'Adi!, he called and signalled me to follow.

We passed the closed khans and went down an alley. There my helpful guide pointed to a low doorway, arched, with the kind of fanlight you would have seen in some derelict Georgian house in Dublin in the seventies.

> – There it is! That's Hammam al 'Adi!

All that was left on the site was a doorway and a bit of a wall. As I surveyed the walled-off building site, I couldn't tell if my guide had had a wicked sense of irony, or genuinely thought I would be pleased with the find, but off he went, delighted with himself. Apparently Hammam al Gadi had been closed for some 40 years and then used as a store; completely neglected, some of the walls were damaged and a fire brought about its complete closure.[48] A street sign now commemorates the hammam.

Maybe a year or so later – when I had forgotten all about this hammam – I popped into the Hammam al-Umari in Suq Saruja, opposite the shrine to Sheikh Umari. This most definitely had the feel of a hammam on its last legs, and as there were no bathers the attendant had plenty of time to chat. We did the usual litany of naming hammams, and the attendant, who had been working in hammams some 50 years, came up with Hammam al 'Adi. I had forgotten about the business of dropping the 'G' and got all excited at the thought of an undiscovered hammam in Damascus. But then, when he described its location, I clicked, and told him they had knocked it down. He refused to believe me, and I wanted to take him to the site, to see it with his own eyes.

It's not just Hammam al Gadi. I went in search of Hammam al-Sultan, a hammam once frequented by the Ottoman sultan Selim, in Faisal Street, a street earmarked for 'redevelopment' (i.e., destruction). M. Kayall writes that it is described by the Department of Antiquities and Museums as 'one of the greatest hammams in Damascus'.[49] The medallion that had once ornamented the entrance was now gone, but the *barrani* smelt sweet for it was used as a carpenters' workshop. But in

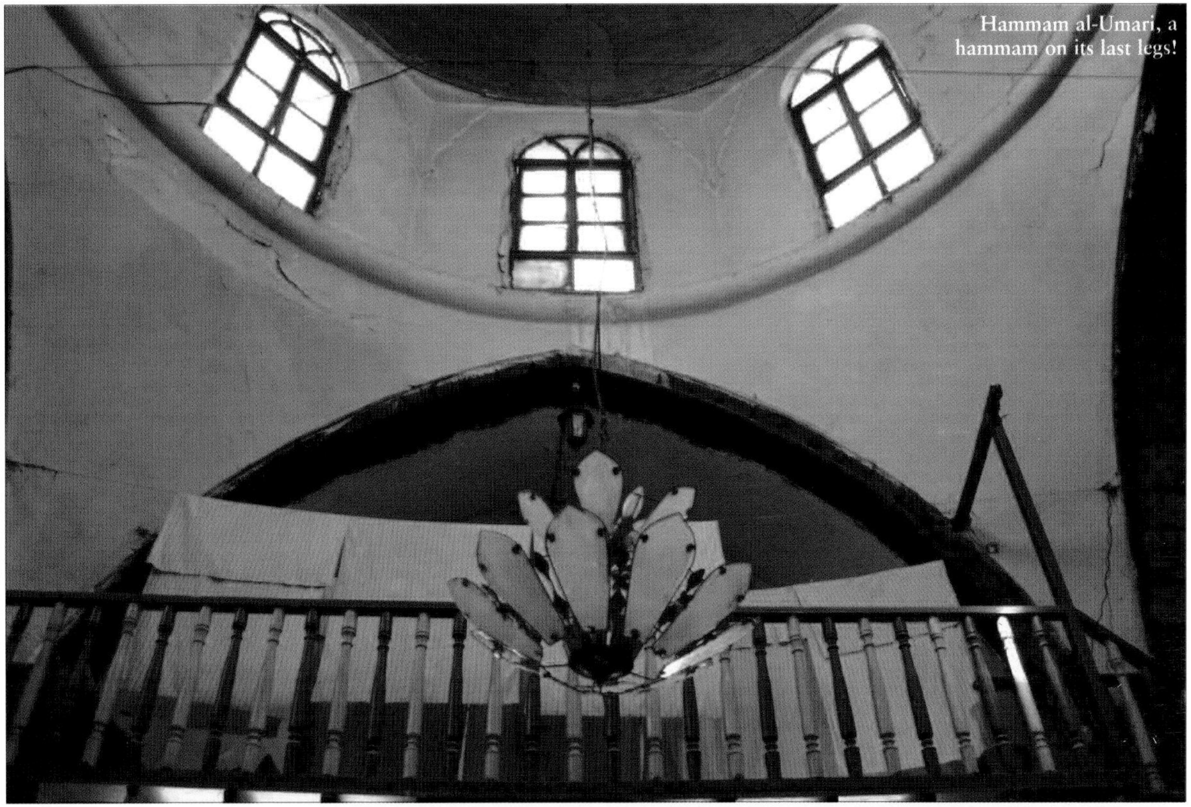
Hammam al-Umari, a hammam on its last legs!

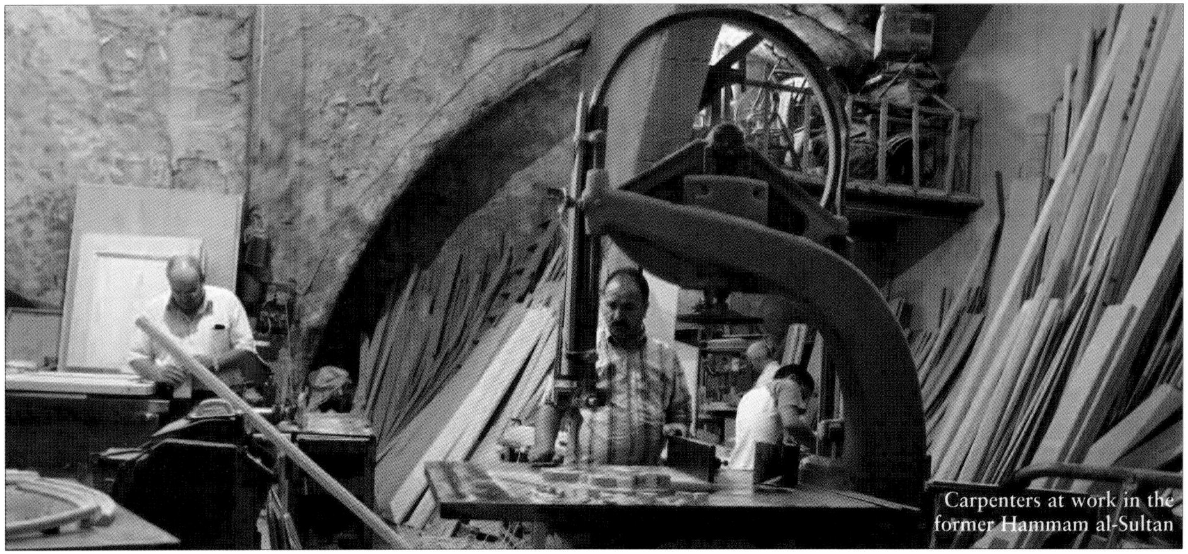
Carpenters at work in the former Hammam al-Sultan

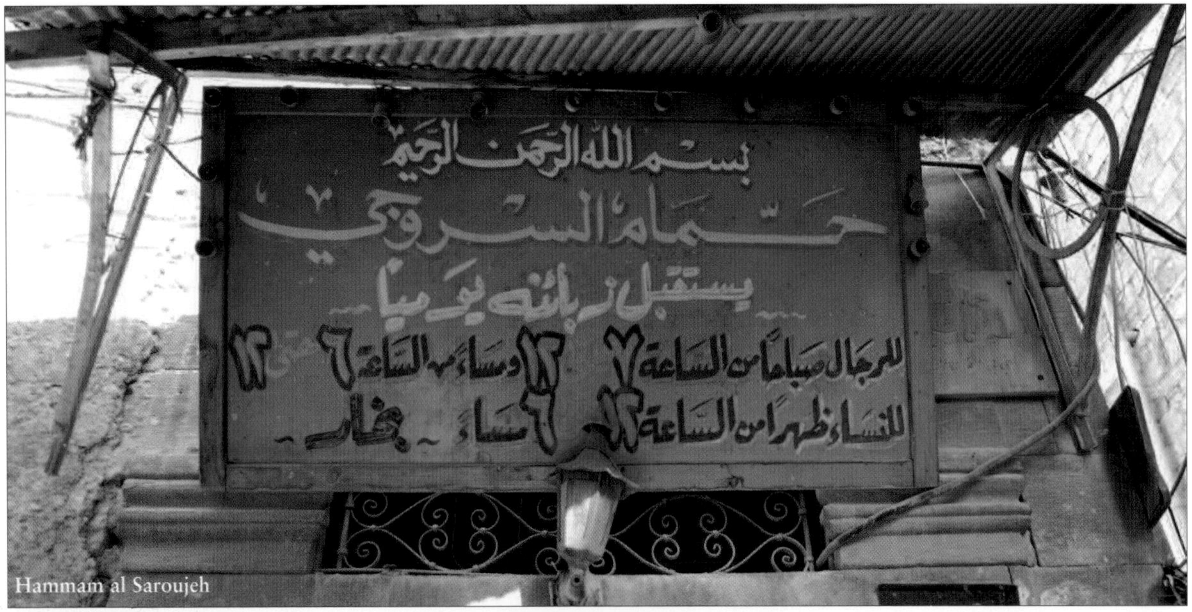

Hammam al Saroujeh

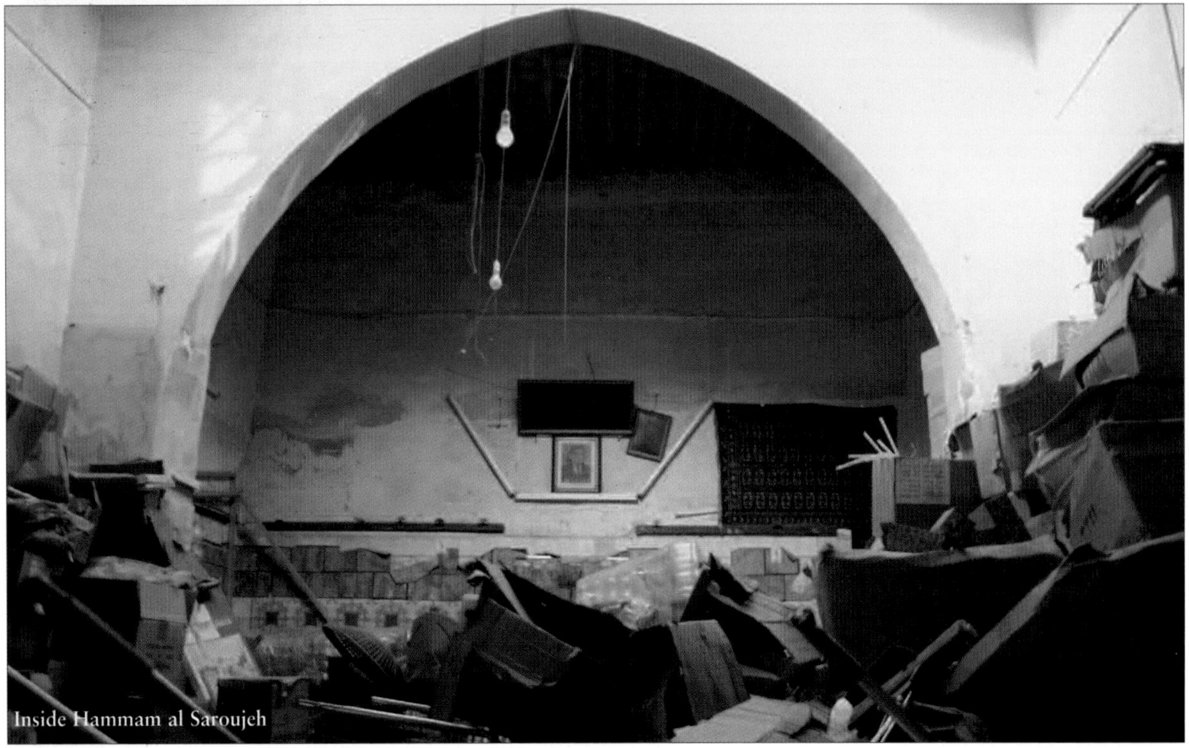
Inside Hammam al Saroujeh

one sense hammam traditions did survive, for the rooms of the hammam were still given over to different pursuits: the *wastani* and *jouwani* were used for packing seeds and nuts and the manufacturing of cloth.

Right in the heart of the city hammams have fallen into disuse. Not far from Hammam al-Silsileh I stepped curiously into an arched entrance and found myself among aproned workers standing by great barrels for dyeing; Hammam Amjak may have once been been a mini-paradise, but now it was functionning as a Dickensian hell.

Other hammams seemed to be just about surviving when I was first in Damascus; once I found Hammam al Saroujeh open, though not particularly inviting, and I should have bathed there and then. When I returned it was closed, but on one occasion I did manage to talk my way into the hammam and found it not so much used as a store but as a dump, albeit with the hammam effects still on the walls. Similarly, in the suburbs I had heard of two hammams in Jobar, but when I finally got round to checking them out I found only one remained. And the fate of some hammams still hangs in the balance: I did once manage to bathe in the hammam in Jeramana – apart from the manager there was just myself – but upon returning I found a phone number on the closed door; they were looking for a buyer.

Once I took a friend from the Yemeni island of Socotra around some of the sites of

Damascus and he quoted poetry about the Barada, for even on an island in the Indian Ocean the River Barada is celebrated. And so I took him to where the river resurfaces after its underground passage through Merjeh Square. Looking down on the stinking trickle, my companion turned to me with disbelief:

– You are not telling me that that is the River Barada?

I felt a certain cynical satisfaction in his disillusionment; perhaps that's what some Syrians feel when they take a romanticising Westerner to the ruins of a hammam.

Decline

What happened in Damascus was mirrored in Aleppo. According to the French architect Sauvaget, Aleppo had almost 200 hammams in the thirteenth century, but few of these would survive to meet the tide of modernity that the French presence heralded.

I would hear of a hammam, and wander through alleys until I found it entirely boarded up like Hammam al-Mileh near Bab Qinnesrin, or Hammam al-Jawhari opposite the *maristan*. Since the fourteenth century the *maristan* housed Aleppo's mentally ill; the curious tourist can still wander around the cells and courtyards where music was played to sooth the mentally ill as they sat by the pool. The hammam, however, described by Abdullah Hadjar as 'spacious and magnificent',[50] with

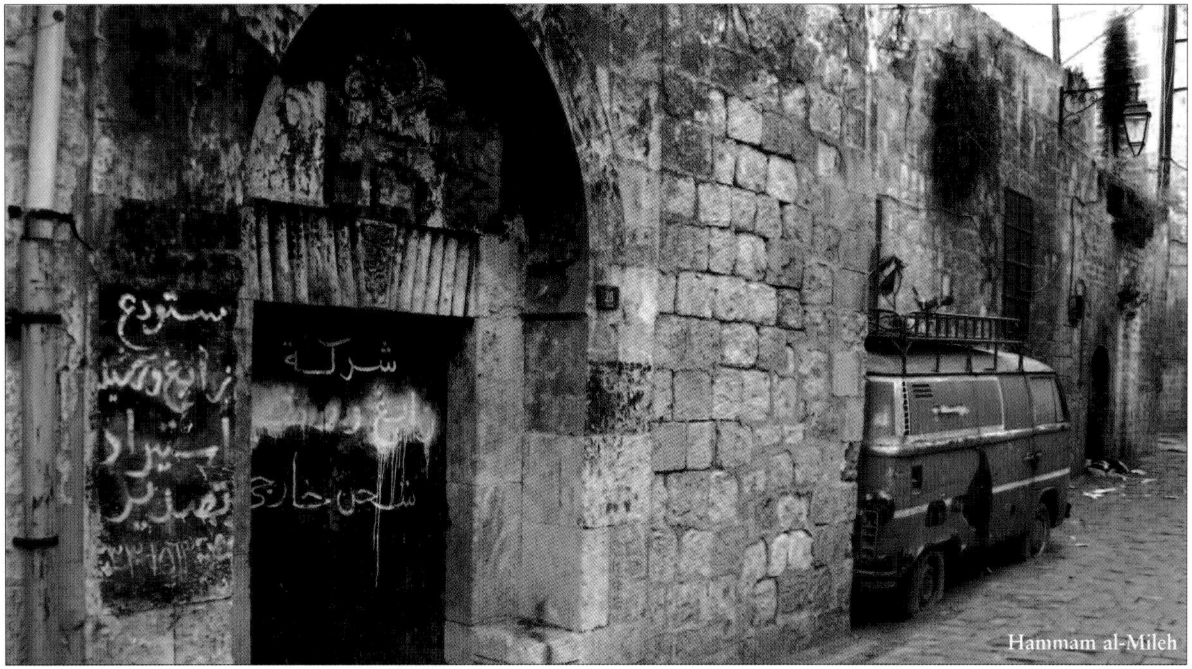
Hammam al-Mileh

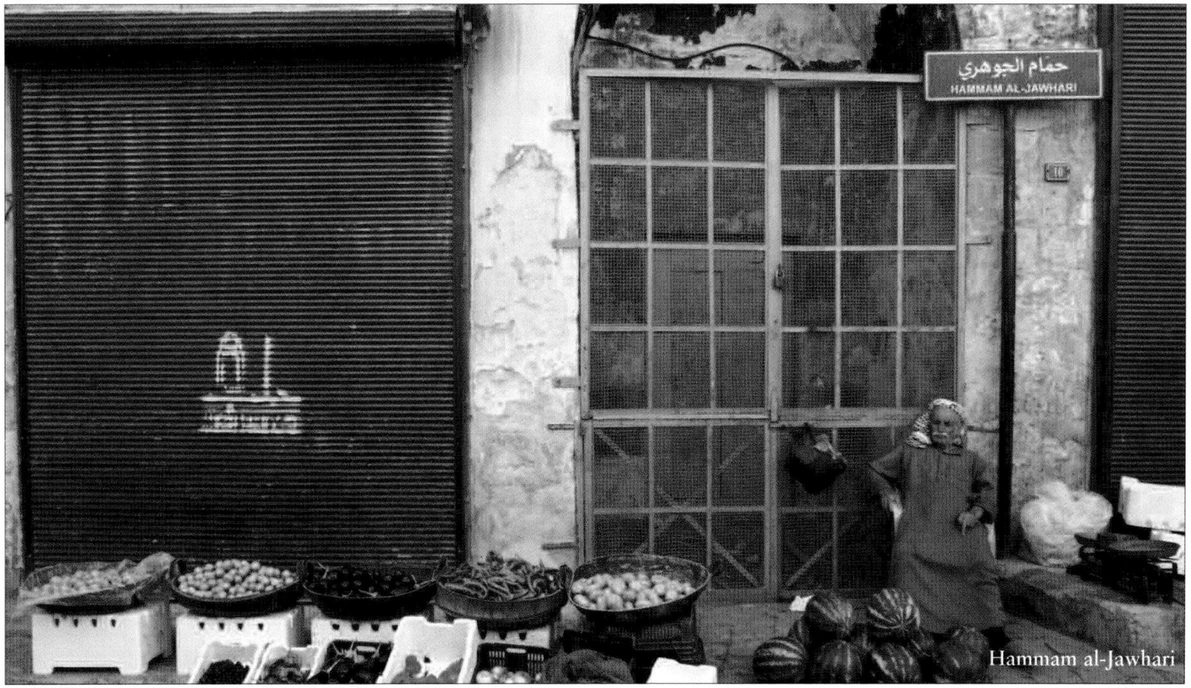

Hammam al-Jawhari

a large yard in which to keep horses, is utterly closed.

In Aleppo in recent years they even knocked down hammams that went back to pre-Islamic times; if we are to believe oral traditions, it seems that the prophet Ibrahim not only milked his cow in Aleppo, but hammamed there. His own font, some say, was preserved in one of the hammams – preserved that is until the hammam housing the holy font was demolished for some exercise in modernisation.[51] It is ironic that monuments that survived earthquakes and wars and the rise and fall of empires should finally succumb to some road-widening scheme brought about by the Municipality.

Near Bab Antakia I have gone in search of a hammam, and found the tiled entrance leading down into its depths, only to see someone carry out boxes from a warehouse – a typical contemporary use of an ancient hammam. I have found another hammam, opposite a mosque of course, the inscription above the door indicating a hammam going back a thousand years, only to find it is now a sort of factory making elastic for underpants. But at least these buildings survive.

The pace of loss beggars belief. I photographed a hammam in Calasseh, an Ottoman hammam if I remember rightly, massive in size, but closed, with fruit sellers on the pavement outside. Returning another time, I wandered here and there in search of it, only to be told that the multi-storied block in front of me had been the site of the hammam.

It is not just in Damascus and Aleppo but up in ancient Antioch on the Orontes that municipalities have set to work. As recorded in a little book (now sadly lost) I found in the Antioch museum of mosaics:

> The streets were so preserved in their original form until 1987, when the municipality destroyed the cultural heritage by concreting all the old streets in Antakia.

Fortunately Antioch's hammams, perhaps by an oversight, escaped. Kociejowski, seeing the destruction around him in Aleppo, rails against the loss of the lines of beauty of Aleppo's architecture and demands, 'Where's the punishment to fit the crime?'[52]

Indeed. In Cairo it is no different. It is hard to believe that the closure of the hammams there is just a matter of neglect. The Egyptian novelist May Telmissany writes that public perceptions of the hammams have suffered badly from the way they have been portrayed in Egyptian films, and there is public indifference to their closure. She writes of Hammam Al-Sukariya, the most beautiful of Cairo's hammams:

> The Supreme Council of Antiquities pledged to renovate it some years ago, but to this day it is in ruins.[53]

How long can hammaming last? Soon it might all be a memory – the rooms vibrant with singing generations, the bather stretched out on the tiles, the attendant standing with the towels – except for a couple of hammams preserved for tourists. The *shebab* dousing each other with dishes of cold water, the bather recovering on the cushioned seats; the attendants pampering the bathers with tea – soon it might all disappear, and just a sign on a wall will remind passers-by of times past. On a summer's day in Straight Street I was directed to a verse on the wall of the street commemorating Hammam al-Muna – the Hammam of What you Desire – stating that in 1141 (HJ) Ismail Basha had this hammam constructed for *hanna*, the good life. Labourers now carry sacks through the emptiness of the solitary surviving dome.

Perhaps in the future hammams will just be remembered by some old men smoking in the café. Or maybe an idle passer-by will stop and read a street sign commemorating a way of life that has passed, like in the Aleppo *suq*, near the sellers of herbs and the sheep carcasses strung up on the great wooden gates, where the cobbled way promises Hammam Atab, but if a hammam of that name ever existed, there is nothing left of it now.

A Contemporary Use for a Hammam

Seduced by the play of sunlight on a wall – light has a way in Aleppo of squandering

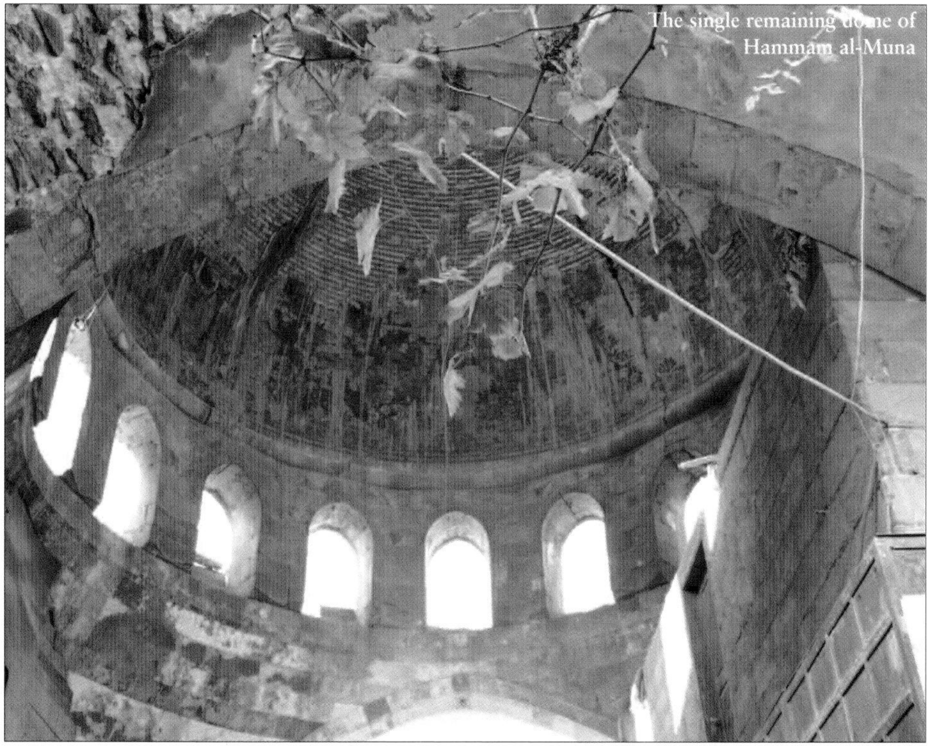

The single remaining dome of Hammam al-Muna

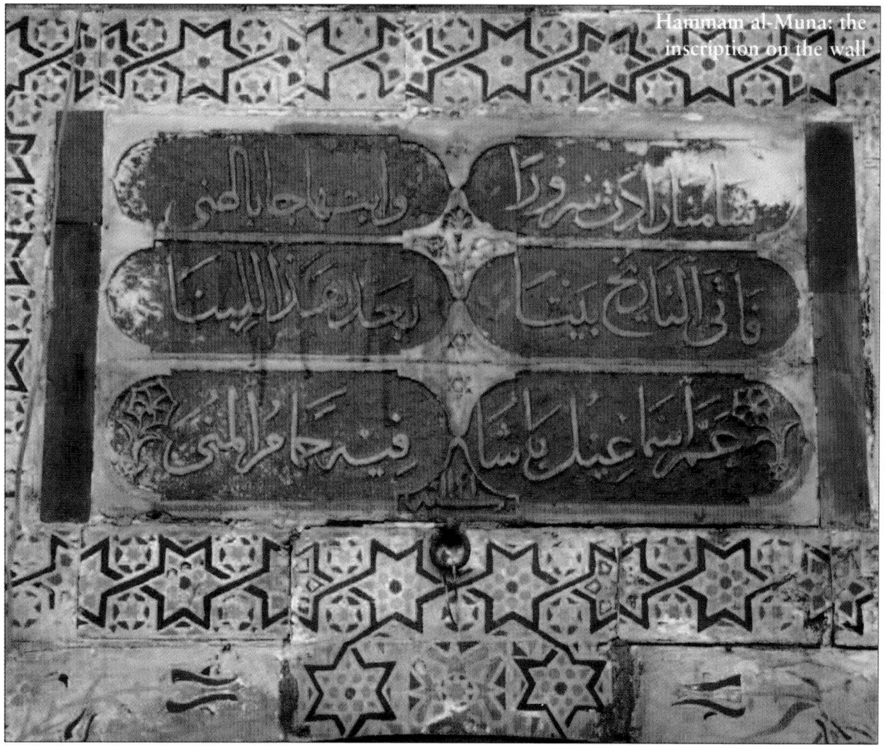

Hammam al-Muna: the inscription on the wall

itself on a patch of stone, or spilling onto cobbles – I followed archway through archway, past men with shopping bags and school kids with satchels.

The streets of Aleppo have a way of enclosing themselves – one distant arch is mirrored by another, which itself mirrors a third archway – as if the streets were framing themselves for viewing. In time I came to a cobbled intersection within the city walls, and there, like an explorer who comes across his goal when he is no longer searching, I found a dome – like the dome of a small mosque, rising above a lane, but with a many-sided glass casing: the characteristic turret of an Aleppan hammam.

Above the door I could make out what seemed to be the date 1353 inscribed in Arabic; within was the semi-darkness of a building that was once a hammam. In the lane outside there was just a sound like running water: the wind soughing through the dried-up leaves of an ash tree.

In the foyer the dome was still perfect, but with a false ceiling, and even the fountain was still intact. Where bathers once reclined for their après-hammam there was now a glass-partitioned office. Nearby the cabinet still stood where bathers once locked away their valuables. I was told that the owner had died decades ago and there had been no-one to inherit.

Inside the glass partition the boss was angry with someone on the phone, but with the usual Syrian courtesy he invited me in for coffee. The hammam is now a tailors' workshop, but the last bathers could have left Hammam Al Saugheer just yesterday.

The View from the Hammam

The hammam looks inward, like the Arab home. The one exception I know is a private hammam. The great houses of Aleppo and Damascus had their private hammams, but they are mostly in a sad state of repair – the hammam and the house in similar states of neglect – like the seventeenth-century Beit Ghazaleh in Jedaidah with its pillared bath room.

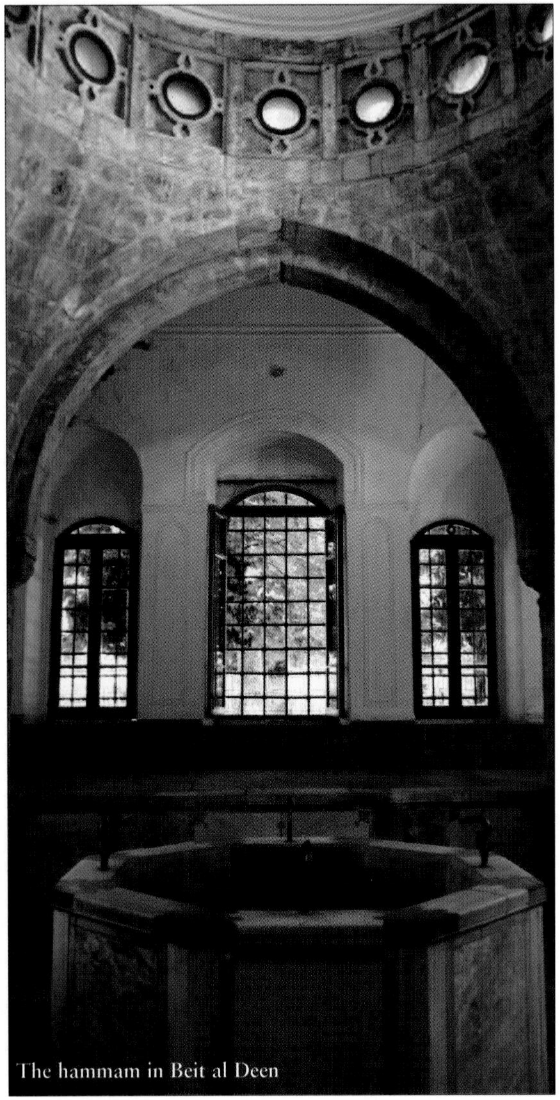
The hammam in Beit al Deen

The most wonderful private hammam in all of *Bilad al-Sham* is not within the Syrian Arab Republic. Beit al Deen in Lebanon was constructed by Italian architects; they brought the Oriental as envisaged by Europeans to the Druze mountains, and featured a hammam in the palace they designed.

The palace has not only extensive courtyards and wonderfully ornate ceilings, but has *mashrabīyat* – sort of bay windows on the first floor once common in Cairo, overhanging the street below, from which those within can view the street but not themselves be seen. In the case of this hammam the windows overlook not the bustle of a street but gardens. This is the only hammam I know of which is not inward looking and focused on itself, but leads the eye out of the hammam to an outer world.

So what then is the view from the hammam? Just as Lebanon looks out to the Mediterranean and to Europe, so Syria I feel looks not out to the West but in on itself, or at least to things Arab or Eastern. The Arab conquest re-orientated Byzantine Damascus away from Europe towards the East, and that is how it has been ever since. The very anti-Lebanon mountains cut Damascus off from the Med and Europe, and Syrian politics have until recently kept coca-cola-burger-king culture at bay.

Just as the hammam encloses itself, so Syria too is a very self-contained world, almost an anachronism given current forces of globalisation. What I am documenting here is the world within the enclosed walls of hammams, but it reflects the society beyond.

A Dying Tradition

I remember going once to a dam in the Alawi Mountains with a student of mine, an officer in the Syrian Navy, Revolution Dam (now there's a romantic name!) I think it was called.

It was that time of year when the air is sweetly scented with the wax of orange blossom and the geraniums flower in their careless way by flat-roofed farmhouses, and we took a boat, and rowed out to the island that had once been a hill top, passing by the remaining stones that had been some holy man's mountain shrine before modernity flooded the valley. There were still a few remaining houses on the island, half-abandoned, but with gardens neatly tended after all the years, with apricots still growing in what remained of orchards.

Hammaming is a bit like that perhaps, a kind of clinging to the old ways – even after the valley has been flooded – a kind of rowing out to what hasn't quite been entirely lost.

I remember standing in the doorway of a massive hammam in Aleppo, a hammam desperately empty of bathers, and talking to the manager, now dead, and his son, now running the hammam, about how things had changed. I asked the meaning of the inscription above the door and the proprietor, in obvious ill health replied:

– That was from the time when people had religion.

I then asked about the running of the hammam. He pointed to the emptiness within and said:

– There were once seventy-seven hammams in Aleppo, but only the *derawish* hammam now.

By *derawish* he meant the poor who don't have a bathroom at home, and I suspected there wouldn't have been enough *derawish* coming to wash to pay the rent.

In Cairo the situation is dire. Considering Meunier's images in *The Last Hammams of Cairo*,[54] the reviewer in Egypt's *Al-Ahram* newspaper writes:

> The problem is that the traditional bathhouses are now widely regarded as unhygienic, and well-off Cairenes would not be seen dead bathing in such places. Indeed, the bathhouses of today are largely associated only with the poorest of the poor.[55]

Meunier's exquisite images record solitary figures, bathed in light, in desperately empty hammams.

Syrian hammams have not reached that sad state of affairs, but you might upset someone nowadays by asking if they ever go to a hammam – they might be living a very modern life in a flat by the motorway, with a car and a mobile phone and satellite TV – and they look at you indignantly and exclaim: why, we have hot water at home!

What is more Syrian than hammaming? Even as far as Irwad Island in the Mediterranean beyond Tartous, on the black rock by the sea wall built by Phoenicians, the ruined sandstone dome of a hammam still stands beneath the fishermen's houses. How many hammams will soon be mere ruins? In this book I am recording the way of life of the last remaining hammams in Syria, and the traditions that somehow survive beneath their domes – before they, apart from a few showpiece hammams set aside for tourism perhaps, go the way of those who built them.

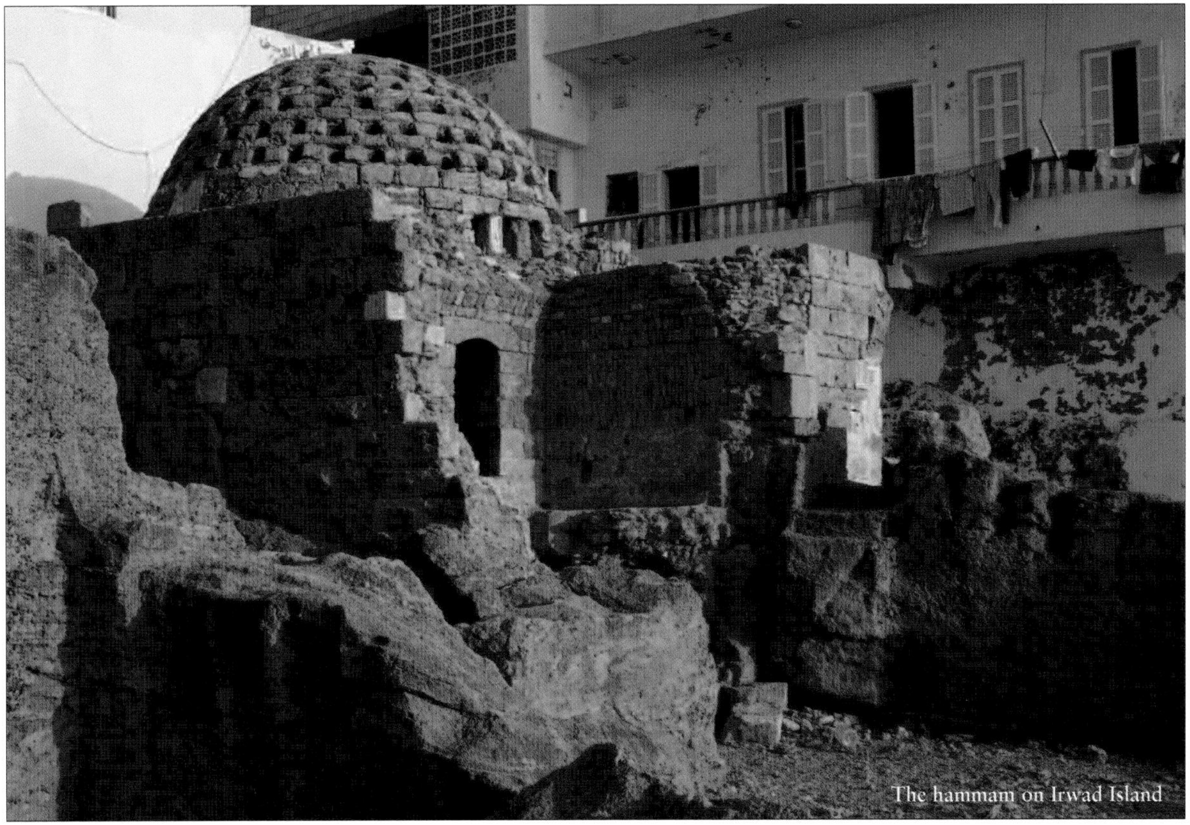

The hammam on Irwad Island

Notes

1 Brue, Alexia, *Cathedrals of the Flesh: My Search for the Perfect Bath* (Bloomsbury, 2003), p. 45.

2 Thubron, Colin, *Mirror to Damascus* (Penguin, 1966, 1967), p. 3.

3 "If you will climb into the fringe of Salhiyeh you will see the curious shape of Damascus – a jagged comet-form, all the angles and serrations of the brown tail defined with unnatural clearness by the depth of the green about it." Dinning, Hector William, *Nile to Aleppo, with the Light-horse in the Middle-East* (G. Allen & Unwin Ltd., 1920), p. 90.

4 Burckhardt, John Lewis, *Travel in Syria and the Holy Land* (Echo Library, 2006), p. 102.

5 Burns, Ross, *Monuments of Syria An Historical Guide* (I.B. Tauris & Co. Ltd, 1994), p. 46.

6 Russell, Alexander and Patrick, *The Natural History of Aleppo* (G. G. & J. Robinson, 1794, 2nd edition), quoted in Kociejowski, Marius, *Syria: Through Writers' Eyes* (Eland, 2006), p. 139.

7 Sibley, Magda, 'The Historic Hammams of Damascus and Fez: Lessons of Sustainability and Future Developments', The 23rd Conference on Passive and Low Energy Architecture, Geneva, Switzerland, 6–8 September 2006.

8 Burns, Ross, *Monuments of Syria: An Historical Guide* (I.B. Tauris & Co. Ltd, 1994), p. 128.

9 Kociejowski, Marius, *The Street Philosopher and the Holy Fool, A Syrian Journey* (Sutton Publishing, 2004), p. 25.

10 Irwin, Robert, *Night and Horses and the Desert* (Penguin, 1999, 2000), p. 65.

11 Ibn Battuta, *Travels in Asia and Africa 1325–1354* (Routledge and Kegan Paul, 1983), p. 65.

12 Qur'an Sura 13.

13 Ibn Battuta, *Travels in Asia and Africa 1325–1354* (Routledge and Kegan Paul, 1983), p. 65.

14 Burns, Ross, *Damascus: A History* (Routledge, 2007), p. 260.

15 Bell, Gertrude, *The Desert and the Sown* (William Heinemann, 1908), p. 135.

16 Dinning, Hector William, *Nile to Aleppo, with the Light-Horse in the Middle-East* (G. Allen & Unwin Ltd, 1920), p. 93.

17 Kayall, M., *Les Bains Damascains* (Ibn Khaldoun Press, 1989), p. 88.

18 Thubron, Colin, *Mirror to Damascus* (Penguin, 1967), p. 116.

19 Translation of *Sunan Abu-Dawud*, Book 26, no. 3998.

20 Translation of *Sunan Abu-Dawud*, Book 26, no. 3999.

21 Mackintosh-Smith, Tim (editor), 'The Travels of Ibn Battuta' (Picador, 2002), p. 21.

22 Lane, Edward, *Manners and Customs of the Modern Egyptians* (M. A. Natali, 1846), p. 349.

23 Arnold, Thomas, *Painting in Islam: a Study of Pictorial Art in Muslim Culture* (Georgias Press, 2004), p. 86.

24 Kayall, M., *Les Bains Damascains* (Ibn Khaldoun Press, 1989), p. 163.

25 Foss, Michael, *People of the First Crusade* (O'Mara Books, 1997), p. 222.

26 Hillenbrand, Carol, *The Crusades: Islamic Perspectives* (Routledge, 2000), p. 278.

27 Hillenbrand, Carol, *The Crusades: Islamic Perspectives* (Routledge, 2000), p. 278.

28 Fedden, Robin, *Syria and the Lebanon* (John Murray, 1965, 3rd edition), quoted in Kociejowski, Marius, *Syria: Through Writers' Eyes* (Eland, 2006), p. 194.

29 Burns, Ross, *Monuments of Syria: An Historical Guide* (I.B. Tauris & Co. Ltd, 1994), p. 176.

30 Kandiyoti, Deniz, 'The Paradoxes of Masculinity: Some Thoughts on Segregated Societies' in Cornwall, A. and Lindisfarne, N., *Dislocating Masculinity* (Routledge, 1994), p. 204.

31 Burns, Ross, *Damascus: A History* (Routledge, 2007), p. 219.

32 Dinning, Hector William, *Nile to Aleppo, with the Light-horse in the Middle-East* (G. Allen & Unwin Ltd., 1920), p. 151.

33 Bell, Gertrude, *The Desert and the Sown* (William Heinemann, 1908), p. 222.

34 Dinning, Hector William, *Nile to Aleppo, with the Light-horse in the Middle-East* (G. Allen & Unwin Ltd., 1920), pp. 152–53.

35 Lukach, Charles, *The Fringe of the East: A Journey through Past and Present Provinces of Turkey* (Macmillan, 1913) in Kociejowski, Marius, *Syria: Through Writers' Eyes* (London: Eland, 2006), p. 204.

36 Watenpaugh, Heghnar Zeitlian, *The Image of an Ottoman City: Imperial Architecture and Urban Experience in Aleppo in the 16th and 17th Centuries* (Leiden: E. J. Brill, 2004), p. 91.

37 Bell, Gertrude, *The Desert and the Sown* (William Heinemann, 1908), p. 222.

38 Watenpaugh, Heghnar Zeitlian, *The Image of an Ottoman City: Imperial Architecture and Urban Experience in Aleppo in the 16th and 17th Centuries* (Leiden: E. J. Brill, 2004), p. 91.

39 Azemeh, Basheer, *The Generation of Defeat* (Arab Institute for Studies and Publishing, 1998), p. 49.

40 Mernissi, Fatima, *The Forgotten Queens of Islam* (University of Minnesota Press, 1994).

41 Kayall, M., *Les Bains Damascains* (Ibn Khaldoun Press, 1989)?

42 Malouf Amin, *The Crusades through Arab Eyes* (Al Saqi Books, 1984), p. 184.

43 Moaz, Abd al-Razzaq, 'Processes of Urban Development in an Islamic City: The North-Western Suburb in Damascus from the Twelfth to the Nineteenth Centuries' in *Lichiko*, no. 47, Spring 1998, p. 70.

44 Moaz, Abd al-Razzaq, 'Processes of Urban Development in an Islamic City: The North-Western

Suburb in Damascus from the Twelfth to the Nineteenth Centuries' in *Lichiko*, no. 47, Spring 1998, p. 70.

45 Thubron, Colin, *Mirror to Damascus* (Penguin, 1966), p. 184.

46 Hadjar, Abdallah, *The Historical Monuments of Aleppo* (Automobile and Touring Club of Syria, 2000, 2nd edition 2006), p. 75.

47 J. Sauvaget, 'Un Bain Damasquin du X111e siecle', *Extrait de la Revue Syria 1930* (Paris: Libraire Orientaliste Paul Geuthner).

48 Kayall, M., *Les Bains Damascains* (Ibn Khaldoun Press, 1989), p. 110.

49 Kayall, M., *Les Bains Damascains* (Ibn Khaldoun Press, 1989), p. 90.

50 Hadjar, Abdallah, *The Historical Monuments of Aleppo* (Automobile and Touring Club of Syria, 2000, 2nd edition 2006), p. 107

51 Hadjar, Abdallah, *The Historical Monuments of Aleppo* (Automobile and Touring Club of Syria, 2000, 2nd edition 2006), p. 29.

52 Kociejowski, Marius, *The Street Philosopher and the Holy Fool, A Syrian Journey* (Sutton Publishing, 2004), p. 25.

53 Nkrumah, Gamal, 'Tales from the hammam', *Al Ahram* weekly online, issue no. 957, 23–29 July 2009.

54 Meunier, Pascal; Telmissany, May; and Gandossi, Eve, *The Last Hammams of Cairo, A Disappearing Bathhouse Culture* (American University in Cairo Press, 2009).

55 Nkrumah, Gamal, 'Tales from the hammam', *Al Ahram* weekly online, issue no. 957, 23–29 July 2009.

2

Cathedrals of the Flesh

'...Are you ready for your gommage?'

'Gommage, that means erase, like pencil eraser, in French, doesn't it?'

'Exactly.'

'What is she going to erase?'

'Your sins.'

'Have you brought me to a church?'

'Yes, a cathedral of the flesh.'

Alexia Brue, recalling a conversation in a Parisian hammam[1]

Doorways and Domes

You could wander past a hammam if you did not have an eye for them.

The main dome of a hammam is not unlike the dome of a mosque, and sometimes in my search for a hammam I would mistake one for the other. But what marks out the hammam from any other building is the characteristic 'hat' or lantern – I have read it called a candle-snuffer somewhere – a distinctive turret above the main dome that allows natural light into the expansive *barrani*.

The lesser domes above the other rooms are distinguished by inlaid ribs of 'elephants' eyes' running across the surface of the dome through which light sifts into the rooms beneath. And so the architect's dilemma – to minimize heat loss, but to allow light into the hammam – is solved by circles of coloured glass, hand-blown in Damascus, ribbing the hemispheres of the domes.

But that is really the view from above. Down at street level the doorway itself would often be nondescript, as if the hammam did not wish to draw attention to itself, apart from its name written on the wall and maybe a striped curtain pulled across the door if women were within. Alternatively, there might be a luminous sign with the hammam's name at the entrance porch or running over the lane, for from the street itself a hammam can be fairly indistinguishable from the buildings around it.

Occasionally, however, the hammam would announce its presence with a magnificent doorway. Below Aleppo's citadel, Hammam al-Yalbougha's entrance is as grand as the honeycombed doorways of the Mamluk mosques nearby, with the *ablaq* of the façade – the bands of black and yellow stone that characterize Mamluk architecture in Syria – announcing the presence of the hammam in all its solitary splendour. There are hammams which draw attention to themselves – here we are in all our magnificence, seven hundred years after our rebirth! – and there are more discreet affairs down some laneway, known only to the neighbourhood and the discerning few.

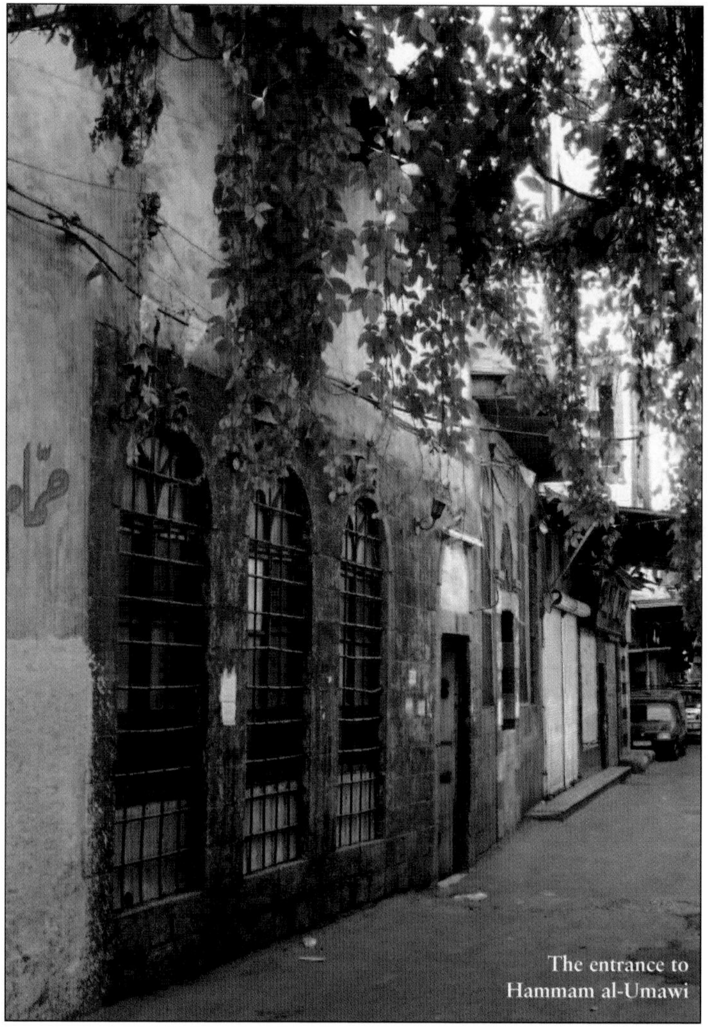

The entrance to Hammam al-Umawi

Occasionally the doorway would be ornate, like that of Hammam al-Zain near Bab al-Jabiya in Damascus. The hammam itself would be scarcely noticeable, blending into the drab walls of the street, were it not for the baroque excess of the ornamentation above the door, and its horseshoe promising good luck to those who enter. (Indeed, hammaming was often a bit of a lucky dip, for you never knew who you might find within.) 1289 (*al Hijri*) is written above the entrance, but the plaque suggests the hammam is more like eight centuries old. A poem refers to the health-restoring properties of hammams:

> This is now a hammam, that was once hammima*
>
> It brings life to the bones, even the bones of a corpse...

* hot material

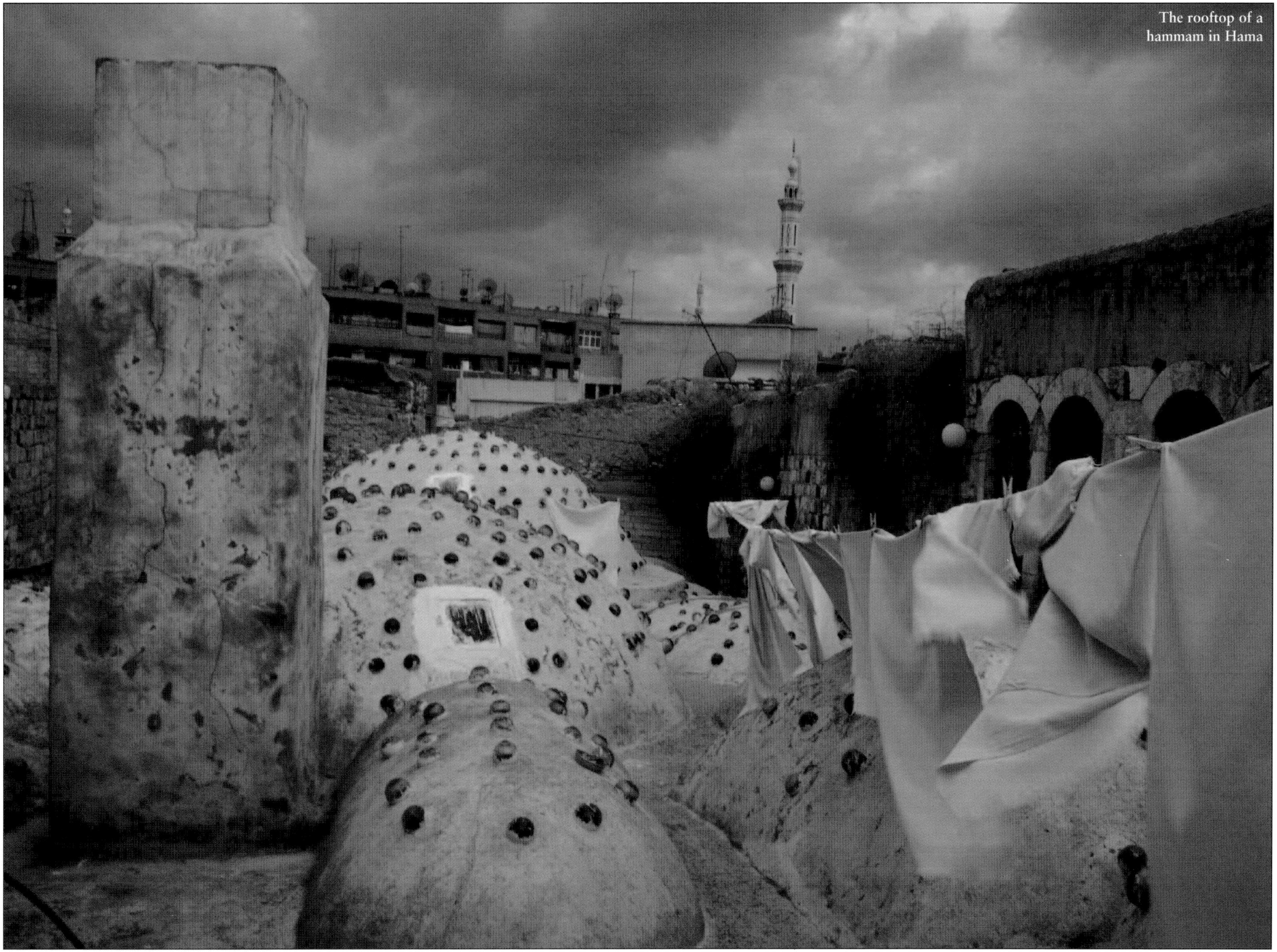
The rooftop of a hammam in Hama

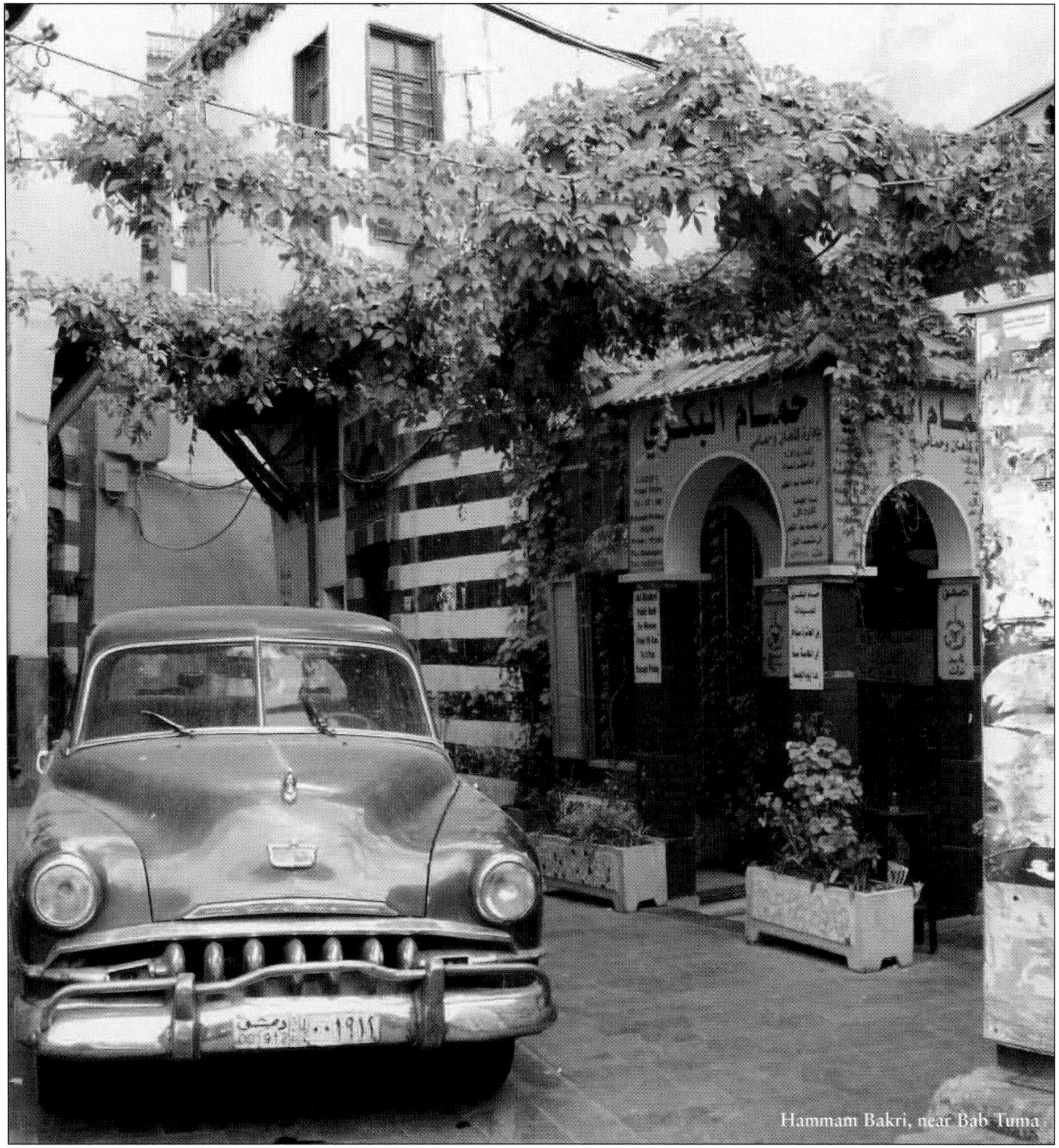

Hammam Bakri, near Bab Tuma

In the *barrani* of Hammam al-Zain a musket hangs on the wall, used by the manager's grandfather to fight the French I was told. In contrast to the drabness of the exterior wall, the inner rooms are painted in zany colours – blues, greens and reds – as if hippies had been commissioned as decorators to compensate for the street's dowdiness.

One of my favourite doorways in *Bilad al-Sham* was in Tripoli, Lebanon. Here I am using the broad geographical term *Bilad al-Sham* to extend far beyond the borders of the Syrian state, for in the past 'Syria' referred to a much wider region. Also, Syria did have a very real presence in Lebanon when I lived there, whether it was the labourers in the fields or the soldiers at the checkpoint.

At the Mamluk heart of the city of Tripoli I found four hammams: one tastefully restored and in use, one preserved, and two in a state of dereliction. It was by the doorway of the thirteenth-century Hammam Ezzedeen that I used to sit and drink Tripoli's bitter coffee with the labourers, below the citadel scarred with missiles from the civil war. Pilgrims' shells and the inscription 'SCS IACOBUS' decorate the entrance to the hammam, the inner door exhibiting a Pascal Lamb and an inscription in Latin reading 'Behold the lamb of God'. In the construction of the hammam he built for Tripoli, the Governor Izz al-Din Aybak clearly borrowed heavily from the monuments of the expelled Crusaders; perhaps the very doorway commemorating

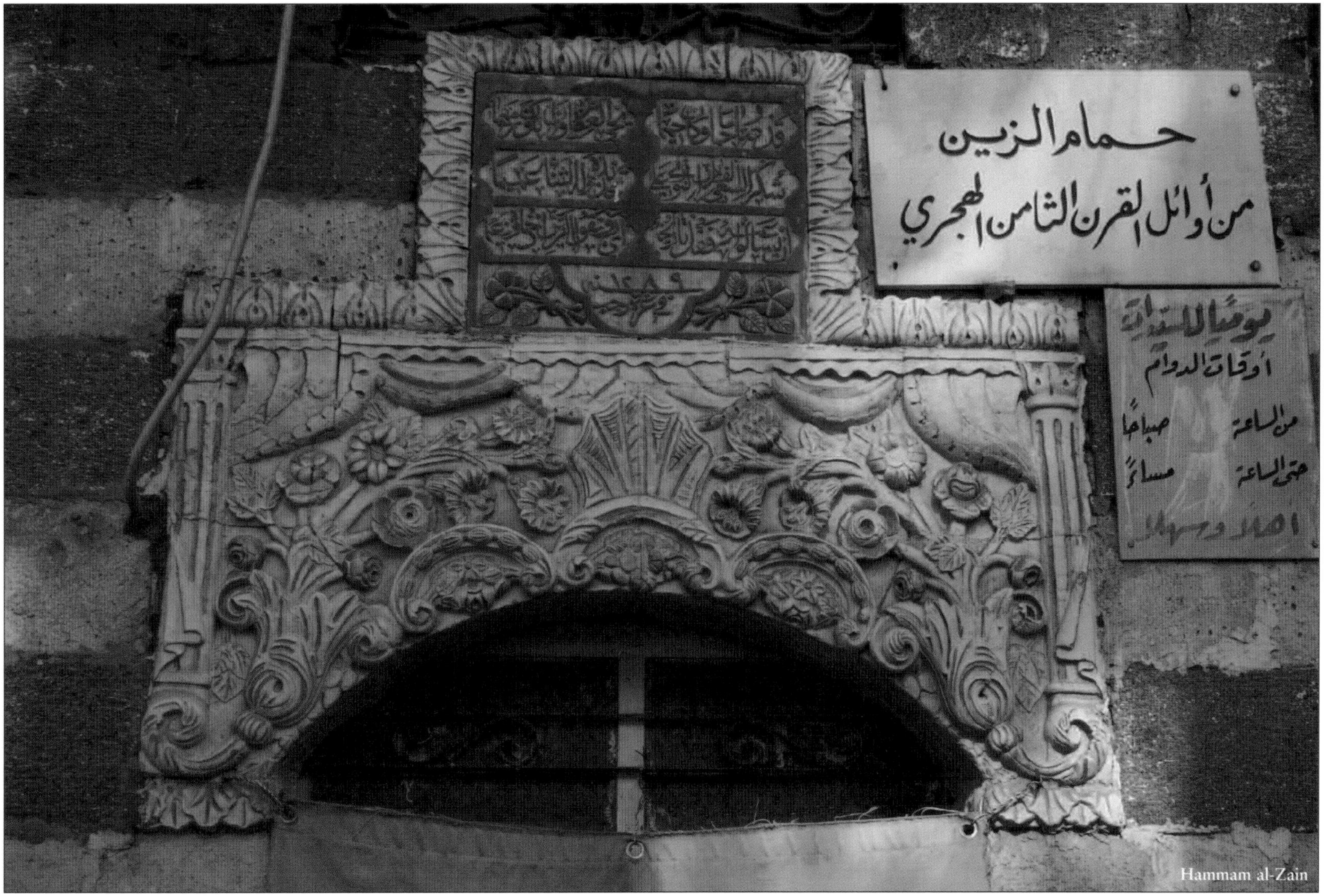

Hammam al-Zain

Saint James, the saint of pilgrims, had once led to a pilgrims' hospice.

Six centuries after its construction, this hammam was almost derelict, for it had been seriously damaged during the war when rival factions had fought it out in Tripoli. The man with the key let me in, and I was able to savour its pastel shades and neglected fonts and crumbling walls. When he stopped off in Tripoli, Ibn Battuta was much impressed by its hammams, but he does not record his thoughts of this Mamluk hammam, with its scallop shells. A consecrated hammam indeed! Its founder chose to have his tomb not by the mosque but beside the hammam.

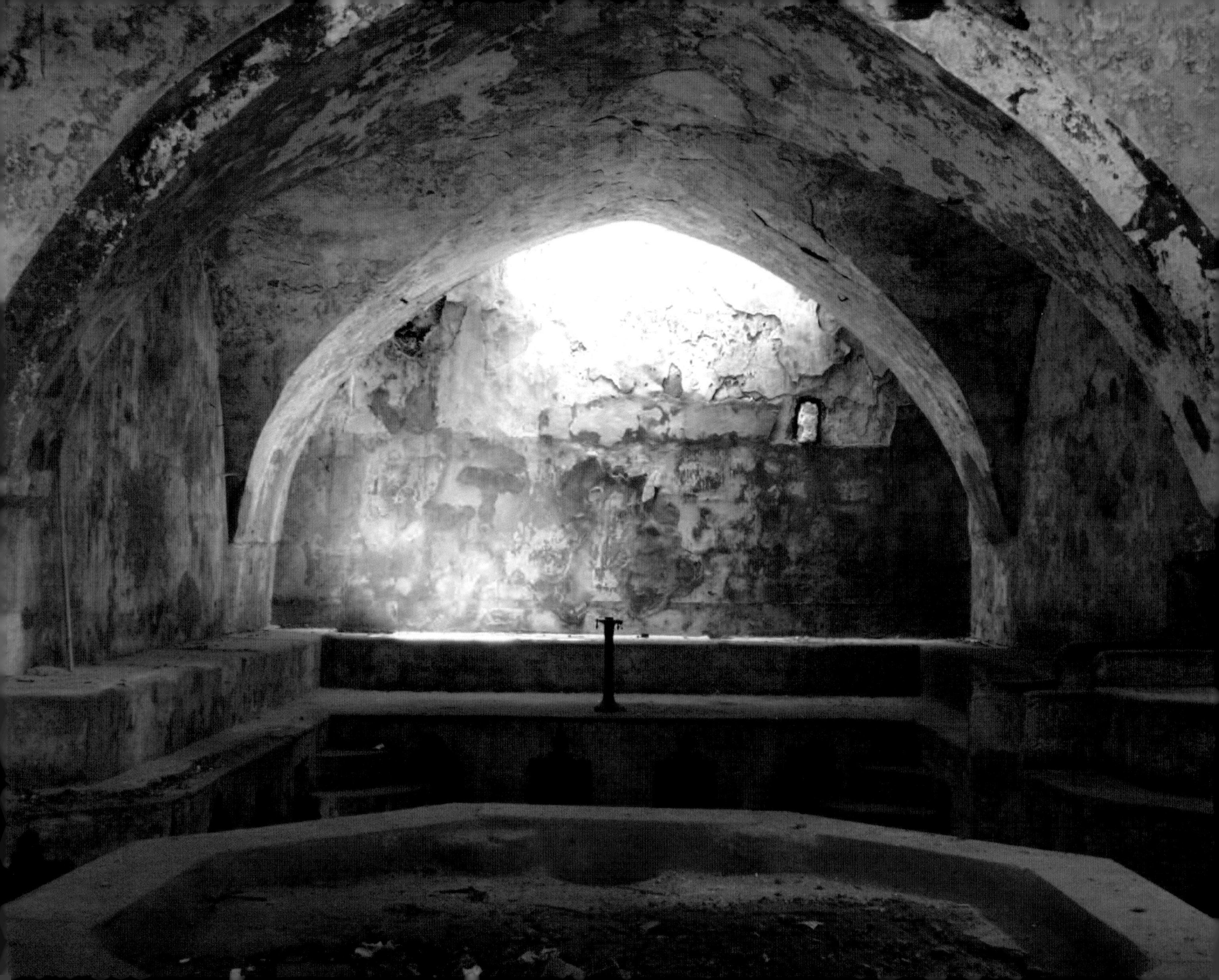

Perhaps Ibn Battuta also bathed in Tripoli's Hammam Nuri. Near the Great Mosque, Hammam Nuri's seriously solid grey dome still speaks of the presence of a hammam among the clutter of buildings near the mosque; I suppose the hammam would have warmed its neighbours as they helped to insulate the hammam. The shopkeeper nearby kindly let me through and I stood within its empty domes, reverently, the quietness in the hammam like the silence in a church when you have it all to yourself.

One of the most magnificent hammams in the world, Hammam al-Jadid, is found in Tripoli, near where the Hanging Mosque arches over the laneway. It's an Ottoman hammam, built in the middle of the eighteenth century by the same governor of Damascus who constructed the Azem Palace in the heart of the city and the more intimate Azem Palace in Hama. The Governor clearly enjoyed his cut from the *hajj* that left Damascus annually in all its pomp and splendour (trade and Islam go quite naturally together; there is none of that Christian angst about serving God and Mammon) and with the funds he graced the region with the most elegant of Ottoman buildings.

The hammam doorway hints of the splendours within – its portal echoing Mamluk grandeur, but with a stucco of fleur-de-lis. The links of a basalt chain carved from a single rock still hang in the entrance, but without the bucket that was once suspended from the chain. The

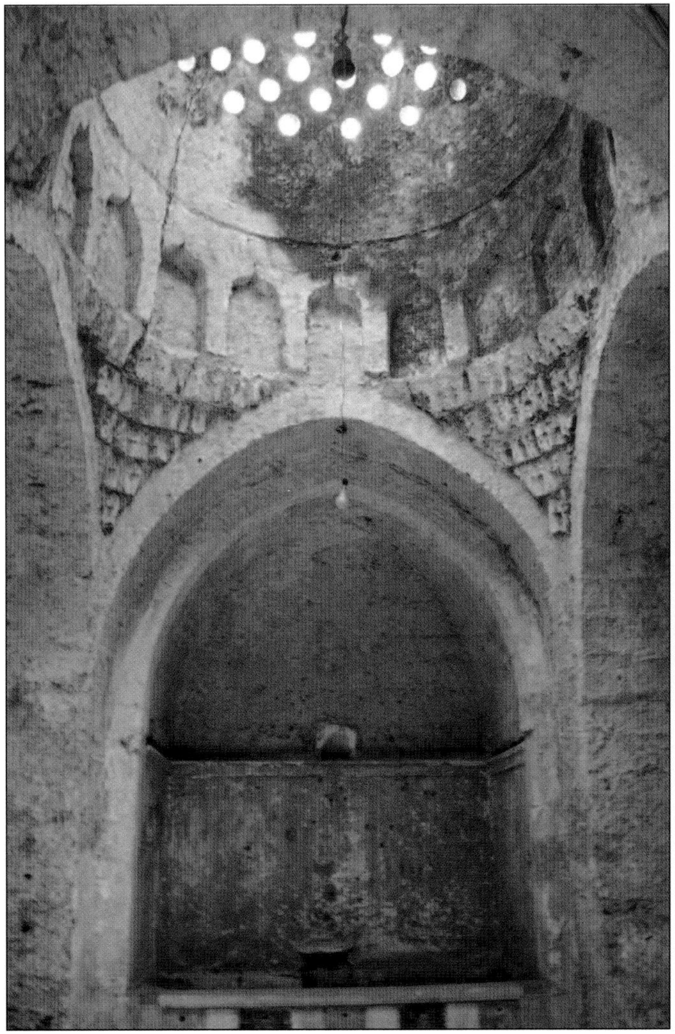

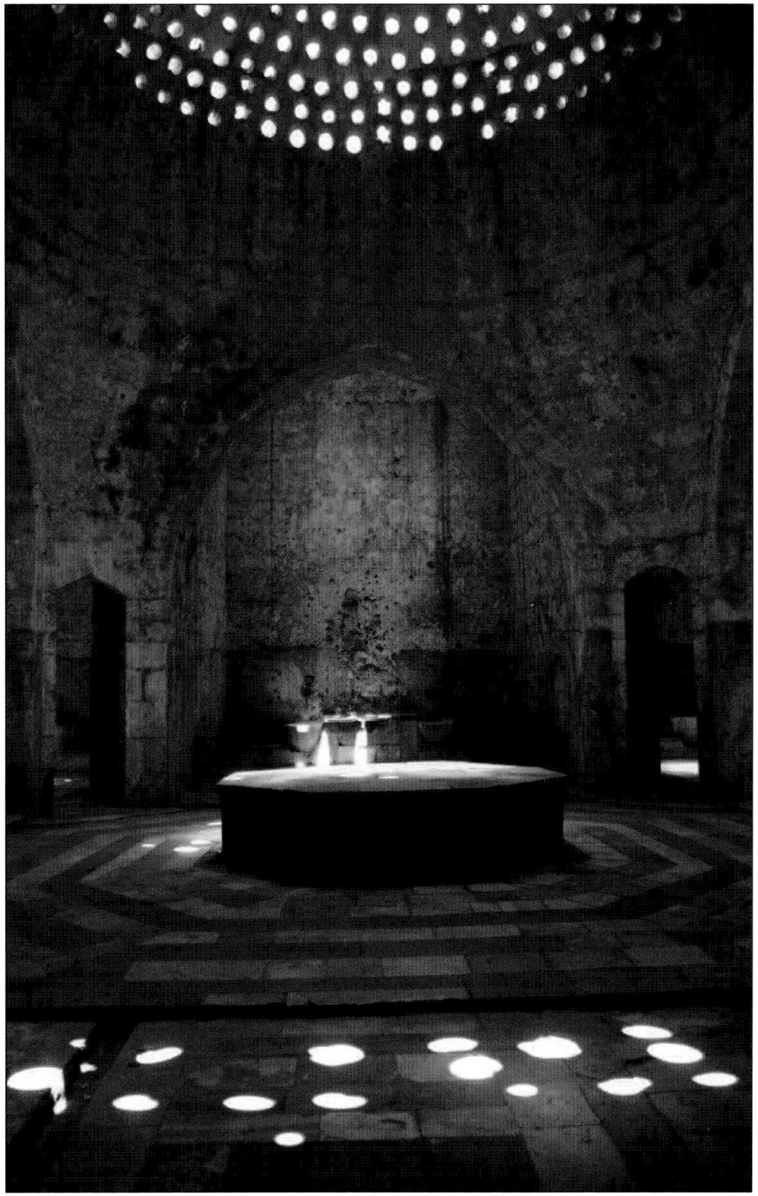

Previous page: Hammam Nuri, in Tripoli, Lebanon
Right: Hammam al-Jadid, Tripoli

proprietor of the hammam told me how he had spent his nights armed in the hammam during the worst of the conflict, to protect it from being looted.

Like any self-respecting hammam, Hammam al-Jadid has a *sebil*, a water fountain in the wall facing the street, to supply the neighbourhood. The *sebil* within a hammam façade or in the street opposite could be exquisitely decorated, usually with an inscription above a cup on a chain asking the drinker to pray for the soul of the departed.

Finally some hammams would advertise themselves through their line of coloured *futas* drying on the wall outside, brightening up the laneway on some grey winter's day – like in Aleppo's Hammam Granada. If it weren't for the *futas* you would walk right past the hammam, for architecturally this hammam is utterly nondescript, having been converted from the stable that was part of the neighbouring khan.

At night some hammams come into their own with a string of fairy lights across the street. Fairy lights, however, are not unique to hammams; even the riot police have a ring of lights around the back of their vehicle. In the Middle East there is often a happy blend of khaki and kitsch.

Veiled Beauty

The traveller in search of the hammams of Salihiye, the once-gardened area of Damascus below Qassioun Mountain, is likely to be disappointed. Of the eighteen hammams that once graced Salihiye, only one remains: Hammam al-Moqaddam – the Hammam of the Commander. It stands near where Ibn 'Arabi is buried, below the Jadid Mosque – the New Mosque ('new' in the Damascene context being about six hundred years old!)

Like any hammam with a history you go down a series of steps into the earth – thus, before our concerns with global warming and the insulation of houses, hammam builders preserved the heat in winter and kept the *barrani* coolish in summer. The traveller expecting authentic stonework and the ambience of those Tripoli hammams will be in for a bit of a surprise however; the décor within Hammam al-Moqaddam is more to local taste.

On walking into this Mamluk hammam you find the raised platforms of the *barrani* fitted out like an Irish bar in the seventies, the red velvet still protected by its transparent plastic covering. Opposite the desk of the elderly manager, portraits of the President are respectfully placed. But these are not the only pictures: reproductions of Constable's English landscapes contribute to the eclectic décor of this fourteenth-century hammam. In the centre of the floor, sea horses spout water into an oval fountain, above which is the mustard-yellow dome of the hammam, from which coloured lanterns are suspended.

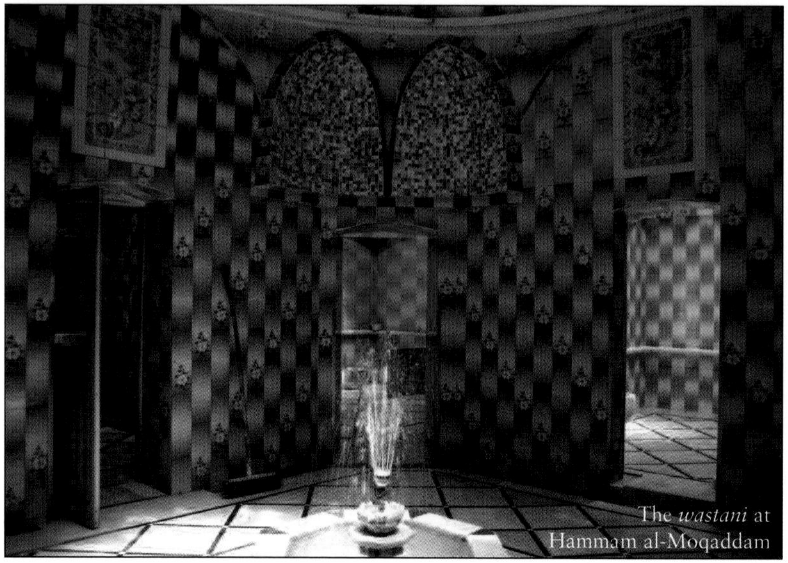
The *wastani* at Hammam al-Moqaddam

A small room leads to the main *wastani*, with boxes for toiletries and sisal scrubs. Here are the toilets in avocado tiles to your left, and also the massage room with its walls converging in a V of glowing pink. In contrast is the rather sombre sauna where you can wait for your massage.

Going through to the *wastani* there is a central fountain, smallish, below a plain dome where mist from the steam room lingers. The walls however are a rhapsody of ochre tiles, and in the spacious bathers' rooms are tiles of every hue. In the corners, tiny multi-coloured tiles create the kind of mosaic once found in bus depots and shopping centres.

Finally there is the Pink Room. The *jouwani* is the tour de force of the interior designer, for this long narrow

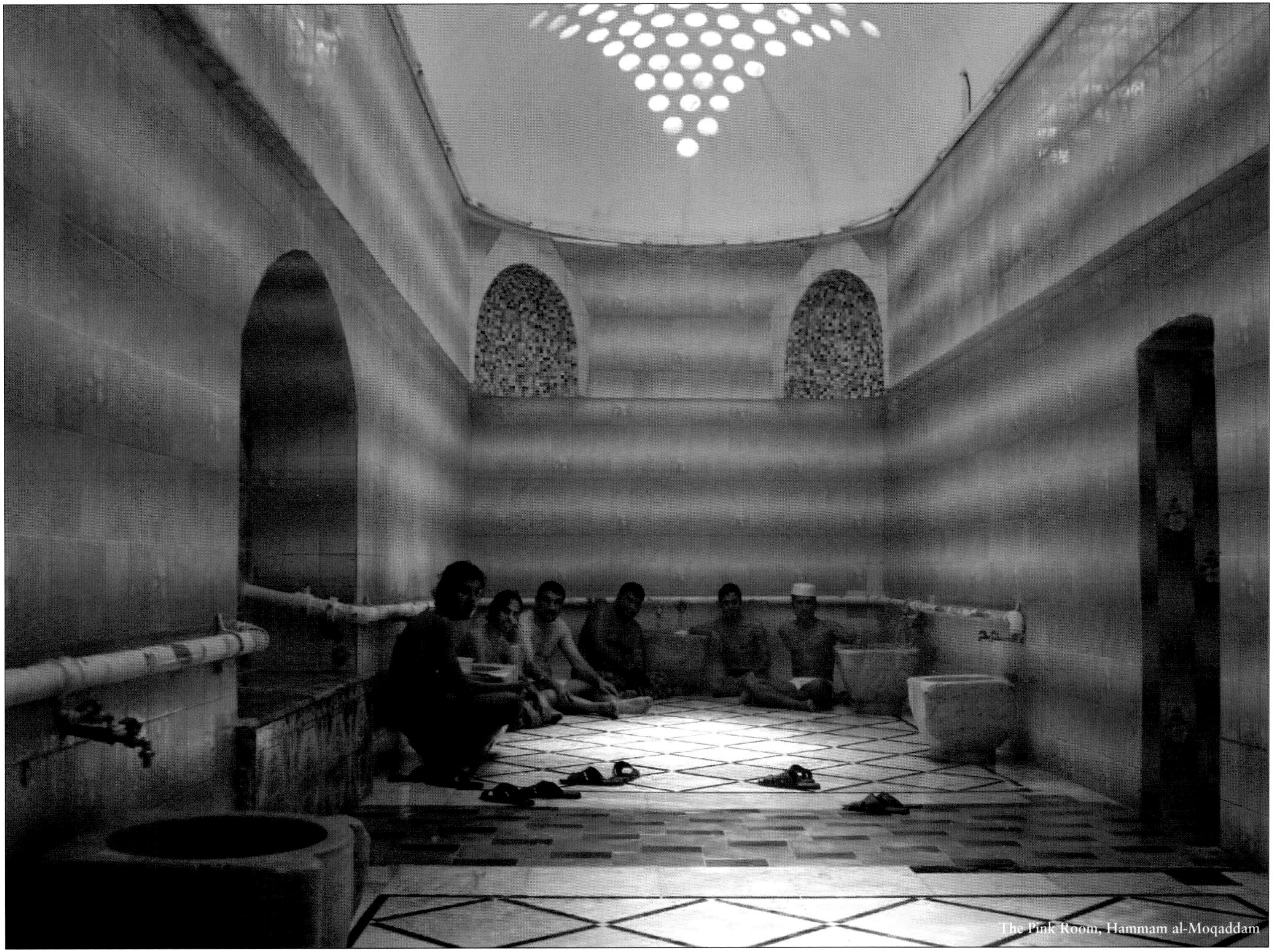

The Pink Room, Hammam al-Moqaddam

room is a unity of shocking pink tiles. Today's bather has been spared however; the ceiling is now a plain white, but peeling paint suggests that even the ceiling was once glorious pink.

And so the decor of the suburban bathroom has been brought to the eight-centuries-old hammam. The aesthetics are not quite to the taste of the former Australian ambassador, Ross Burns:

> The original layout is preserved but covered, in a recent renovation, with a violent concatenation of new bathroom tiles in showroom-style profusion.[2]

I could not argue with that, for Ross Burns is the living Western authority on the monuments of Syria.

In contrast, only a few hundred yards away, the mausoleum of Mohi al-Din ibn 'Arabi is walled with exquisite blue and white Ottoman tiles. (Is this where Ottoman beauty lies, not in the view of the monument in its entirety, but in the detail, like when you notice the bending tulip of a tile?) While the saint's tomb lies amid patterns of ocean blue, his font in the hammam, of grim basalt rock, is surrounded in an extravaganza of jarring tiles.

When it comes to hammaming in the Sham, however, there is no better hammam than this, the last remaining hammam in Salihiye. From its courteous managers, to the attendants who welcome you with their banter, to the affable brothers who work as masseurs – this hammam is the authentic bathing experience in Damascus.

On its roof are simple flats, with jasmine growing in tins; the rooms once housed the hammam attendants before they settled outside the city. Given the view of hammam domes and Qassioun Mountain, this makes the tiny dilapidated flats on the hammam roof for me some of the most desirable real estate in Damascus.

And the décor of the Mamluk Hammam al-Moqaddam? I wouldn't want to change a single tile.

The Manager

The first person you encounter when you enter a hammam will probably be the manager, the *mi'allim*, seated at his desk. To me, *mi'allim* is a very Syrian word. It is a term that suggests knowledge – and therefore used to address the owner of a small business or workshop who teaches others his profession. I believe I also heard it used to refer to a superior in the forces – for in the Arab world who can say when military life ends and civilian life begins?

The word carries a sense of authority. It is with the *mi'allim* that you deposit your valuables before you go to undress; he'll place them in one of the boxes by his desk and hand you the key on a band to wear around your wrist. He'll also pass you the soap and the circle of sisal scrub that you will need for the hammam. Such is the honesty of these managers, I'd willingly deposit for safekeeping a month's salary with the *mi'allim* of any mainstream Damascene hammam.

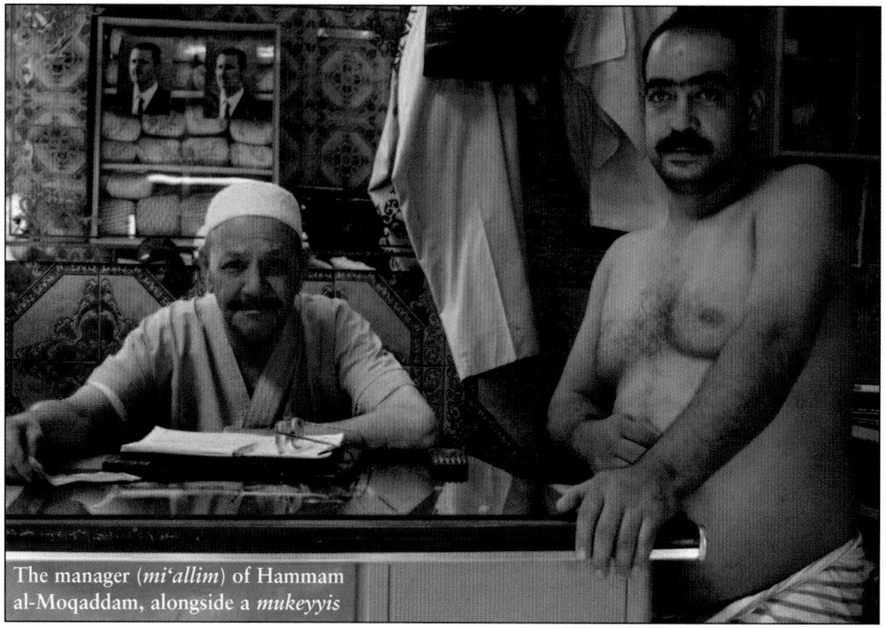

The manager (*mi'allim*) of Hammam al-Moqaddam, alongside a *mukeyyis*

Each manager has his own style, and with the double shift – why shouldn't you bathe twice in the same day, but maybe not in the same hammam? – you might encounter one *mi'allim* in the morning and another in the evening. In Damascus the hammams traditionally close at 11.00 p.m., although some might stay open now until the early morning hours as things have loosened up a bit. In contrast, in Aleppo the hammams are open day and night, and when the hammams are emptying in Damascus they are just beginning to fill up in Aleppo.

It's the *mi'allim* who sets the tenor of a hammam. If he should be absent for even a couple of hours there will be no satisfaction and the whole tone of the place will deteriorate. On such occasions it might be better for a foreigner not to understand Arabic, unless he is particularly thick-skinned.

The *mi'allim* may not own the hammam but he certainly manages it. There is no doubt as to who is in charge, and with one word from the *mi'allim* the staff jump. The hammam has a definite hierarchy, from the manager at his desk down to the lad who shines the shoes in the entrance, and each has his specific role: the attendant in the *barrani* does not later scrub you down in the *wastani*. This hierarchy is also reflected in the style of Arabic spoken, the manager often speaking a 'cultured' Arabic, the hammam attendants tending towards something less educated.

Although there is a hierarchy there is also a kind of social equality; you might see this late some morning as the staff have breakfast together, a kind of brunch around midday. You see this social equality in the hammam with everyone seated around breakfast on the floor, tucking into dishes of eggs and *foul* beans, the bather often invited to join in.

I'm not sure however that I have often seen the manager eat with his staff – he is that bit apart, and above. In Hammam Ezzedeen the manager would simply press a buzzer when a customer walked in and the attendants – dressed in tracksuits like a football team – would leap into action with a raucous chorus of *Ahlan wa Sahlan* to welcome the bather as he started to empty his pockets to deposit his valuables. Then an attendant, towels in hand, would escort him across the foyer to undress.

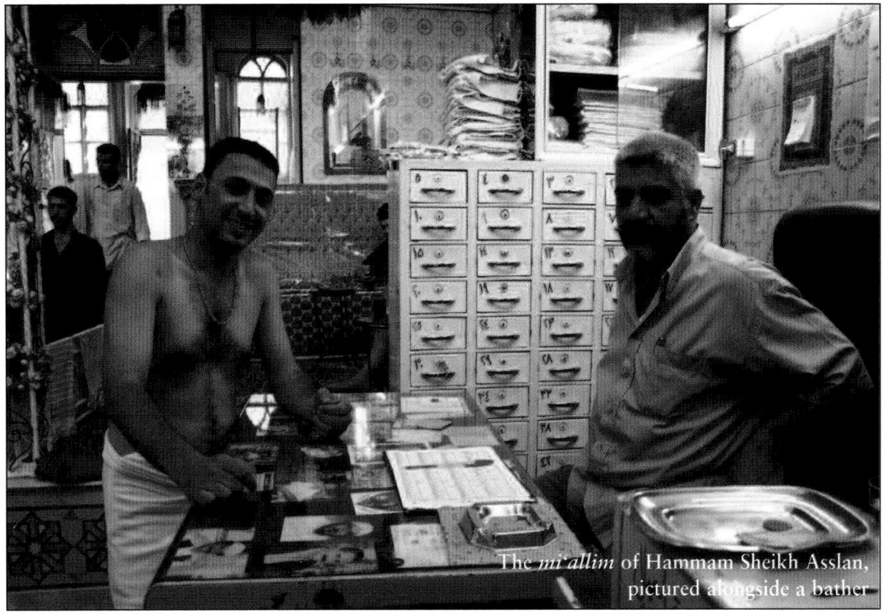
The *mi'allim* of Hammam Sheikh Asslan, pictured alongside a bather

Each manager has his own manner. There is Abu Sayed in Hammam al-Qaramani – all calm and inquiring and cultured in his way, now sitting alone in the empty foyer of the hammam now that it is disused. In Hammam Silsileh the manager would give the warmest of welcomes – generous, laughing, tolerant – and approving of my recording of the life of his hammam. Up in Aleppo there is the elderly *mi'allim* in the Granada, himself showing the years, catching a nap under a blanket as winter approaches, fussily urging me as I leave on a winter's evening to be sure to cover my head properly and not get a cold... And then there is Ibrahim of Hammam al-Nahasin in Aleppo – the most down to earth of the hammam managers, with the most colloquial of Arabic and the bawdiest of songs. I suspect he has never been to school – or if he has, education hasn't spoiled him.

Dropped Vowels

Hammam Ezzedeen is found down through the market at Bab al-Jabiya – outside the city walls, opposite the Ezzedeen Mosque where circles of bread just bought at the baker's are left out to dry on bicycles and even on the pavement itself. At the entrance, arches of fairy lights hint of the splendour within, as if the bather were walking into an amusement arcade, not a public bath.

The overall effect of the décor of Hammam Ezzedeen is that of the *suq*: the floor and pillars are not unlike the mosaic veneers on the tables they sell in Suq al Hamidiye, and above the fountain, mock electric lanterns compete with splendid hanging lamps of a golden texture, fringed. It's not all oriental however: the walls of alternating maroon and black metal stripes give something of the ambience of a barber's shop.

Within the hammam, the *jouwani* rivals Hammam al-Moqaddam for the effect of its tiles, but it was once explained to me that Damascenes favour hammams that are tiled for their greater cleanliness. The only relief from the Orientalism is the employees in their plain blue cotton tracksuits with *Orintal Bath* written on the back. (The mistake in the dropped vowel is, of course, not sloppiness; the tourist guide to Syria, *Culture Shock*, assures us that imperfections in the work are out of pious respect for He whose creation alone is perfect.)

Above the drinking water taps is the inscription *al ashak al nabai, yasalaih al nabai* (love the Prophet, pray for the Prophet). I once asked one of the attendants to write it for me. He did so, but warned me not to let the paper on which the words were written fall to the ground.

Even though it is a desert city, I wouldn't say that there is much reverence for the water that gives Damascus life. It's not uncommon to find the water spilling over the marble basin onto the floor, both hot and cold taps running, the bather having long departed to get dressed. The attitude among some bathers seems to be 'I've paid for the hammam, so I'll waste as much as I want.' Ross Burns quotes Ibn Jabar as describing Damascus as 'sickened with the superfluity of water'.[3]

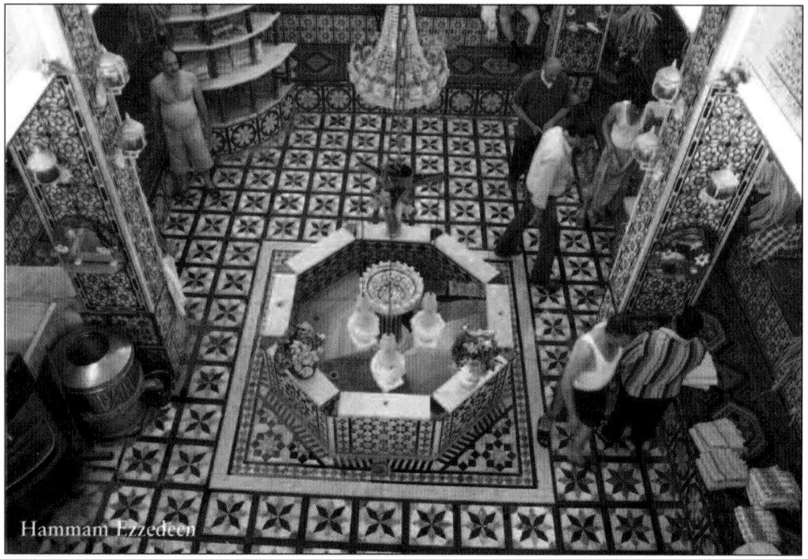
Hammam Ezzedeen

The excessive décor of some hammams was for me not unlike the classical Damascene house: the richly panelled walls within, the oriental excess of the ceiling, all olives and gilt and a wealth of reds, the elaborate script running across the walls beneath. The furniture itself would be grossly studded with mother of pearl. It might even be a bit like Syrian hospitality – sometimes it is all just too much, and you want to be left alone, for you cannot eat another morsel.

Homes and Hammams

The structure of the hammam parallels the traditional home. The Ottoman house in Damascus was built around three courtyards, although this could be reduced to two: the external courtyard or *selamlek* that was a public meeting place for the men, and the second courtyard or *haremlek* that was private and for the family. The third courtyard was a more modest place for the servants.

In her *Hidden Treasures of the Old City* Brigit Keenan quotes an American in the mid-nineteenth century as saying 'Each Damascus house is a paradise.'[4] Indeed, when you escape the traffic, and enter the courtyard with its scented trees reflected in the coolness of the pool, who could argue with Curtis's statement? The architects of Islamic homes would have consciously mirrored the watered gardens of paradise. However, a lot has been lost, and Keenan's book is almost elegiac in its descriptions of Damascene homes; she herself bought one small paradise to save it from destruction.

Although the lower walls of the traditional house were constructed of stone, the higher parts of the Damascene house were built of wattle. I suspect some hammams would have originally mirrored this design. Keenan writes:

> ...though the walls on the ground floor of a Damascus house are built in stone ... the upper storeys are made with a framework of slender poplar trunks filled in with sun-baked mud bricks...[5]

So the Damascus house is a strange being: stone and elaborate design within, humble mud and wood without – the reverse of the saintly prince wearing sackcloth beneath his silken garments.

A colleague of mine married into a family who have one of those Ottoman houses in the old city, and her husband graciously gave me a little tour of the family home. Given the materials used in their construction, the Ottoman houses were easily ignited in the bombardments of the city when Syrians rebelled against French rule, and the area I visited is still affectionately known as 'The Burning'. Similarly nowadays some Ottoman splendour might unfortunately catch fire some Friday afternoon, burning down to its stone walls before the fire brigade can arrive, another half-vacant plot becoming available for 'developers'.

You wouldn't have noticed the house from outside – there was just a door opening on to the *suq*, but within was a splendid courtyard with its pool and citrus trees. We had coffee in a room not unlike the drawing room of some Anglo-Irish house, with black-and-white photographs of his aunts on the table – elegant women, from a time perhaps before a public dowdiness became the norm.

His family had the second biggest courtyard, with their own hammam with its traditional domes on the first floor. This was the family home. He and his wife however actually live independently in a modern flat near the motorway to Homs – not the Ottoman house in the old city that foreigners would die for, but perhaps not wish to share with the extended family.

A century ago Gertrude Bell called in on the women of the Azem Palace in Hama, and admired the courtyard with its fountain and the intricate workmanship of woodwork and mosaic within the rooms. It was within the palace, in its interior rooms, that the real beauty lay:

> The women of the house of 'Azam have even a greater reputation than the sumptuous walls that hold them; they are said to be the loveliest women in all Hamah.[6]

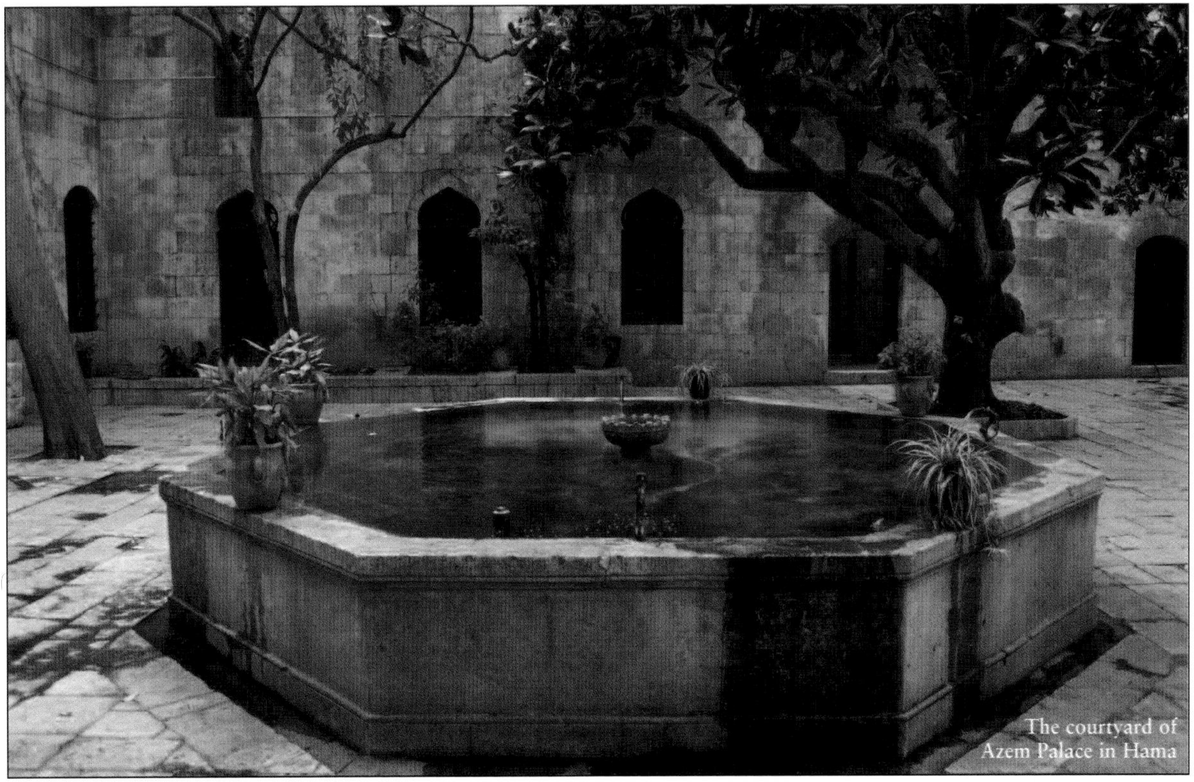

The courtyard of Azem Palace in Hama

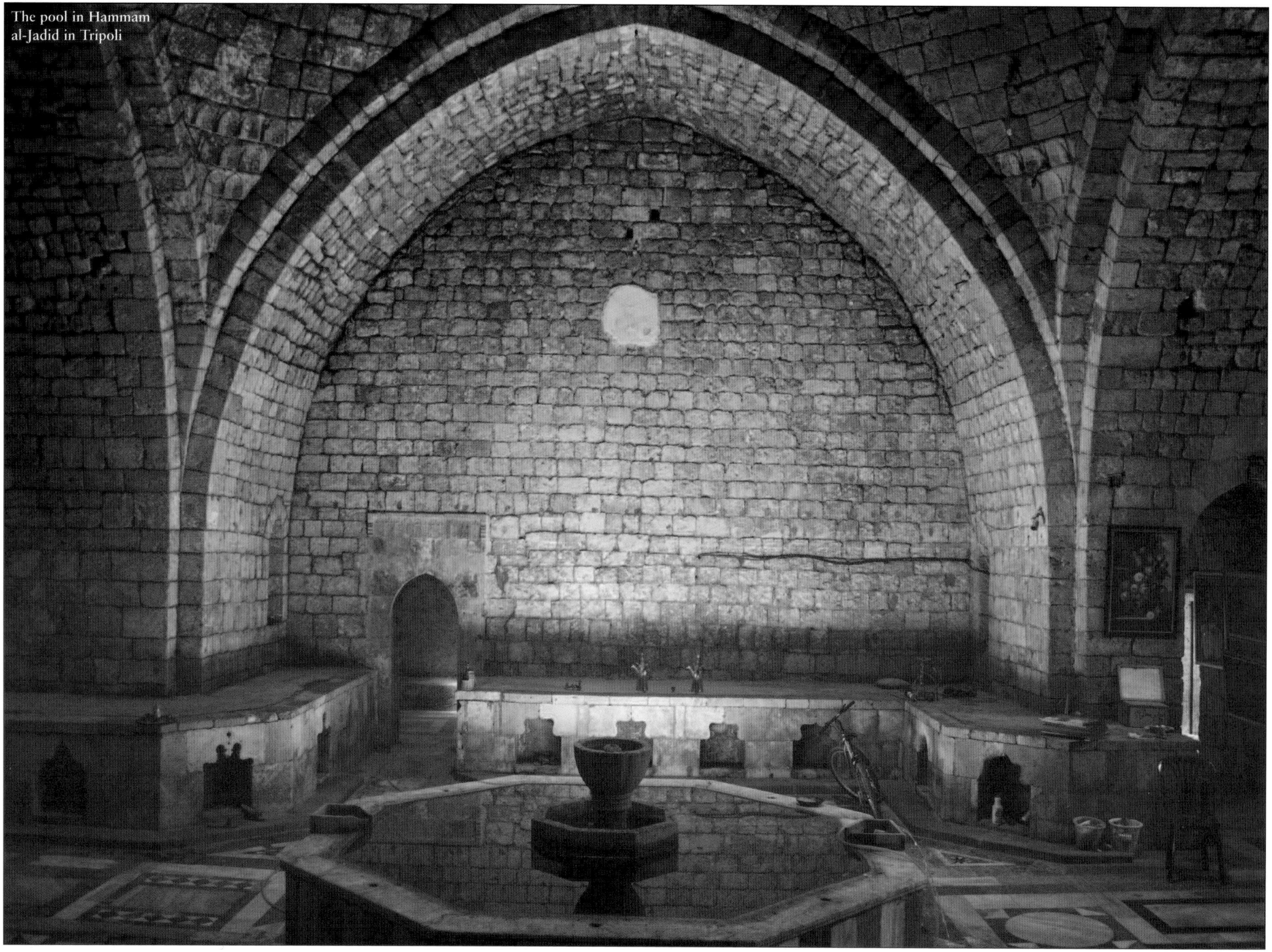

The pool in Hammam al-Jadid in Tripoli

Today the pool in the outer courtyard still reflects the shady trees which surround it, just as the fountain in the outer room of a hammam is its focus. The reflecting waters of the Azem Palace in Hama are matched by the waters of the pool in Hammam al-Jadid in Tripoli, built by the Azem Governor of Damascus. (The fountain, by the way, incorporates an optical illusion, so that no matter from what angle it is viewed, the floor of the pool seems to slope.)

In almost every hammam I know there is at least one fountain, just as the courtyards of a Damascene house are graced with a cooling pool. Fountain styles vary: it will be of impeccable taste in the likes of the upmarket Malek al-Zaher, or reflect more popular style in a hammam like Hammam Sheikh Asslan in Bab Tuma, with its tower of plastic fruit. The fountain, however, is not just ornamentation; buckets are lowered into the pool and the water flung across the marbled floor to clean it.

Gertrude Bell found ranunculi and narcissi growing in the fountained courtyard of the Azems. The typical hammam plant unfortunately is rather dull: the aspidistra, for it can tolerate low levels of light. Sometimes a hammam with its ageing furnishings and dusty aspidistras can have the air of a neglected parlour room.

Hammams have parallels to the traditional homes; just as the home gets more private as you move from one courtyard through to

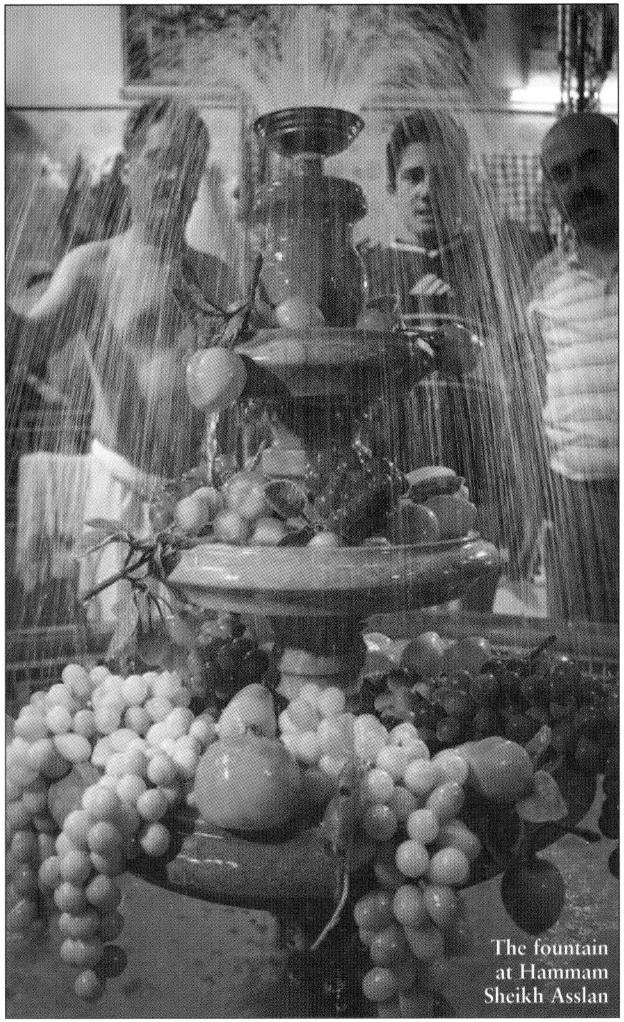

The fountain at Hammam Sheikh Asslan

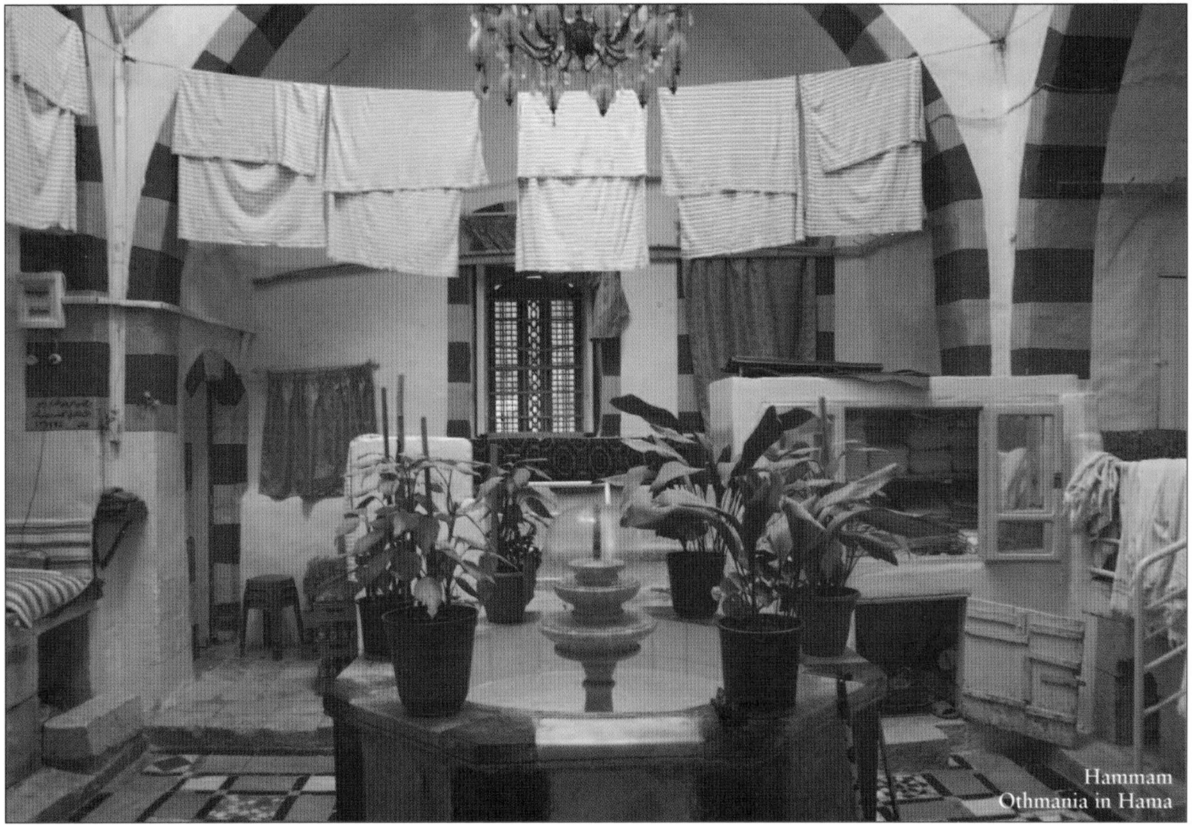

Hammam Othmania in Hama

another, so within the hammam bathing becomes a more private affair. I felt that this structuring however goes far beyond the architecture of homes and hammams; it reflects the society.

Even the Arabic language of Damascus is full of set ritual phrases – as if conversation were a game of well-oiled minimal pairs that people play, set up to keep the other at bay, with one speaker giving the set phrase and the other the set response. There are phrases for every kind of occasion – from funerals (so much easier in the Islamic world where everyone has their set words to say) to events like having a hair cut or just sneezing. To every such utterance there is a set response.

With Palestinians and the Kurds and people from the coast it was somehow different – these were people I felt I got to know. But it seemed to me that the Damascenes keep you in the public, external room with that traditional politeness of theirs. (What's the conversation like when Damascenes get together on Fridays and sit stiffly in those upright chairs, replete with a lunch of stuffed vine leaves and *kibbeh* cooked in yoghurt, the mother-in-law complimenting the woman she chose for her son to marry on her culinary skills?)

Given the political history of Damascus, that distancing is understandable. But after some years in the city I would say that unlike other Syrians, Damascenes never quite let you through to the inner rooms – to what is personal or even intimate – but keep you out there in the public courtyard.

A Trinity of Rooms?

Hammam Nur al-Din is likely to be the bather's first port of call in Damascus. This hammam is in the old city, between the Azem Palace and the vaulted domes of Khan Asad Pasha al-Azem, with its central dome open to the heavens.

If you walk into Hammam Nur al-Din, ignoring the barber's shop at the entrance, you enter the domed grandeur where the bathers modestly undress, or enjoy their post-hammam tea, pampered with towels, their heads too wrapped in a mini-towel, acclimatizing to near-normal temperatures before returning to the wintry street – for a hasty hammam in winter is likely to be followed by a lingering cold.

Sometimes, like a hotel which hides rather tacky rooms by deceiving you with a refurbished foyer, so with some hammams the inner rooms do not quite match the expectations raised by the outer – like in those Aleppo cinemas, where the foyer displays all kinds of enticing shots which have been censored from the actual film. Hammam Nur al-Din however doesn't deceive – and if the splendid room where bathers undress seems somehow out of joint with the rest of the hammam, it is because although the hammam goes back to the time of Nur al-Din, I was told the first main room is Ottoman.

Black-and-white photographs in the entrance show the hammam's former dereliction before restoration. Hammams have suffered not just from neglect but from conflicts with colonial powers; in Medan the French bombed Hammam Rufai in an air strike when the women were bathing, and the crimson of the modern *barrani* somehow does not hint of the hues of the stone within.

Just as Dante's hell had its circles of various intensity (Saladeen was confined to the coolest portion as a reward for his honourable deeds; he brought the defeated Crusader leaders sherbet iced with snow), so the hammam has its rooms of various temperatures. Indeed Dante himself most probably modelled his circles of heaven and hell from Islamic concepts of the afterlife.

What I am presenting as the tripartite structure of the hammam should not be taken too literally however. Some hammams seem to have a dressing room and then the three main rooms of the hammam, according to the architectural vogue at the time of their construction. It might be best to see Nur al-Din as basically a triple-roomed hammam that had a spacious dressing room added to it. And often off the main rooms there will be *maqsuras* or chambers, quite spacious, for washing in. So when you reach what you think is the intense heat of the *jouwani* in Hammam Silsileh (now there's a hammam

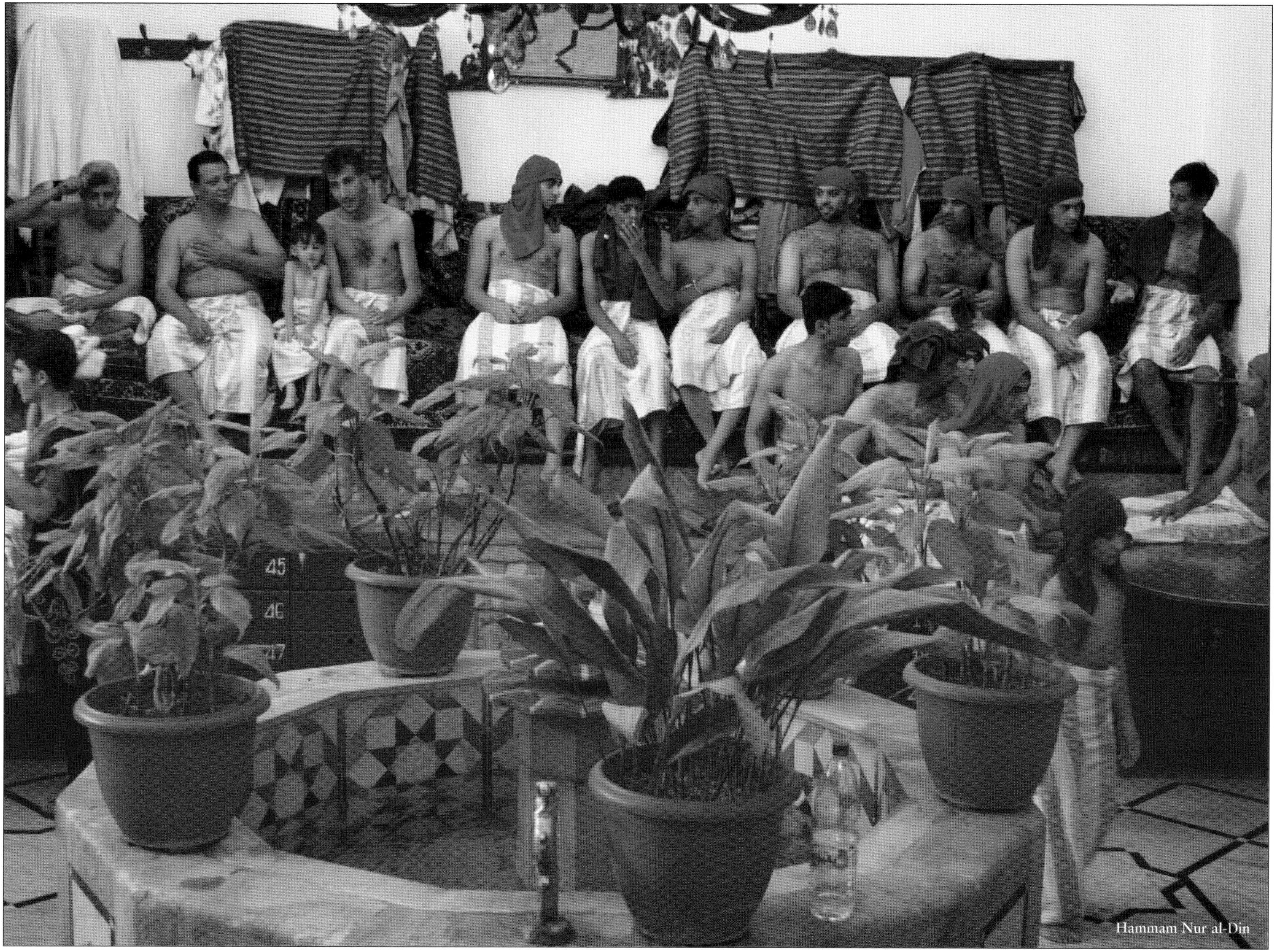

Hammam Nur al-Din

that pulls no punches!) you find yet another room beyond it which leaves you gasping.

In the dressing room beyond the fountain there are further dressing areas, for the first room is often the most expansive room of the hammam. The Australian cavalry officer Hector Dinning aptly describes the room where bathers dress as an '...open, divaned cooling-off room, an amphitheatre of couches upholstered with a kind of gay-coloured towel'.[9]

This 'amphitheatre of couches' varies very much from hammam to hammam. Up in Aleppo, Hammam Bab al-Ahmer has some of the ambience of an Indian restaurant. The attendant might be seated in the porch, all wrapped up in his *abayah* (like a university gown, but lined with a sheep-skin), the mirror behind him reflecting the cold greys of the citadel. But beneath the ornate dome of the *barrani*, it is all dark greens and rich reds, with poetry inscribed in gilt in the corners. Vertical strings of beads give privacy to the alcoves where bathers undress.

In a hammam like Nur al-Din, the dressing room is often a melee of activity – as someone undresses, another is doing his prayers a few metres away. Islam is comprehensive: there is no compartmentalizing of public behaviour and prayer – religion is absolutely part of the public domain. As one bather unselfconsciously prays, another sips his coffee. In contrast it would be something worthy of comment to see someone in Ireland say their prayers in the public sphere of the City Council swimming baths.

Temperatures increase as you put on your clogs and pass through what is possibly the original *jouwani*, which is a cool room where the bather, having finished his bathing, slips out of the wet *futa* into something dry. Beyond this is the *wastani* – the connecting room. *Wasta* is a key word in Syrian society, for you will need a *wasta*, a person with connections, to arrange your residence visa or deal with the traffic police if you ever have a scrape with them. (The most civilized bribery I have ever seen was when travelling through the *badieh* – the desert plain, the heart of things bedouin. The traffic policeman who stopped us simply wished the driver *Ramadan karem* and the driver dutifully reached for his wallet.)

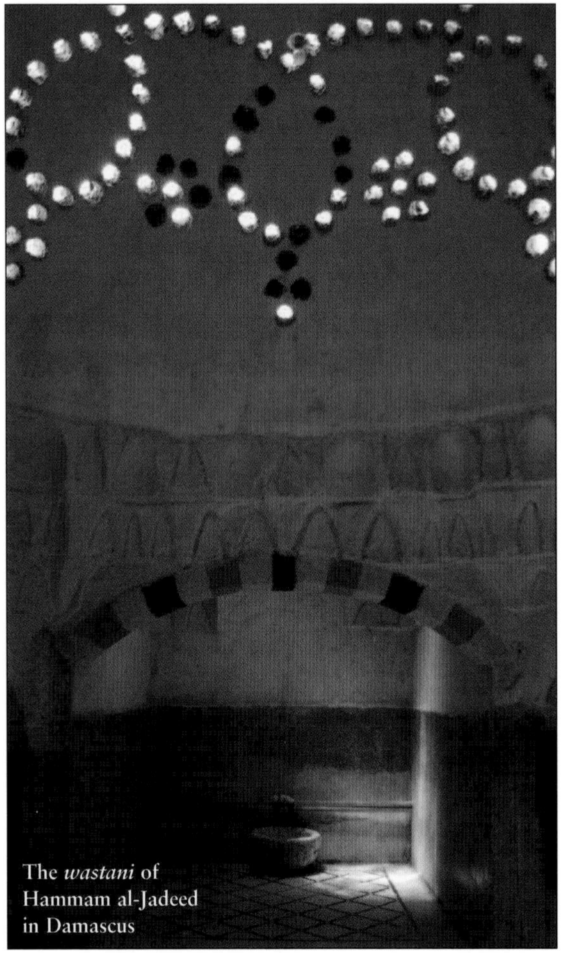
The *wastani* of Hammam al-Jadeed in Damascus

The *wastani* is often where the *mukeyyis* (the attendant who scrubs your skin clean) hangs out, and there are usually small rooms like alcoves for this purpose. In Hammam Nur al-Din such are the numbers of bathers, it's a bit like a conveyer belt, with men hanging around the alcoves waiting for their turn. It is here in the *wastani* that the discriminating bather might choose to linger – leaning against a shell-shaped font, languidly scooping a copper dish of cooling water over his steaming body. The fonts for bathers are usually in the alcoves of the *wastani* and the rooms off the *jouwani* within – they can be of solid basalt or quite delicately carved stone.

A rather foreboding wooden door opens into the *jouwani* – the innermost room of the hammam. Here bathers are in a state of near collapse, such is the intensity of the steam. Men hug the floor or sit hunched over in benches so as to breathe somewhat easier, for as the steam rises the heat in the lower regions tends to be less intense; others retreat into the private alcoves to douse themselves with cooling water. It is in the *jouwani* that you are most likely to see bathers under the full impact of the steam; Dinning describes them as 'drooping comatose forms'.

In Hammam Nur al-Din there is still one more room for the foolhardy – most stand by its door, gape, and never enter, for the heat of the steam room is enough to give a short sharp scorch to the skin. *Abandon hope all ye who enter here* might be appropriately written above the entrance to the steam room.

I had sensed a smell that I could not quite place in the hottest hammams of Syria; that Australian cavalry officer's senses were at work as he explored Damascus and again he got it right:

> Room after room you pass with swinging doors; each is hotter than the last. In each there is a stronger smell of man.[7]

Indeed! And I suspect the smell of maleness that the cavalry officer identifies is not far from the smell of scorching flesh.

Even an unused hammam can be described as hellish: the *Aleppo Visitors' Guide* of fifty years ago describes the palatial Hammam Yalbougha below the citadel when it was used as a felt factory:

> The jerky movements and the unintelligible sounds of these half-clothed felt-makers as they work in the deceptive shadows of the old bath may remind the educated visitor of a scene from Dante's 'Inferno'.

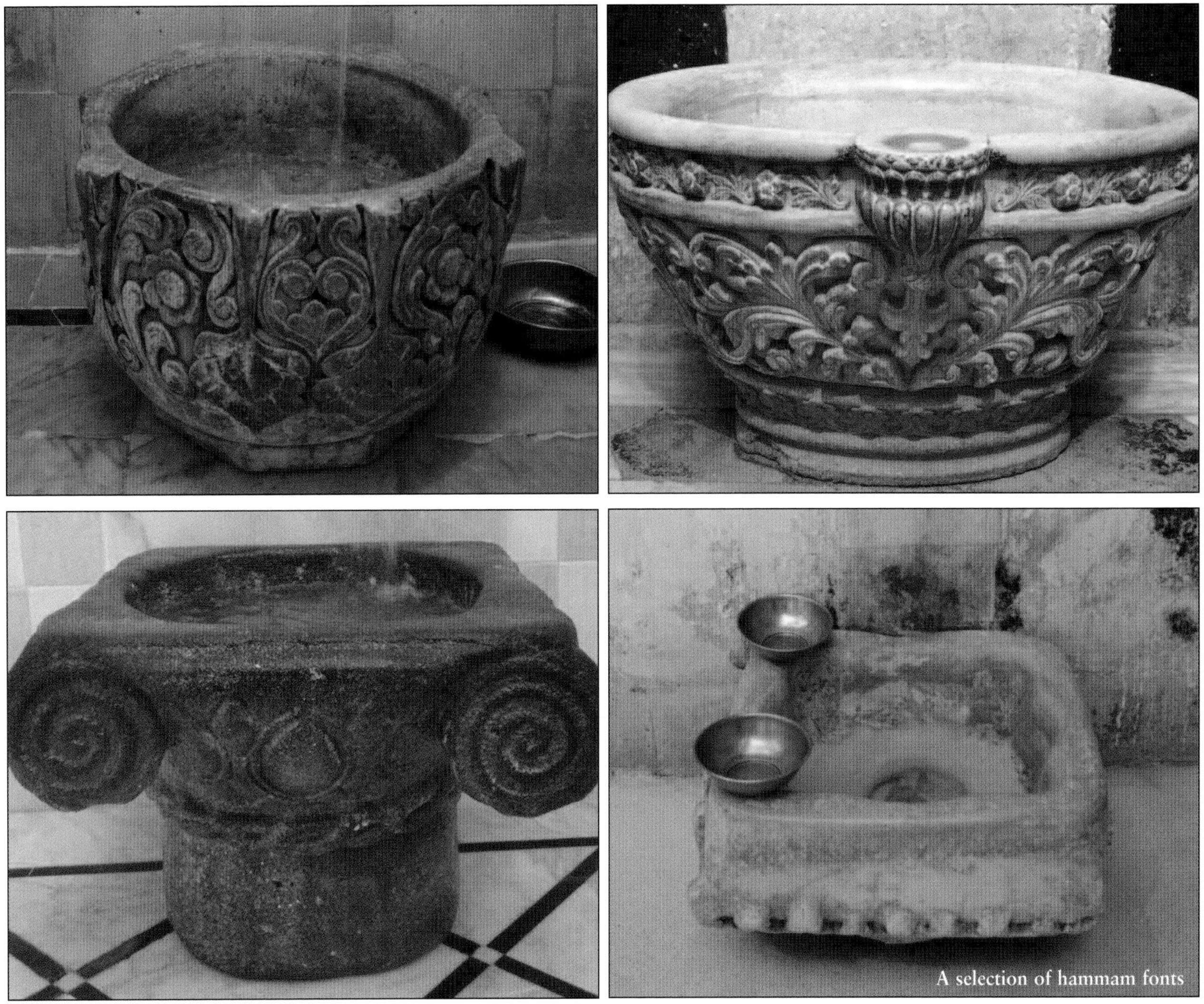
A selection of hammam fonts

So much for hell! If Captain Hector Dinning is to be believed, the fires of the hammam might be a taste of the eternal punishment to come. Having captured the distinctive smell of the hammam, he summed up the bathers thus:

> They give you strongly the impression that they are seeking recovery from a debauch; and for this impression there is very good ground. The race is steeped in lasciviousness.[8]

From Arabia to India the standard Western perception of 'Oriental' morality has been one of 'hot climes, hot desires'. If Dinning's thoughts on hammaming reflected the realities of his day, things must have got a bit tame since then, although there are a couple of steamy exceptions.

When it all gets too much the bather can retreat to the *wastani* – have a cold shower – (a not unregrettable innovation in my opinion) and change into fresh towels, before going out to collapse on one of the couches. Showers are not the only recent innovations: a *wastani* nowadays might host some recent western imports like a sauna in the case of Hammam Nur al-Din or even a jacuzzi in some other hammams.

Both intrigued and appalled, having captured the essence of hammaming in the Sham, Dinning retreated to the 'sweetness of the bazaars'. And indeed, outside Hammam Nur al-Din, the stall keepers still tempt you with sugared fruit, and liquorice, and walnuts and rainbowed sweets that must contain every E number known to humanity.

Hair Matters

In the foyer of at least three hammams in Damascus a barber is in service, often in front of a massive mirror ornately decorated with mother-of-pearl. It's all part of the pampering, with the barber attacking any nasty spots on the face with a piece of thread held between the teeth and dexterously pulled around any protruding blackhead. It is here that the hammam most resembles a hairdresser's; in one hammam, bathers swathed in towels avail of a Lady Diana face mask.

It is not just the face that is attended to. Within a couple of hammams, just as you go to enter the small room before the *wastani*, a more specialized hair removal service is offered: the bathers line up, the attendant reads the number on their bracelet so that they can be later billed, and matter of factly shaves each bather's armpits, with the same blade.

Apart from hair on the face of the male, bodily hair is not much encouraged in the Islamic world. The Russells' record of hammam life includes their analysis of a paste which was used to remove body hair:

> The depilatory is composed of quick lime, and orpiment, in the proportion of one dram of the latter to an ounce of the former. These are intimately rubbed together in a mortar, to a powder, which is moistened a little with water...[9]

Nowadays hair removal is just a matter of shaving. And it is not just the armpits that are shaved: as part of bodily hygiene, privately the bather may himself remove the body hair of other more intimate areas. It has a lot to do with hot climates, and on seeing me with a razor an attendant voiced his approval and expressed his disgust at the body odour of foreigners.

In Syria, beards are not much more common than in the West, although *shebab* do tend to sport a carefully trimmed beard. The growing of a beard as an expression of masculinity is quite encouraged in Islam, but the more 'fundamentalist' style of beard (I distance myself from the word as it is normally used, for there is nothing extreme in observing the five fundamentals of Islam) has not been much encouraged in government circles. A significant beard nowadays seems to be more visually present in the streets, along with a dress style which is believed to emulate that of the Prophet.

A moustache is essential – what Syrian male would shave off his moustache, except if he wanted to prance around with the *firasha*, the 'butterflies', as they ham it up in the baths? Beirut is different: on leaving Syria it is the shaved moustaches of the Lebanese officials at the border, somehow emasculating, that announce your entrance to another country. A second wonder is the ability of the Lebanese officials recording your passport details to type with more than one finger.

The attendant has a rather specialized job, and it goes with handing out the soap, sisal scrub and shampoo. (The *leefah* by the way, or sisal scrub, is one of the few things in Syria to be recycled – the plate of radishes and scallions on the restaurant table as you wait for your meal being one of the others.)

One of the attendants once asked me if there was work for him in Ireland, but I had to reply that there was not a great demand amongst Irish men for his particular skills.

The *Mukeyyis*

When you enter a hammam you will usually find the *mukeyyis* hanging about with the other attendants, smoking or maybe catching a nap if you should arrive on a quiet afternoon. To have a hammam without being scrubbed down by a *mukeyyis* would be like having a wash without soap.

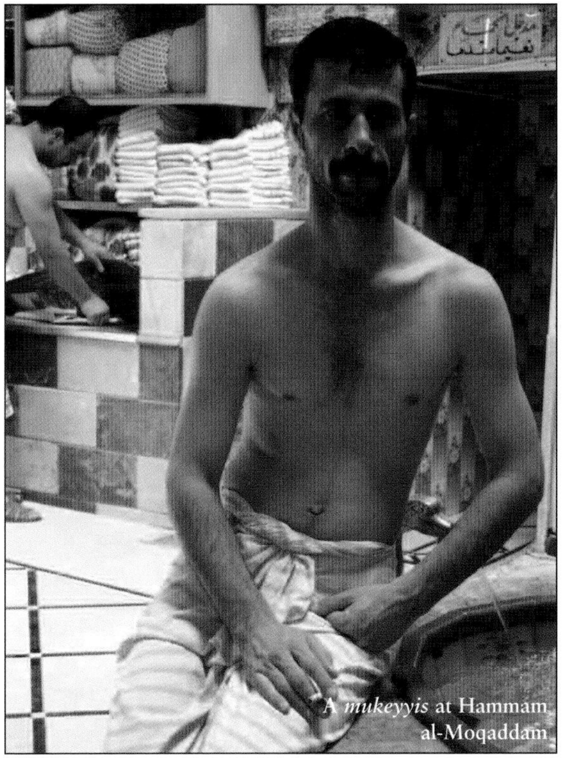

A *mukeyyis* at Hammam al-Moqaddam

The *wastani* is the area where the *mukeyyis* actually works, for here it is not too hot. You may also find him in one of the arched alcoves which are set aside for his work, sitting by the massive copper bowl of warm water in which the leftover soap of the day is recycled.

Any decent *mukeyyis* will let you sweat it out first for as long as you want, and the bather who knows anything about hammaming will not wash with soap until after the *mukeyyis* is done. After a whispered *bismillah* he sets to work, using a kind of coarse mitt made of goat hair for the purpose. Starting with the right arm, he works his way from limb to limb, scouring the body clean so that the skin is left pinkish and invigorated. After the arms and chest, he'll move on to the legs, and then tell you to turn over to do the back and the rest of the body. It's an intimate, but not necessarily a sensual, experience – lying there on the marble floor, staring up at the echoing dome of the side-room, as the *mukeyyis* sets to.

If you have ever heard a *mukeyyis* shout for one of the other attendants, you will know why I call the dome echoing. There is a kind of intimacy, but I wouldn't describe the typical *mukeyyis* as gentle in his approach. Once I asked a *mukeyyis* if the mitt he used was made of camel hair. He looked at me with contempt – 'Camel hair is soft!' – and went on with his task of scouring me clean.

It's probably the sedentary life style that leads to the typical *mukeyyis* figure, for nowadays given the decline of the hammams they might have quite some wait between bathers. But not between smokes. A *mukeyyis* may happily light up before he starts to scrub you down, for political correctness has not quite reached the hammams.

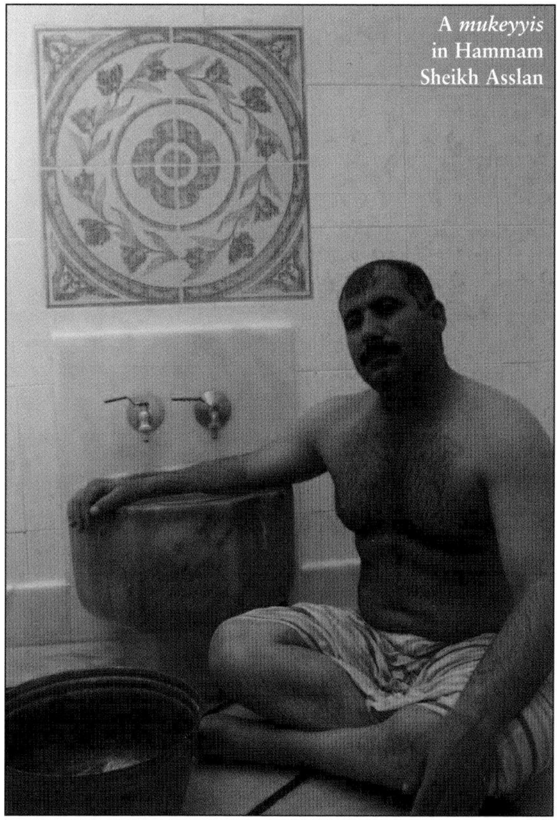

A *mukeyyis* in Hammam Sheikh Asslan

The owner of Aleppo's Hammam al-Atiqa told me it was all the good food that the bathers bring to eat and share with attendants, eating it all from a tray on the hammam floor, which gives the *mukeyyis* in Aleppo his recumbent figure. The *mukeyyis* will probably have worked at least a decade in the hammams, and his overhanging belly is a source of pride, suggesting a life of leisure and good living. A *mukeyyis* in Hammam al-Moqaddam takes the prize; his pendant belly would be the envy of even a traffic policeman.

In a hammam in Hama – the wonderful Hammam al-Assadia in the *suq* – I asked the *mukeyyis* Abu Rubai about his life in the hammam:

- And how long have you worked in the hammam?
- 37 years.
- So how old were you when you started?
- I was about 11. I did the towels.
- And served tea?
- We didn't serve tea in those days.
- What! No tea? I can't imagine it – a hammam without tea! And was your father a *mukeyyis* too?
- Yes, and my grandfather too.
- And will your son be a *mukeyyis* like you?
- God no! He goes to school. He wants to study military engineering.

It's not unusual for a *mukeyyis* to be the son of a *mukeyyis* (as the Syrian proverb says – the son of a duck knows how to swim) and in Damascus almost every *mukeyyis* is from one village – the village of Mazamia about half an hour outside Damascus on the Aleppo road. But Abu Rabai's comment about his son shows how the job is seen as incompatible with an education, and the Arabic of the *mukeyyis* reflects this.

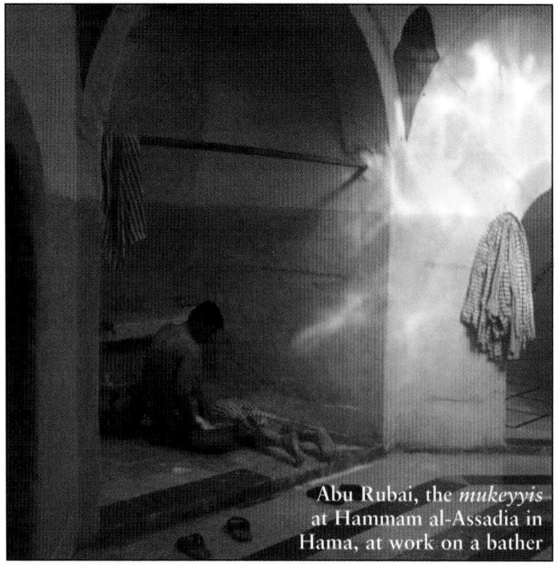
Abu Rubai, the *mukeyyis* at Hammam al-Assadia in Hama, at work on a bather

A conversation with a *mukeyyis* is likely to be just as down to earth as his scouring of the body. I once asked a *mukeyyis* in Hammam Granada in Aleppo if he spoke any English. His reply showed the uneducated Arab's humility before his mother tongue: 'Me? I don't even speak Arabic.' Only the classical is seen as the language; the colloquial does not count. Not knowing a word of classical Arabic myself, I was in no position to judge, and yielded to Abu Jameel's no-nonsense scrub down.

I was flattered one day to be summoned by a bather in Hammam Aramani to be scrubbed down, and as I worked away he asked how long I had been working in the hammam. It was with delight that I told him I wasn't a *mukeyyis* but an English teacher. Richard Burton may have passed for a pilgrim in Mecca, but my Arabic had been sufficiently 'street' to be mistaken for a Syrian *mukeyyis*. I had been shamming in the hammam.

Once in Tripoli I asked the attendants if they were Lebanese. They claimed they were and I laughed at that, and asked why they had the accent of the village of Mazamia near Damascus. Even in Lebanon the *mukeyyis* network extended from this Damascene village, but the political situation has changed now, and with the withdrawal of Syrian troops the attendants have also moved back to the hammams of Damascus.

I have heard that the network from this village extends down as far as to Petra in Jordan, where there are a few hammams set up for tourists, and so of no interest whatsoever. I imagine the *mukeyyis* network as a kind of bush telegraph; they must know everything that goes on in the city. Apparently in Ottoman times the hammam workers were also in the service of the state; if some bathers were plotting insurrection in the hammams, the *mukeyyis* would be the first to hear it and dutifully inform the authorities. I would not wish to comment on whether this tradition survives today.

I have even met one or two Iraqis working as *mukeyyis* in Syria. The Iraqi *mukeyyis* in Aleppo told me his story as he scoured me clean. (How the hammam is like a confessional – what stories have I heard inside the hammam!) His father had had a family business in Iraq, but was murdered in

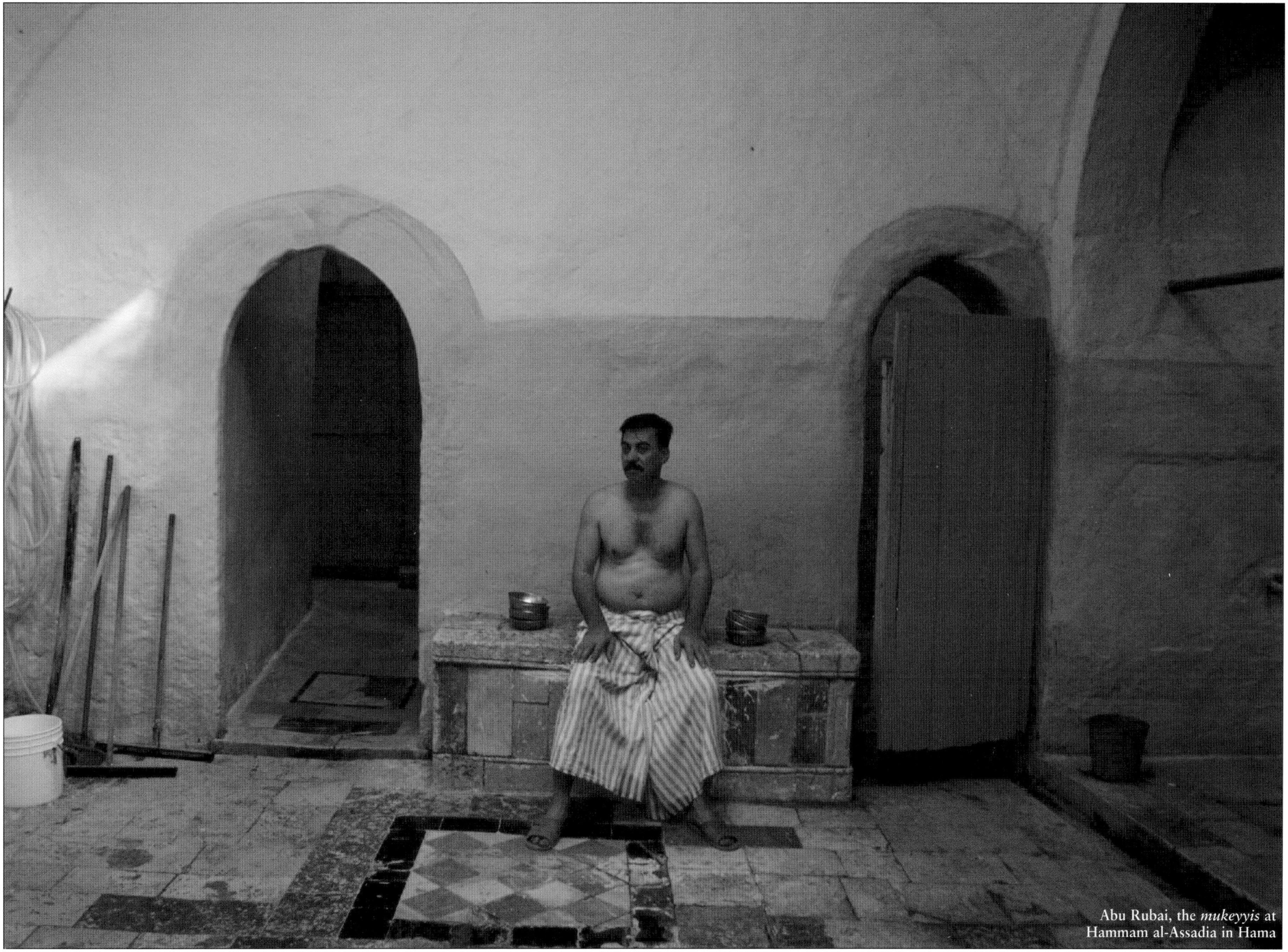
Abu Rubai, the *mukeyyis* at Hammam al-Assadia in Hama

the conflict brought about by the invasion. And so the son now lived in exile, making a living not as a young businessman but as a *mukeyyis* in a hammam.

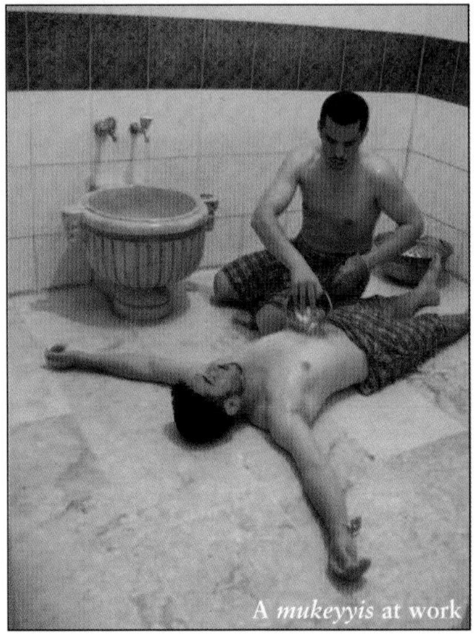
A *mukeyyis* at work

When I say the *mukeyyis* scours the bather clean, I do not mean the circular motion like when you're at the kitchen sink doing the dishes. It's more a kind of up and down movement, like when you are hoeing the garden. The *mukeyyis* leaves you cleaner than you have ever been in your life, although the mitt used might have a particular whiff that might suggest a lapse in standards of hygiene.

When the *mukeyyis* scrubs you with that coarse glove he puts over his right hand, the dead skin comes off in tiny greyish rolls – so much sometimes it is almost embarrassing to think of what has accumulated in the days since the last hammam. As Gavin Young wrote of the effect of being scrubbed down in a Baghdad hammam:

> This produces black rolls of dirt from your skin, and you feel deeply ashamed of the inadequacy of European washing habits: not enough real soaking, not enough serious scrubbing, not enough running water.[10]

You haven't washed properly until you have hammamed.

At the end of the scrub, before he soaps you down with soap scented of bay and myrtle, the *mukeyyis* takes a dish of clean water from the font and throws it over you. It's all washed away – you see it – you see the water taking away the little rolls of your own dead skin. So many little pellets, like rolled up scrolls, float towards the drain, the water carrying it all away, like so many past years. To me it is a thing of disgust, those grey residues of skin (but then if you're not in the mood the whole experience can be nauseating, like when you have been too long among the crowds of Suq al Hamidiye and long for the light at the end of the star-roofed tunnel – for the light coming through the rusting holes in the corrugated iron hints of desert stars).

I suppose everything is in the eye of the beholder. To at least one Mamluk poet, observing his beloved in the hammam, the material world went under a miraculous transformation: his lover's beads of sweat became the unstrung pearls of a necklace, the pellets of dead skin, strands of musk.[11]

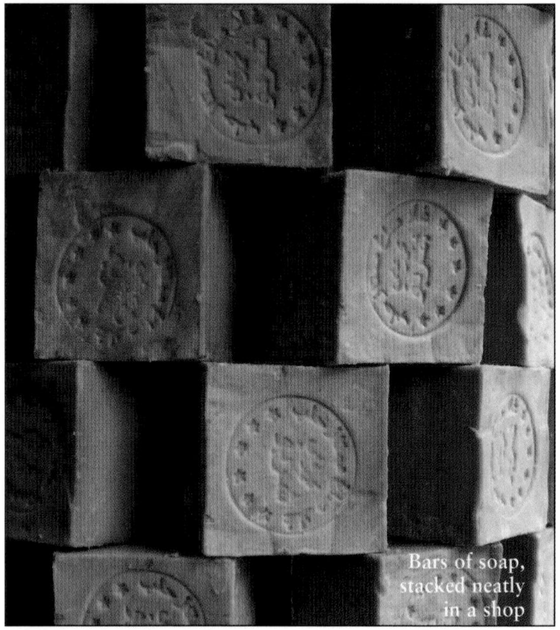
Bars of soap, stacked neatly in a shop

The Brass Dish

Western concepts of 'cleanliness' – like soaking in a hot tub of bath water – would be anathema to Syrian Muslims. Islamic cleanliness is about running water, and a brass dish or *tasai* is used to scoop the water from the basin on to the body. No-one washes in the font itself; washing means pouring water over the body. Given Islamic concepts of cleanliness, 'innovations' like the jacuzzi seem doomed to fail, for what Muslim would wish to soak in the bath water of others?

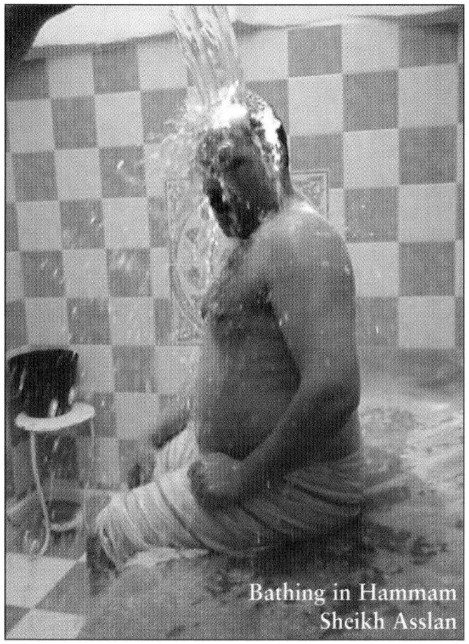
Bathing in Hammam Sheikh Asslan

Many a Syrian proverb comes from hammam life and at least one focuses on the brass dish of the hammams; the proverb *tasai sukhan, tasai barid* reflects the way life is likely to treat you: one day it throws a dish of hot water at you, the next day it splashes you with cold.

Unfortunately cheap plastic bowls have replaced the brass dish in many hammams, and they are now most likely to be found in an antique shop, for the bowls are sometimes beautifully worked.

Once I heard a *mukeyyis* describe the amount of money earned daily in the Tailors' Hammam, right in the *suq*, as a couple of *tasai* of gold coins per day. The hammam was one of the most successful in Damascus, not surprising given its location, until its water supply dried up. Under the fading patterns of its dome – like some wallpapered room that has lost its colour from exposure to the sun – underwear is now sold.

Massage

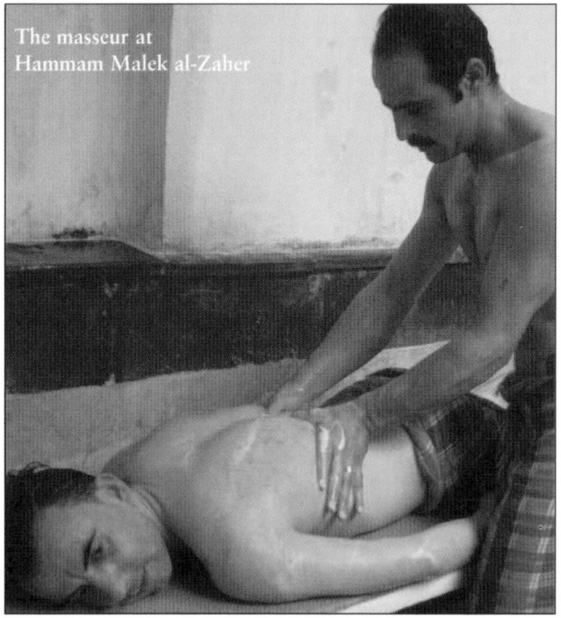
The masseur at Hammam Malek al-Zaher

After the *mukeyyis* has scrubbed you down, it might be time to indulge in a massage, often in a side room or *maqsurah* off the *wastani*. Contrary to Western expectations, however, the massage is not fundamentally part of the hammam – to have a hammam without a massage is quite acceptable.

The bather who expects to be handled daintily by the masseur would be better to go straight out to the *barrani* for his infusion of flowers or his Lady Diana face mask. A massage in Syria is not so much a tender working of the flesh as a pummelling, a cracking of joints, a twisting of limbs, and, to cap it all, a dexterous jerking of the head from left to right.

Massage techniques have not much changed since the Russells' stay in Aleppo at the end of the eighteenth century:

> ...one of the attendants begins to press and handle the tops of the shoulders, the muscles of the whole body... The attendant then taking hold of the bather's fingers, with a dexterous jerk makes each joint crack successively; after which, laying him flat on his back, and bringing the arms across the breast, the shoulder joints are made to crack in like manner.[12]

Similarly, Lane speaks of his operator in an Egyptian hammam cracking almost every joint in the frame:

> He wrings the body, first one way, and then the other, to make several of the vertebrae crack...[13]

It is certainly a relationship of trust, for the masseur has one final parting gift for the Russells:

> Last of all (and to strangers a part of the process the most alarming) the neck is made to crack, by raising the head and bringing the chin forward to the breast.

Lane's man in Egypt has a slightly different technique:

> ...the neck is made to crack twice by wrenching the head round, each way.

Even a much experienced bather like myself baulks at the final touch. Finally the bather (I almost wrote patient) is doused with a bucket of cold water emptied over the head.

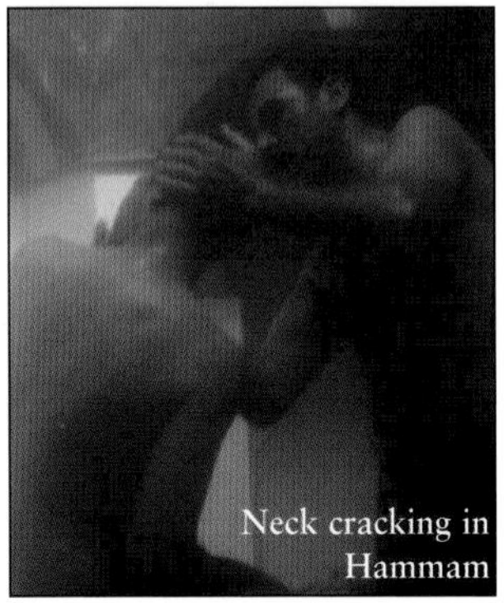
Neck cracking in Hammam

Perhaps the massage is the Arab answer to the Roman work-out in the gymnasium, for it puts the body through almost as much.[14]

The Attendants

If the heat is getting too much the bather can retreat back to the *wastani* to recover, rather than suffer the embarrassment of fainting in public. On such occasions the attendants' role is to bring refreshments.

Hammam Malek al-Zaher is not for the faint-hearted; it is an intrepid bather who stretches out on their *beit al-nar* for the heat to permeate his body. (The *beit al-nar*, the fire-house, is usually the raised area running across the floor to the wall which conceals the tank of water heated by the furnace.) And so, one Friday, I retreated for a half-time breather in the *wastani*.

What I really wanted was a herbal tea with a little sugar, but I asked the attendant for a herbal tea with no sugar. He seemed amused at the request, but I knew the scene: I could have heaps of sugar, or no sugar, but a little sugar was out of the question. The masseur told me how he liked his tea: he put in one third tea, one third hot water, and a third of sugar. I'm sure he was not exaggerating.

Time for tea

The attendant returned with not just the herbal tea but a glass of cool water on a tray, just as it should be:

- 'One herbal tea without sugar!' he called.
- 'And a glass of water too! But maybe you have sweetened the water?'
- 'No, it comes as sweet as the God of the worlds has made it.'

The Après-Hammam

As you have your final rinse the attendant will run off and return with towels balanced on his head, like a kid returning from the bakers with the flat circles of unleavened bread that is the staple with every meal. He'll pat you down with a fresh towel, then as you drop yours there'll be a flick of the wrist and a fresh towel will be already around your waist. *Naemun* he'll say – this is the set phrase for the occasion – and show you the door to the *barrani*.

It is after the hammam proper that the true pampering begins. Fresh towels are brought, ear buds are presented for cleansing the ears, and the bather recovers from the hammam in pampered splendour. The après-hammam is a time of recovery; that captain of Australian cavalry rather nicely captured the mood: 'The bathed sit swaying in the ecstasy of reaction from the steam, with closed eyes.'[15]

If *nargilehs* are on offer, the smoker might reach an ultimate state of relaxation. Richard Burton, the greatest explorer of the Victorian era (who lived next to a hammam in Salihiye, but strangely remained silent on what he observed there), said there was no English word for the Arabic *kaif*. Burton saw *kaif* as a characteristic of the East: the ability to enjoy a kind of total mental relaxation (mental 'shut down' might be a fair translation) where a different, more sensual plane is enjoyed.

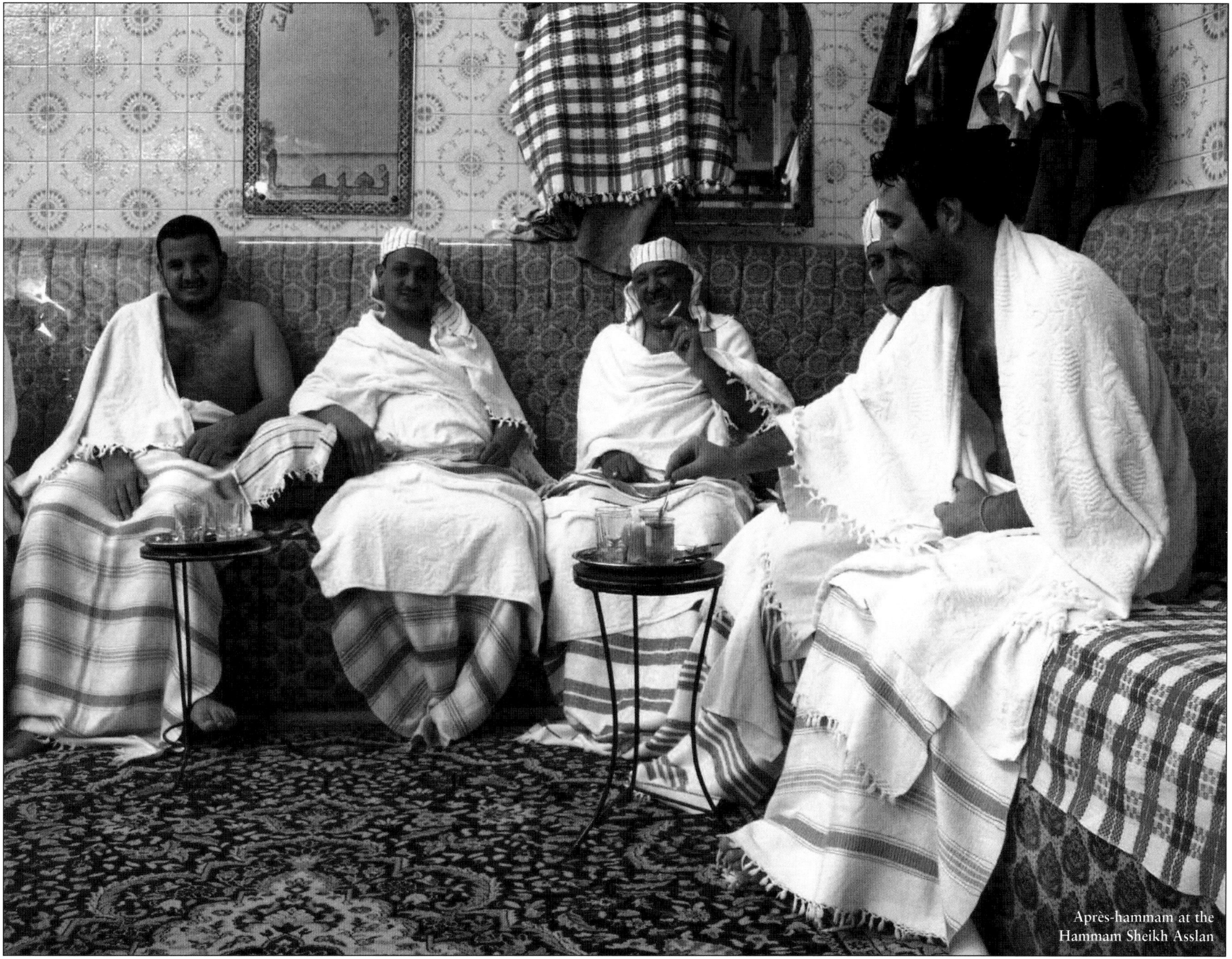

Après-hammam at the
Hammam Sheikh Asslan

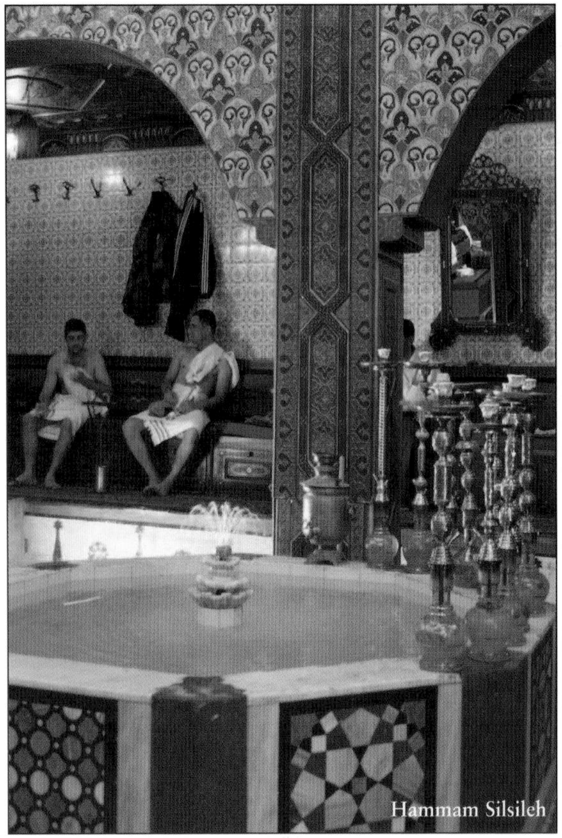

Hammam Silsileh

Gavin Young quotes the Palestinian-Iraqi novelist Jabar on hammams: 'They expressed man's love of sensuous abandon by alabaster troughs...'[16]

Maybe in Syria the hammam carries this function – the intense heat and the steam can bring something similar to a sensuous abandon. The *nargileh* would be the icing on the cake; for after the hammam's heat the tobacco goes to the bather's head. Wrapped in towels like some pampered film actress, he puffs contentedly on his pipe, reclining like one of those figures carved on a tomb in Palmyra – slightly corpulent from all the good living, raising the cup of wine from Roman days when Queen Zenobia ruled the oasis city, as if to our health.

In one sentence Dinning sums up the experience of hammaming in the Sham: 'No Roman bathed more voluptuously.'

Pay and Conditions

The *mukeyyis* does not so much work for a regular wage as for tips; the tradition is that the bather should tip according to his means. The service rendered however is also likely to be in proportion to the expected tip. And so the bathers from Derazor by the Euphrates, who are not renowned for their generosity, or the soldiers on military service on their few Syrian pounds a month, will get the briefest of rub downs. So too will foreigners, who, having received the most cursory of service, are expected to give the biggest tip. (The thing to do here is to return your arm to the *mukeyyis* and tell him it is not your first time in a hammam.)

One summer afternoon Hammam Nur al-Din was like a gathering of the Arab League; from Yemen to the Gulf, men were nipping in for a holiday hammam. I suspect there wasn't a single bather from Damascus present, however, for the *shebab* go off to the outdoor pools in summer – the water pumped up deliciously cold from the ground beneath. The hammams are left for those on vacation.

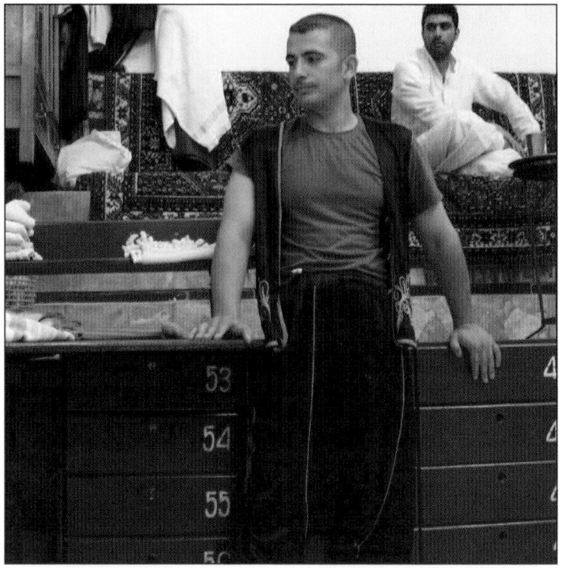

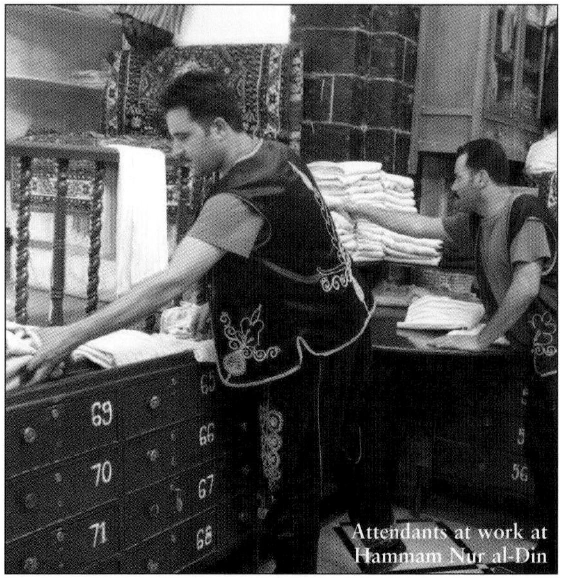

Attendants at work at Hammam Nur al-Din

Summer in Aleppo is a different story. One summer evening I came across the *mi'allim* of Hammam al Naem and a rather grumpy *mukeyyis* sitting outside in the street. I greeted them cheerily: 'Any customers this evening?' It can be boring if you have the hammam all to yourself. The reply was curt enough: 'No-one.' 'You mean it's nine o'clock on a Thursday night, and there's not a single person in the hammam?' The explanation was simple enough: 'In winter they bathe here; in summer they go to the sea.'

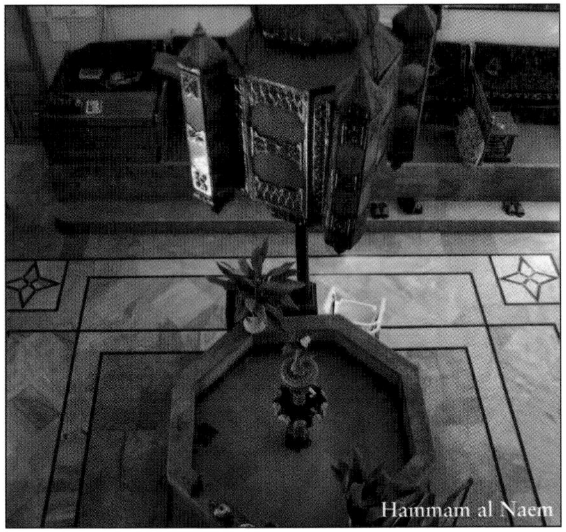

The *mi'allim* was resigned to the seasonal rhythms of the hammam year; in summer the *shebab* take the train through the mountains to the coast. But unlike in Damascus, when the locals desert the hammams in summer they leave them empty; Gulf tourists rarely make it up the road to Aleppo.

In Damascus however, the attendants were kept especially busy that day, but one was enjoying a breather. I asked how long he'd been working:

- From 8.00 this morning.
- And you finish at midnight? That's a long working day!
- But tomorrow's off.
- Yes, I forgot. And do you work on the farm or anything on your day off?
- No, I just take it easy.

Around us, Jordanians were undressing for their hammam, and in the main foyer *shebab* from the Gulf were enjoying a sweet tea.

- And do you mind if I ask about pay?
- It's 600.

I hesitated a while, trying to work out 600 what per what...

- So that's not so bad, 18,000 a month.
- Ah, but you forgot we work every other day...

That would make it about 200 dollars a month. At the manager's desk an attendant would be offering a little *finjan* of coffee – a little cup with no handle – to the bathers as they left, subtly reminding them to leave a tip in the box. The tips would later be shared out among the staff, although in most hammams the bather tips the hammam worker directly. And as the departing bather tosses back the proffered coffee – it is really just enough strong, bitter coffee to fill the bottom of the cup – he might say the traditional *Daimai* or 'Always' (something not to be said by the way when coffee is offered at a funeral).

I continued probing into the matter of finances:

- But then you have the tips – that might be more than the salary.
- True, but it depends on business.
- And who are the best tippers?
- Maybe the ones from Qatar.
- And the Saudis? I asked mischievously.

The attendant paused a little.

- The Saudis who come here to Damascus...

He hesitated again so as to find the right words.

- The Saudis who have money go to Europe... The ones who come here...

I laughed. The attendant didn't need to complete the sentence for me, and he wasn't just talking about financial status, for the nightclubs of Damascus depend on the Saudis for their existence.

But in that very hammam I chatted to some *shebab* from some rural area of Saudi. They weren't exactly reaping the benefits of all that oil money, and were modesty itself – educated in some training institute, making a living as a carpenter or whatever, and probably married to a cousin at the age of seventeen.

And that's what hammaming is like: in the hammam you meet all types. Gavin Young reports the *mi'allim's* description of the clientele in the Baghdad hammam he visited:

> 'All sorts come here,' the owner told me. 'Taxi drivers, students, office workers, army officers, a minister or two. See those young men there? They are in the Iraqi football team. A hammam is a democracy you see.'[17]

With everyone wearing just a *futa*, or perhaps less in an Iraqi hammam, a kind of levelling process is at work, for without clothes it's not easy to maintain pretensions. And so Gavin Young notes the text in the hammam foyer: 'Let man see himself as he was created.'[18]

A hammam is a democracy. Indeed! Especially with regard to the range of people you meet; you might find yourself with a boxer, or a tailor, or even someone just out of prison. Young quotes Jabar on hammams:

> ... in the voluptuous mist, philosopher and merchant, pimp and angel, found communion in nudity, water and conversation.[19]

I have rarely found myself mixing with a wider range of people in one room than in a Syrian hammam, except in a Yemeni qat chew perhaps.

Chatting with a *Mukeyyis*

In Hammam Ezzedeen an attendant handed me a couple of dates as I went in to bathe – leftovers from Ramadan.

With the *Eid* festival that marks the end of a month of fasting you get people coming for a hammam who only come once a year, like people who go to church just at Christmas. A man with scars slashed across his belly asked me, the foreigner, for guidance on hammam procedures. (I never really got an explanation for this occasional feature of Syrian manhood – the way someone will have scars, as from a knife, slashed across the arms or chest. When I challenged someone on the issue, his explanation was that he had fallen out with his mother, and inflicted the scars on himself.) The next bather asked

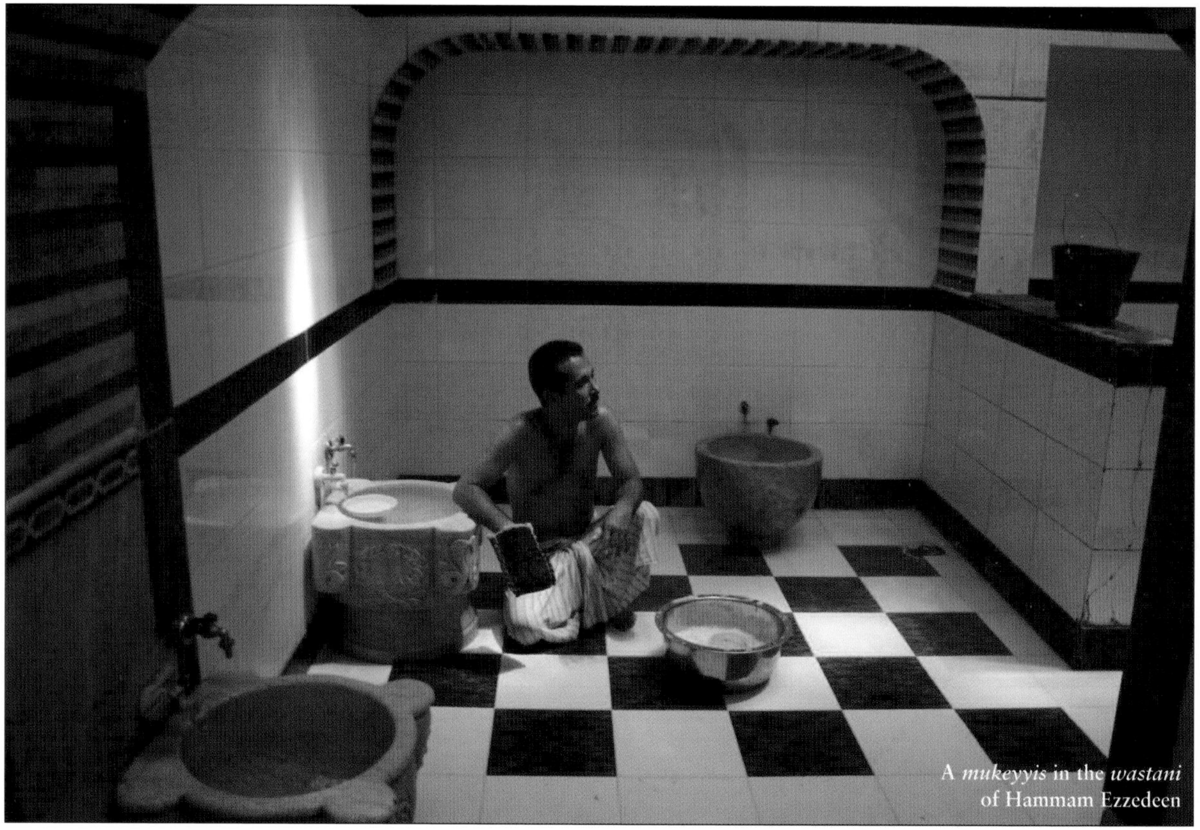
A *mukeyyis* in the *wastani* of Hammam Ezzedeen

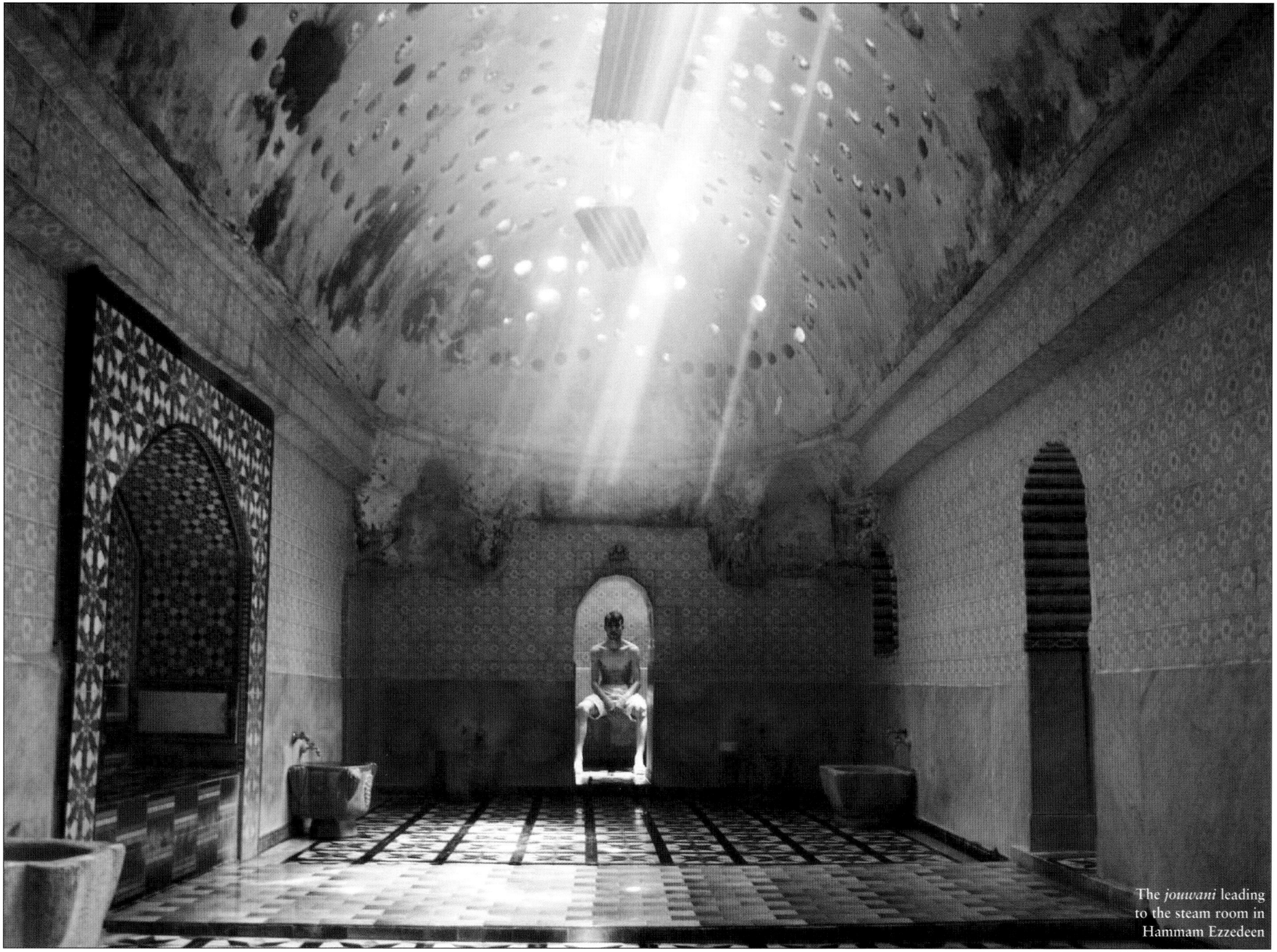

The *jouwani* leading to the steam room in Hammam Ezzedeen

about emigration to Italy. And then the *shebab* (young men) came in – cocky affability itself – and took over the steam room. They looked like lads doing their military service – muscled, without an inch of indolent flesh – one with a Syrian icon tattooed on the chest.

I asked the *mukeyyis* if he was ready. As he cleaned me I pumped him for information.

> – Why is the hammam called Ezzedeen?
>
> – He must have been the builder of the hammam.
>
> – And the water, is it Ein el Fiji water?
>
> – No, the hammam has its own well.
>
> – So, it's free?
>
> – Well, we pay for the pump and fuel.
>
> – And how many hammams are there now in Damascus?
>
> – Something like twenty now.

The scrub down, like the conversation, was a bit cursory – as if it were my first visit. But the *mukeyyis* warmed to his story at last:

> – You know it used to be that before a wedding the bride and the groom's mother would go to the hammam together, along with the other female relatives. And the groom's mother would inspect the bride – when I say inspect I mean she would inspect everything, everything – for in those days a man would not have seen the woman he was to marry.

The *mukeyyis* grew nostalgic, even moralistic:

> – But it's not like this nowadays. Young men and women sitting together in cafés and smoking *nargilehs* and the like – it wasn't like that in the old days.

For the traditions regarding women and hammams, I am afraid I have to go to a male source and that a Turkish one, not Syrian. In the Islamic world the visit to the hammam was one of the rare occasions when a respectable woman could leave the confines of her home and meet others. In his memoirs, Irfan Orga recalls his regular visits – at the age of five – to the hammam with his grandmother. Regardless of how the boy might have seen things at the time, the adult Orga portrays the hammam of his childhood thus:

> Hamams or the Turkish baths were hotbeds of gossip and scandalmongering, snobbery in its most inverted form, and the excuse for every woman in the district to have a day out.[20]

The hammam was also the marriage market; within the privacy of the hammam, mothers of eligible bachelors would sit aloft and survey the young girls bathing for a suitable match. There would have been no rush:

> Nobody ever dreamed of taking a bath in anything under seven or eight hours.[21]

Perhaps in Syria things were not much different, but nowadays, as the *mukeyyis* complained, a young couple might meet up in a trendy cafe. Traditions still survive, however, although it is not like the days when the *khatbeh*, the match-maker, showed the eligible bachelor's mother photographs of suitable girls in the area, and arranged for her to see the desirable ones. And an inspection of the potential bride in the hammam would have been par for the course. I'd guess nowadays the *khatbeh* has been made redundant by the mobile phone, but it is still often the mother who chooses the bride for her son.

Hammams are not just linked to weddings. Once when I wanted to visit Hammam Fathi in Medan, I was asked to come another day, for it was given over to readings from the Qur'an to mark the passing of a former *mi'allim*. The 'milestones' in life – childbirth, weddings, and so on – have been traditionally marked by a visit to a hammam.

In some societies, the very act of hammaming must have marked the passing of childhood to adolescence. The boy would have been a very young male among females as his mother brought him to the hammam; in some parts of the Islamic world he would have enjoyed hammaming with females even until there were hints of puberty. Then he would have been catapulted into the world of adult men. A Tunisian writer puts his 'eviction from paradise' thus:

> For the boy the hammam is the place where one discovers the anatomy of others,

and from which one is expelled once the discovery takes place.[22]

Stag Night

One traditional function of the hammam is to act as a venue for the stag night. Traditionally before a wedding the groom would be taken to the hammam and scrubbed clean by family and friends in preparation for the big day.

In Aleppo I have seen such a wedding party in Hammam al-Nahasin, and observed the village lads teasing the skinny groom, and enjoyed the accompanying banter, and innuendo... And I was welcomed as the Aleppans do with offerings of fruit, affable conversation and a dexterously thrown dish of cold water.

Later in the foyer I helped the groom put on his tie, as it was the first time he had ever worn one. Dressed, he looked much better in his clothes than out of them. They would be having a kind of wedding breakfast, they said, with drumming but no music (I think they probably saw music as something *haram* or forbidden). And indeed, seeing the preparation for the wedding, it did seem somewhat different from *our* stag nights, and perhaps none the worse for that. The wedding itself, with its segregation of the sexes, would probably have seemed to Western eyes a fairly joyless affair.

As the wedding group left at midnight, another group of lads came in, and another – for in Aleppo bathers come to the hammam long after they have closed in Damascus, and given the popularity of the Hammam al-Nahasin it seemed that a visit to the hammam for the groom and his mates was still an essential part of Aleppan wedding traditions.

The best wedding party I have encountered was not, however, in Aleppo but in Damascus, at Hammam Silsileh. In the early evening the welcoming party were lined up in the street against the hammam wall with drums. The groom arrived carried on the shoulders of his best friend, like a Nuban wrestler in Sudan carried victorious by his vanquished opponent, except that the groom was dressed smart casual. The manager kissed the groom on the cheek in welcome, as the street musicians chanted. Twins, dressed in white, were the pagan votaries of the celebration.

Friends now de-robed the groom – first his shirt, then trousers, the groom wrapping a *futa* over the nether regions... He was first carried aloft on the shoulders of some hirsute friend, but was then passed from companion to companion so that the honour of carrying the groom could be shared.

Meanwhile the *barrani* was beginning to feel as hot and humid as a sauna. The hammam

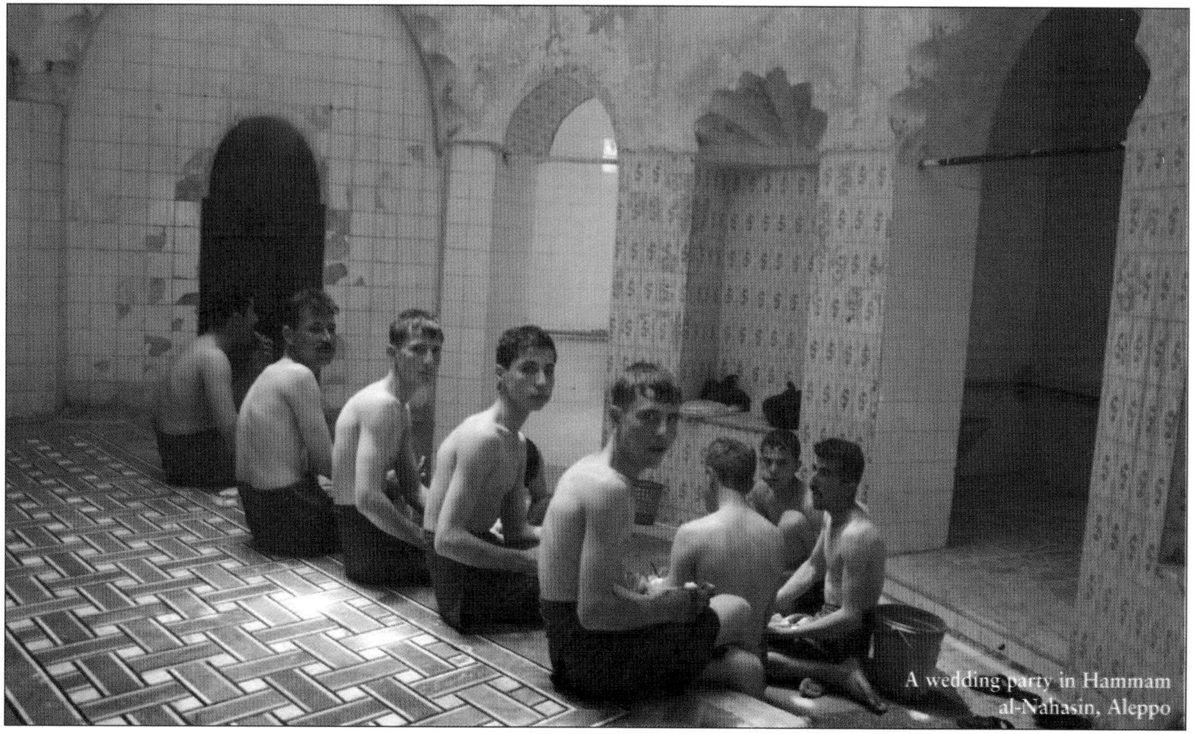

A wedding party in Hammam al-Nahasin, Aleppo

was beginning to take on some of the atmosphere of a disco as the guests gave themselves up to the music. Friends danced on the fountain, as others undressed to bathe. The groom was an expert dancer, with a graceful, feminine (but not effeminate) movement.

Only men were present, but a stag party in Hammam Silsileh is the nearest I am ever likely to come to a disco in Ibiza.

The Disappearing Bride

It was in a hammam in Aleppo that some *shebab* invited me to join them as they reclined in the *barrani* after tucking into a plate of fruit. They laughed when I spoke about the hammams of Aleppo, and said they had a test for me. I was game:

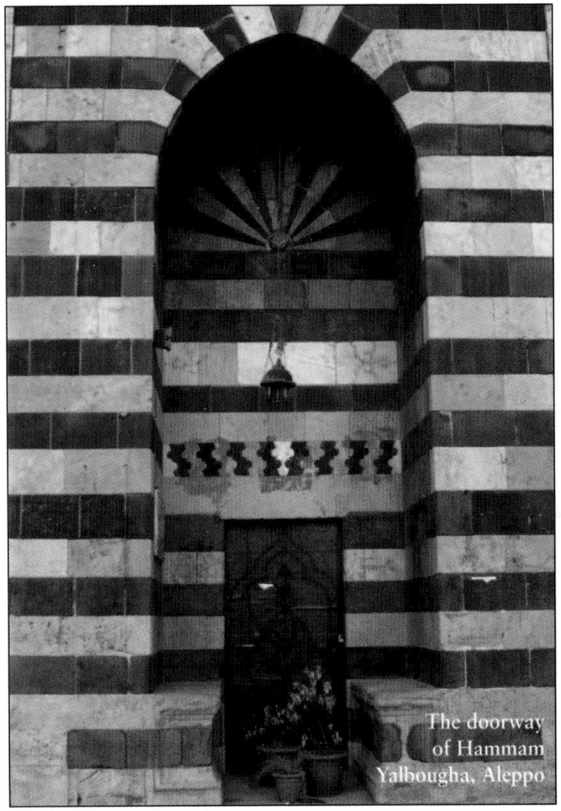
The doorway of Hammam Yalbougha, Aleppo

- Well, you know Hammam Yalbougha under the citadel?
- Of course, but it's closed now.
- Yes, but why was it closed before?

I had bathed in this cathedral of hammams, but now it had been completely closed for at least a year – I could never ascertain why, but perhaps it was a matter of a new contract to be signed for the renting out of the hammam. Surely it couldn't need to be restored again, after the successful restoration programme of the 1980s? The biggest risk of hammam closure is, however, when the owner dies, and the children quarrel over the inheritance.

But I knew a little of this hammam's history, and that its location was by the old horse market in Aleppo. After Tamerlane's ransacking of the city, the hammam had been rebuilt by the Mamluks. More recently it had fallen into disuse, and had had the undignified role of functioning as a manufacturing workshop:

- It used to be a factory, a factory for ...

And here I struggled to find the Arabic word for 'felt', even though the former name for the hammam had been Hammam al Lababidiya.[23] The Aleppans knew, of course, that it had once been a factory – but why had it been closed?

I had failed the test and one of the locals told the story:

- There was a wedding party in the hammam, with the bride taken to the hammam by the groom's female relatives.

This so far seemed pretty standard to me. They would all bathe and the groom's relatives would check there were no blemishes on her body.

- Well, at the end of bathing they looked for the bride and no-one could find her; she had disappeared.

I expressed disbelief and awaited the explanation:

- The *jinn* had taken her!

Here the *shebab* were not mocking some old wives' tale, for jinn are a 'fact' of Islamic life; they were telling me something that they themselves believed. I suspect rather than *jinn*, it had been a matter of family honour, even virginity perhaps...

- The hammam was haunted and the bride was never seen again. The hammam was closed.

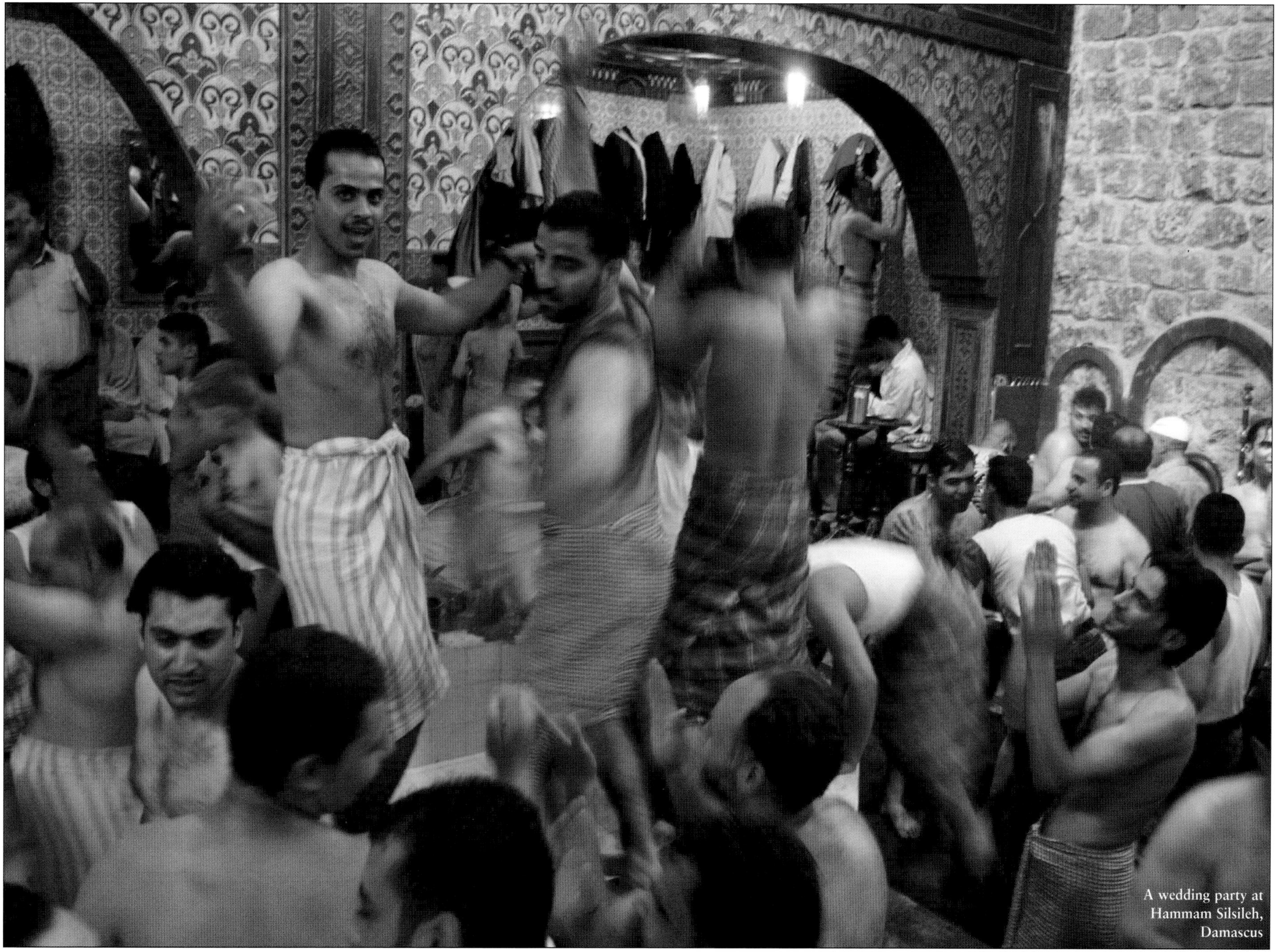
A wedding party at
Hammam Silsileh,
Damascus

The haunted hammam is not something unique to the Yalbougha. In the back of my mind I'm sure I've heard a similar story about a hammam in Tripoli – as if it is almost an urban myth in El Sham – the haunted hammam and the disappearing bather.

The *Jinn*

I asked the *mi'allim* at the historical museum why the *jinn* seemed to be associated with the hammams. For the West, the *jinn* appear on stage in the genies of the Christmas pantomime, but in the Islamic world they are thought of as a reality (although ghosts are a Christian invention), for they are written about in the Qur'an.

I was given a very simple explanation for the presence of *jinn* in the hammams:

– Nakedness... It's the nakedness.

And I suppose by that the speaker meant the temptations of the flesh, especially in a society where the flesh is usually very much covered. He went on to say that *jinn* have been believed traditionally to be found in hammams and markets.

His explanation for the *jinn* inhabiting the markets was the presence of *ghashash* – cheats and swindlers I suppose – and any foreigner who has been in Damascus will have had some experience of being ripped off; nowadays it's likely to be on your first taxi ride when the driver will brazenly try to fleece you. But until recently it was all done with a kind of courtesy – like when the taxi driver charged you twice the fare but said as you handed it over the set phrase for the occasion: '*Halal* money returns to its owner.'

I'm not sure what it ultimately says about me, but it was these '*jinn*-haunted' places – the *suqs* and the hammams – that I loved above all others.

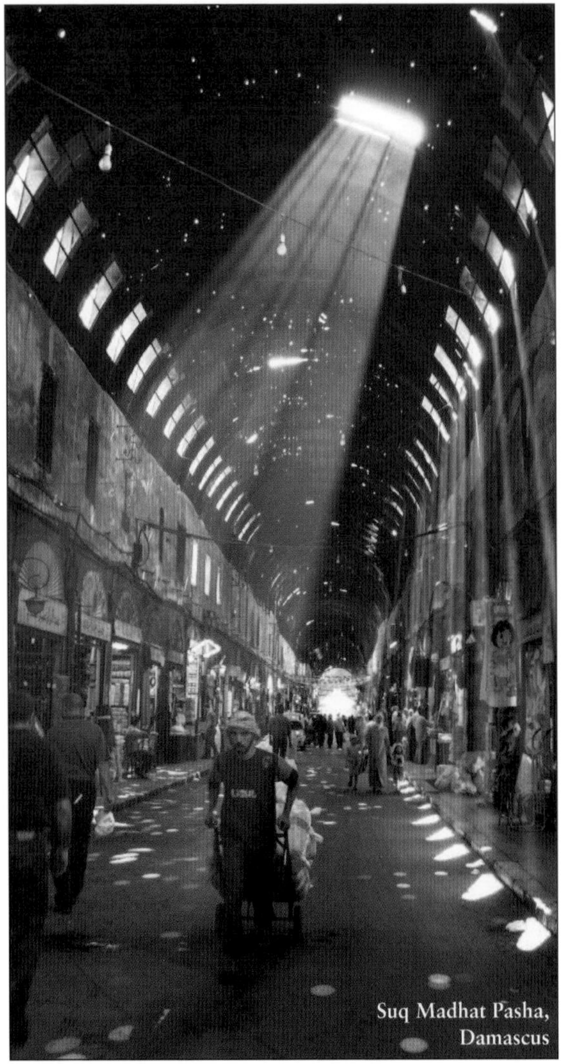

Suq Madhat Pasha, Damascus

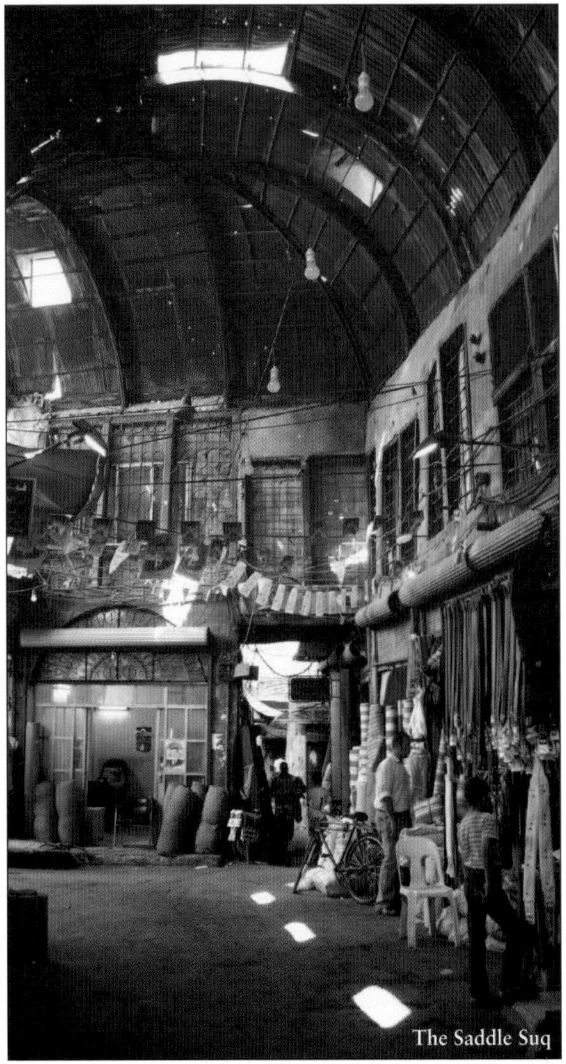

The Saddle Suq

The Haunted Hammam

Lane, in his *An Account of the Manners and Customs of the Modern Egyptians*, writes of Egyptian hammams that:

> The bath is believed to be a favourite resort of ginn (or genii), and therefore when a person is about to enter it, he should offer up an ejaculatory prayer for protection against evil spirits, and should put his left foot first over the threshold. For the same reason, he should not pray nor recite the Kur-án in it.[24]

In Syria today there seems to be no issue with praying in a hammam, but the belief that hammams are haunted persists.

It was the first lieutenant who told me about the supernatural associations of hammams, although he had never been to one. He liked to emphasise the simplicity of the people of Lattakia, and indeed when I hiked through the terraced hillsides there, the frugality contrasted with the excesses of the Damascene middle-class. Even in Ramadan the restaurant tables have an ostentatious display of cuisine; the fast is broken with a feast.

One evening when the orange blossom below the balcony was fading in all its waxy sweetness, he started to tell me about a hammam in the Saruja area, probably after a few glasses of arak had loosened our tongues. I know the hammam well, of course. It's just by Beit Khalid al Azem, where the photographs of Druze revolutionaries are displayed in all their moustachioed glory, and the wonderful collapsing splendour of Beit Yussuf, its late Ottoman excesses falling off its mirrored ceilings as plaster gives in to the years. (Within a few years it will be totally beyond repair; there's nothing like conscientious neglect – a gardening term I will apply to Ottoman Damascus – to set the scene for 'development'.)

In the summer, the walls of the hammam are all dappled with *nafnufa,* the vine that winds its way over the old city streets, and there's a kind of unofficial *suq* where lads from Dera'a sell water melons and the like in the street, and a lorry of police arrives every so often to half-heartedly disperse the market, only for it to re-form later in the day.

The first lieutenant's story went like this. One night, after midnight, the *mukeyyis* came to rub down the last remaining bather, but the bather, sensing something was not quite right, refused the offer. The *mukeyyis* however forcibly caught hold of the man, who, following his instincts, looked down at the feet of the *mukeyyis* and found them to be less than human (just as that visitor to Aleppo, Othello, looked down at the feet of Iago to see if he was a devil or not). The lone bather fled into the main room of the hammam to tell the *mi'allim* of his discovery. But then he caught sight of the manager's feet, and saw that they too had the cleft foot of the devil.

A *Jinni* in the Hammam

In Hammam Nur al-Din I asked the attendants about the *jinn* story. The mild-mannered and courteous Ayman confirmed it, but said that kind of thing happened a long time ago; *jinn* are only found in empty, isolated places, not in popular places like Hammam Nur al-Din.

Ayman went on to explain:

> – Just like humans, there are two kinds of *jinn*, believers and non-believers.

This would be the typical Islamic point of view: the *jinn* existing before the creation of Adam. *Jinn* in the Islamic world are a fact of life. To this day, when doing their spring cleaning the more traditional housewives of Damascus will actually apologise to the *jinn* who might have congregated in some dusty corner of the house, before disturbing their habitat with a broom. The other attendant, however, was having none of this *jinn* stuff:

> – I've seen some people worse than *jinn*!

And he mentioned his time in Beirut.

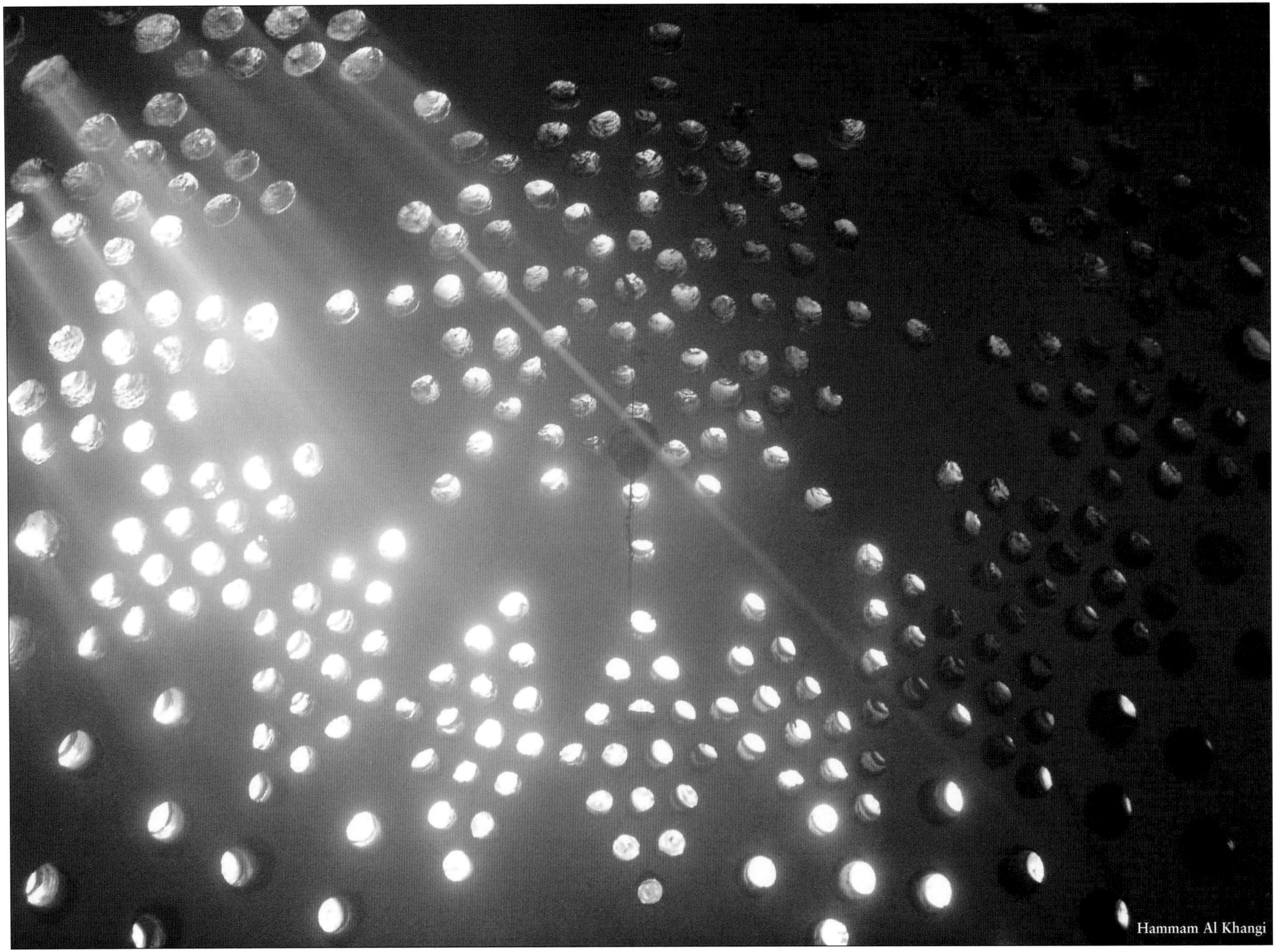
Hammam Al Khangi

The elderly *mukeyyis* also pronounced on the presence of *jinn* as he scrubbed me down. He said he had heard of the *jinn*, but this was before the days of electricity, when people used to bring in the beans to cook overnight on the embers of the fire that heated the hammam's water. But the other *mukeyyis*, lean and wiry but some fifty years old, laughed as he described the night sounds he himself had heard in the hammam, like the beating of drums and cries. (In fact, according to the scholar Robert Irwin, the Arabic word for a certain kind of colloquial poem, *zajal*, is also the word to describe 'the soft humming sound made by the jinn at night.')[25]

Back with the other attendants, Ayman explained further:

> – The *jinn* are like us, there are Muslims and *kuffar*, the unbelievers.
>
> – So where does that leave me, then? I asked.

At this point, a very respectably dressed man from the Gulf came in. He had come not to bathe, but to have a look round, and had been given a pair of clogs with which to negotiate the wet floors of the hammam. He had also kept on his shoes as a kind of double barrier against any contact with anything 'unclean' in the hammam.

We were all amused at the spectacle of someone wearing both shoes and clogs, for there are those who give great importance to the outward forms of religious purity. On observing our unnaturally-footed visitor the attendant put it rather nicely:

> – Would you look at that, did you ever see the like of it in your life?

He reverted to our earlier topic:

> – There it is! That one! Now that's a *jinni* for you!

Orientalism?

It is not only Westerners who cast curious eyes on the hammam. Seated in the wonderful Hammam Silsileh, its foyer draped in the black and red stripes of 'genuine bedouin rugs', I noticed that there was hardly a passing woman in the street who didn't peek in the doorway to catch a glimpse of men enjoying their hammam. In most hammams, public modesty is very much the norm; all that can be seen is a row of men wrapped up very decently in towels.

Although there is decency, there is also a kind of homoeroticism. I think of the *shebab* up from Jordan in Hammam Nur al-Din sitting in a group of three on the marble floor. One of the youths is sitting upright as the second lies languidly across his crossed legs. Tenderly, affectionately, one rubs away at the other's skin – so close that their faces almost touch.

I don't think anyone else would have noticed this scene that I am remembering (some might say creating, for there is a long tradition of Europeans building an Orient of their imagination). The late Palestinian academic Edward Said shows how Europeans in literature and art fabricated an Orient of their own imaginations – a place of exotic delight. For example a painting of the Orientalist school, 'The Nargileh Lighter', shows a curvaceous Caucasian slave, naked, stretched out languidly by the harem pool where other women bathe; the exotic was also the erotic.

Orientalism wasn't just a matter of art, however; travel in itself was Orientalism, with the Orient as the stage and the Westerner dressed in Ottoman costume for the play. Some of today's Western converts to Islam continue this Orientalist tradition by donning what they see as an appropriate costume for their time in Damascus – the men wearing a *jelabiyah* and *sirwal* hoisted well above the ankles, oblivious that the indigenous male Muslims around them are wearing jeans and t-shirts.

From the apparent straitjacket of Victorian times, where public conformity to *deen* – the public expression of religion – was very much the norm, the Orient, it seems, offered sexual licence. And so Oscar Wilde explored new territory in the north of Africa with Gede (what would Oscar have made of Hammam al-Moqaddam's bathroom tiles?) and Flaubert travelled throughout Egypt, starting off with a medical inspection of the country's last syphilis-ridden Mamluk soldiers. Cruising on the Nile, he sampled not only

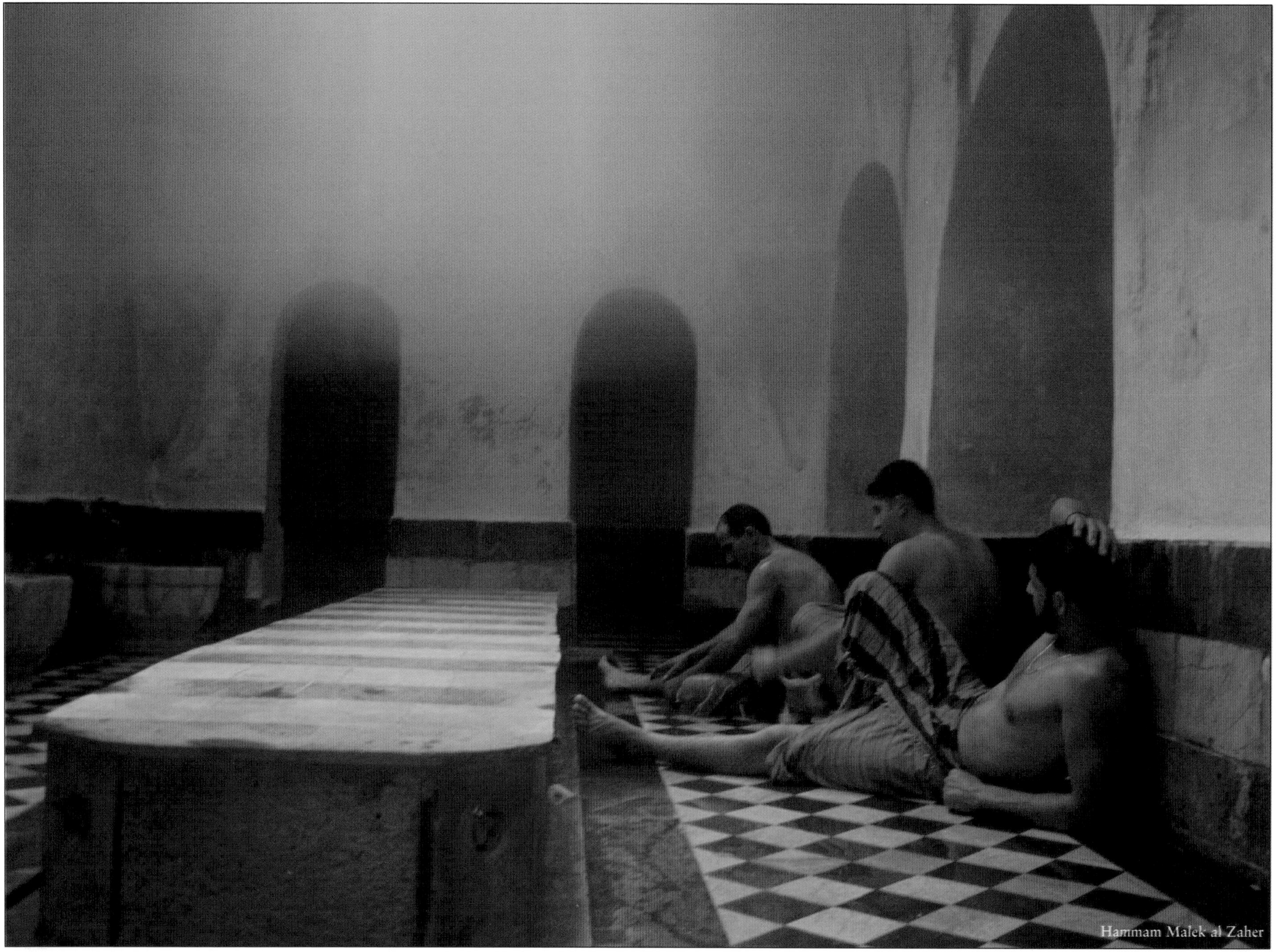

Hammam Malek al Zaher

the delights of the fleshy courtesan Kuchuk (the odour of her bedbugs mingling with the scent of sandalwood) but, ever so catholic in his taste, Flaubert also hopped into a hammam for a little light relief with the Egyptian lads.

When it comes to donning a costume, no-one could have outdone T. E. Lawrence. Wadi Rum was his arena, but any young middle-class British man could have continued his schooldays in the Great Public School of the Middle East. In the Orient too, females were excluded from public life, manly virtues were extolled, and in the desert a kind of homoerotic bonding was the norm. As William Dalrymple wrote of the decaying Baron Hotel in Aleppo, it was no wonder Lawrence felt so at home – it was not just the dining room that looked like a college hall; the food itself was like a school dinner.

Now, in more modern times, it is perhaps the hammam which is the last refuge of the Orientalist. In contrast to the often insipid light of an Irish winter, in Damascus there is the sharp intensity of desert light that so attracted painters. (Where does the charm of Damascus lie, in the midday sun piercing the holes of a rusting corrugated roof overhead, or in a lane dappled with autumn sunlight before the vines have shed their leaves?) Within the hammam there can be a wealth of colour, from the rainbowed patterns of the *futa* to the pomegranate split open in the dish, its ribbed sections crimson with beaded seeds.

The *nargileh* lighter (not that she ever existed outside a painter's imagination) has gone. Today's traveller to Damascus is more likely to have his fire lit by a young Kurdish man in a waistcoat and polyester trousers. The Westerner, however, as a traveller and voyeur of other societies, can still enjoy the Oriental world beneath hammam domes; I do not entirely exclude myself. The 'otherness' sought for when travelling is embodied in the hammam.

But perhaps the hammam nowadays does not so much preserve an Oriental world for Westerners (with Sufi rhythms sounding over the music system in the upmarket hammam) as create one for Arabs themselves. And so, after the Mamluks and the Ottomans, some hammams now embrace the new hordes: the Gulf Arabs who flock to Damascus in the summer. To accommodate their summer visitors, a taste of the Gulf is brought to Damascus; some Damascene hotels are now graced with plastic palm trees that light up at night. The phenomenon is really unique to Damascus; Aleppo for some reason is beyond Gulf reach, or interest.

Having embraced McCulture in their own countries, Gulf Arabs search for 'a truly Arab experience' in the hammam. And in some hammams a local photographer with his instamatic Polaroid camera (now there's a dying hammam tradition if ever there was one!) is there to record the experience for it to be taken back to the Gulf.

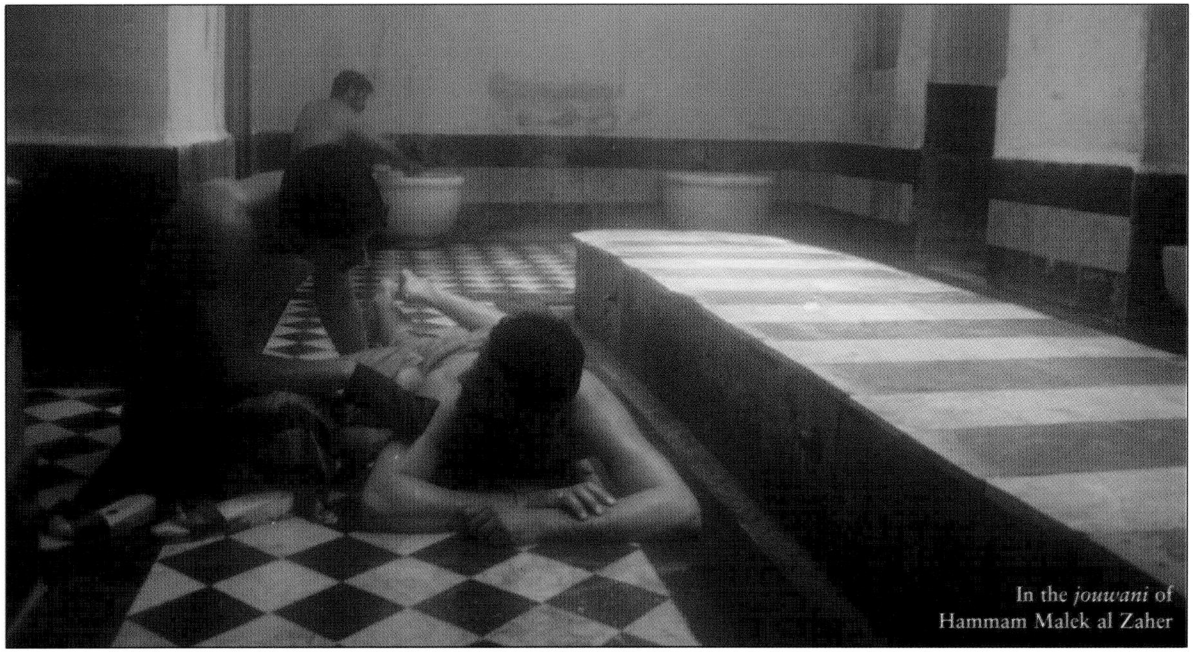

In the *jouwani* of Hammam Malek al Zaher

Occidentalism

I would often step out of my flat and catch a minibus into town. A century ago Richard Burton lived just by, his home right by an old hammam that has since been demolished and replaced by a block of flats. No doubt that Orientalist with an insatiable sexual curiosity (his first research was on the activities of British army officers in Karachi; his last a translation of *The Scented Garden*) would have popped into the local hammams. But I suspect anything Burton wrote about hammams was cast into the fire by his widow in order to protect reputations and public morality.

As I sat on a minibus nothing could have been more contrary to the myth of the licentious Orient than the reality confronting me: the passengers changing seats like so many pieces on a board game so that no woman would have to sit next to an unknown man; the women in front of me sitting with seriously grim faces, as if any expression of personality, even just the hint of a smile, would be the ruin of reputation.

The last rain in Damascus had been six months before, but in temperatures of almost 35 degrees every woman on the bus was wearing the ubiquitous lightweight raincoat, although Christian areas like Bab Tuma are of course a different story. In public the women cultivate a deliberate drabness, right down to unflattering stockings and inelegant heels – as if aspiring to look like their grandmothers.

Perhaps – although here I think I am running dangerously near to cliché – it is all a bit like the traditional Damascene house with the dull walls of the exterior hiding the internal treasures of the courtyard. Drawing a parallel between the walls of the house behind which women were confined and the veil drawn over a woman's beauty, one scholar even sees the Arab house as 'a stone veil'.[26]

Female beauty is not something to be displayed, although again the Christians of Bab Tuma heading off for a night on the town might disagree. A woman's beauty, or otherwise, is for the husband only to enjoy, although she might dress up for a few female companions. And here I will discreetly refer the reader to the coffee-table book *The Secret Life of Syrian Lingerie*;[27] it's not just the taps in a hammam that have produced birdsong.

The rule with regard to dress and gender seems here to be that the more the woman is covered, the more visibly masculine will be the husband she accompanies. Similarly it is the most conservative areas of Syria, where the women walk veiled, that you are likely to find the best hammams. They know how to hammam in Hama! And if the woman in question is not with her male guardian she may be with a group of women all wearing the same shade of coat – navy blue or washed-out grey – with the headscarf pinned around the face in a distinctive way. These details of dress are not by accident, but reflect a system of values.

It is not just the more conservative women who appear drab; after a few days in Beirut with its unrestrained capitalism and embrace of the Mediterranean, Damascus, with its concrete flats of the 1970s and polyester greys, can seem like some dowdy old maiden aunt devoted to the Party. However,

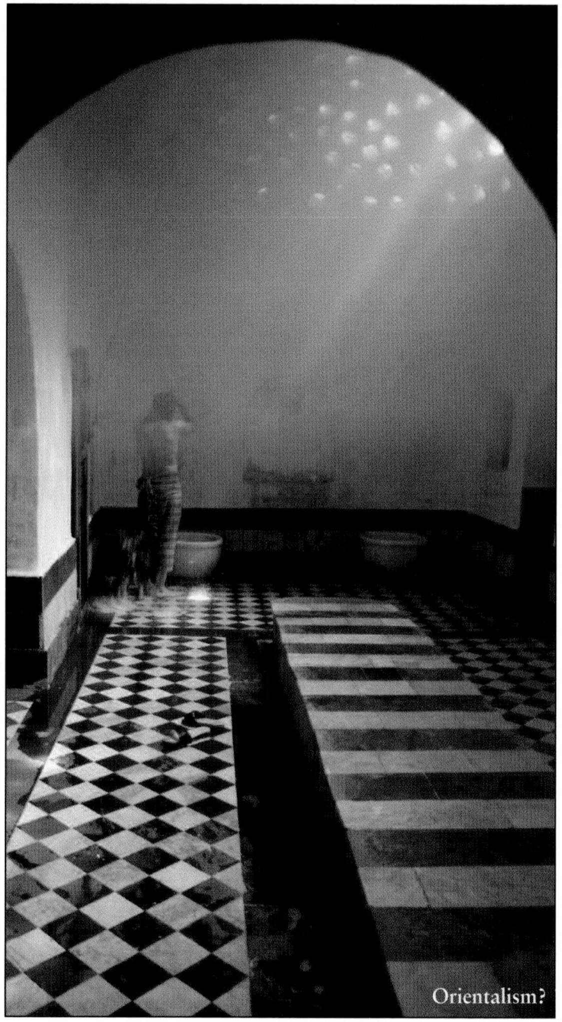
Orientalism?

in my case at least, after the superficial attractions of Lebanon, I'd soon be longing again for Damascus.

The old myths are now somehow reversed, and the West is now the Arab world's mirror-image of how Orientalists once portrayed the East. For some, fed on internet images and satellite TV, the West is seen as a place of sexual licence beyond dreams. And so Victorian Orientalism is matched by a current Occidentalism. In some perverse way the West is almost a parody of paradise – for unlike the Christian heaven which seems an eternal yawn of angels and harps, the believing Muslim goes to a heaven of sensual and sexual gratification. Female believers are rewarded with an eternity with their husband (a dubious reward for some, perhaps) but the male believer gains access to the *houris* – the virgins of paradise.

It is not just the *houris* who attend believers; beautiful androgynous cup bearers will also attend the faithful, offering cups of heavenly wine. I would discuss all this with the first lieutenant when the local arak by some strange alchemy had turned milky white in the glass. He had a reverence for the Qur'an, but had beliefs that were quite at odds with mainstream Sunni beliefs. I'm sure, like many a member of a religious minority in Syria, he tended more towards a belief in reincarnation than in some afterlife with a physical heaven and hell. The first lieutenant expressed his scepticism quite succinctly:

– In the next life you can enjoy what is forbidden in this... there in the Big Duty Free in the Sky.

Hammaming in the *Arabian Nights*

Unsurprisingly, a hammam features in the *Arabian Nights*. On the four hundredth and ninety-fourth night, Shahrazad begins to tell the story of a barber who, on arriving as a stranger in a city, asks for the hammam. The inhabitants do not understand the question, but after the barber's explanation point him towards the shore: 'We do not know what you mean by a hammam. When we wish to take a bath, we go to the sea.'

The barber, Abu Sir, arranges for an appointment with the king, in order to express his disbelief that such a city could lack a public bath, for '... a hammam is the

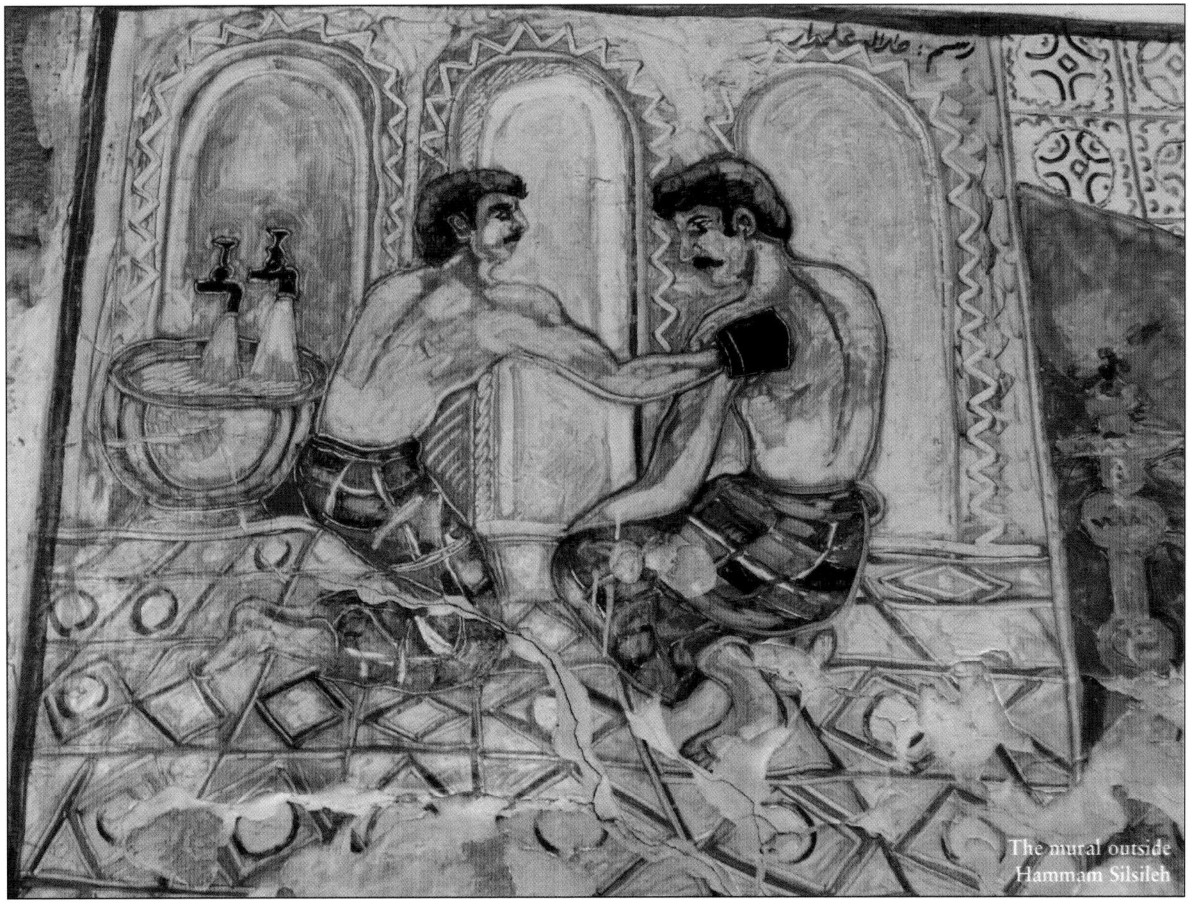

The mural outside Hammam Silsileh

chief ornament and centre of delight of any city'. The king, feeling somehow inadequate, sets the best palace architects at Abu Sir's disposal.

The hammam built is indeed fit for a king, with many-coloured marbles, and 'far-brought curiosities such as ravish the soul'. The central pool is of transparent alabaster, where the fountain would have 'turned aside the spirits of the blessed'. Towels of linen and silk are provided, and 'precious essences, perfumes, incense and the like' scent the hammam. The hammam attendants are 'twenty well-built and beautiful boys'.

The king is not disappointed. Having passed from stage to stage of the hammam, culminating in a bath of scented rose water, he feels much rejuvenated by the experience. 'Unnatural strength came to him so that he felt himself to roar like a lion. "As Allah lives, I have never felt so robust in all my life..."'

After being dried with musk-scented towels, the king's verdict concurs with the barber's first impressions of the city: '...my city was no city until this place was built...'[28]

But the barber has an enemy, the dyer, with whom there had been an apparent reconciliation. Just as the barber had seen the city as lacking only a hammam, so the dyer tells Abu Sir that his hammam lacks just one thing: a paste for the removal of body hair. And so the dyer offers Abu Sir a recipe for the perfect paste:

> I can give you the prescription of a paste that has no equal. Listen, take yellow arsenic and quick lime, pound them together in a little oil, mix in musk to remove the unpleasant smell, and store in an earthenware pot.

Innocent of the dyer's wish to bring about his downfall, Abu Sir has the paste prepared. Meanwhile the dyer warns the king that Abu Sir has been sent as a spy to kill him. He warns the king that the next time he hammams, Abu Sir will suggest that the king's body hair be removed. It being the *Arabian Nights*, it is not just to the armpits that the paste will be applied:

> He will suggest the paste to you by saying it will remove the hairs of your bottom comfortably and without shock.

No details are spared:

> He will apply the paste to the anus of our king and thus kill him by poison through the most painful of all channels.

Abu Sir is arrested as a spy, the wonder he has created becoming his downfall. He is sentenced to be cast overboard at sea in a sack of quicklime – so that he would both burn and drown at once – but is saved by his friend the captain with whom he had hammamed, and eventually returns to the kingdom after a fish brings him the Sultan's magic ring. But that is another of Shahrazad's stories...

A Hammam, a Mosque and a Fish

The intense heat of the hammams nowadays is fuelled by the local heating oil. It is still delivered by horse and cart through the streets of Aleppo, the hawkers crying out with such a plaintive mournfulness that you would think they were calling on the inhabitants of the city to bring out their dead in a time of plague.

Traditionally the hammams have been fuelled by animal dung and the like. Indeed, there is still one hammam in Damascus – Hammam Ammoune just outside the walls – where the original heating system fuelled by wood shavings still stands intact. (In contrast, in Yemen a bag of butcher's bones outside a doorway might indicate a place to bathe, for this has been the traditional fuel for the hammams the Ottomans left behind in Sana'a.)

On the Syrian coast in Jiblai below the Ansariye Mountains, I came across a hammam – Hammam Sultan Ibrahim – which was still being fuelled with the husks of ground nuts. I popped into the hammam of course – it was still functioning, but temperatures within were not much more than in the street outside – and had a tour of the mosque with its tomb of a Sufi saint. The men around the tomb were affability itself; they were not so much worshippers as men hanging out of an afternoon in the mosque.

The Mosque of Sultan Ibrahim was tastefully constructed and welcoming, but it

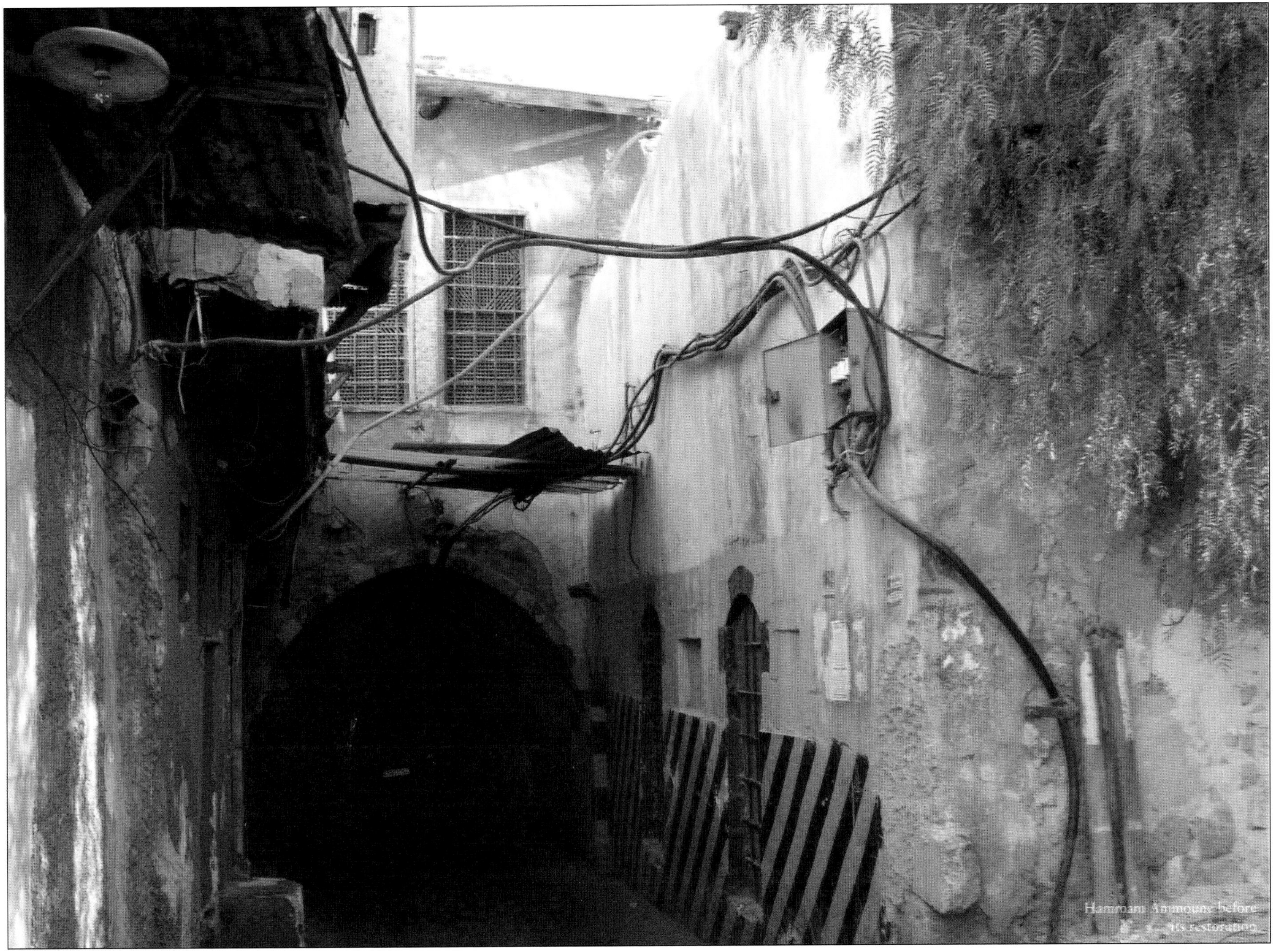

Hammam Ammoune before its restoration

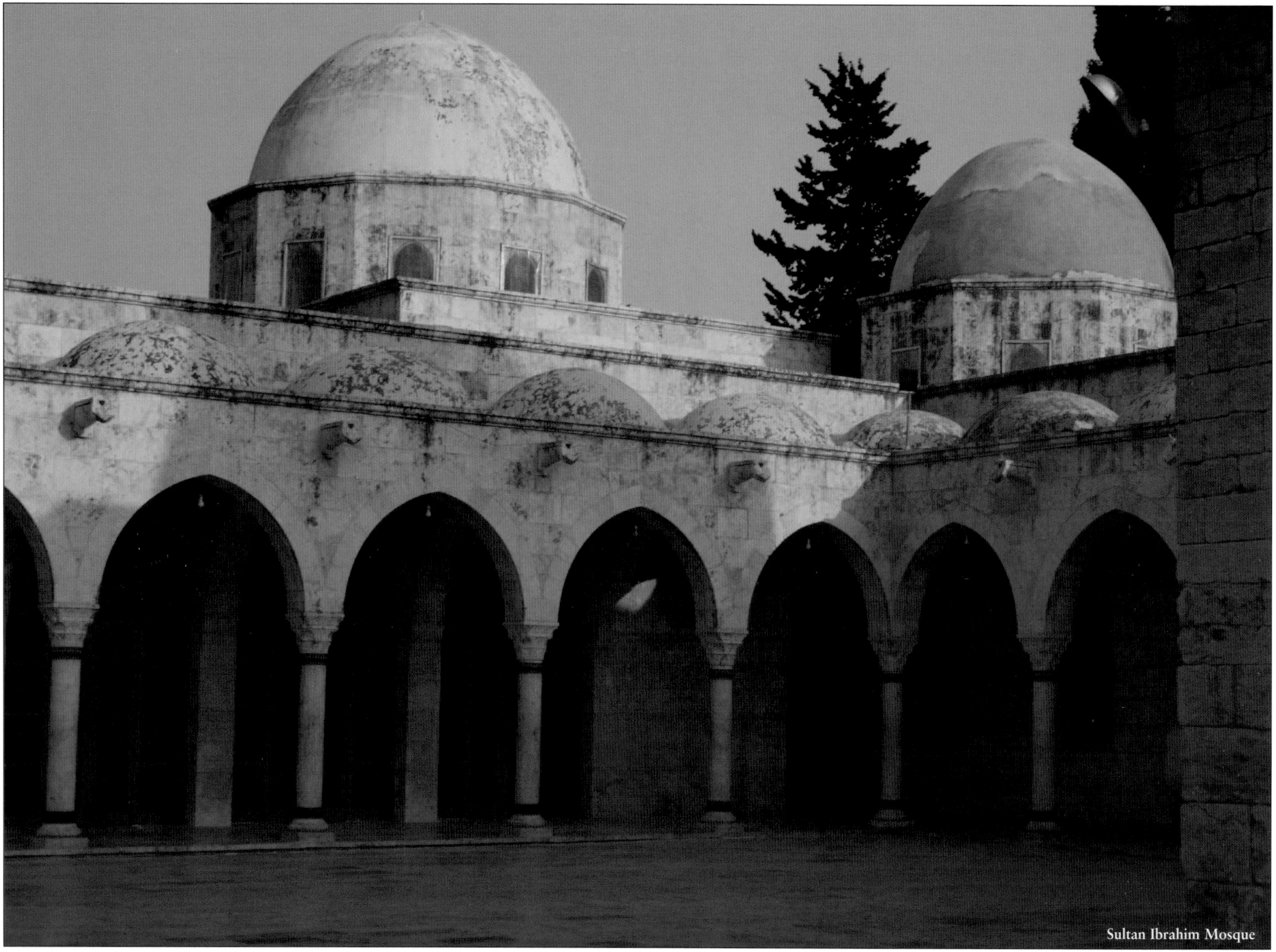

Sultan Ibrahim Mosque

would be fair I think to say that in the mountains above the coast the spiritual centres are not so much mosques as shrines; there is scarcely a hilltop that is not graced with some Alawi shrine in its sacred grove. A century ago Gertrude Bell wrote of the dead holy men enshrined on the mountain tops:

> These high-throned dead, though they have left the world of men, have not ceased from their good offices, for they are the protectors of the trees rooted among their bones, trees which, alone among their kind, are allowed to grow untouched.[29]

When Ibn Battuta travelled along the coast he was appalled at the people's disregard for the mosques forced on them by the conquering Malek al-Zaher. He approved, however, of the Persian mystic who had settled not far from Lattakia, giving up a life of royal luxury for the self-denial of an aesthete.

Ibn Battuta was as much interested in the circumstances of Sultan Ibrahim's birth as in his life. Self-denial was obviously in Sultan Ibrahim's genes, for his father Ad'ham had lived a life of abstinence. One day, however, temptation had come in the form of an apple floating downstream. Ad'ham ate it and, ridden with guilt, set out to ask pardon from the orchard owners. The first gave forgiveness freely; the second would absolve Ad'ham only if he married his daughter.

Ad'ham reluctantly agreed, but, ever the aesthete, spent the wedding night in prayer, and the next, and the next. No absolution came, for the marriage had not been consummated. Finally Ad'ham did the deed, did his ablutions and died on the spot. The posthumous son was Ibrahim, who in time inherited his father's kingdom, but rejected it for a life of Sufi asceticism.

Today in Jiblai the mosque and the hammam built by the saint's mother are named after him. More unusually, a fish also bears the sheikh's name, and if your pocket allows it, you can order a kilo of Sultan Ibrahim in a trendy restaurant in Lattakia overlooking the Mediterranean. How did a fish get the name of a saint? According to legend the former monarch was stitching his threadbare clothes by the river but dropped his needle; thousands of fish then appeared with golden needles in their mouths for the saint. With Sultan Ibrahim we seem to have travelled back into the world of *The Arabian Nights*, but his hammam – dilapidated though it is – is most definitely a reality.

Hammams and Saints

The basics of any hammam are water and heat, so in the hammam you encounter the essentials: water, the essence of life, and fire, the element of punishment. The fires of the hammam would have been fed by the rubbish dumped nearby to fuel its furnace.

The periphery of the hammams became a favourite abode of mystics. The dunghill by Hammam Nur al-Din was a haunt for holy men verging on the edge of sanity, the *muwallah* (one madly enamoured of God) in the wastes outside the hammam perhaps as scantily clothed as the bather within.[30]

Why the outskirts of the hammam should have been the *muwallah's* hang-out of choice is hard to explain: perhaps the dunghill expressed their scant regard for concepts like ritual purification, for they were more interested in the soul than in public ablutions. Or perhaps the hammam's furnace was a good visual aid for the fires of divine punishment.

These mystics trod the sanctified ground between sainthood and madness. They were viewed as righteous possessors of *barakah* by the common people who came in droves in pursuit of their blessing, but were sometimes seen as dangerous heretics by the religious authorities, for they threatened the public norms of religion.

One modern scholar, Mari, writes of the rivalry between two *muwallahs* who used to hang out near the same hammam. One 'saint' according to the Damascene writer Ibn Kathir was even named after the furnace of the hammam where he held court:

> He was known as al-Iqmini because he used to reside in the furnace of Nur al-Din al-Shahid's bath. He used to wear long garments which dragged on the ground and urinate in his robes [with] his head bare. It is alleged that he possessed spiritual states and many illuminations.[31]

While some authorities suppressed these mystics, others embraced them. As Damascus passed from Mamluk to Ottoman rule, one of the priorities of the first Ottoman ruler of Damascus, Selim the First, on entering Damascus was to pay tribute at the shrine of the mystic Ibn 'Arabi. Finding the Andalusian saint's tomb much neglected, he ordered the building of a mausoleum and mosque to honour him – giving the holy man his official blessing, and perhaps hoping for the mystic's *barakah* in return.

Under Selim's rule the massive soup kitchens built almost opposite the mosque to feed those making their *ziyārah* or pilgrimage to the tomb were designed by the Ottoman Empire's greatest architect (and designer of hammams) Sinan. Of course I went to visit and was welcomed. In the Friday *suq*, a bearded seller of artichokes took me by the hand and led me into the Spartan spaciousness below the domes. In fact, although a key function of the building would have been the feeding of pilgrims making their *ziyārah* to the tomb of the saint, this was more a religious complex than mere kitchens. The tiled surface was interrupted only by some sheikh's tomb at the end, and the remains of a mill where donkeys had once circulated in their daily grind.

Someone who had been hosing out the great sunken basins that are used for cooking, each the size of a jacuzzi, broke away from his work to talk. I said I was interested in Ibn 'Arabi because I had seen his font in Hammam al-Moqaddam nearby. (What I didn't say was at that time I had imagined the holy man to have been as miserably dour as his basalt font.) But the attendant disagreed. Sheikh Ibn 'Arabi – who to this man was the first and last of the Sufis – was, he told me, linked to Hammam Rufai in Medan.

He went on to tell me the story of how the Sheikh and Sultan Selim met in the hammam, and I asked him to write the story down for me. But he couldn't, for he had never gone to school, and yet this man's manner was more civilised than many a university graduate. His companion recorded it for me, and I asked my friend Yussuf over supper to translate it. The story goes as follows.

Sultan Selim wasn't aware that Ibn 'Arabi was in Damascus, and when he entered Hammam Rufai he found an old man bathing alone. The Sultan said to the old man:

> – I see you are not protected by anyone. If a man had been good to his father and mother, there would be someone with him to look after him.

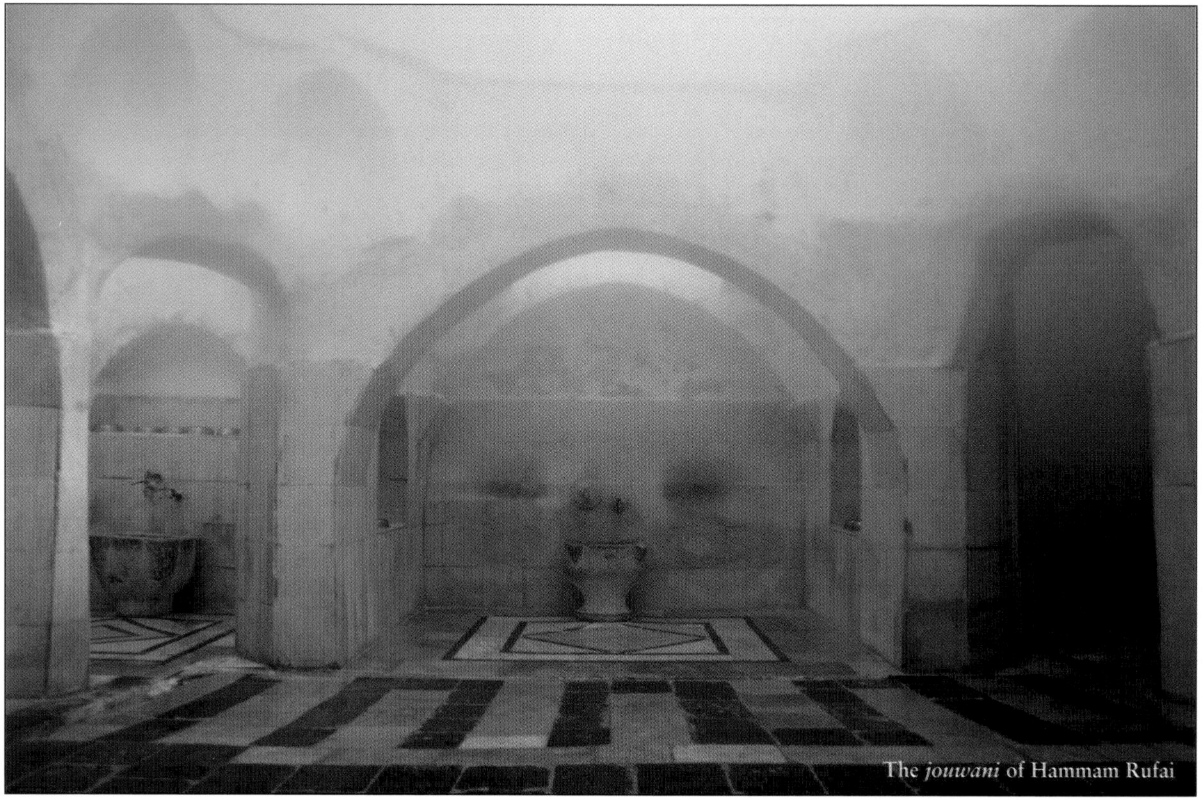
The *jouwani* of Hammam Rufai

And the sheikh replied:

> – Because I respected my parents, you have been sent all the way from Istanbul to protect me.

In popular belief, the ruler of the Ottoman Empire and one of Islam's greatest mystics met up in a hammam in Medan, and the mystic's power was greater than that of the ruler of the Ottoman Empire. That one should have built the other's tomb is a matter of historical fact; in terms of popular belief, however, they bumped into each other in a hammam – even though Ibn 'Arabi had died by the time Selim came to Damascus.

Mari quotes an account of Selim's building of the mausoleum and mosque and *takiya* (the religious complex I have inaccurately called the kitchens):

> He ordered that a dome be built over Ibn al-Arabı's mausoleum, a congregational mosque beside it, and a *takiya* across from it. The Sultan charged the ... Chief Qadi with these tasks. He built it as the aforementioned building. It turned out to be the most splendid and most perfect construction.[32]

The final comment on the building of the tomb is revealing:

> All this was made possible by our master the Shaykh Ibn al-Arabi, may the clouds of Mercy rain over him.

It was not the ruler of the Ottoman Empire, but the sheikh buried within the tomb, who enabled the mausoleum to house his own remains to be built. Even after their deaths, these saints are seen as God's agents on earth, appearing to their devotees in dreams and performing miracles from beyond the grave.

These holy men are a headache for the bringers of modernity. Imagine the architect of a five-star international hotel like the Four Seasons, or the civil engineer designing a major road, who finds the tomb of some sheikh on the site. Demolishing the tomb would be out of the question, for, apart from the public outcry, the builder might find his machines no longer working, or have workers stricken down with some unidentifiable illness. And so the road divides to avoid the tomb, or the hotel incorporates the tomb intact into its overall design, rather than invoke the wrath of a holy man who died centuries ago.

Hammams, however, have been a different story. The moderniser simply knocked them down or, as in Lattakia's sole surviving hammam, demolished whatever got in the way of the road, leaving the *jouwani* for posterity.

Ibn 'Arabi left us his poems. Yussuf gave me this translation, which shows the mystic's religious tolerance and the breadth of his beliefs. Nothing could be further from the dour fundamentalist I had imagined, or from the preachings of some of today's religious leaders:

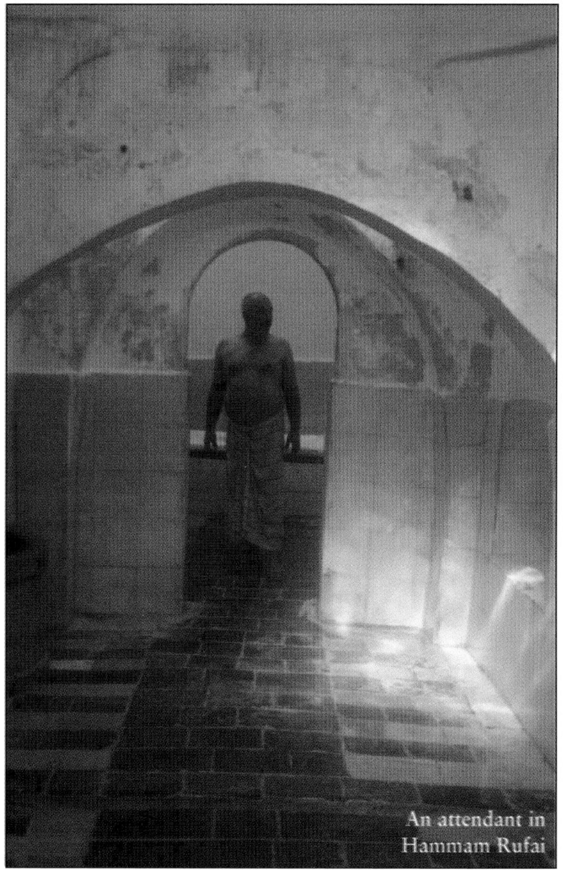
An attendant in Hammam Rufai

> My heart has become capable of all forms
>
> It is a meadow for gazelles and a monastery for Christian monks,
>
> A temple for idols and the pilgrim's Ka'aba
>
> The tables of the Law and the book of the Koran.
>
> I profess the religion of Love, and whatever direction
>
> Its steed may take, Love is my religion and my faith.

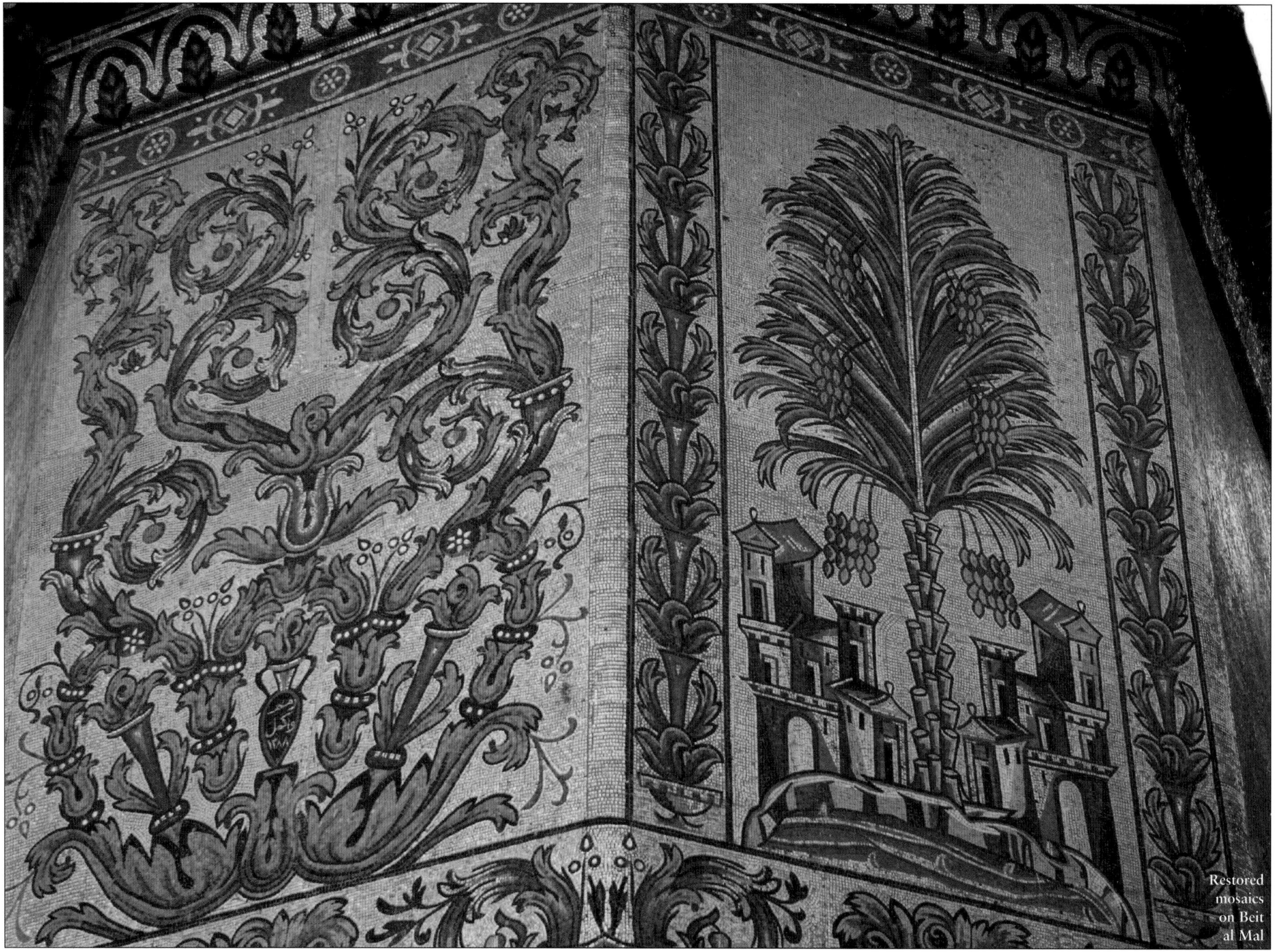

Restored mosaics on Beit al Mal

Paradise

In Syria there is a phrase for every occasion, and as you leave the hammam, the attendants call '*Naemun*' to you. Once I challenged the hammam employees as I was about to leave, and asked them to explain what the phrase meant. They looked at me, flummoxed. The tall, balding *mukeyyis* began explaining:

- It's like this... When someone leaves the hammam we say *Naemun* and he replies *Naemallahalek*.
- That's not what he's asking, retorted the *mi'allim* at the desk, amused by my question. He's asking what the word means.
- Of course, I said. I know what is said, but why do you say it fifty times a day?

The traveller Alexia Brue, as she travelled across the world sampling different baths, compared being scrubbed down in a Turkish bath to entering a powerful, unrelenting car wash. The attendant too used the car image to explain *Naemun*:

- It's like this. When you leave the hammam you feel good and refreshed – so it's like a new car! You're congratulating someone on their new car!

I wasn't getting the most academic of answers. But perhaps the most practical one was from the lad who did menial tasks in the hammam, like emptying pails of water over the floors:

- Me, I'm just a *fela'ah* – a peasant farmer. I have never worked in any hammam other than this one. In fact I've never even been to a hammam other than this one.

But then he cast his gaze on the box for tips that sat on the counter.

- When we say *Naemun* it's to remind the bather ...

And the others chimed in:

- To put in a couple of thousand!

We all agreed on that one. I was hammaming in Tripoli where they have restored the last working hammam to reveal the lovely worn stone of the *barrani*. But the workers were all Syrian, and a discreet photograph of the Syrian president was by the manager's desk. The couple of thousand referred to Lebanese pounds: a tip of something just over a dollar.

Just as we spoke, a bather picked up his valuables and paid. '*Naemun!*', the attendants called. The departing customer ignored the hint and walked out the exit door to the whitewashed walls of the lane. His departure was met with silence, which showed a certain restraint given that it is from the tips that an attendant earns his living. In Damascus the *mi'allim* often calls out the amount given, and a generous tip is met with an enthusiastic chorus from the attendants. Meanness can be met with some phrases mumbled under the breath referring to the bather's sister.

It was the balding *mukeyyis* who gave the explanation I was looking for:

- *Naemun* refers to paradise. To the eternal. So the bather has enjoyed the hammam. And as he leaves, you wish him the pleasures of paradise.

Notes

1 Brue, Alexia, *Cathedrals of the Flesh: My Search for the Perfect Bath* (Bloomsbury, 2003), p. 6.

2 Burns, Ross, *Monuments of Syria: An Historical Guide* (I.B. Tauris & Co. Ltd, 1994), p. 104.

3 Burns, Ross, *Damascus: A History* (Routledge, 2007), p. 207.

4 Keenan, Brigid and Beddow, Tim, *Damascus: Hidden Treasures of the Old City* (Thames and Hudson, 2008), p. 91.

5 Keenan, Brigid and Beddow, Tim, *Damascus: Hidden Treasures of the Old City* (Thames and Hudson, 2008), p. 99.

6 Bell, Gertrude, *The Desert and the Sown* (Heinemann, 1908), p. 227.

7 Dinning, Hector William, *Nile to Aleppo, with the Light-horse in the Middle-East* (G. Allen & Unwin Ltd., 1920), p. 97.

8 Dinning, Hector William, *Nile to Aleppo, with the Light-horse in the Middle-East* (G. Allen & Unwin Ltd., 1920), p. 98.

9 Russell, Alexander and Patrick, 'The Natural History of Aleppo' in Kociejowski, Marius, *Syria: Through Writers' Eyes* (Eland, 2006), p. 140.

10 Young, Gavin, *Iraq: Land of Two Rivers* (Collins, 1980), p. 42.

11 Rowson, E. K., 'Two Homoerotic Narratives from Mamluk Literature' in Wright, J. W. and Rowson, E. K., *Homoeroticism in Classical Arabic Literature* (Columbia University Press, 1997), p. 177.

12 Russell, Alexander and Patrick, 'The Natural History of Aleppo' in Kociejowski, Marius, *Syria: Through Writers' Eyes* (Eland, 2006), p. 140.

13 Lane, Edward William, *Manners and Customs of the Modern Egyptians* (John Murray, 1871), p. 346.

14 'Alternative Therapy and Islam', http://www.TurnToIslam.com/.

15 Dinning, Hector William, *Nile to Aleppo, with the Light-horse in the Middle-East* (G. Allen & Unwin Ltd., 1920), p. 97.

16 Young, Gavin, *Iraq: Land of Two Rivers* (Collins, 1980), p. 42.

17 Young, Gavin, *Iraq: Land of Two Rivers* (Collins, 1980), p. 42.

18 Young, Gavin, *Iraq: Land of Two Rivers* (Collins, 1980), p. 42.

19 Young, Gavin, *Iraq: Land of Two Rivers* (Collins, 1980), p. 42.

20 Orga, Irfan, *Portrait of a Turkish Family* (Eland, 2003), p. 11.

21 Orga, Irfan, *Portrait of a Turkish Family* (Eland, 2003), p. 11.

22 See Kandiyoti, Deniz, 'The Paradoxes of Masculinity' in Cornwall, A., and Lindisfarne, N., *Dislocating Masculinity* (Routledge, 1994), p. 203.

23 Hadjar, Abdallah, *The Historical Monuments of Aleppo* (Automobile and Touring Club of Syria, 2006), p. 84.

24 Lane, Edward, *An Account of the Manners and Customs of the Modern Egyptians* (Ward, Lock and Co., 1890), p. 308.

25 Irwin, Robert, *Night and Horses and the Desert* (Penguin, 2000), p. 278.

26 Bouhdiba, Abdelwahab, *Sexuality in Islam* (Routledge, 1974), pp. 30–42.

27 Halasa, Malu and Salam, Rana, *The Secret Life of Syrian Lingerie: Intimacy and Design* (Chronicle Books, 2008).

28 Mathers, E. P., *Book of the Thousand Nights and One Night* (Routledge, 1996), Vol. iii, p. 15.

29 Bell, Gertrude, *The Desert and the Sown* (William Heinemann, 1908), p. 213.

30 Meri, Josef, *The Cult of Saints among Muslims and Jews in Medieval Syria* (Oxford, 2002), p. 61.

31 Meri, Josef, *The Cult of Saints among Muslims and Jews in Medieval Syria* (Oxford, 2002), p. 94.

32 Meri, Josef, *The Cult of Saints among Muslims and Jews in Medieval Syria* (Oxford, 2002), p. 172.

3

Aleppo and Beyond

'… a hammam is the chief ornament and centre of delight of any city.
In fact, O King of time, a hammam is an earthly paradise.'[1]

NIGHT TRAIN

Getting a train in Syria is a dying but not ignoble tradition – a bit like going to a hammam or the cinema perhaps. And so I found myself one evening in a taxi on my way to the station, Aleppo bound.

The driver played some kind of traditional music as we passed through the urban landscape, and among the drab concrete flyovers and high-rise blocks of the city, the traditional singers, in their gaiety, were like visitors from another life. Soon I would be at the station: not the delicate façade of the Hejaz station built to carry pilgrims to Mecca, but the dour suburban station of Qaddam. It was from this area that the Prophet is said to have rejected Damascus for the paradise of the hereafter.

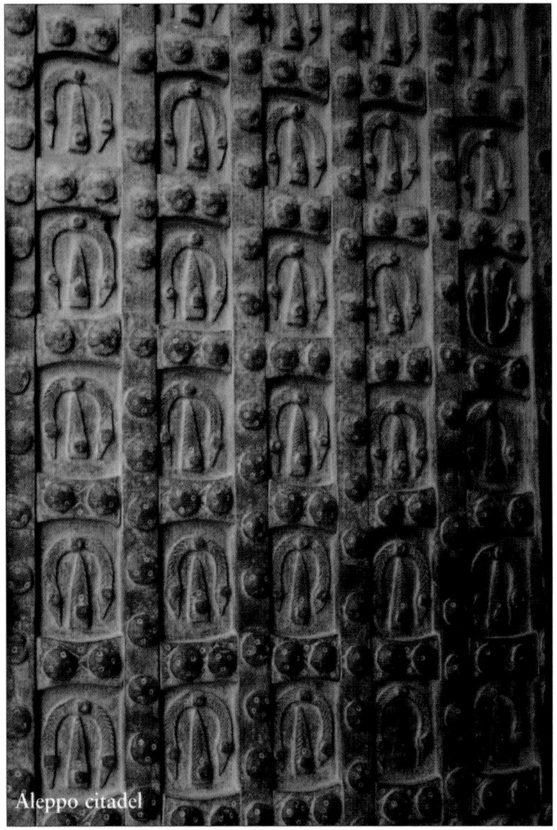
Aleppo citadel

Clearly the traffic was somewhat lighter then – before the tide of modernity had engulfed the olive groves and wheat fields of the city, for there was once a green girdle of orchards around Damascus. But from the station platform, while the last passengers boarded the midnight train, I could still see the great mountain of Qassioun rise above the city. In the night sky, with all the flat-roofed houses piled on its side, clinging to the mountain as limpets to a rock, the sheer drop of Qassioun was a wall of lights.

The train was ready to depart; the compartment clean, the bed linen crisp. The Aleppo train was not like those Sudanese journeys I made in my youth, sleeping on the roof by night, hiding in the crammed compartment from the heat of the sun by day. I handed my passport over to the guard and settled down, trying to remember some words of Freya Stark:

> The beckoning counts, and not the clicking latch behind you, and all through life the actual moment of anticipation still holds that delight.[2]

On the platform a young soldier, ticking off the days of his youth until the two and a half years of military service finally came to an end, envied, I think, my freedom as I set off on a journey just for the pleasure of it:

> – It's fine for you foreigners travelling all over the place!

I would not be crossing any borders on this journey – at least not formal, political boundaries – but Aleppo is in some sense a different world from Damascus. T. E. Lawrence put it like this: 'Aleppo was a great city in Syria, but not of it.'[3]

ALEPPO

Unlike Britain and Ireland where every town is beginning to look like the cloned copy of another, the cities of Syria are remarkably different.

For T. E. Lawrence, Aleppo was very much Ottoman, and today the city still has that Ottoman, multilingual feel. Like in many a city the crumbling area by the clock tower had once functioned as a red light area, but the hotel signs – the Umayyad Palace, the Khambra, the Andalusia – still advertise accommodation in Arabic and Armenian and English.

The polyglot nature of Aleppo is written on its walls, but the Ottoman buildings of Bab al Faraj might not last much longer. As I was driven past latticed balconies, lovely in their decay, the driver turned to me and said, perhaps not without pleasure:

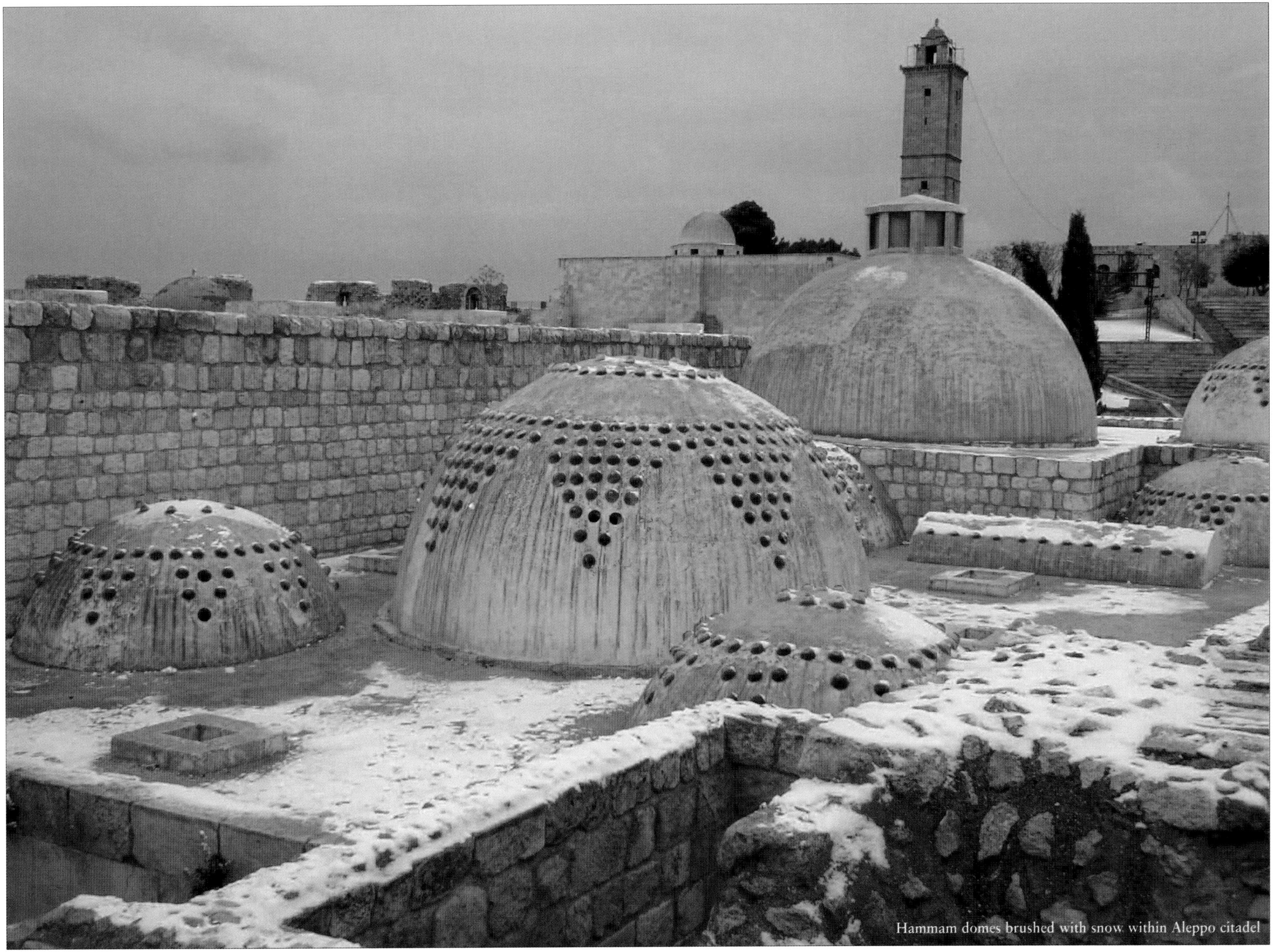
Hammam domes brushed with snow within Aleppo citadel

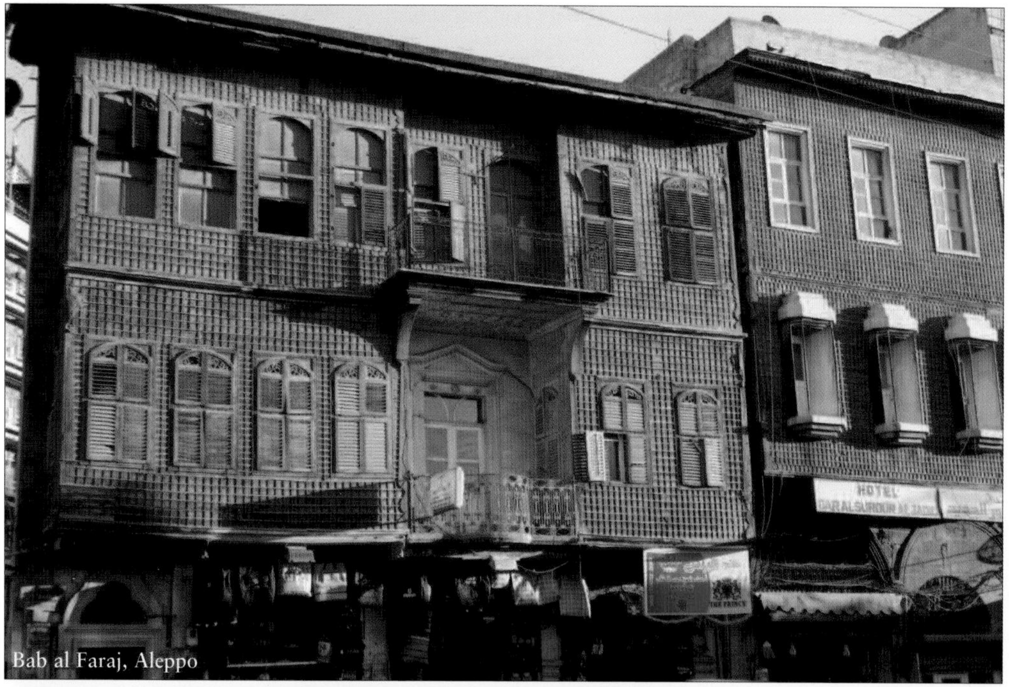

Bab al Faraj, Aleppo

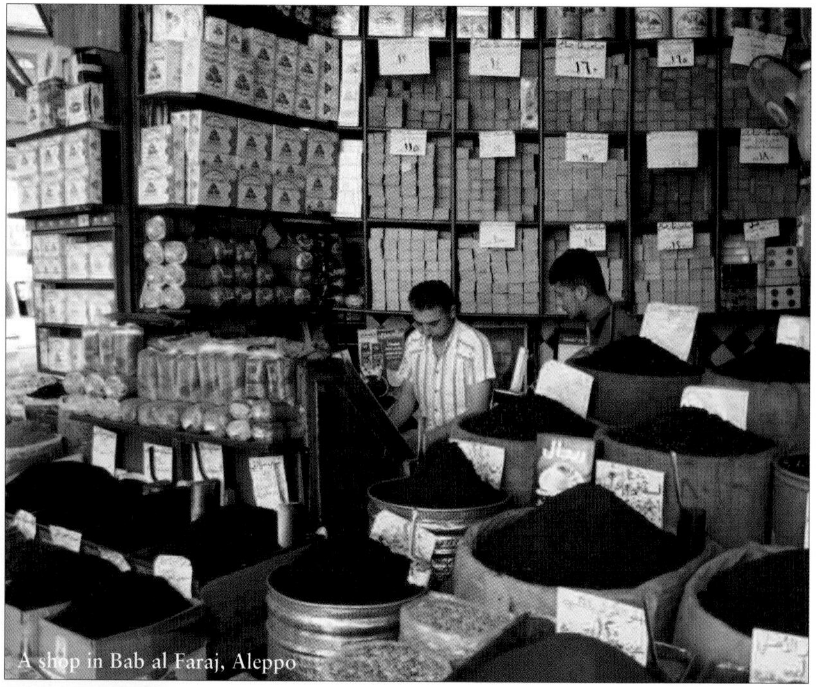
A shop in Bab al Faraj, Aleppo

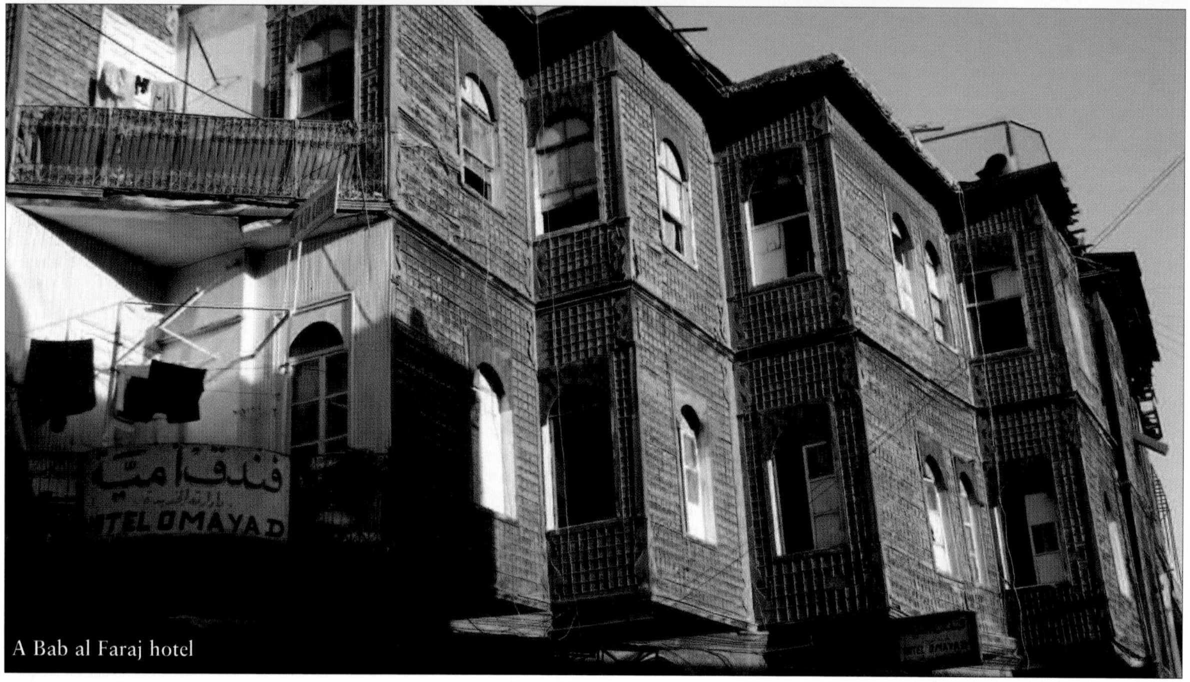
A Bab al Faraj hotel

– Do you see this? They're going to knock it all down.

Right in the heart of the city, the lovely shops selling Aleppo soap stacked in pale green towers near pyramids of spices, dates and tea, were all earmarked for 'redevelopment', and the days of the hotels too were probably numbered.

It is to Aleppo the displaced have come. The hotel waiter was a Palestinian in his seventies, and had the courtesy of people of that age. He had been expelled from Palestine in 1948, put on a train, and carried his son with him to Aleppo. Almost a century ago Aleppo gave refuge to Armenians; more recently the city has given asylum to thousands of Iraqi refugees.

In Baron Street the atmosphere in the café was thick with smoke and I enjoyed a good espresso. The waiter had fairish hair; he was Kurdish, and spoke Arabic as a second language. His village was in Afreen, not far from Qala'at Samaan. There is still something archetypal in the stony landscapes of Afreen: women at wells, men on horseback, villagers offering tea, the water drawn from some cistern green with duckweed.

Here in the fifth century a monk had perched on a column for thirty-seven years; such a religious stunt did not go unnoticed and the site became a centre of pilgrimage. To commemorate a stylite's lifetime of perching, the Cathedral of St Simeon was built in the shape of a cross around the celebrity's pillar, a church unmatched in Christendom until Justinian built his Church of the Holy Wisdom in Constantinople.

As Gertrude Bell travelled on horseback throughout Syria, relating 'the talk that passed from lip to lip round the camp-fire', she was not quite seduced by the ruins of St Simeon, despite its acanthus-leaved arches, sculpted so that the leaves hugging the pillars might seem to be caught by a breeze.[4] 'Rosy with a deep content' the night she camped there, Bell caught sight of a star above the cathedral's arcade, and comparing it to the holy man who had been stuck on a pillar for most of his life, thought it 'better

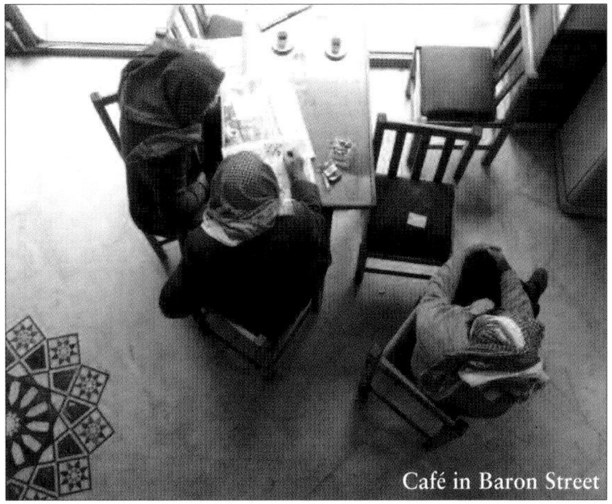

Café in Baron Street

to journey over earth and sky than to sit upon a column all your days'.[5]

I'll drink to that! But holy men were often wanderers, and Aleppo's association with them goes back some time. The pharmacy opposite my favourite café is called *Heleb al Shebwa*, the traditional name for Aleppo, for according to legend, the Prophet Ibrahim (Abraham of the Old Testament) used to milk (*heleb*) his black and white cow (*shebwa)* within the site of the citadel, and distribute the milk to the people. A mosque still commemorates the milking place.

Viewing the 'barren, treeless, featureless world' that surrounded the city, Gertrude Bell summed up the geography of Aleppo with a rather nice domestic image:

> The site of the town is like a cup and saucer, the houses lie in the saucer and the castle stands on the up-turned cup.[5]

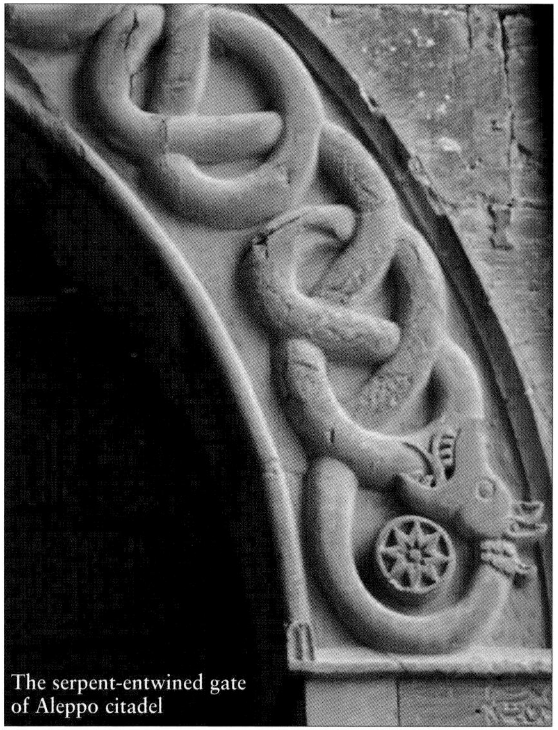

The serpent-entwined gate of Aleppo citadel

She was less interested in what lay within the walls of the citadel than in the view of the great plain that the citadel granted. Languidly, she writes:

> ... you might see Baghdad but for the tiresome way in which the round earth curves, for there is no barrier to the eye in all that great level.[6]

Unlike the houses of Syria, the citadel is at its best from without. Nothing within matches the entrance inscribed with Mamluk glories (a building was something to be read) and the serpent-entwined gate, each head swallowing a tail. Then there is the shrine to al-Khider (who travelled over to England as Saint George, but for the first lieutenant is a fertility myth paralleling Adonis) and the twin-lioned gate, one laughing, one weeping. Within, there is the Mosque of Ibrahim and two restored hammams, but the wax dummies of bathers seated by a font in a hammam-museum are a sad parody of the real thing below the citadel walls.

For me, what marks Aleppo out from any other city is not the citadel but the *suq* beneath – an ancient labyrinth, where donkeys still transport produce along cobbled ways. Its shoppers, village women in bright unsophisticated clothes, hint of a country fair, with their primary colours and embroidered golds and velvets.

The feel of Aleppo is different. The country women may be brightly dressed, and the Christian women might have their own styles, but often the women of the Muslim neighbourhoods go veiled and wear a uniform black. Aleppans are not ones for half measures; when they eat, they feast, and when they drink, they really drink, a hundred men and more knocking back the arak in the smoky affability of a restaurant.

Even the *futas* in Aleppo tend to be more colourful, like the wrap-rounds they have in the hammams in Turkey. Walking into Hammam al Naem just off the *suq*, with its spacious private cubicles for undressing and socialising on a balconied area of the *barrani*, it seemed to me that I had stepped into a hammam in Turkey itself.

Linguistically even the Arabic is different; in hammams the word *futa* is almost unknown, for Aleppans have their own vocabulary. And the men don't sing their Arabic in the way Damascenes do; it's more guttural and masculine. Traditionally, an Arab city is written about as feminine but, for me, despite the curves of its domes, Aleppo is most definitely male: in Baron Street you might not see a woman at all, just aimlessly roaming *shebab* tempted by cinema hoardings.

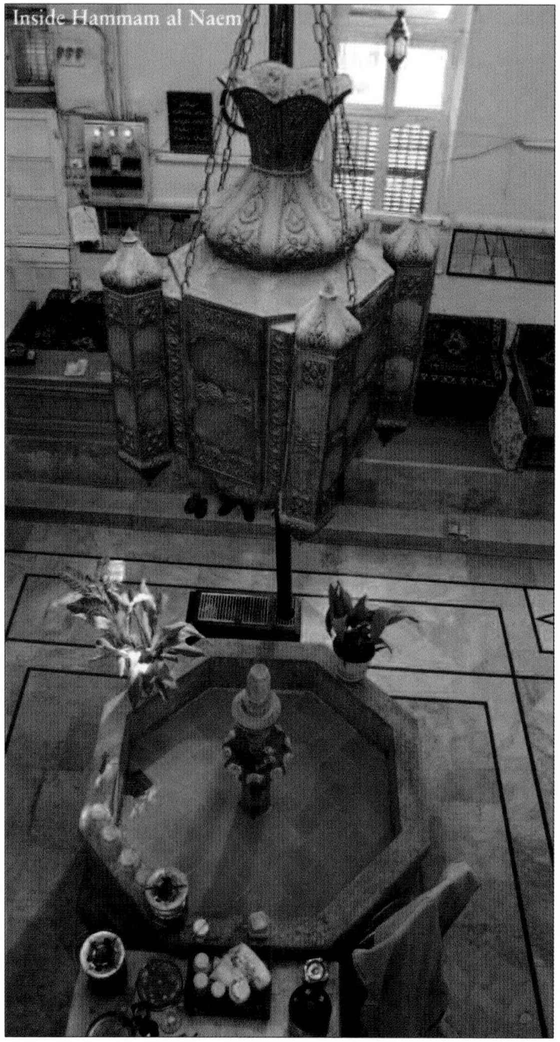
Inside Hammam al Naem

Everything is that bit more extreme. The summers are hotter, the winters greyer and harsher, which makes hammaming even more desirable. I have seen the domes of Aleppan hammams brushed with snow, and heard that some *shebab* will hang out in a hammam the whole winter's day to escape the bitter wind that blows across the plain. After a few days in Aleppo even Damascene cuisine seems that bit blander, for even the kebabs are laced with cherries.

It is the Aleppans who set the standard when it comes to hammaming; no-one hammams like they do.

Popping in For a Hammam

It had rained so much one winter's night in Aleppo that my shoes were letting water in, and under the sheets of rain it had not been easy to get a taxi. But finally I had taken one to the Iron Gate below the citadel and now I was walking down into the bowels of the earth. At the end of the twenty-two steps stood a hammam attendant, his greeting as warm as the hammam itself:

– Welcome, my soul!

They are like that in Aleppo – they are a little excessive in their greetings, and one might address another even when his name is unknown with words like 'my soul', 'my love', 'my eyes', 'my beloved'.

At the reception desk sat the sober manager of the hammam, beneath a framed photograph I assumed to be the late father of the *mi'allim*. For that's how it is in even a grocer's shop in Syria – the father enshrined in a black-and-white photograph above the shelves, serious and unsmiling, the dead still supervising the work of the living. On the manager's desk were photographs of pilgrims and the black, veiled cube of the Kabbah, where, in 'the days of ignorance' before Islam, poets had inscribed their verses.

The manager, surrounded by photographs of holy sheikhs, warmed to a smile as I deposited my valuables and wrapped the key to the box around my wrist:

– Where have you been all this time?

It was some months since I had hammamed in Hananu, the hammam named after a Syrian revolutionary. The dressing room had its fountain tiered like a rather vulgar wedding cake, and the chequered ceramic tiles set on the walls like a chessboard hid the original stone, but the hammam itself was probably at least five centuries old.

I undressed and walked through to the *wastani*. Here a couple of kids were playing in the plunge pool, for almost every hammam in Aleppo has some kind of pool that the bather can dip into. It is this that distinguishes Aleppan hammams from those in Damascus: an Aleppan hammam might

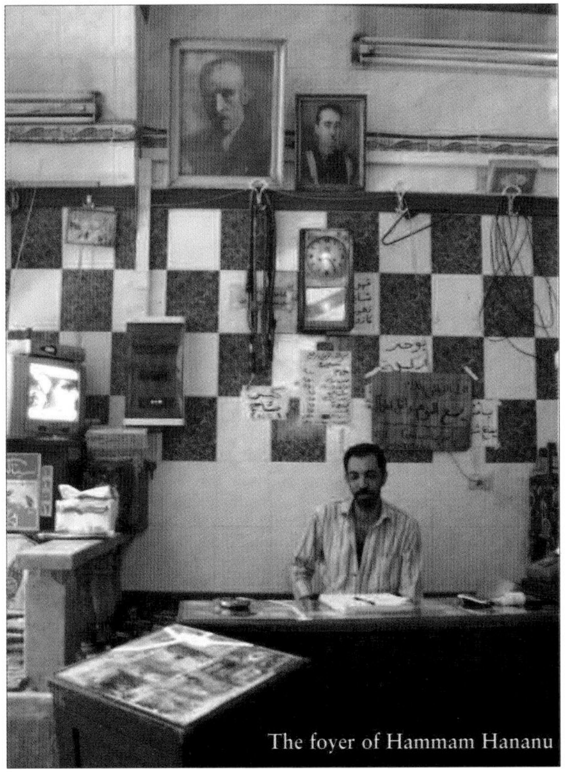

The foyer of Hammam Hananu

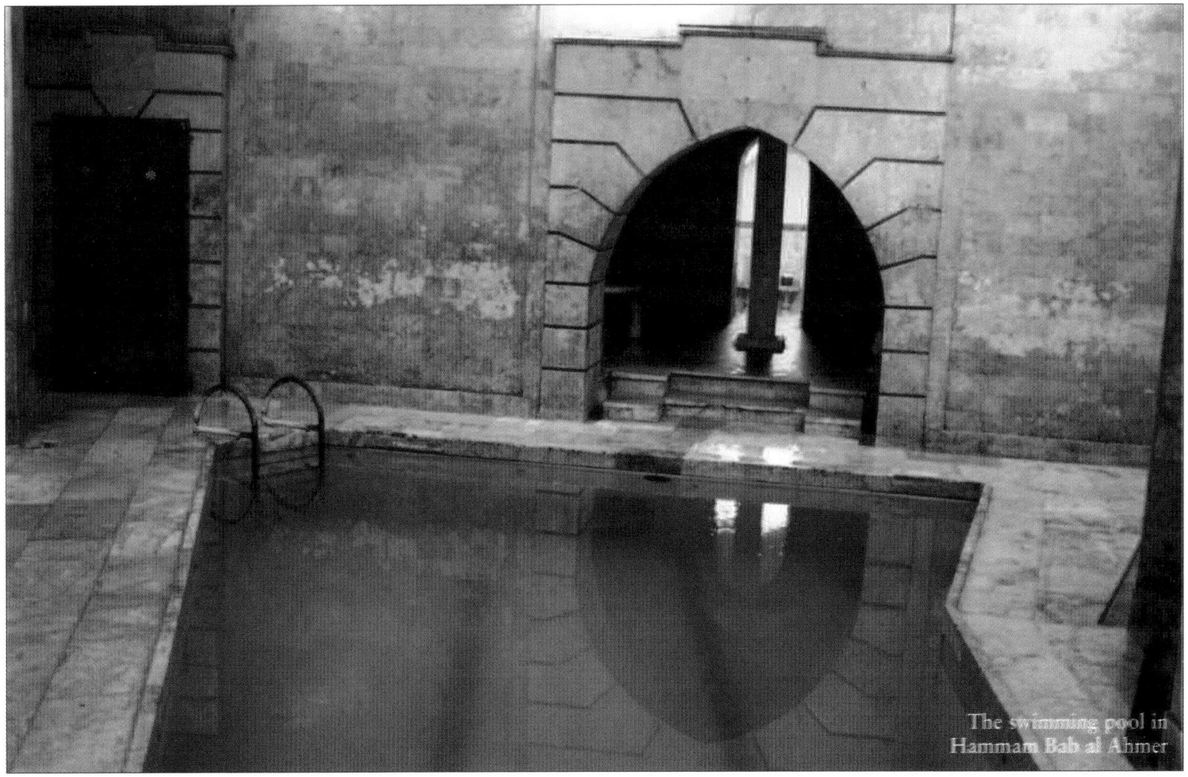

The swimming pool in Hammam Bab al Ahmer

even have, like Hammam Bab al Ahmer, its own covered swimming pool. If the hammam is an annexe to the mosque, then in Aleppo the pool is the annexe to the hammam. And this is maybe why hammams in Aleppo remain popular; they swim as kids then hammam as adults.

I walked into the innermost room – the octagonal *jouwani* – with the firehouse running its length giving off a cosy winter warmth. By one of the bathing fonts a solitary middle-aged man, great in girth, lay collapsed on the marble floor, like a beached whale. In two of the side rooms sat groups of *shebab*, the entry to one room blocked by a great silver-coloured tray.

The bather seated next to me on the firehouse was affable enough:

– I can see you speak a little Arabic.
– You could say that, I replied, not exactly flattered.
– And where are you from?

The usual conversational routine was interrupted as half a kilo of carrots, washed but unpeeled, were thrown into my lap. The Aleppans were welcoming me with a warmth that is not quite so common in Damascus. Half a dozen clementines followed, then apples. In Aleppo the hammam is not just a bathing place; it also functions as a restaurant – a little incongruous to the visitor perhaps, for who in Ireland would bring in their supper to eat on the tiled floor of the city baths?

I threw a clementine to one of the bathers, who courteously replied:

– The generous have given to you, and you have generously given!

And so this is the second feature that distinguishes Aleppan hammams from those of Damascus: in Aleppo, hammams function as eating places. Rather than go out to a restaurant, you can bring your supper in with you to eat, say to the *wastani* of Hammam al-Nahasin. I'm sure any Aleppan bather would agree with Irfan Orga's recollection of a hammam's effect on the taste buds:

> Food always had twice its appeal if offered in the hammam.[7]

And the hammam has its traditional food: *mejedderah:* a time-honoured dish of rice and lentils, although nowadays bathers are more likely to bring in a takeaway.

Together we chatted about the number of working hammams in Aleppo, and the *shebab* made it three or four. They laughed as I claimed it was around ten (although I was once told that in the past there had been seventy-seven hammams in Aleppo) and started to go through them, beginning with the citadel.

– There's Hammam Bab al Ahmer under the citadel, and Hammam Yalbougha. Then go down in to the *suq* and there is the Coppersmiths' Hammam, Hammam al-Nahasin. And a few minutes away there is Hammam al Naem.

I moved on to another finger, and continued my litany of hammams.

– Then by Bab Antakia there is that small one... what's its name...? And then further along Hammam Granada...

The naming ritual was interrupted as the other group invited me to join them for supper. I politely refused, but a bather with a wonderful gut insisted. I thanked him with the usual phrases, but he took me by the arm to the alcove where they were all seated around the half-eaten dishes on the floor – chicken pieces, cut cucumber, mayonnaise... As I dipped in, out of politeness one of them continued eating to accompany me. Between mouthfuls I asked about their work: the young lad on my left said he worked with silver; the fat one told me he was an optician.

– But I'm a doctor as well.
– Really? I asked, for he had given the word a rather dubious intonation.
– Yes, I do a bit of circumcision on the side.

Now it was time for the little steam room, suitable for only a couple of bathers. Seated next to me was Mohammed; he was working on the coast but had come up to Aleppo to visit his mum for a day and to hammam. He had heard the *shebab* tell me a joke about a Syrian who went to China, and brought a Chinese back for a hammam, so now he launched into a joke of his own. For reasons

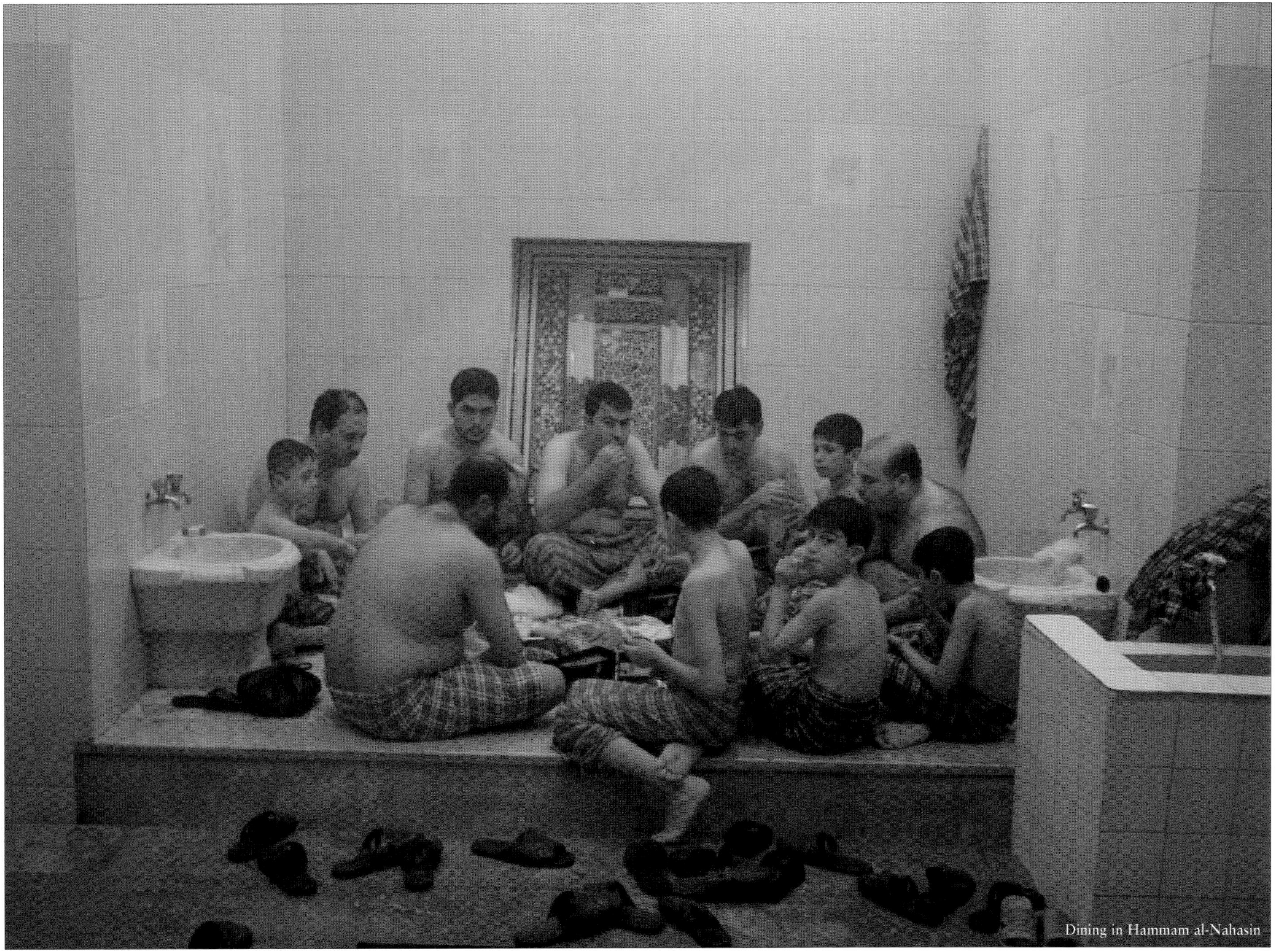

Dining in Hammam al-Nahasin

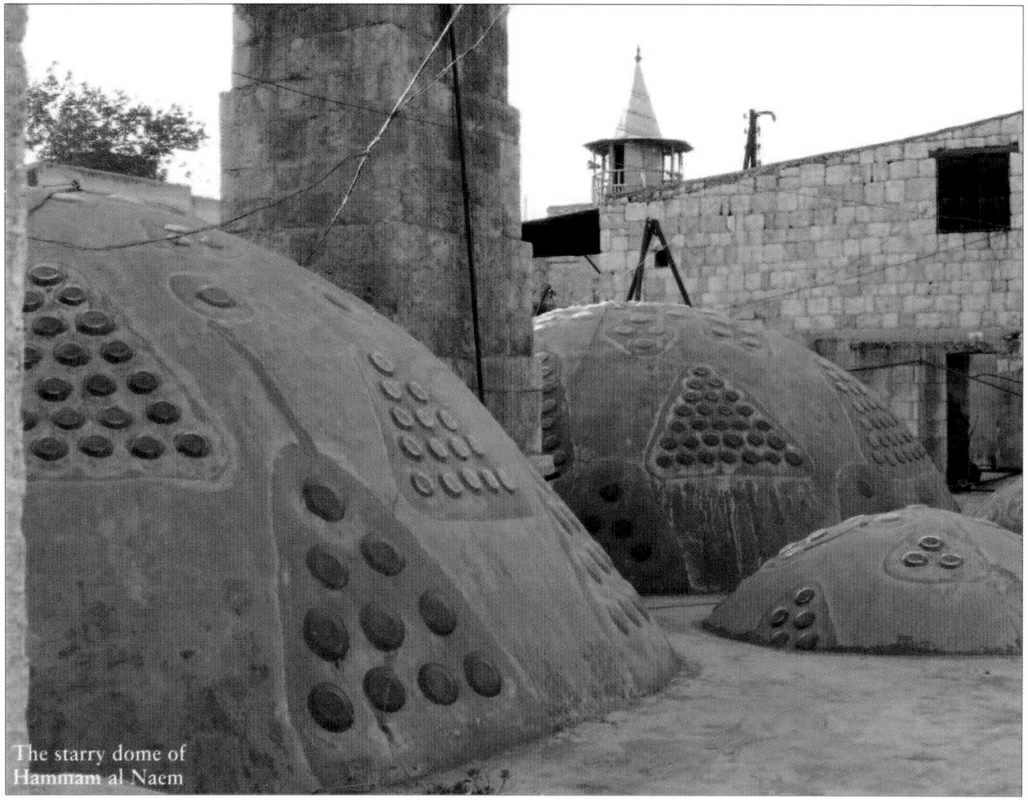
The starry dome of Hammam al Naem

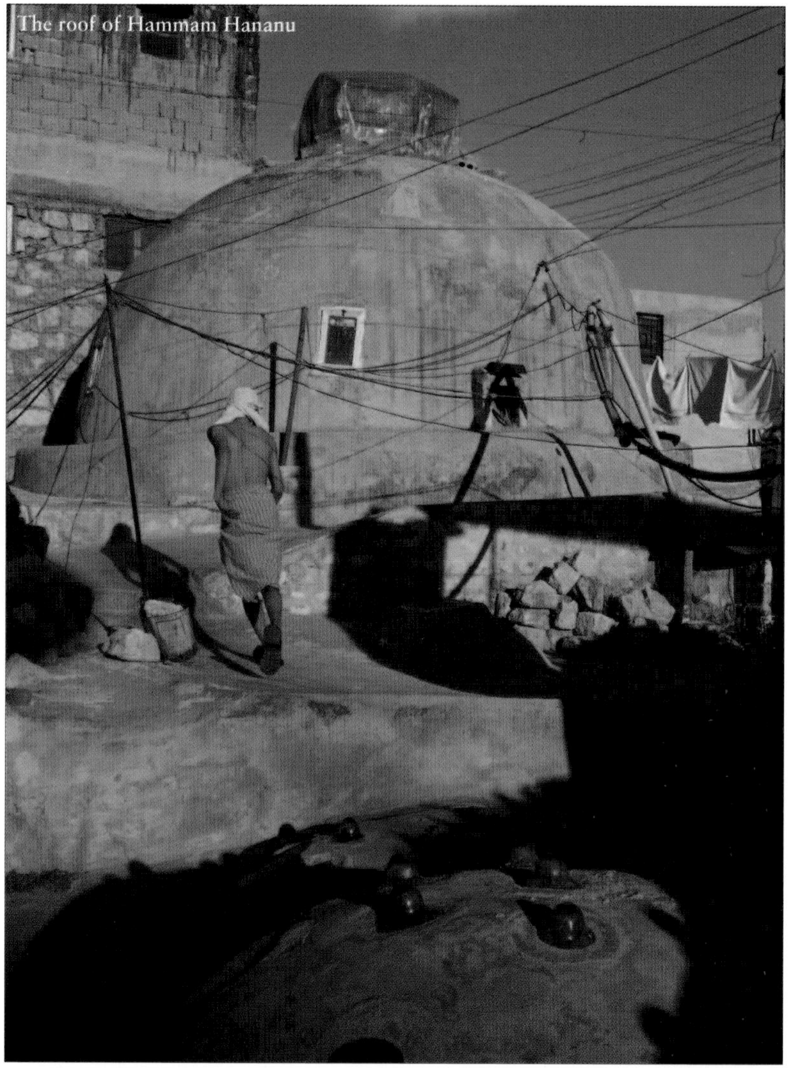
The roof of Hammam Hananu

of etiquette I won't repeat the joke here; people confide things in you in a hammam that they wouldn't dream of saying elsewhere.

It was now well past midnight. In Damascus the hammams would have closed by this time, but in Aleppo they stay open and bathers will come until dawn. One with a splendid tattoo entered, and sat cross-legged at the font. I myself sat under the starry dome of the hammam – the dome itself, whether from faded paint or from a kind of algae spreading in the humidity, had hints of green, like the green sheen of a racing pigeon's feathers where they blend with a softer grey.

I call it a starry dome for the overarching dome had stars cut into it – like the plastic stars that cooks use to mark their pastry. I lay back on the firehouse, where the towels were stretched out to dry on a clothes-line above my head, almost intoxicated by it all – such was the effect of the steam and the heat. The indolence however was interrupted by a call from the roof; someone was shouting for the attendant to see to the heating system.

– Expecting more customers? I asked.
– They drink, and then they bathe.

Now the bather with the tattoo lay stretched out on the floor in a state of perfect indolence, one hand reaching up every so often to scoop a bowl of water over his chest. Framed by the arched doorway to the side room, the bather formed almost a tableau, like in those Orientalist paintings of bathers of the East. Aleppan streets themselves seem to frame themselves for viewing – as the sunlight squanders itself on some stone wall – with one arched way mirroring another more distant arch.

The *mukeyyis* asked if I was ready. He was a wiry, muscled man, and not without a sense of humour. When I asked his name he told me Hajj Ibrahim – *Hajj*, the honorary title of one who has returned from the pilgrimage to Mecca. However, I wasn't going to fall for that one, nor was I going to settle for the cursory rub down that they give the tourists in the hammams below the citadel; when the *mukeyyis* had finished the first arm I returned it to him and told him to do the job properly. As he scrubbed me down I told him I had heard a snore coming from the tattooed bather:

> – You know one of your customers is lying there on the floor asleep?

He laughed. A *mukeyyis* is not one to give himself airs:

> – Asleep? That one's pissed.

New bathers were still coming in, but it was time for me to go. In one of the alcoves I dropped my *futa*, hung it over the rod across the door for privacy, and had a final rinse. The attendant hung new towels for me into which I would change. Outside, another attendant arrived with a pile of towels balanced on his head, like a boy carrying the morning's bread home through the *suq*. He rubbed me down and changed me into the final towels. I then reclined in the pillowed comfort of a kind of snug, as the final act of cleansing was performed: Johnson's ear buds for babies.

The foyer now had the air of a pub after closing time. But as I lay alone in pampered splendour a man came down the steps, calling that with him was a *derwish* who wanted to bathe. A *derwish* is a man who gives up the material world in pursuit of the spiritual, a traveller on a spiritual plane rather than someone like me in pursuit of the exotic. This *derwish* was not one of those *mulawiyah* who entertain tourists in Damascus, their immaculate skirts encircling the dancer as he rotates, the spirituality of the Sufis reduced to a secular display for diners.

The word *derwish* can also be used simply to refer to someone who is poor, and this old man, clearly in a state of poverty, was much in need of a bath. In a slow voice he called that he would pay '50 notes'. The attendants were having none of it:

> – The last one we had like this bathed, left, and died not long after. Questions were asked.

Outside, it was bitterly cold, with the rain lashing down on the fruit sellers' empty stalls where the *derwish* sought shelter. I gave him a coin, just a coin, and, not unconscious of the contrast in our circumstances, splashed through the rain to the taxi that would take me back to the warmth of my exquisitely restored hotel.

Hammam Granada

Given the nostalgia for a lost world displayed in the names of Aleppo's hotels, it's not surprising to find a hammam named after a city in Spain where the Umayyads ruled on long after they had lost the Arab world.

What names can be more evocative of lost kingdoms than Cordoba and Granada? The palace walls in Andalusia were themselves inscribed with poetry, for the word and not the human form is the appropriate ornamentation in Islamic architecture:

> Although his Diwan has not survived, so much of Ibn Zamrak's was used to decorate one of the palaces of the Alhambra and its garden that the place can be read as if it was a book of poems fashioned in stone.[9]

When I was staying in one of the downmarket hotels near the clock tower, some of my fellow guests were the head-scarf wearing bedouin of the *badieh*. The *badieh* – the desert wilderness – is perceived perhaps as the very

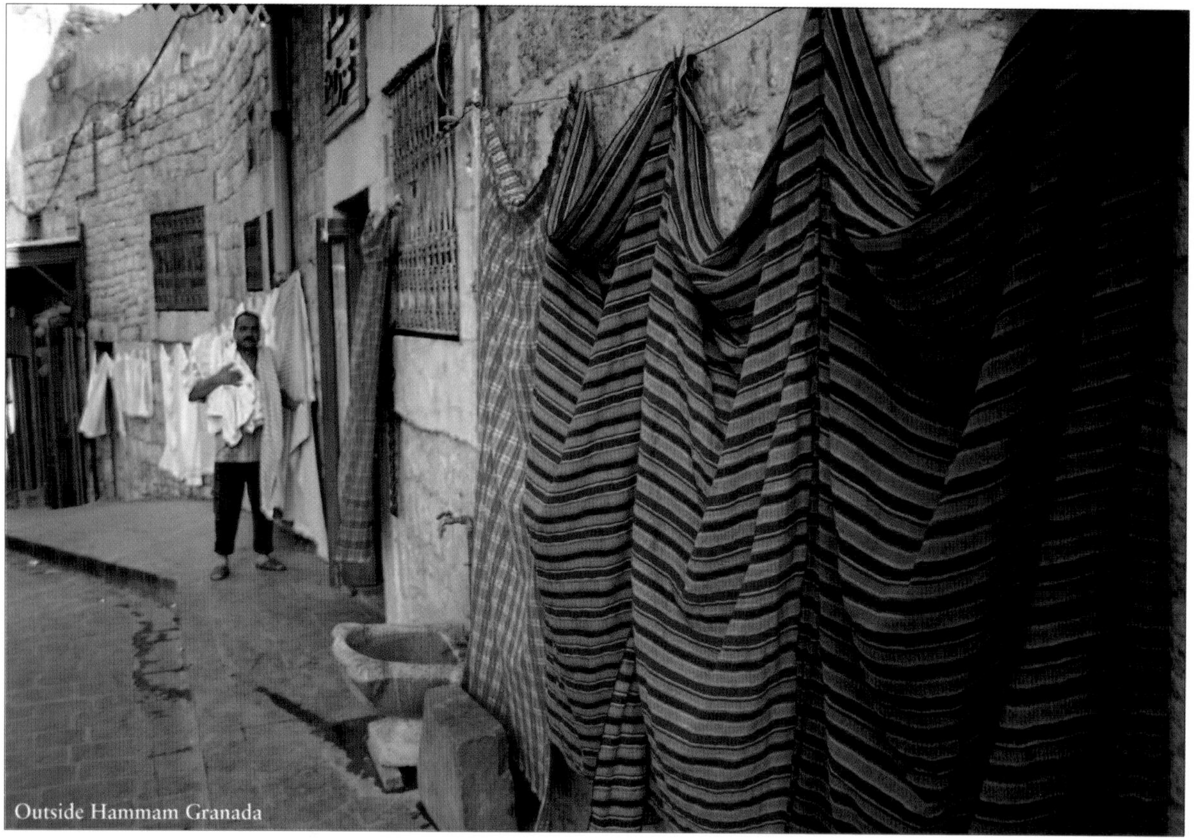
Outside Hammam Granada

soul of things Arab, just as in Ireland it is not the capital but some remote western isle that is seen as the essence of things Irish. They were from some one-horse-town where I had stopped one day for a few minutes on my way to an Umayyad palace in the desert. City folk are more likely to call such people *chawi* than bedouin: country bumpkins.

As we chatted together I asked one of the men – handsome, smartly bearded, with bedouin leanness – why anyone would give the name 'Granada' to a hammam in Aleppo. I was matter-of-factly informed that there was not just a place called Granada in Spain, but a Homs as well. And we laughed at that, to think of a Homs in Spain, for although Homs is perhaps the ugliest city in Syria, its people are maybe the loveliest, with the richest sense of humour, and, like the Irish, the butt of many a joke. Even Tamerlane spared Homs when its people greeted him with jokes and buffoonery.

Seeing my disbelief, my fellow guest quoted from an Andalusian poet, reciting in the loveliest-sounding Arabic – not like when the urban dweller changes into classical and speaks as if he has marbles in his mouth.

– And did you learn that in school?
– No, in the *jelsah*.

I think I know what he meant by the *jelsah*. It was like in Yemen when people sat together chewing qat, and it seemed the most natural thing in the world to say a few lines of poetry as the gathering got high on the national weed – for poetry in the Arab world, like prayer, is not something to be embarrassed about.

He wrote down the words for me, and then we sat on, watching the latest cartoon on Syrian TV. Back in Damascus the first lieutenant did a translation for me:

Where is Homs and its lovely gardens?
Its river full of fresh sweet water all year
You, the one who is sleeping,
Don't forget that the days don't sleep!

Of all Syria's hammams, Hammam Granada seems the least likely candidate for its name, for there's not a lot within it to evoke Andalusia. It doesn't even have a fountain or a pool, a requisite of any Umayyad building, be it mosque or palace; the *barrani* is more like a parlour room than a fountained courtyard. If anything, the atmosphere is rather severe; there always seems to be someone spreading out a prayer mat in the *barrani* – it is not the place to recline and have a leisurely nap.

The manager once confronted me about my behaviour in his hammam, but my offence seemed a rather innocent one:

– Why do you go round talking to people?

My words to another bather had been reported, and the manager was irate:

– Why did you say that this hammam was a stable?

I had not been commenting on the off-white ceramic tiles but on the hammam's history; it had once been a stable for the neighbouring khan and hence was missing a *wastani*; the stable architecture had lent itself to only a two-roomed hammam.

Hammam Granada has its own style. It has a kind of homely or even dowdy air, what with the furnishings and its utter lack of pretensions. Perhaps it is the bathers who make the hammam what it is; they are not exactly Aleppo's nouveau riche, and don't come in noisy groups and throw water at each other. One evening the hammam's clientele were:

(1) a carpenter with the Arabic equivalent to *Time Flies* tattooed on his biceps;
(2) a moustachioed farmer, with not ungenerous tummy, who told me his land was planted with olives or wheat;
(3) two lads from the Turkish border, cousins, who import bicycles into Aleppo.

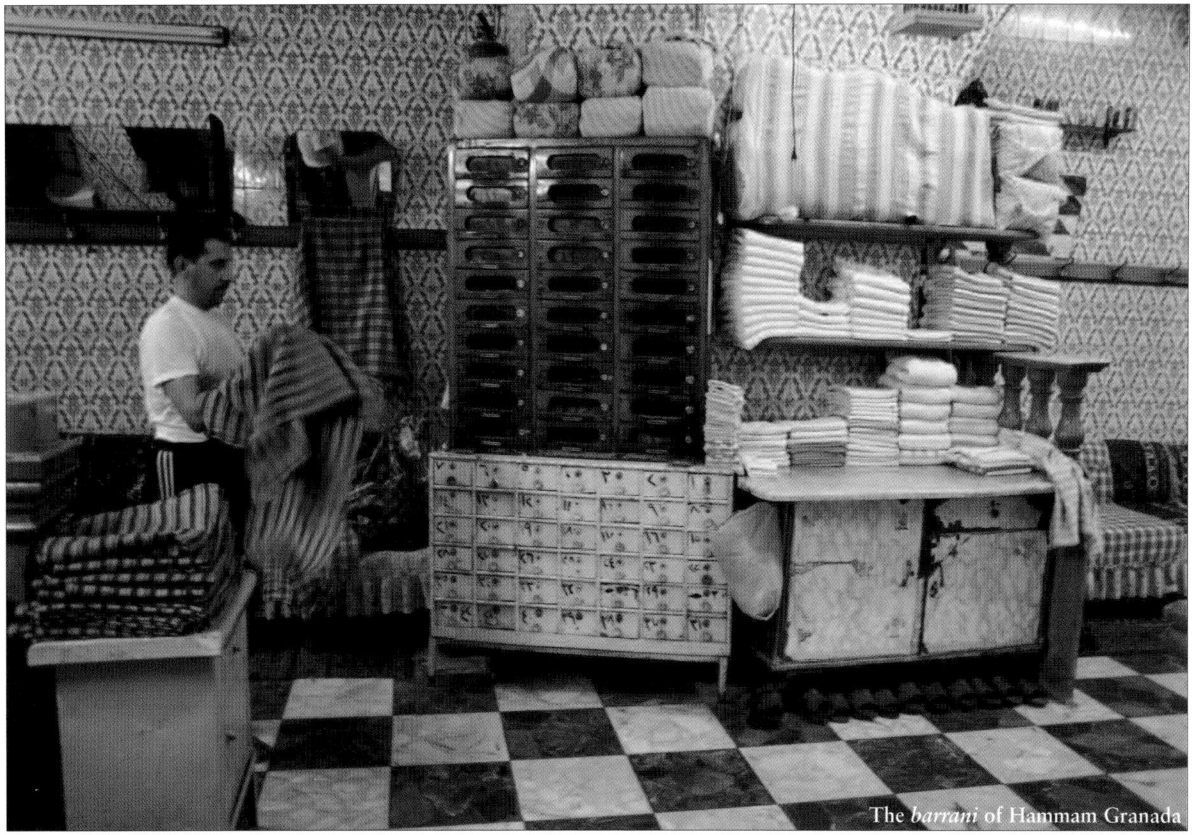
The *barrani* of Hammam Granada

Hammam Granada is anything but pseudo-Oriental. This hammam is a real one, and without doubt is one of the most authentic places to bathe in Aleppo – I'm tempted to say it's my favourite.

Hammaming with Yahia

It was in front of the Kindi Cinema, just before it finally closed, that I met Yahia. I'm not sure whether he was a cinema attendant or just ran the test-your-strength machine on the pavement. In response to my question about Aleppan hammams, he went through the usual ones – Hammam Bab al Ahmer, Hammam Yalbougha etc., but then mentioned Hammam Saddat, the Gentlemen's Hammam.

The name to me seems almost a contradiction in terms, given that nowadays most of the Syrian middle-class would not be seen dead in either a cinema (they have their pirated DVDs at home) or a hammam. An assistant librarian once explained to me, as I rummaged for information about hammams,

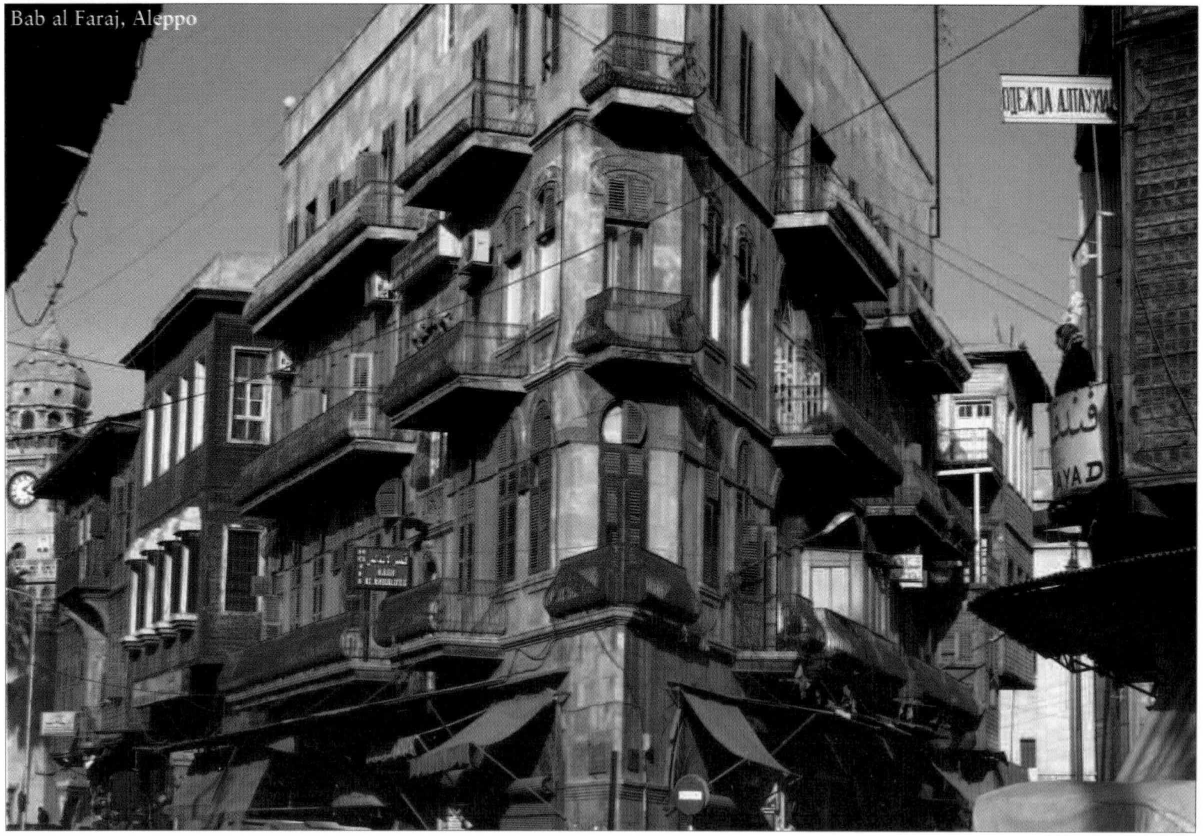

Bab al Faraj, Aleppo

that two kinds of people frequented them: the really well-off who could afford to pay a couple of hundred Syrian pounds for a wash, and the poor who didn't have bathrooms.

Yahia and I went through the streets to find the hammam, past the Ottoman clock tower with its stars and pikes. The Ottomans, as their empire collapsed under the weight of five centuries, built clocks all over their disintegrating world, as if an emphasis on punctuality would somehow hold it all together, or at least accurately record its passing. As his empire fell apart Sultan Abdul Hamid retreated into the world of detectives stories; the chief of the imperial wardrobe would read him Sherlock Holmes from behind a screen.[10]

We followed the streets up past Hammam Granada, asked for directions, followed the directions, and found nothing. Finally someone pointed to a nondescript building and told us Hammam Saddat was closed.

We settled instead for Hammam Miliki and walked along the city walls, past alleys whitewashed and inscribed with '*mabrouk al hajj*' painted the length of the alley wall, congratulating pilgrims just returned. We walked past the mosque with Byzantine pillars built into walls with Babylonian inscriptions, and down the steps towards Bab Antakia where the Sufis commune together in a tiny mosque in the city gate.

Hammam Miliki clearly had seen better days. Like a great house whose owners live in genteel poverty, with half the rooms lying unused and unheated, the darkened rooms and empty fonts of the hammam told of an institution on its last legs. It seemed the hammam had a dual function – a local resident could come for just a perfunctory shower in the *wastani*, or he could go through, as we did, and have a hammam proper.

We threw some water on the *beit al-nar* but it didn't seem to be doing much to heat the room. As I lay down there was the sound of my *futa* ripping – not, I believe, from the extra pounds gained by a love of Syrian cuisine, but merely through the weight of the years that the *futa* had borne. Yahia called for another, and patted my paunch, as if in contrast to his own physique. I made an excuse:

> – It's the food – it's so good here. And the drink!

There were two other bathers in the hammam – a boy who we might describe in Ireland as being a bit simple, and his relative. They had both finished bathing, and the older man was telling the boy to cover himself properly as they left.

– In Sudan, I said, they call it *barakah*. They believe that such a person will give others a blessing.

Yahia corrected me:

– No, it is not that he gives a blessing. He himself *is* the blessing.

I was feeling pretty blessed myself as I hammamed in Aleppo, and thought of my time in the Arab world:

– There is a *hadith* of the Prophet saying that Yemen and Al Sham are the blessed places in the world. I've lived in both! So, Yahia, does that make me twice blessed?

Lying that evening on the *beit al-nar*, I wasn't exactly feeling, like the hammam, down on my luck. We had taken the mitt from the *mi'allim*, for where other hammams seem sometimes to have a score of attendants, everything here was managed by one man. Yahia set to, working on my chest as if he were scouring a particularly nasty saucepan after Sunday lunch.

– It's camel hair, he said, commenting on the mitt.

He went on to attack my back, an experience more invigorating than sensual. I took the mitt from Yahia, but before I could start, he reminded me that I should rinse myself first. In the Arab world there are still times when I am caught out – like that evening in the *Shebab* Restaurant, when I had dropped two tiny bits of bread on the floor, and the Kurdish waiter stooped down and returned them to the table – as if the bread used to help the kebab and arak on their way was in itself something sacred.

Yahia extended an arm for the mitt, and with each touch of my mittened hand the blood rose to his skin, giving it a certain bloom – like the veined blush of the pink marble of the floors of a Damascene hammam. But my scouring was having no effect; this guy was spotlessly clean, except for his back where the unwashed walls of the hammam had left their mark.

As we lay on the *beit al-nar*, Yahia became contemplative:

– Syria is like a flower which has not yet opened; just a couple of petals have been revealed.
– And what's lovelier than that?

To what kind of flower was Yahia comparing Syria? To the unfolding petals of the geraniums grown in tins in the farm yard? Or to the delicate pink of wild cyclamen, hidden on a bank below a citadel, its petals folded back against the stem?

Yahia might have been talking about himself rather than the country – with just his primary education, and his youthful physique, he was not unlike a flower that would soon go to seed. And outside the *suqs* the people themselves, perhaps because the mountain range of the ante-Lebanon cuts much of the country off from the Med and Europe, still can have an innocence in their encounters with a foreigner.

Aleppo is not without its flowers; it was from Aleppo that the Tulip King, Sultan Ahmet III, transported his spring flowers for the fêtes in Istanbul, the Sultan seated in his pavilion as caged nightingales sang from overhanging trees.[11] The great favourite of the Ottomans was the tulip; such was its popularity, fortunes were won and lost in the search for a rare species.[12]

The wild flowers of the dead cities of Byzantium outside Aleppo are still brought into the grey streets of Aleppo with the New Year and sold as little bouquets: red anemone, muscari the blue of stained glass, fragile narcissi, all tied together into a buttonhole to sweeten some city flat. A tenth-century poet of Antioch, Al-Sanawbari, portrays the hills of Al Sham as dressed in spring flowers:

> The hills are in wondrous reverie...
> Anemones their gowns of silk
> Purple engrossed with black.[13]

After that hammam I'm not sure that I ever saw Yahia again; sometimes it seems that this is how I lived in Syria – I would have some chance encounter and then move on from one brief interaction to the next, like some taxi driver moving from fare to fare.

A Holy Man's Resting Place

I handed the address of the latest hammam I was chasing to the taxi driver. He knew the area below the citadel, but not the hammam itself. As we drove I made the usual polite conversation:

– And where are you from in Aleppo?

He named some area that I have now forgotten.

– And where's that?
– It was just here, ahead of us.
– 'Was'? What do you mean 'was'?
– It was here beyond the park... They have knocked it down.
– Was this thirty or forty years ago then?
– No, just last year.

I had arrived in Aleppo to find yet another area cleared, with just a minaret or two surviving above the rubble.

– Near the Pullman station?
– Yes, that's where our house was.

The whole thing to me seemed really Syrian, with the driver stating some of the facts of the matter, but without making any actual criticism.

– And was it a traditional Arabic house? With fruit trees in the courtyard?
– Yes, with fruit trees.
– I would weep to lose such a home.

Now we were driving up towards the citadel. To the left an area had been cleared to make way for some not unpleasant, but unremarkable, buildings.

– And where are you living now?
– In rented accommodation.
– But you owned the other house?
– Yes, it was my father's.

We were now coming up to the citadel, the pearl in the crown of this ancient city that boasts a UNESCO heritage site.

– And were there any hammams in your area?
– Yes, there was one, but it was knocked down some time ago. I used to bathe there when I was a child with my mother.
– And nowadays, do you ever go to a hammam?
– Oh, no, never. We have a bathroom at home.

We arrived at an iron-roofed market of fish and vegetables, which had somehow survived all the 'development'. Unless it too had been demolished, I would find the hammam I was looking for somewhere here. When I got out of the taxi one of the market men lost no time in shaking my hand and, abandoning his work, he marched me down the street towards my goal, my arm linked in his.

Soon we stood before a totally nondescript block of flats.

– This, said Hussein, clearly delighted with himself, is the hammam.

The owner had been standing in the street with a group of *shebab* and with the usual Syrian courtesy obligingly gave me a tour:

– This is the biggest and oldest hammam in Aleppo.

It had become a sort of cliché – I don't know how many hammams in Syria lay claim to the title 'the biggest and oldest hammam...'

– You're not telling me that this hammam, I said, looking around at a fairly run of the mill foyer, is bigger than say, that hammam in Jedeidah, or Hammam al-Nahasin, for example?

The *mi'allim* said little in response, but took me on a little tour of a *barrani* with its fountain intact, a balcony at one end that would not be out of place in a Methodist church, and a collection of racing pigeons housed in tins against a wall. Over a quarter of a century ago the hammam had been in use; all it seemed to need was a good scrub down and it could be functioning again.

Its history was not lost on the current owner, who had inherited the hammam from his father:

- The hammam is named after a sheikh, Mohammed Asshak Tummer, who built both the mosque and the hammam.
- And is he buried here?
- He is.
- Is it not strange to bury a holy man in a hammam instead of by the mosque he built?
- Every hammam must have its sheikh. People say the hammams are haunted by *jinn*, and the sheikh keeps the *jinn* away.

We all laughed at that. Here was a potential marketing slogan for Syria's hammams: 'A sheikh a day keeps the jinn away'. But this belief in the power of a dead holy man went beyond hammams: when Simeon the Stylite's life of perching on a pillar came to an end, the people of Antioch petitioned the Byzantine Emperor Leo for his remains, for their city walls had been destroyed in an earthquake and they wanted the saint to be buried there as the city's defence.[14] Why build battlements when the bones of a saint can protect you? But holy bones have their place in modern Ireland too: the 'blessed remains' of St Thérèse were escorted ashore by the Irish army in 2001; the relics then did a tour of the country in a Thérèsemobile.

We went through to the *jouwani* where I was soon to learn the history of the hammam:

- This was once the biggest hammam in Aleppo, but it was destroyed during the rebellion against the French.
- Like the hammam in Medan in Damascus maybe?
- Perhaps. My father restored this section of the hammam. The old *wastani* is now part of the *barrani*. The original hammam is over 2000 square metres – it stretches right to the end of the street. In fact there is another small hammam attached where people came for a quick wash.

The *jouwani* seemed cross-shaped, with the *beit al-nar* running along the length of the cross, and side-rooms leading off. To the right was where the bather hung his *futa* over a bar and washed privately. Opposite was the room for the *mukeyyis*. But what interested me most was a small area of *muqarnas* in an alcove, the honeycombed decorative style favoured by Mamluks for their mosque doorways, above what seemed to be a tiled bench and a cracked, grey marble font.

- This, said the *mi'allim*, this is the sheikh's burial place.

Indeed it was a strange final resting place for someone so devout – not to have a tomb in sanctified ground, but in a room where the dead would have been surrounded by playful Aleppan youth throwing dishes of cold water at each other. I thought I caught one of the men mumbling a prayer as we stood before the honeycombed shrine:

- Ahmed, are you standing there asking for protection from the *jinn*?

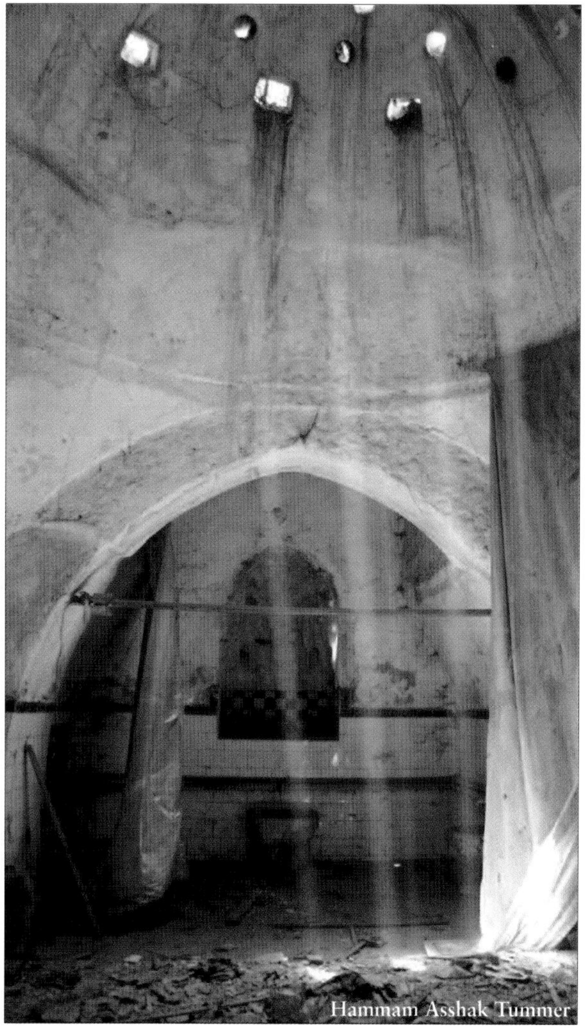
Hammam Asshak Tummer

- No, I'm saying a prayer.
- Asking the holy man to intermediate for you, to be your *wasta*, your mediator with Allah?

They laughed, for everyone could relate to the Arabic word for intermediary; indeed, who could live in Syria without one?

Back in the *barrani* we sat around the fountain, drinking coffee, talking about life with a capital L.

- I don't know what it is you want to achieve, but for us... What matters to us is to have children, bring them up... work, eat and sleep.

I nodded over at Hussein. I knew the proverb about the Aleppan interest in food, but an orientation towards the stomach was only half of the proverb:

- But there's something you've forgotten! There's another thing dear to Aleppan hearts!

We moved away from innuendo on to politics, but here Aleppans were about to preach to the converted:

- Don't get us wrong. We love the USA and France and Germany. But there is one thing...
- You don't have to mention it. I know what it is. And it is our support for that neighbour of yours that is the source of the problems in the region.

We moved on to the arts. I challenged them:

- Give us a few lines of an Aleppan poet!

There was silence.

- A few words then!

Amused silence. A girl (I assume she was the owner's daughter) was sent off to get her school books and some of Hamdani's poetry was then recited. I was given the background:

- He wrote his poetry in prison while his cousin ruled Aleppo and failed to negotiate his release.

Ahmed recited the poetry in a suitably poetic voice – it was as if he had moved to another language, such is the difference between the colloquial and the classical. The poetry was Greek to me:

- I couldn't understand a word. I learnt my Arabic in the fruit and vegetable market of Khartoum. What about you, Hussein?
- I could hardly understand a word either. I can't even write my name.

We left poetry to return to hammaming issues. The *mi'allim* explained:

- What you see around you is all new – the *jouwani* was rebuilt only fifty years ago.
- But isn't it strange – to rebuild a hammam just fifty years ago, and then close it, say, thirty years later?
- It's a matter of economics. Those hammams in the *suq* have customers who have money. But this is a working-class area, and also so many people have moved out. And then there's the price... If a working man earns 300 Syrian pounds for a day's work, is he going to spend 200 to have a wash?

Soon it was time to go. My guide was Hussein, and my transport was his motor – a noisy, polluting three-wheeled vehicle that took vegetables to the market and gas canisters to homes. As Hussein negotiated the narrow cobbled lanes on the way to his home (a courtyard where he shook down oranges from the trees for the guest; a roof top where racing pigeons pranced) I felt that I was living like a king, going from hammam to hammam in the warm winter sunshine, far from the world where I now worked, where knowledge was merely a product to be marketed, students were primarily customers, and education was oriented towards performance management and customer care.

At least the hammams of Syria had so far escaped the effects of McDonaldisation.

The Sultan's Hammam

Under the citadel I had found the Sultan's Hammam decidedly closed, with a wealth of vegetation growing among the stones. But down the laneways I came across the offices of a restoration project for the old city.

One of the restorers told me he had gone against his parents' wishes and had become an artist. He was a sculptor whose workshop had once been in the hammam I had visited the previous day.

- The women used to come to pray before the tomb of the sheikh buried in the hammam. But I would be busy in

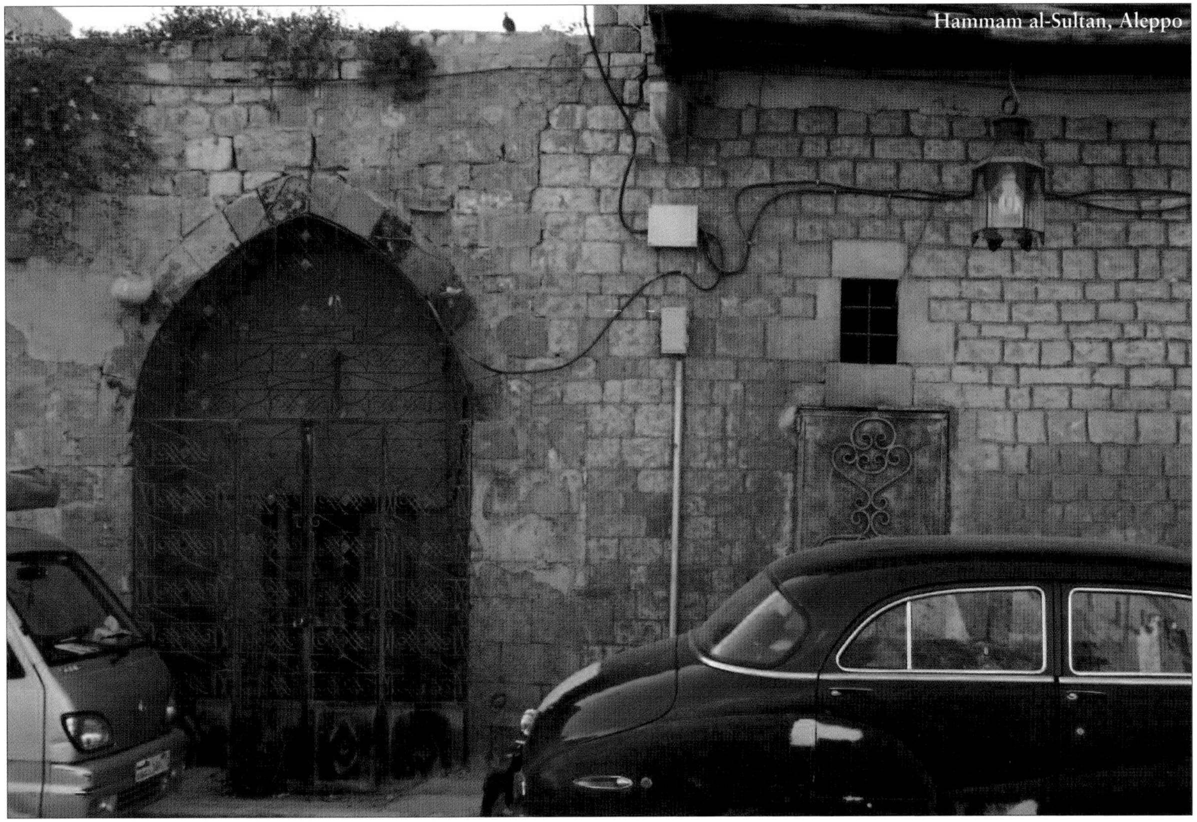

my workshop, for it was the *jouwani* that I used. I would take the candles and light them for them – which was good for me, because every so often there would be power cuts.

- Devotions at the tomb of the saint! There's a tomb in Saruja in Damascus where they fasten locks to the iron grid over the tomb's windows, you know.
- Yes, that's like the mosque here. People pin their locks when they make the request, and when it's been granted come back to remove the lock. But often they have lost the key, so that creates problems for the caretaker!

I asked about his time working in the hammam.

- I had some problems you know. I like my glass of arak, and I would be accused of drinking from the smell of my breath. But I would deny it: 'This hammam is haunted with *jinn*!'

We laughed. This was a man generous with his time, and I would love a glass of arak with him some day.

- And the story of the haunting is like this. The owner at that time, say in the twenties, was a rich man and a collaborator with the French. So the people put it around that the hammam was haunted to ruin his custom. And in the end they attacked the hammam.
- So it wasn't bombed by the French?
- No, it was damaged when the people rebelled.
- And then the father of the current owner bought the hammam? It must have been going for a song!

Here I had a different version of the hammam's history. My host laughed as he remembered his former workplace:

- You know there is another little hammam, around the corner from the main door, where people would go for a quick wash before the dawn prayers. The old men would like to be seen going there – it would be for the ritual cleansing after intercourse – for they would announce to the world: 'I'm still young – I can still do it!'

I was taken for a tour of the palace with its three courtyards. The two main courtyards had been immaculately restored, but the third courtyard was still in a state of beautiful neglect. I stood staring up at the embellished wood of the great arch:

- I can't believe this was the courtyard for the servants!
- Let's just say that the prince would have had more than one wife. You have that other small courtyard with the fountain by the ovens that servants would have used.

- But a fountain for servants?
- Yes, but a fountain in those days was not just something ornamental, you know.

We passed back through to the courtyard and up to the first floor.

- This was the door to the hammam.
- Was it a connecting tunnel then?
- No, on the other side is the hammam. And directly opposite here, is, what I believe, was the prince's bedroom.
- So he might have had private access to the hammam! Interesting!

Finally I was taken to see the work in progress – the restoration of the formal meeting room of the palace. It was all dark wood and embellished silver and gold, except the ceiling, which was bare white paint. The original ceiling, however, was no longer with us. Perhaps it was just as well, given the years my artisan host had spent restoring the walls.

From his words I would now see the hammam of the previous day in a different light; the truth – if that is the right word – seemed to come in many layers, like an onion.

Reading the Hammam

I stood before the unattainable: Hammam al Bai'ada. The hammam dates back to Mamluk times, having been built according to Abdulla Hadjar[15] by Ibn al-Nafis, and is in the heart of a quarter that stretches from below the

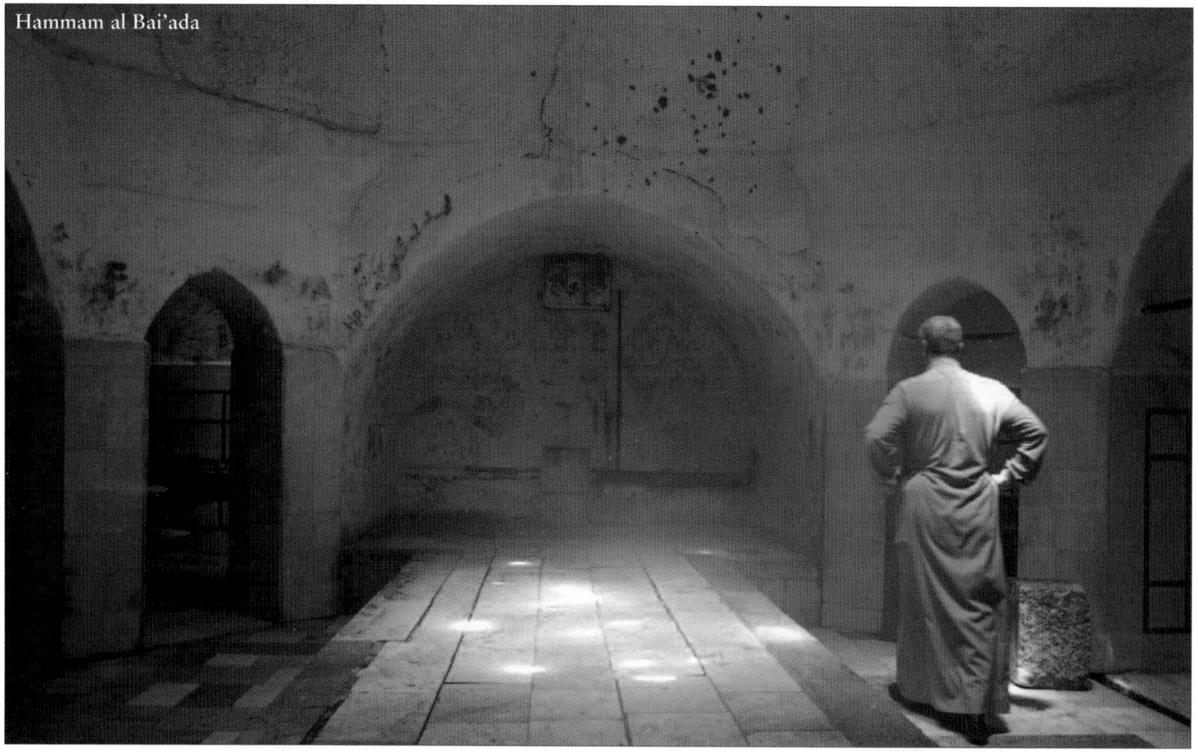
Hammam al Bai'ada

citadel to the Bab al Hadid – the Iron Gate, named after the forges beneath the gate. Centuries after the building of the city gate, blacksmiths still work their bellows within.

I stood before the unmistakable turret of a hammam and took in the warped corrugated iron of the shop fronts and the blocked-up main door. However, as I read the signs of apparent dereliction, a woman dressed in black exited from a minor door; the hammam was still in use. Standing in the street with tomato vendors and a water-melon seller with his horse and cart, I took the requisite photo then spoke to a man idling near by:

- And what do you do?
- I'm the *mi'allim*. The hammam's about a thousand years old.

His wife managed the hammam, for it was only for women. There was no way I could enter that day, but like drink, one hammam often leads to another, and the *mi'allim* kindly pointed me down the road, instructing me to turn left after the carpenters. (I did get back to the hammam another day for a little tour; sadly, it too was a hammam that had most definitely seen better days.)

Finding Hammam Balaban was not quite as simple as it might at first have appeared,

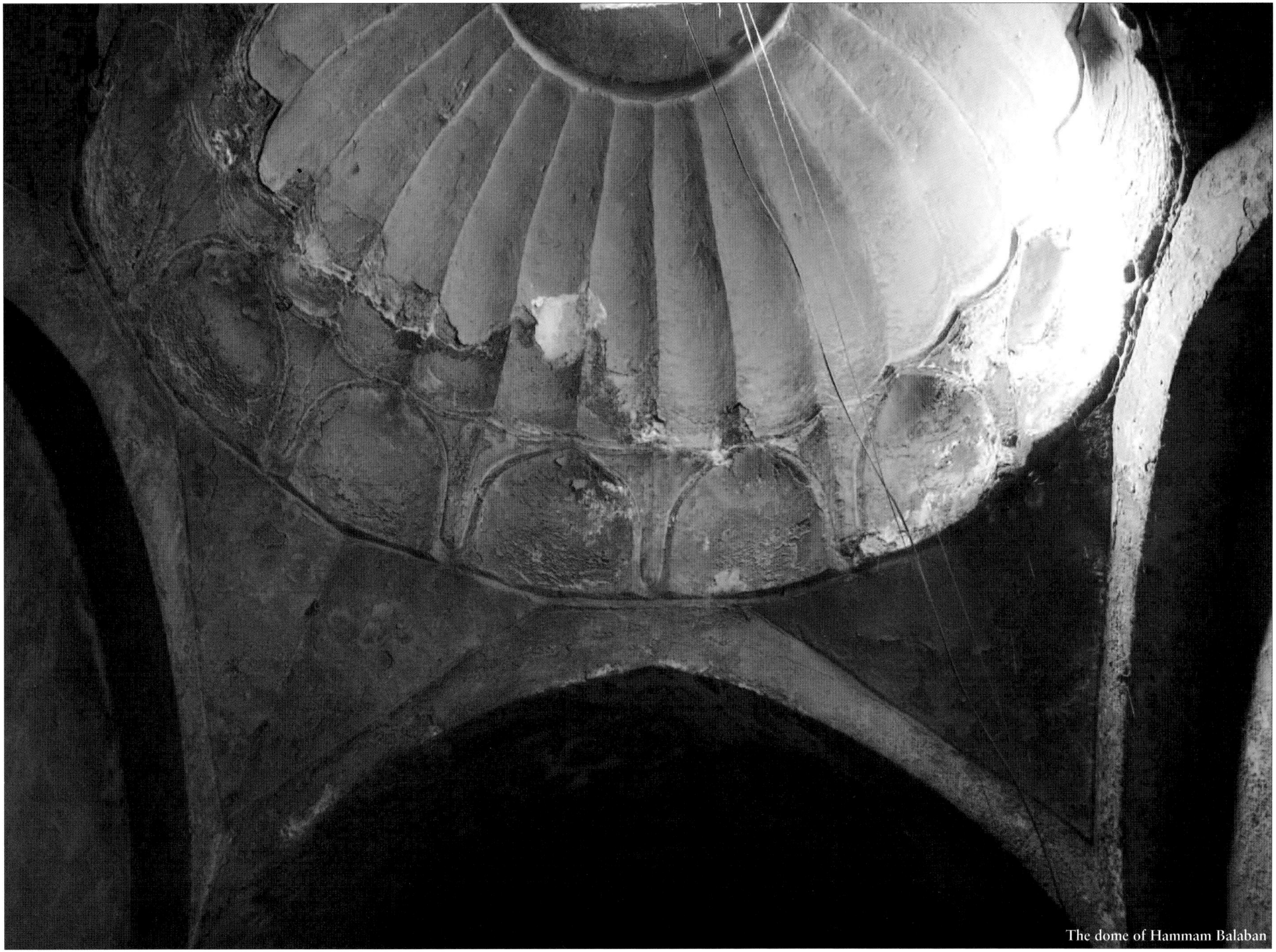

The dome of Hammam Balaban

for I greeted someone on the way and was invited for coffee in a yard with citrus trees and jasmine and an overspreading vine. Eventually, I turned down an alley, and found myself in an area that had the feel of a thriving neighbourhood. Before me was a doorway and steps down into Hammam Balaban, now sweet with the smells of a carpenters' workshop.

I had my guide, a young lad not much more than twelve years old and impeccably polite, who pointed to the dome above. The dome, he told me, was a sun clock. I searched the dome for the metal rod that would cast its shadow and point the time, like the sundial still intact on the wall, unseen by the passing crowds, opposite the mosque of Ibn 'Arabi in Damascus. (Some mosques also have their dials, like a mosque in Tripoli where someone pointed out to me the sundial on a wall, his companion too noticing the dial for the first time: 'I've been praying here for twenty years, but I've never noticed that clock!')

Here, however, there was no sign of the rod and Arabic numerals, only the great dome of the hammam unfolding above us like the bell of a flower. The boy explained:

- You can see the inner ring is divided into 24 – these are the 24 hours.
- And the next is made up of 12 *antarrah* – these are the 12 months of the year.
- And here, here we have the four arches representing the four seasons.

The *mi'allim* of the workshop had now appeared, and as he sent his son off to get tea he asked me to write my name. I did so. He then asked for my ID card. It all felt rather too Syrian for me – and I objected; I was just a teacher of English with an interest in hammams. The *mi'allim* protested; from the letters of my name he then went on to do some character analysis that wouldn't have been out of place in some new age fair. I was merely dealing with eccentricity.

But back to the hammam – if I got it right, 1329 was written above the door, but this was likely to be the date of re-construction. And I think someone said something about the hammam once having belonged to a prime minister, but I could not vouch for that... But what I do remember about Hammam Balaban is that just as some might read a holy book to find some esoteric meaning hidden from others, so those working in the hammam read the building in which they worked, and saw in the dome of Hammam Balaban a recorder of time.

Hammam Bizdar

One Friday afternoon I had taken a photo of Abdul and his brother packing wool into cushions above one of the cobbled paths inside Bab Antakia. A few days later as I was walking through the near-deserted *suq*, Abdul called me in for tea. I had half-heartedly been looking for Hammam Bizdar, for in Hammam Balaban someone had mentioned it. I followed Abdul to a door and climbed up to a raised platform that was furnished with a mattress on the floor.

Below us lay a rather spacious building that had a rather familiar feel, with a ceiling arching into the four-pointed style that is typical of the khans, so I felt that I was sitting in a great cellar. The kettle was put on to boil on a kind of picnic stove, and a couple of *shebab*, brothers from next door, joined us.

I was with the men of the *suq*, and with the rough vibrant speech I remembered from my days in Sudan when I had spent much less time with the respectable middle classes and much more time with local life. When someone mentioned something about learning English, Abdul replied:

- I don't even know Arabic, so how on earth would I know English? I'm illiterate.

I didn't see anything to be ashamed about:

- I've travelled, I said. And I've met people with university degrees who know next to nothing. And I've met people who can't read or write who know a lot.

Abdul sat next to me, shirt off, with a lean, muscled torso. He continued:

- I didn't even do a year at school. And when I was there the teacher would send me out to get bread and the like.

He took a pen and showed me that he could write his name...

The *shebab* told me they were employed in a workshop that made underwear. We chatted about the traditional house, and Abdul told of the buried treasure he claimed to have seen with his own eyes dug up from his neighbours' yard. And then, on the subject of things historical, Abdul casually referred to the building around us:

– This was once a hammam.

The self-styled expert on hammams hadn't recognised that he was sitting in one. I looked down over the edge of our platform; there still remained a small dome through which light had once filtered on to bathers.

– And do you know the name of the hammam?
– Bizdar.

I pulled out my notebook.

– Yesterday someone told me about this hammam. Look, the name's here in Arabic.

(The shopkeeper in front of Hammam Balaban had got someone to write the name for me.)

– Yes, he has written Bizdar Hammam.
– I was looking for the hammam. And now I'm having tea in it!

It was a wonderful cavernous place, with an underground feel. But there was something

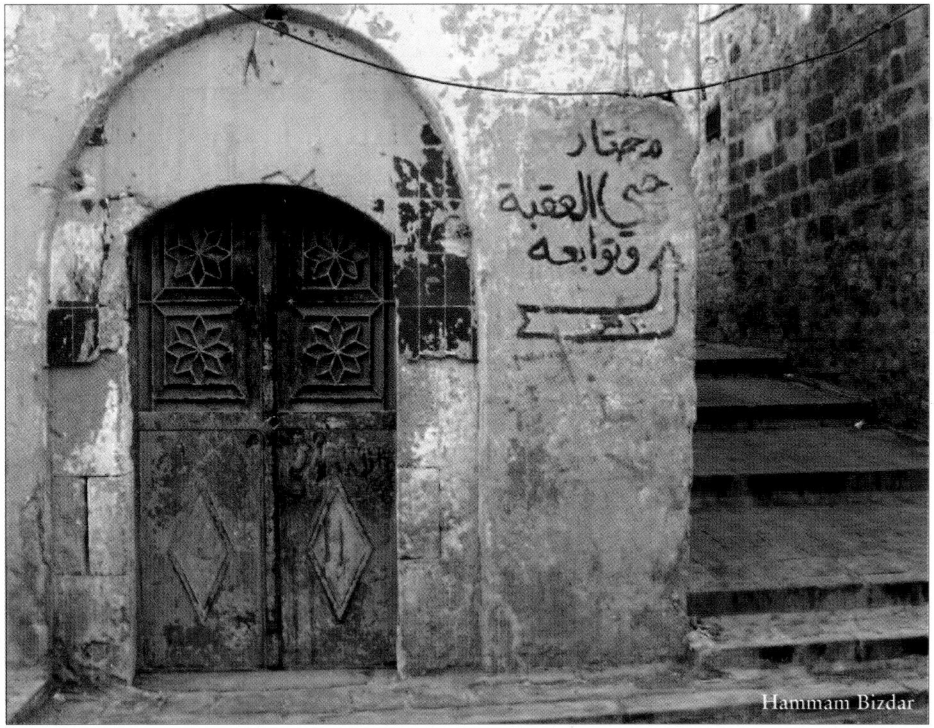

Hammam Bizdar

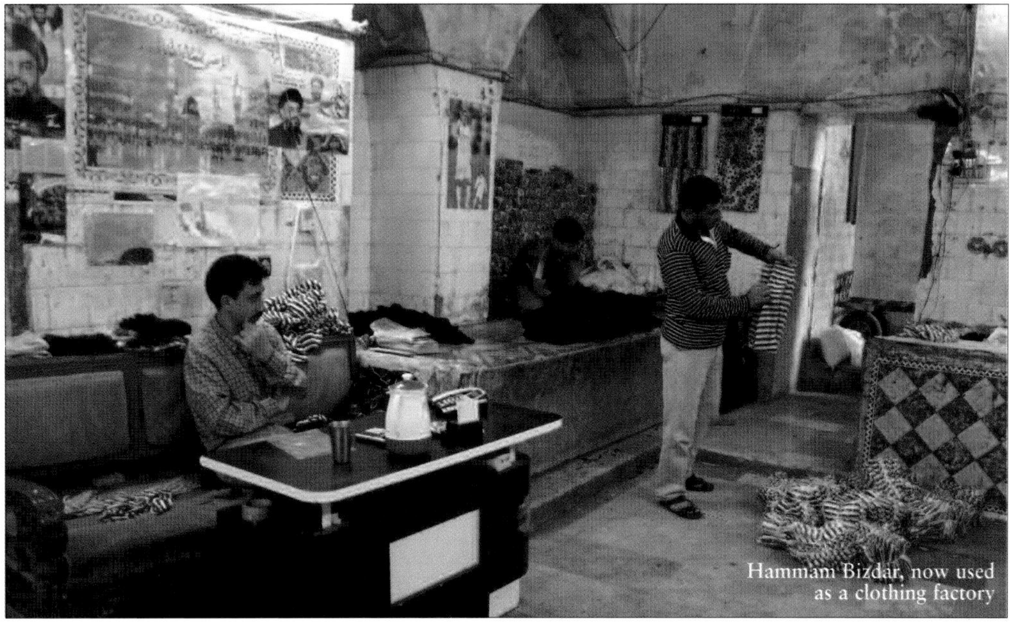
Hammam Bizdar, now used as a clothing factory

not quite right about the hammam: it was as if half was missing.

- It's blocked off with this wall. Their workshop is on the other side.

It looked like the hammam had been out of use for a century – but Abdul's brother actually remembered bathing in it.

Now it was nearly eleven, and I sensed that the *shebab* wanted to go, but we went out into the street, walked up towards the mosque, and entered a door to the other half of the *barrani*. There I found the current function of the hammam: it was the workshop where the lads made underwear. Before I left, the *shebab* dropped another pearl:

- There's another hammam you know in our area.
- Called what?
- Hammam al-Salihiye.

I had been looking only the day before for this very hammam, near Khan al Saboun.

- But it's closed now, isn't it?
- No, by day it's for women; by night it's for men.

I was sceptical. If it was a working hammam surely I would have heard of it! But I walked down the cobbled path toward Bab Antakia with a new address in my pocket.

Hammam Salihiye

My taxi driver had a sense of the area, and stopped to ask a pedestrian where we could find Hammam Salihiye.

- He's a foreigner, explained the Kurdish driver, and he wants the hammam.
- It's closed.

The driver turned to me, and repeated the man's words, as if I couldn't understand, even though we had been chatting away in Arabic throughout the journey.

- It's closed.
- Never mind, I still want to see it.
- But it's closed!

In the street was Abu Hassan, the local teacher. He had a quiet, gentlemanly manner, but unfortunately spoke English. As usual I was unprepared for recording historical detail:

- I'll just get a pen from the grocer's.

Abu Hassan spoke to the grocer for me, as if I couldn't do that myself, and then pointed to the beautiful arch in the wall with a drinking fountain:

- It's a *sebeel.*
- It's Ottoman, I'm sure. I bet you it's the same date as the hammam.

I could well have been wrong in that assertion, but this was the most beautiful street corner

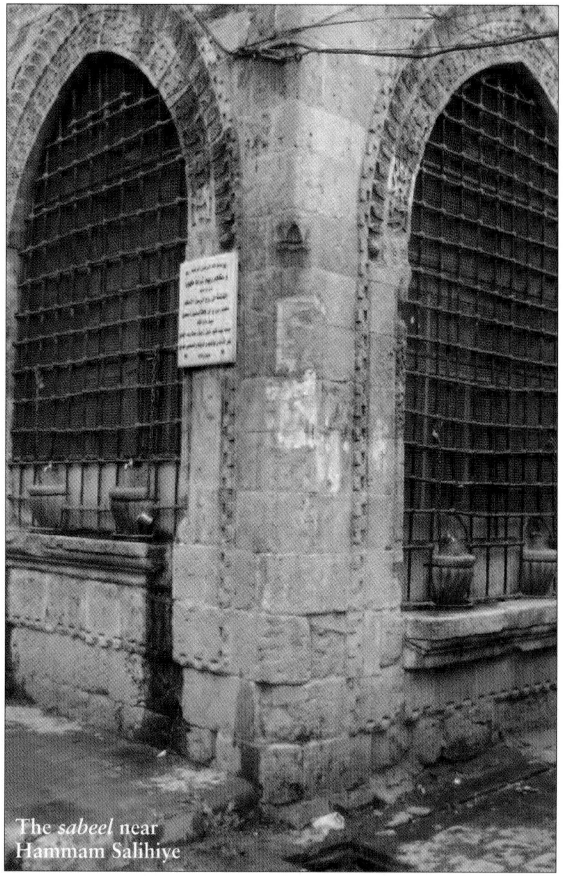
The *sabeel* near Hammam Salihiye

I had seen, with little metal drinking dishes still chained for the thirsty.

We went over to the hammam and tried to decipher the inscription above the door, which seemed to be dated something like 1100 *Hijri*. Abu Hussain explained that we could decipher the inscription later, and took me down the steps into the hammam. I greeted a worker at his machine, for the first part of the building was used for making insoles for shoes, then walked into the hammam proper, which seemed to have been closed for some months.

The whole building seemed a little uninteresting, but the people around me were anything but. The hammam had been in Ahmed's family for generations. He explained:

- The hammam is for women only.
- But I heard it was for men in the evenings!
- Maybe, if there is a group.

I didn't feel that I was missing out on much. Instead of the lovely black and yellow stone that make up the *madrassahs*, here black and mustard blocks had been painted on the wall. The hammam just seemed to me to be maybe a couple of hundred years old. Abu Hussein did some maths:

- If you take the year 1100 and add, say, 623 years, what do we get? 1723!
- So the hammam is around 300 years old.
- And its location?
- Bab al Maqam.

I was talking to people who knew their hammams and their traditions. The city gate was named after the shrine *(maqam)* of some sheikh buried right by the gate. Abu Hussein explained:

- Some might say differently, but Aleppo has eight city gates. We don't count Bab al Ahmer because it was within the actual city. Why do we say eight? Because Aleppo is an Islamic city, and the Islamic city is modelled on the eight gates of our paradise. And every gate in Aleppo has its hammam.

I wasn't convinced by this last assertion, (and even paradise seemed now a little less desirable if it were walled in, like the walled garden of some Anglo-Irish great house) but we went through the ritual, naming the hammams, matching them to the city gate near where they had been built.

- And every hammam has its sheikh or *wali*?

A worker interrupted:

- In Hammam Sahat al Bizeh we have the tomb of Sheikh Sakkah. And he was buried in the hammam by Sultan Ibrahim.

Sultan Ibrahim? I was in some kind of web. I had been to the mosque and hammam of the saint in Jiblai below Lattakia, and now in Aleppo they were claiming he had buried their local saint.

According to the inscription above the door this hammam was about 300 years old. But Ahmed claimed it went back some 700 years, and the hammam had extended far beyond the current building: the problem was the inheritance. Ahmed's family were originally from the Hejaz. But sons argued and the inheritance was divided up and the original building had been divided too. (This was a familiar story: the working life of hammams sometimes ends with the sons squabbling over the inheritance, like in medieval times when the state went to ruin as princes fought over the kingdom.) Part of the family had continued to work in the smaller hammam and had taken the name Hammamji, the Turkish suffix indicating a person's occupation. He made the 'new' hammam to be 291 years old but claimed the original was maybe 750 years old.

It was like that when I had stood at the decaying Hammam al Gadi in Aleppo – the Hammam of the Judge (Damascus had once had a hammam of the same name) up through the iron-roofed *ṣuq* at Bab al Nasser. There was a juice shop by the entrance and a man selling a few water melons, the hammam itself almost hidden from view.

Across the way a shopkeeper of the old school sat back on his counter and surveyed the world. I asked him the age of the hammam – a hammam so neglected I was probably the only one to notice it that day.

- Hammam al Gadi? Eight hundred years.

And then with pride:

- That was when they renewed it.

In fact, the lintel declares that the hammam was restored in 1508,[16] but who knows how

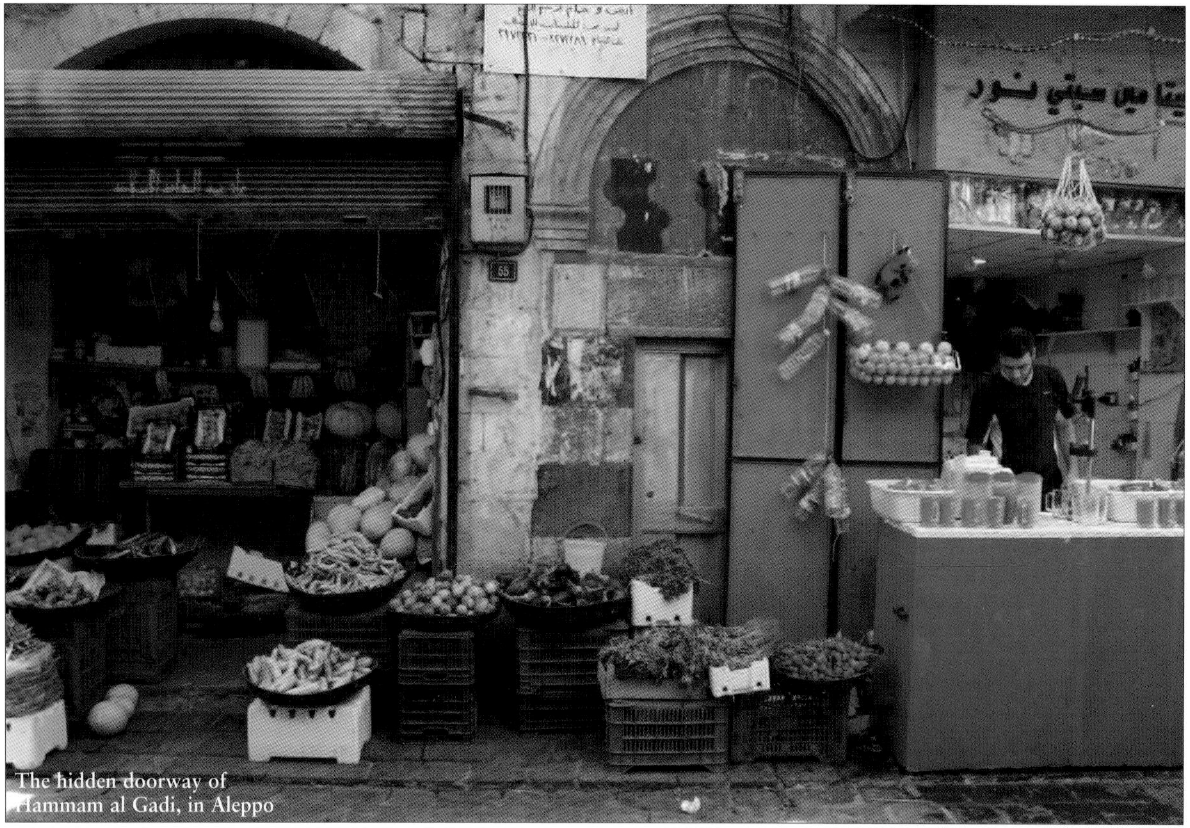

The hidden doorway of Hammam al Gadi, in Aleppo

many 'renewals' had taken place before that date. And what would be the future of the hammam? Another time I passed I found a notice on the door with a telephone number, saying that the hammam was for sale. But given the current state of 'Turkish baths' in Syria, who would invest in hammaming?

Aleppo Suq on the Last Day of Ramadan

Once I happened to be in Aleppo during Ramadan, and right at the end of the holy month I decided to savour the atmosphere of the *suq*.

The citadel was honeyed stone in the late afternoon light of winter, but already the crowds were leaving the *suq* below. At the entrance sat a woman dressed entirely in black: black gloves, black veil, black socks and black shoes – even the shopping bags at her feet were a matching black plastic. Only the veil was folded back in a triangle to reveal a pasty face. If her husband was trying to stop a taxi he would have some trouble, for the traffic is hectic in the last hour before the *iftar* when people break their fast.

Below me was the labyrinth; I stepped down into the mouth of the *suq*, avoided an emerging motorbike and was immediately offered a fox skin. Of more interest to me were the nifty waistcoats of pure sheepskin:

> – Monsieur, monsieur, for you only one thousand five hundred!

Now I passed the tomb of a martyr, with its candles and coins placed on the other side of the grill. The great ball suspended from the roof at Bab Antakia, much bigger than a cannon ball, is said to have been this martyr's favourite missile for throwing at the enemies of Islam. Next there was a glimpse of a courtyard through a half open door lined with aspidistras; a man left and the door locked behind him. Already there was the sound of shop shutters being pulled down. A man sat in his shop reading the Qur'an, mouthing the words as people do here when they read. A cyclist and a man walking collided and they passed it off good humouredly.

Then I passed the apothecary's with his sacks of henna, and tortoise and starfish and curved python – the hallmarks of his trade.

And then it was sacks of pistachio and wine-coloured hibiscus leaves and mountains of olives in their green and black gloss and basins of salty local cheese and Saudi dates. Kebabs were lined up for the oven, as butchers leaned by sheep carcasses alongside huge lumps of fat on hooks, posing among fat and blood.

I stopped at a stall selling headscarves and veils. One of the *shebab* knew my face and called, 'How's the *craic*?' Aleppo's polyglot traditions were clearly alive and well. Now an old, grey-bearded man, his head encircled with a green band, looking for a coin or two, announced to the crowds that it was the last day of Ramadan. Next I was with the brothers who sell the silk scarves and local textiles, with the posters of footballers and Oscar Wilde on their shop ceiling. 'Cheap and nasty!' they would call, advertising their own wares. 'Cheap and nasty!' They invited me to break the fast with them. 'Surely you don't need to be back at the hotel, unless you have a blind date or something!'

Now I was passing through the perfumed air of Suq al Attaria and the mosque doors were open; beneath the chandeliers a row of men were already lined up for prayer. But near the mosque there was a man sitting above his sacks of henna, and tins of paprika and hibiscus and cinnamon, reading Jane Austen.

A blind man shouted out 'Marlboro' as I walked past kids with their hands over the

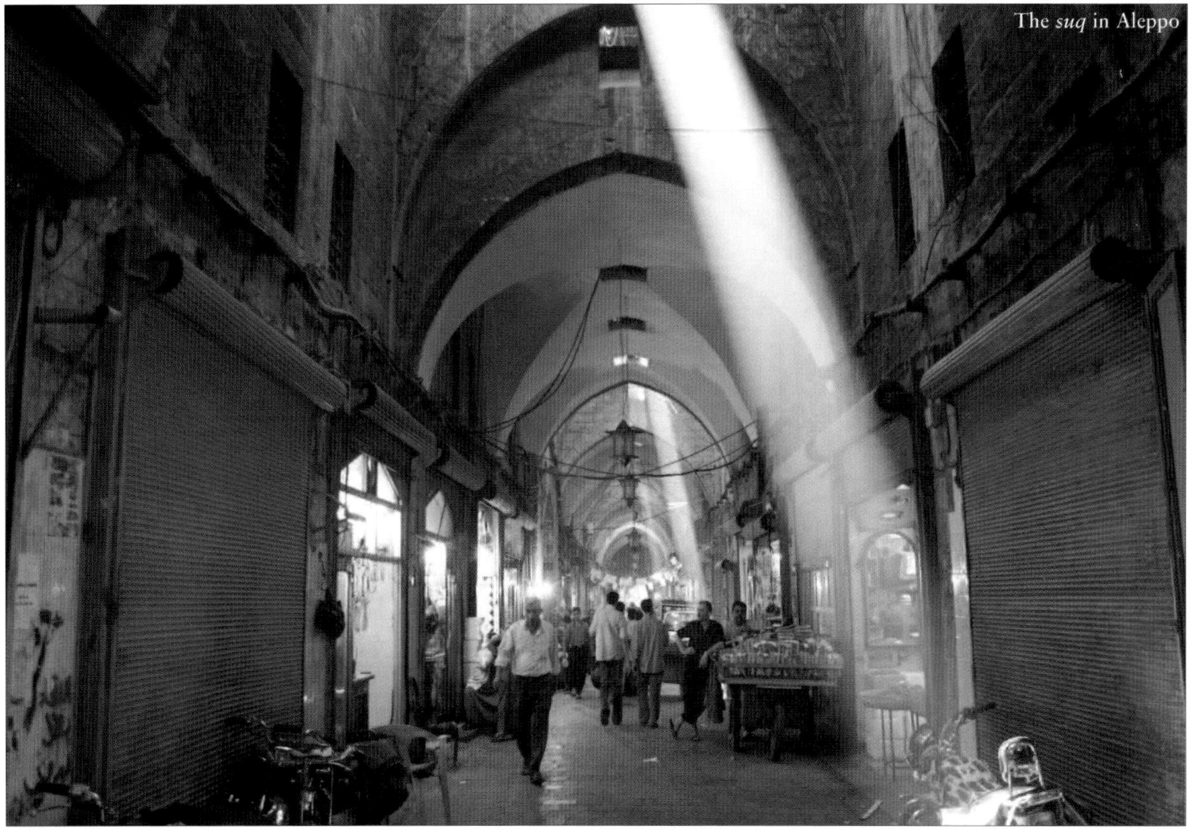
The *suq* in Aleppo

flames of a brazier. Here were the porters and their donkeys and a crowd gathering to buy a fried egg sandwich to break the fast. And now the mosques were starting up, but a man was still selling belts for fifty Syrian pounds, only fifty Syrian pounds.

With the familiar dull thud of a cannon, the first cigarettes were lit. A boy walked past with a great dish of tomatoes and minced meat on his head, while a grapefruit seller pushed his trolley uphill. And now *Mohammed al rassoul Allah* sounded through the great caverns of the half-empty *suq*. Still the biscuit makers were breaking eggs into a tray, and there was the whiff of ground coffee as a woman sensuously ran her hands through falling coffee beans. The dull rotation of salted seeds sounded from a tumble-drier, for vast quantities would be consumed over the Eid festival.

A butcher and a woman were bargaining:

– Liver, kidneys, ninety a kilo. How many kilos do you want?
– I don't want any!
– Okay, for you, seventy-five a kilo.
– I'll have two kilos then.

A glass of tea was offered to me, and then I was out in the winter darkness at Bab Antakia. About a mile down the road was Calasseh, and it was here, as Ramadan came to an end, that I would see how one of the year's milestones, the end of the month of fasting, would be marked in an Aleppan hammam.

Hammaming at the End of Ramadan

Calasseh is a traditional neighbourhood with three hammams: one is now used for wedding gatherings, one was looking fairly derelict when I first went in search of it (but at least it was still standing at that time), and the third, Hammam al-Atiqa, survives. It was here that I planned to bathe on the last day of Ramadan, when in the evening the hammams fill with those preparing for the Eid celebrations. Such is hammam life: the milestones of life have been marked by a visit to the hammam.

The people of the neighbourhood seemed somewhat surprised to see a foreigner:

– It's Bab Qinnesrin that you want!
– No, I've been there already.
– But that's where tourists always go. There's nothing in this area.
– I wouldn't count that mosque as nothing, but I'm interested in the hammam you have here.
– This road up to the left will take you directly to Bab Qinnesrin.

To my disappointment, instead of the expected end-of-Ramadan rush, I found Hammam al-Atiqa empty. There were only the attendants and the owner, corpulent and middle-aged, seated at a plastic garden table in the foyer. *Atiqa* means ancient, but even such a place could not escape the ubiquitous plastic chairs.

The *mi'allim* was a man with a mission. He had been to Germany as a young man but, in terms of civilisation, had not been particularly impressed. Then, back in Damascus, he had visited Hammam Nur al-Din, which had been magnificently restored. He decided that he would restore his own local hammam – not as a commercial enterprise but as a labour of love.

And so he had built a shrine to kitsch: the central dome had been painted to look like red brick, as in a 1960s fireplace perhaps, and now in celebration of Ramadan it hosted a great ball of a Christmas decoration suspended from the dome. In the *wastani*, Aleppo citadel was reproduced in pebbles on the wall.

I'm not sure what the original builder of the hammam – a woman – would have made of the renovations. Apparently the hammam had been built as a *wakf* to finance the upkeep of the mosque she had built. The *mi'allim* explained:

– For you know the building of a mosque, if someone has enough money…

At this point I interrupted, for I knew the story:

– …is a kind of ticket to paradise. But what about those who build not mosques but hammams, where do they go?

And he laughed at that, and we talked about other hammams in Syria. I compared Hammam al-Atiqa to Hammam Sultan Ibrahim near the coast – for it too was a kind of foundation to pay for the upkeep of the mosque. The owner of course knew of the hammam, but told me it was closed. I was the bearer of good news, since I myself had bathed in it. At this the *mi'allim* expressed delight, like a botanist who has found a specimen of a plant thought to be extinct.

The attendant brought us tea but was chastised for his lack of etiquette, for the *mi'allim* knew the ways of Europeans:

– *Chawi*! You put the sugar in the pot! Why didn't you bring the sugar separately, so each could add the sugar according to his taste!

The first customers, teenagers, were now arriving, and the owner advised me to see the hammam before it filled up with the crowds getting ready for the *Eid*.

– But I want to bathe myself!

In the steam room one teenager was massaging the fleshy mass of another. Elsewhere in the *jouwani* a group of farmers were seated around a font. They had that robust, healthy look of country living; a look not untypical of Aleppo, for the people have a certain country earthiness.

– Where are you from?
– Ireland.
– Ireland and Syria are one country.

Syria and Egypt had been united in the year of my birth; I suppose his uniting Ireland and Syria was just a way of saying welcome.

An older man broke into a local song in the folk or *baladi* style, and indeed he had the voice for it. It was a religious song, something not inappropriate for the end of Ramadan, but then there was that typically Arab lack of compartmentalization when I asked for a song by the Arab world's most revered singer, Oum Kulthoum, and he launched into a song of loss or unrequited love.

I had hammamed enough. Outside, the *barrani* was packed. Fathers had arrived with their numerous kids and the *shebab* were undressing leisurely. There was hardly an empty peg for bathers to hang their clothes and at the desk a bunch of youths were demanding a group discount. The hammam buzzed. And so I had a glimpse of how it must have been once: the hammam and the mosque as the meeting places for the community, or at least for the males of the neighbourhood. I said my goodbyes, went to pay and was met with the traditional Arab courtesy towards the stranger:

– No charge for you; this one is on the house.

It was past midnight – Ramadan, it seemed, had finished and tomorrow would be the *Eid* festival. As I walked back to the hotel the traffic was tooting its way along like some frantic orchestra that had lost its conductor, but the shoppers were thinning out. At the roadside, beneath the glare of their light bulbs, the street sellers were dismantling their stalls, and selling the last of their stock. Someone selling a rainbow of loose sweets was calling into a microphone:

– Just 50 notes, 50 notes, *ya derwish*. Pick and mix as you like, just 50 notes!

The cardboard boxes were being torn up to burn in a brazier, for the night was cold, with the flames rising up as if to set the plastic sheeting of the stall alight. Still the vendor tried to rid himself of the last sweets:

– Come on *shebab*! Come on *ya derwish*! Just 50 notes. Just 50 notes!

Tomorrow, I thought, would be the first day of the *Eid*, and silence.

The Gentlemen's Hammam

In the old khan next to Hammam Granada it was the usual afternoon scene: a couple of men were taking it easy around a desk, with one half-asleep on the sofa. Given that I had just wandered in unannounced to their workplace, they couldn't have been more affable. That's how it is in Aleppo; you could be standing contemplating some monument only to be pulled into the place next door for breakfast.

Hammam Granada once had the same name as the neighbouring khan – Aireesh – and this was the very name of the man I was speaking to. As usual we couldn't talk alone; two others arrived on some kind of business. One of them was slightly dark in his looks with that lovely *asmer* complexion – somewhere between darkly tanned and reddish-brown – for which there is no word in English.

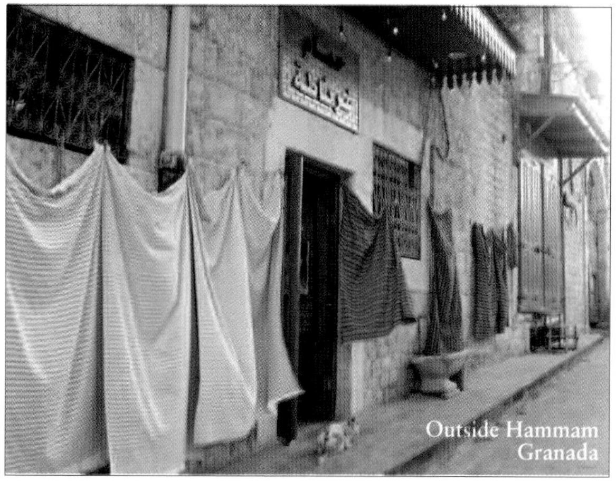

Outside Hammam Granada

- If you are interested in hammams, he has a hammam.
- You're joking!
- Hammam Saddat.

Some time ago I had gone in search of Hammam Saddat, wandering with Yahia through wintry alleys.

- But it's closed, isn't it?
- We're going to open it again in a month or so.

As we left, the keeper of the khan warned my companions to be careful what they said, for their words might be published.

- And are you from Aleppo? I asked. You look like you're from the south of Yemen or the like.
- I'm from Idleb.

It would be an interesting hammam, for the men of Idleb are the butt of many a joke...

We stopped in front of an unremarkable building with an equally ordinary door. The hammam didn't seem to have the traditional layout: the *wastani* was more like an annexe; the *jouwani* a series of cubicles around a square, with a series of sewing machines filling the space. The *barrani* didn't have a fountain but had no shortage of junk.

- Now was this originally built as a hammam?
- No, this was the courtyard of a house.
- And when was it turned into a hammam?
- About forty years ago.
- So this is maybe the last hammam to be built in Syria?

The only other contender for the last hammam to be built in Syria might be the ruined dome of a hammam on Irwad Island, a private enterprise built of sandstone on black rock below the fishermen's houses, just within the Phoenician wall that once surrounded the island. It was a fitting site for an ancient tradition: Irwad gets a mention in Genesis.

I was still curious about the name Aireesh; it sounded none too Syrian to me.

- And are your family originally from Turkey?
- We have been here at least five generations. Our name might be Spanish.

In his companion's hands was a parcel of invitations.

- Come to the wedding. My wedding! Not this Friday but the next. It will be of interest to you.

For Aleppans, even an invitation to a wedding could be spontaneous – unlike our own affairs where every place is counted and costed. I nodded over to the hammam owner.

- We'll take him to the hammam first!
- Ah, that's the kind of thing we did in the past...

I didn't go to the wedding but I have kept the invitation with a heart between his name and hers. And I did return to the hammam to find an extensive plunge pool and discreet spotlights that highlighted the original stone. Where were the obligatory fluorescent lights? Surely the guardians of hammams weren't beginning to realise the beauty of daylight on stone, or a carefully placed bulb highlighting a niche in a wall?

That stag-night tradition might have been dying, but this was a hammam undergoing renewal. Could it be that the ambience of hammams was changing?

A Winter Evening in the Coppersmiths' Hammam

I had heard that there had once been two hammams on the site of Hammam al-Nahasin, a hammam formerly known as Hammam Al Sitt. Many a time I had lain on the *beit al-nar* under the great dome of the *jouwani,* for it is one of the best in Syria. I had watched workmen knock the tiles off the vast *barrani* of the hammam, and replace it all with pine, so that as you go down the steps that take you down from the *suq* it seems like you are entering the biggest sauna in the world.

Before the end of summer I had been taken for a tour of the remains of the other hammam; on the roof penned-up turkeys clucked and towels were hung out to dry. I peered down through the remains of a dome to desolate ruins where Aleppans had once bathed. Walking down into the hammam was a little like walking into catacombs; Aleppans say that tunnels from the catacombs beneath those old houses in Jedeidah link up to the citadel.

Now Ibrahim, the *mi'allim*, was telling me a few months later that the work was complete.

– Would you like to see the new pool?

I was led through a long passage, past alcove after alcove, to the newly built pool, which would certainly contribute to the commercial success of the hammam. There were none of the usual tacky kitchen tiles; the hammam had been decorated in rather stylish Pompeii red. What Ibrahim didn't tell me though was that during excavations treasure had been discovered, contributing to the popular belief that fortunes lie beneath the floors of all ancient monuments in Syria.

Back in the original hammam I sat back with Kurdish brothers who lay indolently on the floor. One had just had his back 'cupped' – a kind of blood-letting endorsed by the Prophet, where by using a heated cup and a superficial piercing of the skin, 'bad blood' is removed by a kind of suction. I have seen the cupping (*hijama*) actually taking place in the *barrani* of another Aleppan hammam, with the tea-glasses used to draw out 'bad blood' from the back. (On this occasion I decided to forgo my usual après-hammam cup of tea.)

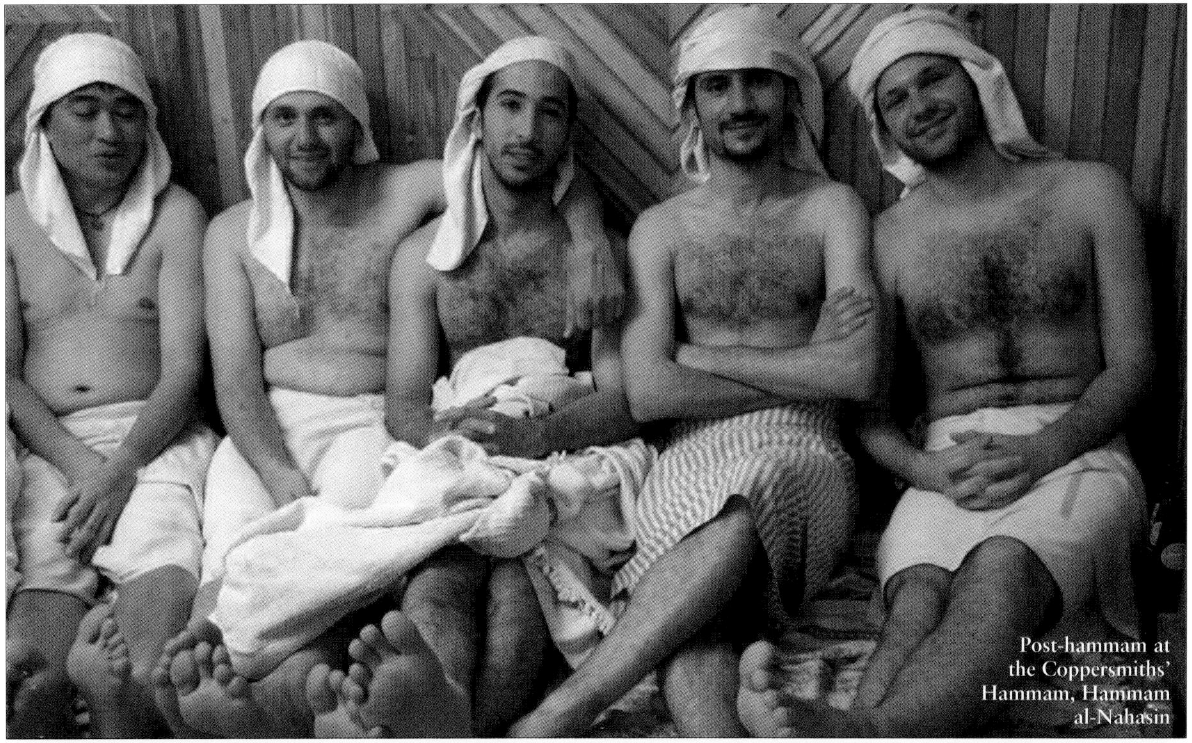

Post-hammam at the Coppersmiths' Hammam, Hammam al-Nahasin

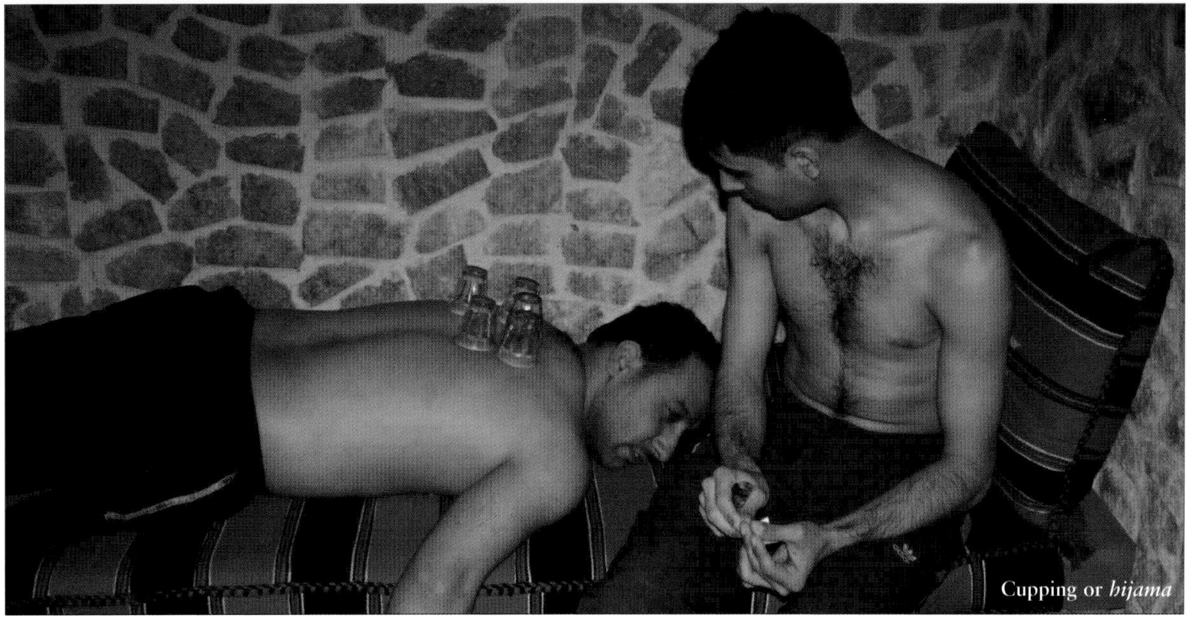

Cupping or *hijama*

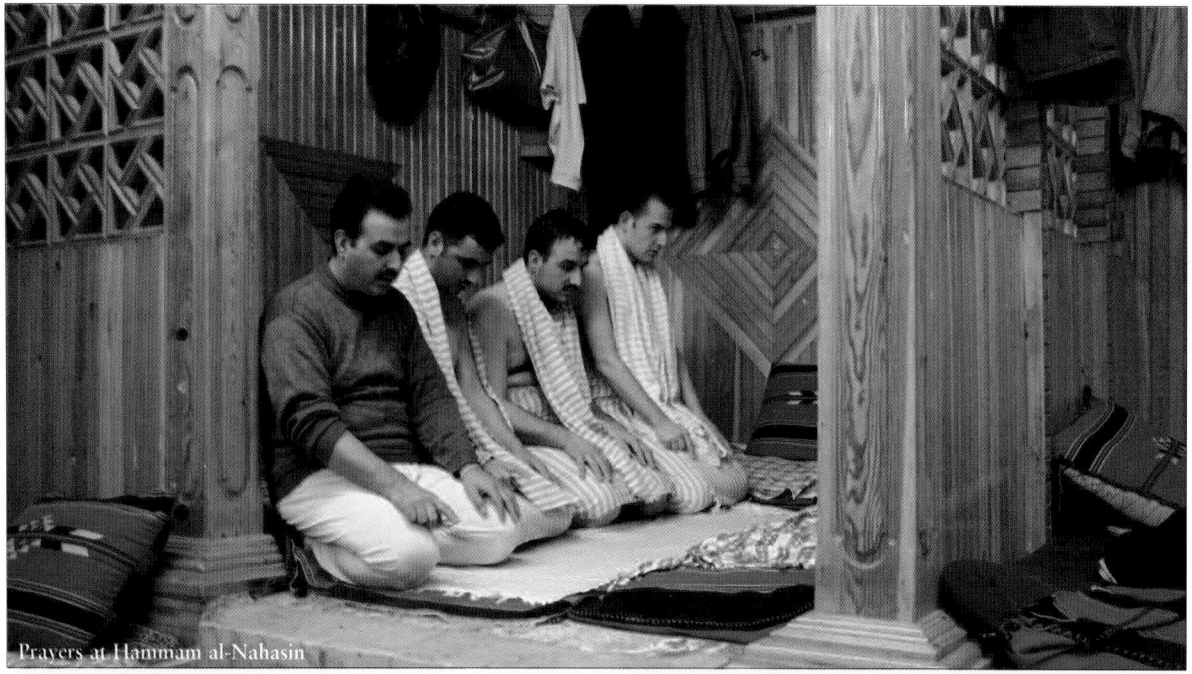
Prayers at Hammam al-Nahasin

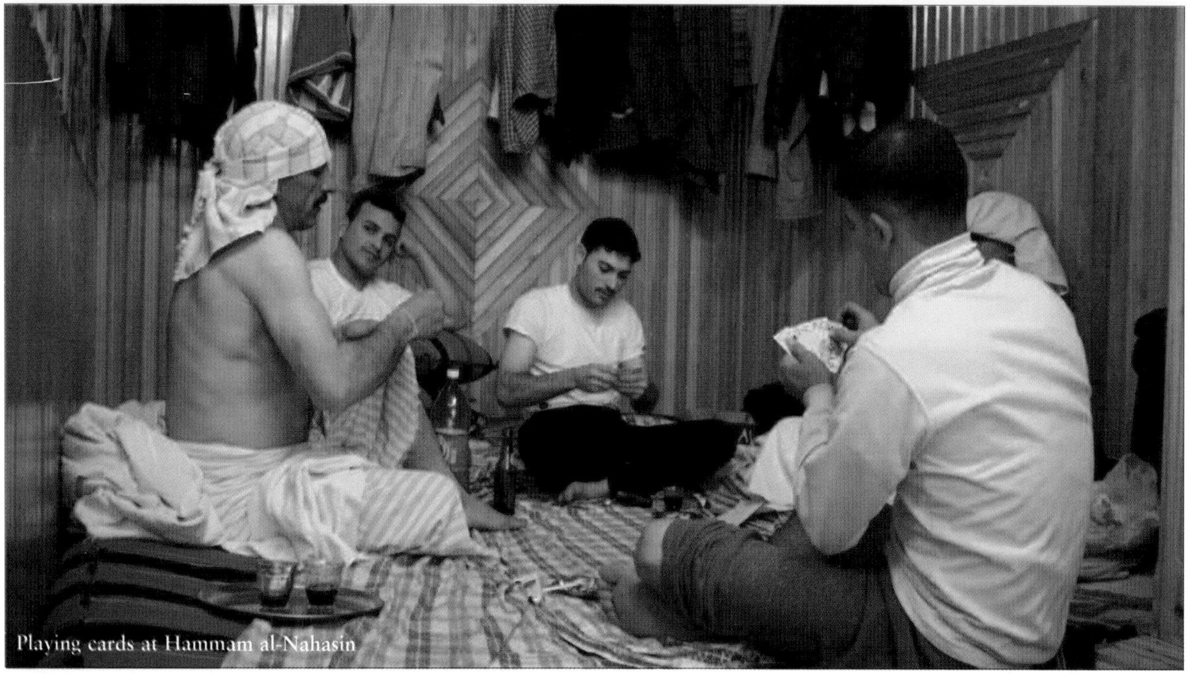
Playing cards at Hammam al-Nahasin

In Damascus there might be half a dozen customers in the hammam of an evening. Here there was the buzz of conversation and Arabic music was sounding out from satellite TV. This was the kind of hammam where as one group did their prayers, another would be hanging about playing cards in the snug where bathers get dressed. The horseplay was already beginning among the *shebab* before they had even entered the hammam proper, and so it would continue into the early hours of the morning.

As the lads came down the steps I thought not so much of a dying tradition but of crowds coming through the turnstile for a football match; there was an air of anticipation. Just before midnight in at least one Aleppan hammam a thousand-year-old tradition was very much alive and well.

Hammam Bizeh

I would go sometimes in the early evening to catch the last light on the citadel when the city streets were already in shade. At that time of day the citadel – the jewel in the crown of the city – would seem almost soft in the evening light.

There would be women dressed entirely in black sitting in a circle and picnicking on the grass. I asked one of the youths sitting at the foot of the citadel how old he thought Hammam Yalbougha was. And to my surprise, if not scorn, even though he lived

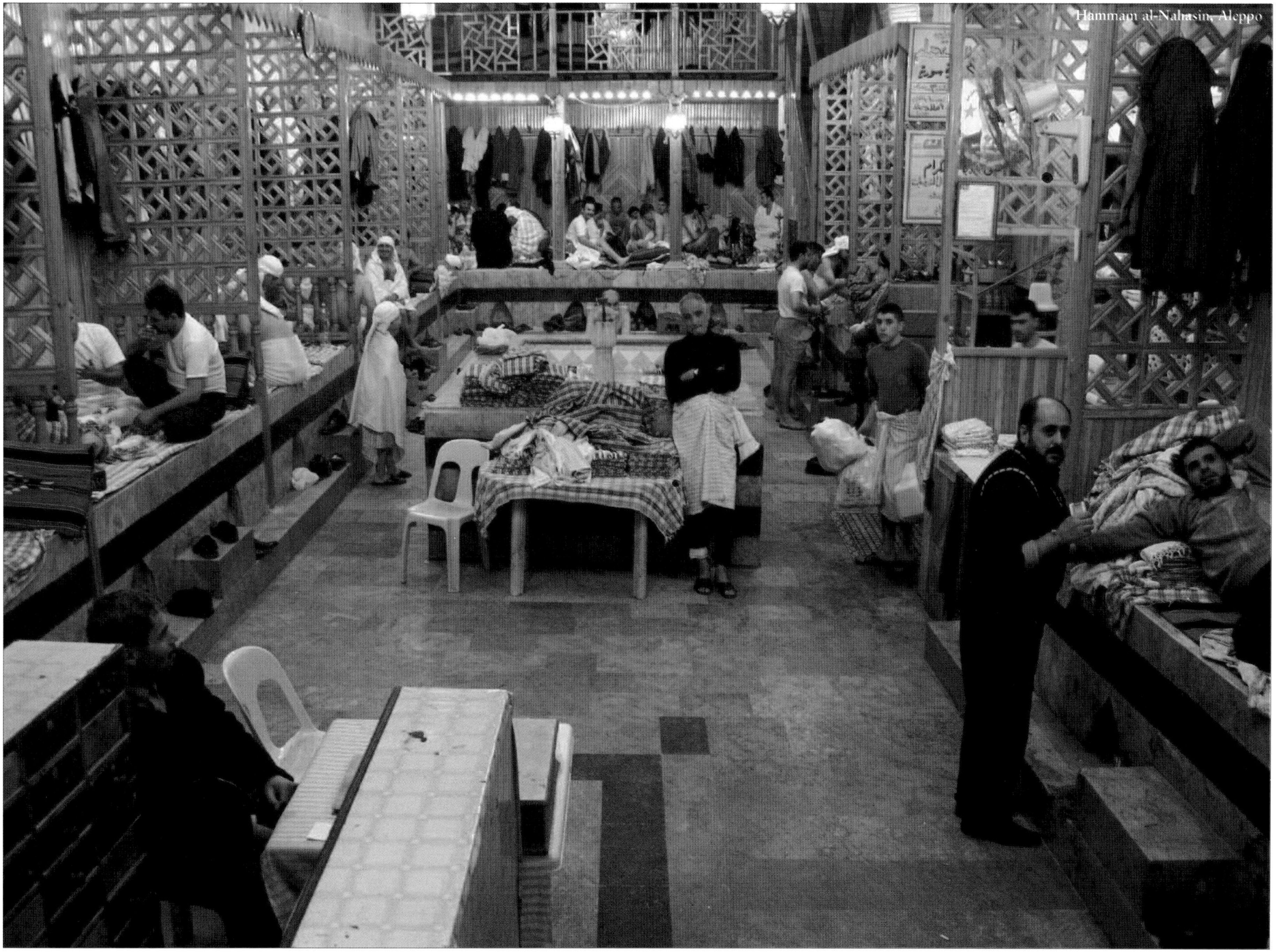
Hammam al-Nahasin, Aleppo

just below the citadel, he said twenty-five years. Given that Tamerlane had destroyed the hammam on the site, he was a few centuries out.

It was amazing how anyone could live in such a city and yet have so little sense of its history. Like the cook in the Kindi Restaurant – often seen moulding the raw meat of cherried kebabs on a skewer – who had told me he lived in the quarter called Al Bai'ada and had expected me to know nothing of it.

- Oh yes, I said, I know the hammam. How old would you say it is?
- Fifty years old, said one cook.
- Three thousand, said the other.

They were probably pulling the foreigner's leg. Or maybe in a city like Aleppo the past and the present blend into one. Although Christianity is mistakenly seen in Europe as a Western phenomenon, in the West any Biblical figure belongs to another world – the world of a holy book. The Biblical is light years away, but in Aleppo it is physically present; the tomb of Zechariah is there in the Umayyad Mosque (or at least there is a plaque commemorating an 'organ' of his – I've never found out which one – which had been found there).

As is the wont in Syria, as Mohammed and I were conversing we were joined by an uninvited third, who confidently asserted the age of the hammam:

- You talk about Sayf al-Daula living in the citadel here. Well, he also restored the hammam.

There had been a hammam on the site before 1400 when Tamerlane ransacked the citadel above it, but this speaker wished to date the hammam back to the tenth century, when Sayf al-Daula's court attracted poets and philosophers. The intruder continued to astound:

- There's a bigger and older hammam than the Yalbougha here in Aleppo and that's my own.

I scoffed:

- If there was a hammam as you say, I would have heard of it.

He was having none of it:

- And when I say it is the biggest... Well, it has twenty-two fonts. Twenty-two!

I remained sceptical.

- Don't tell me, you are Turkish.
- Yes. And the hammam has been ours for generations.
- And do you have another hammam in Turkey by any chance?
- No. But my cousins are butchers there in Istanbul. Our family name – Belourh – is well known in the *suq* there. The hammam is now a furniture workshop. It's only ten minutes away. Would you like to visit it?

This was not the kind of invitation I was going to refuse:

- What about now? I replied.

On the way, Yasser went on to talk about the treasure that lies buried beneath hammam floors:

- Every hammam has its treasure.

That was a very Syrian view of the country's monuments – how treasure was just waiting to be dug up from below any ruin.

- Anything found has to be handed over to the government, of course.

I wondered how long it would be before the treasure from the Coppersmiths' Hammam would be exhibited in the national museum.

Suddenly we came upon a square that was being re-cobbled. There was a small bakery and a stall under the trees with a man barbecuing meat, and people milling around among the vegetable and fruit sellers. In this part of the world, as Thubron has written, beauty is hidden. It seemed that I had come across not just an area of secreted beauty but a way of life, somehow intact, hidden amongst encroaching modernity.

Sharp fluorescent lights from inside the hammam outlined its doorway. Within there was the fragrance of fresh wood shavings, but the scene was not so much carpentry as the assembly of bedroom furniture. The workshop was almost Dickensian in the age of the kids employed. We went down the steps to the *wastani*:

- This is the only hammam I know with steps between the *jouwani* and *wastani* rooms.
- They are not original. We built them.

A green curtain with Islamic script hung over a hole, about the size of a cupboard, in the wall. Within was the tomb containing the bones of a saint – right in the heart of the hammam. Indeed, every hammam has its treasure. I turned to my guide:

- And do people still come to pray at this shrine?
- Of course. Men and women.

In Syria, probably because mosques are primarily men's territory, it is the women who are the real devotees of shrines.

My guide pointed to a star, half hidden by the partly-assembled furniture, carved on the wall, like the six-pointed stars on the walls

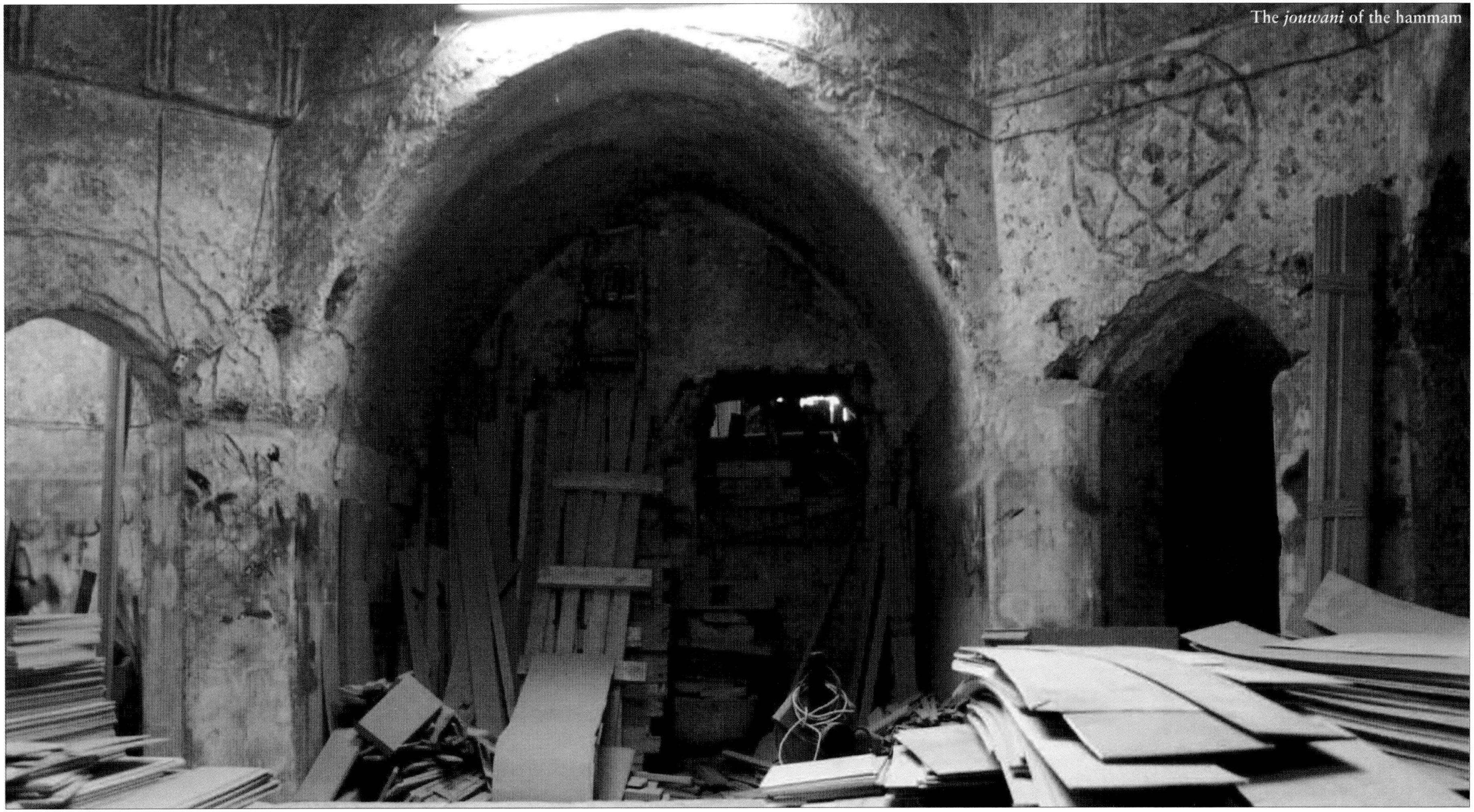

The *jouwani* of the hammam

of Ottoman houses in Jedeidah. I had never seen the like in a hammam – except for the stars sometimes cut into the domes for light.

Outside again in the open air Yasser introduced me to an old man in his *jelabiyah* sitting in the square.

- And how long has the hammam been out of use?
- Thirty years.
- And have you ever bathed in the hammam?
- Of course.
- And the *wali*, the holy man?
- He is Sheikh Bizeh.

So the square and the area and the hammam all shared the name of a sheikh. But it was all rather bizarre – for although in Ireland there might still be pilgrimages up holy mountains, what cleric would choose his resting place in the municipal baths?

Syrian Mosaic

It was like a chain: there would be a casual reference in one hammam to another, and so in Hammam Salihiye, Abu Hussain made a casual reference to Hammam Sultan and Hammam Mustafa Basha nearby.

I had heard that Hammam Mustafa Basha was near the citadel, opening onto one of the alleys. And so I found myself in a lane that was all decaying *mashrabīyah*, and minarets, and mosque doorways, and an

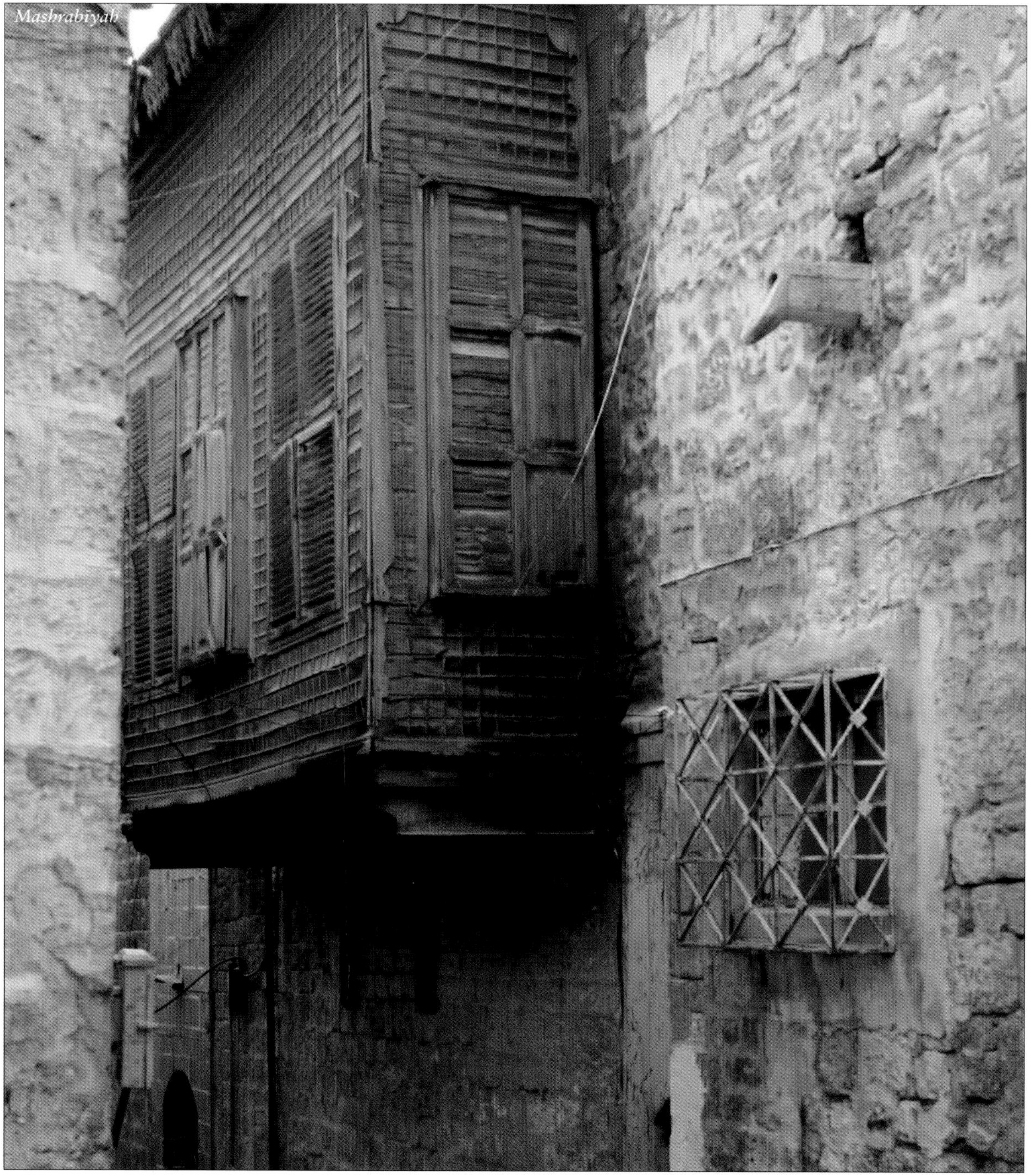
Mashrabīyah

archway leading down into a traditional neighbourhood of cobbled ways.

I asked some of the *shebab* working outside the black door to a warehouse if they knew of an old hammam on that street. They didn't, so I stepped into the mosque to make enquiries there. This mosque with its mausoleum presented an unremarkable exterior to the world, but within was a hidden garden, with a fig tree and a graceful pomegranate bush. There were turbaned Ottoman headstones, and even a purple-leaved tradescantia trailing over a child's grave.

Seated on mats in the courtyard, the mosque elders were getting ready for a late lunch, so I asked permission to enter the mosque and savour its simplicity. They told me that the mosque was called Nasimi, and I felt that was right, for, although it may be a false etymology here, *naseem* is the Arabic for breeze, and the place was like a breeze refreshing the soul.

I turned down the invitation to join them for lunch, but was passed a kind of takeaway.

– Well, if I'm going to eat I'll join you then!

Sitting down in the courtyard to a glass of yoghurt and the local delicacies, I complimented my hosts:

– There's nothing like Aleppan cuisine!

Inevitably the talk turned to things religious, which I suppose was fair enough given that we were in the courtyard of a mosque.

– Are you a Muslim?
– No, I'm a Christian.

I didn't here say that this was in the broadest cultural sense of the word.

– And is there Islam in Ireland?
– No, we're Christians.

And here there was many a thing I could have said about religion in Ireland, but I refrained. These men however had utter certainty in their beliefs:

– May God give you Islam!

Nasimi's religious views were somewhat broader than those of the guardians of his tomb today, who seemed to me a little bit short on multi-culturalism. In contrast, Nasimi would have absorbed a wide range of philosophy and religious beliefs. Like other mystics, Nasimi portrayed himself as 'drunk' with divine love, a love that permeated the elements of the universe itself:

> Wind, water, fire and flame, the world is drunk with love,
> The devil and the ghost, the serpent and the dove.[17]

In Nasimi's time Aleppo must at times have been the Londonistan of its day, a centre for exiled preachers (he was born in the Azerbaijan region) whose ideas undermined governments and states. However, unlike today's so-called 'radical preachers' (to use the BBC's politically correct phrase) these medieval preachers had a message of love: in the words of Ibn 'Arabi, 'Love is my religion and my faith'.

For these mystics, divine love permeated the universe. The writing of poetry however was a hazardous occupation, and verses in which Nasimi seemed to claim that he and God were one (for these mystics the divine and the human were inseparable) were seen as blasphemous. In Aleppo, Nasimi was convicted of atheism, skinned alive and dismembered.[18] According to legend, however, our saint triumphed over the Aleppan authorities. Composing a poem for the occasion of his death, he left the scene in style:

> [He] mocked his executioners with improvised verse and, after the execution, draped his flayed skin around his shoulders and departed.[19]

Hammam Domes

The men in the mosque did at least point me in the direction of the hammam I was seeking:

– It's just by my house! said one.
– That's fine, I replied. But I don't know where you live!

They directed me back to the black gate where men were unloading goods into a kind of store room.

A few yards from the mosque, I found the black door.

– I asked you guys about the hammam…

They looked at me uncomprehendingly.

– Well, you're working in it!

I talked my way into the building and found the essential rooms and the domes that make up a hammam. It was all a bit exasperating; these men were working in a hammam and hadn't noticed.

In my time in Syria, I shuttled forth between hammams and mosques, between courtyards and *barranis*, alternating between worshippers and bathers. The very architecture of the hammams seemed to mirror the domes of mosques, but given that the founder of the mosque was often the builder of the hammam, and that the same architect often designed both monuments, why should the hammam not in some way echo the mosque it accompanied?

In his novel *Young Turk*, Moris Farhi recalls the sacred precincts of the hammam of his childhood in Turkey, where the very material from which much of the hammam was constructed had for him mystical qualities. Marble he portrays as a stone fit for the gods:

> … the primary material for the inner sanctum, the washing enclave itself, must be marble, the stone which, according to legend, shelters the friendly breezes and which, for that very good reason, is chosen by kings for their palaces and by gods for their temples.[20]

For Farhi, the very floor of the hammam embodied the spiritual.

The hammam's architecture paralleled that of the mosque, and it was the combination of columns, domes and high windows that for Farhi created the atmosphere of the hammam:

> … for this combination will suffuse the inner sanctum with a glow suggestive of the mystic aura of a mosque.[21]

It seems as if the hammam architect had consciously set out to create a spiritual atmosphere; Farhi's hammam has a mystical glow.

In Aleppo the skyline of the city around me was defined by the maleness of its minarets and the round female shapes of its domes. Churches, mosques and hammams share a common architecture in Syria; unlike Western cathedrals with their Gothic steeples reaching to the firmament, the domes of the east can be seen as mirroring the heavens themselves. In *The Station*, Robert Byron writes of the Hagia Sophia in Constantinople:

> The lines of construction and means of support are invisible. The shadowless misty interior seems not to rise from the earth, but to swim, poised above it. Gothic reaches to the firmament. This has recreated it.[22]

At the inauguration ceremony the speaker asked if the dome were not suspended from heaven by a golden chain.

The Ottomans took the Byzantine dome but lightened it, not just in their mosques (those cascading domes of light!) but also in their hammams. And so, light does not just enter the dome of Hammam al Jadid in Tripoli; it seems to raise the roof itself – a dim religious light it is not. When I think of an Ottoman hammam, it is the patterned circles of light filtering through the domes that I picture, the honeyed beams spilling on to marbled floors. These monuments built for the body and for ritual purification go beyond the merely religious; they hint of the spiritual.

It even got to the stage where I would wonder if it was all a coincidence – this spiritual feel to the hammam. If anyone has been to certain hammams in the region, they will laugh mockingly at this point, I know, for some hammams might be seen as the antithesis of anything religious. The contradictions are there in Farhi's novel too. The hottest room, the 'inner sanctum', is seen as appropriately

Right: Hammam al Jadid in Tripoli

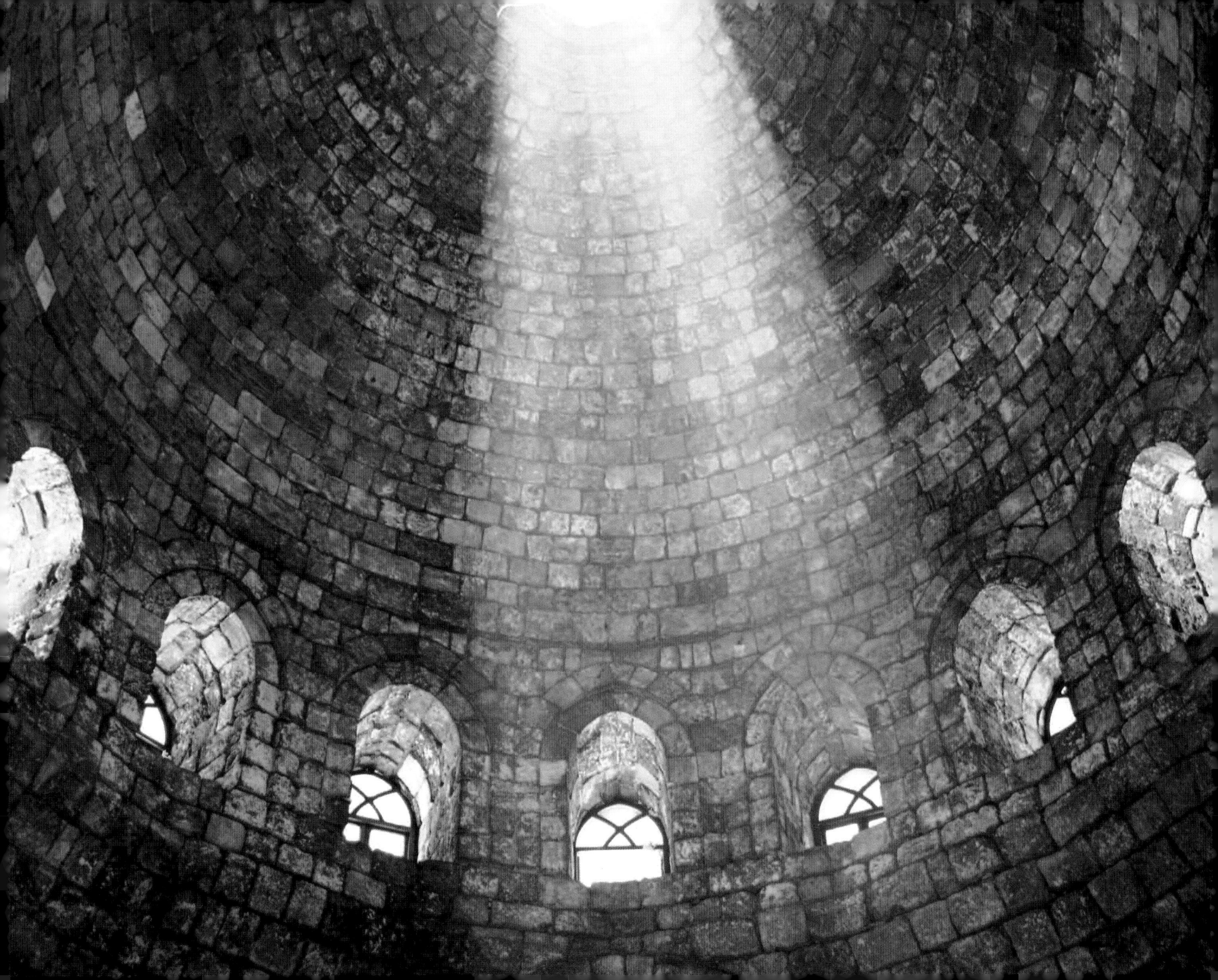

round, or rather oval, and therefore feminine – because here, as a very young boy, brought to the hammam by the family servant, the narrator could observe the female body utterly naked, beneath 'Apollonian light'. Expulsion from paradise comes when a woman sees the boy as sexually aroused among the bathing females.

An English convert to the Greek Orthodox Church, who left Damascus for the expat life of the Gulf (that would be an expulsion from paradise for me), explained it like this:

> – In our Western architecture we have the steeple; man is in the ditch grasping up at heaven. In the East however there is the dome; heaven comes down and touches earth.

Notes

1 Mathers, E. P., *Book of the Thousand Nights and One Night* (Taylor and Francis e-Library), Vol. 3, p. 13.
2 Stark, Freya, *Traveller's Prelude* (J. Murray, 1950), p. 38.
3 Lawrence, T. E., *Seven Pillars of Wisdom* (Wordsworth, 1997), p. 324.
4 Kociejowski, Marius, *Syria: Through Writers' Eyes* (Eland, 2006), p. 164.
5 Bell, Gertrude, *The Desert and the Sown* (William Heinemann, 1908), p. 276.
6 Bell, Gertrude, *The Desert and the Sown* (William Heinemann, 1908), p. 259.
7 Bell, Gertrude, *The Desert and the Sown* (William Heinemann, 1908), p. 269.
8 Orga, Irfan, *Portrait of a Turkish Family* (Eland, 2003), p. 23.
9 Irwin, Robert, *Night and Horses and the Desert* (Penguin, 2000), p. 306.
10 Freely, John, *Inside the Seraglio: Private Lives of the Sultans in Istanbul* (Viking, 1999), p. 291.
11 Freely, John, *Inside the Seraglio: Private Lives of the Sultans in Istanbul* (Viking, 1999), pp. 198–99.
12 Ruggles, D. Fairchild, *Islamic Gardens and Landscapes* (University of Pennsylvania Press, 2008), p. 57.
13 Irwin, Robert, *Night and Horses and the Desert* (Penguin, 2000), p. 226.
14 Kociejowski, Marius, *The Street Philosopher and the Holy Fool, A Syrian Journey* (Sutton Publishing, 2004), p. 242.
15 Hadjar, Abdallah, *The Historical Monuments of Aleppo* (Automobile and Touring Club of Syria, 2006), p. 71.
16 Hadjar, Abdallah, *The Historical Monuments of Aleppo* (Automobile and Touring Club of Syria, 2006), p. 94.
17 'At love's most sumptuous feast was I with love made drunk', translated by Irina Zheleznova, accessible at www.poetry-chaikhana.com, *Sacred Poetry from Around the World.*
18 Hadjar, Abdallah, *The Historical Monuments of Aleppo* (Automobile and Touring Club of Syria, 2006), p. 98.
19 Wikipedia. Wiki: Imadaddin Nasimi.
20 Farhi, Moris, *Young Turk* (Saqi Books, 2004), p. 47.
21 Farhi, Moris, *Young Turk* (Saqi Books, 2004), pp. 47–48.
22 Byron, Robert, *The Station: Athos – Treasures and Men* (Phoenix, 2000), p. 136.

4

REVIVAL

I remember the coloured towels
As they dance on the door of Hammam al-Khayyatin

Nezar Qabbani[1]

Hammam Ammoune

Not far from Bab al Faradis (Paradise Gate) in Damascus, near the graveyard and Hammam Assakari, is Hammam Ammoune. The neighbourhood is the real thing: Mamluk mosques, houses arching over laneways, sheikhs' tombs marked with candles. But when I popped in once or twice to the much neglected Hammam Ammoune, I didn't much care for the place, even though it is one of the most ancient hammams in Syria, its traditional heating system still intact.

But one Ramadan I came across the hammam attendants of Milek al Zaher doubling up as builders, restoring the hammam. It was the slackest time of the year – for who would bathe during the day while they were fasting? – and now the attendants were plastering over the hammam walls, or sleeping away the long hours before the breaking of the fast.

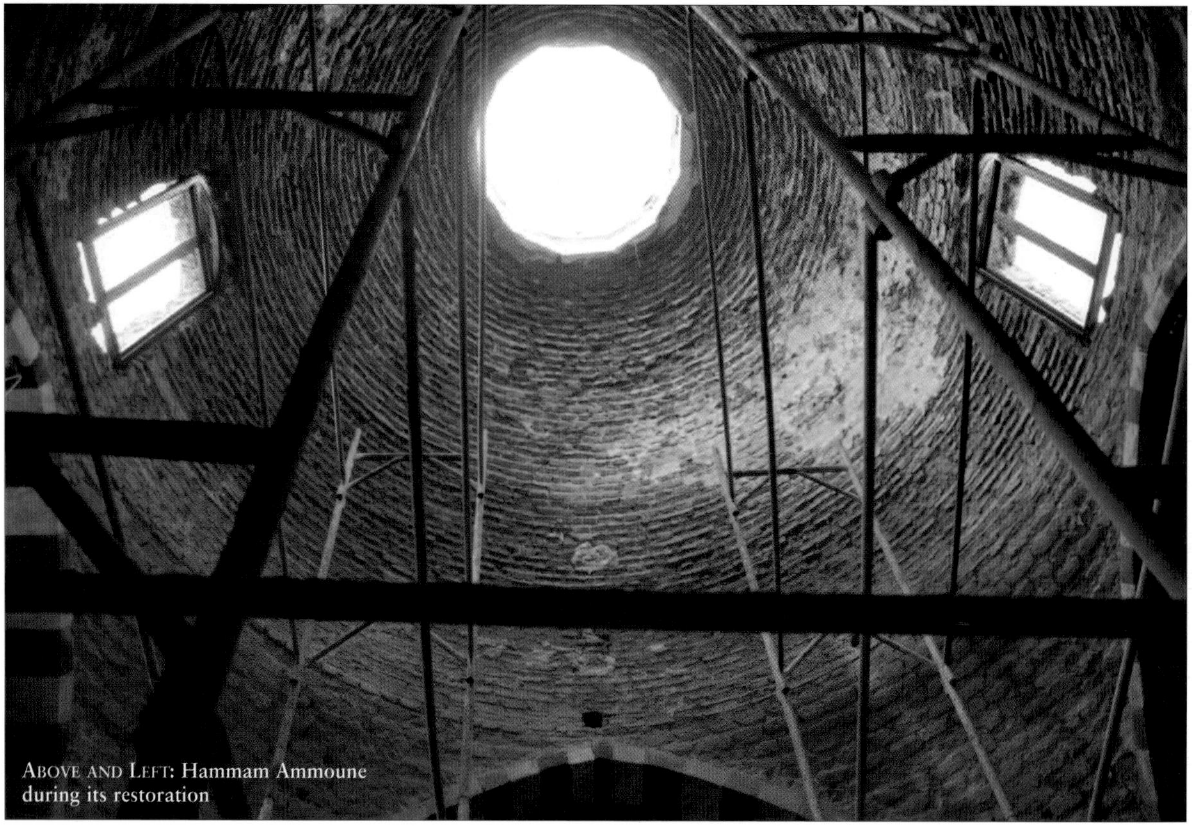

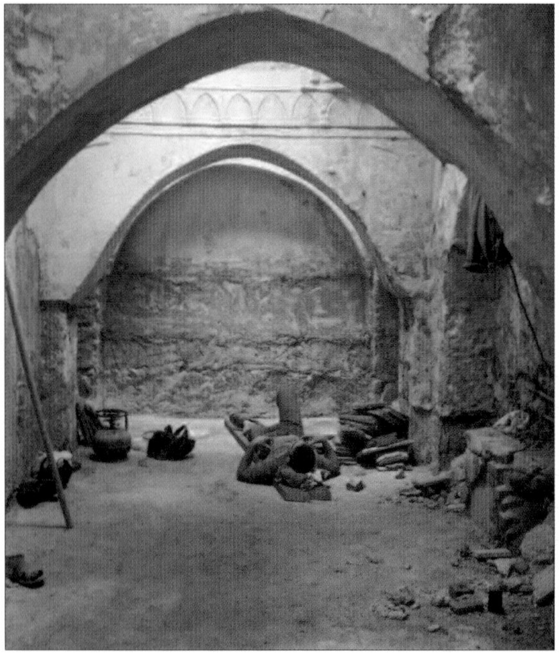

Above and Left: Hammam Ammoune during its restoration

Soon Hammam Ammoune was re-opened, and I was undressing in the exquisitely decorated *barrani*. It is the perfectly intimate small hammam, given over to women by day and men in the evenings. The restoration of this hammam has had support and guidance from a European project; fortunately it is under the same caring management as Hammam Milek al Zaher. From the *barrani* you go straight into the *jouwani*, with its steam room and jacuzzi of basalt blocks, and sauna. It's all in impeccable taste, but happily the attendants are their down-to-earth selves, and steeped in the traditions of hammams. We chatted into the early hours.

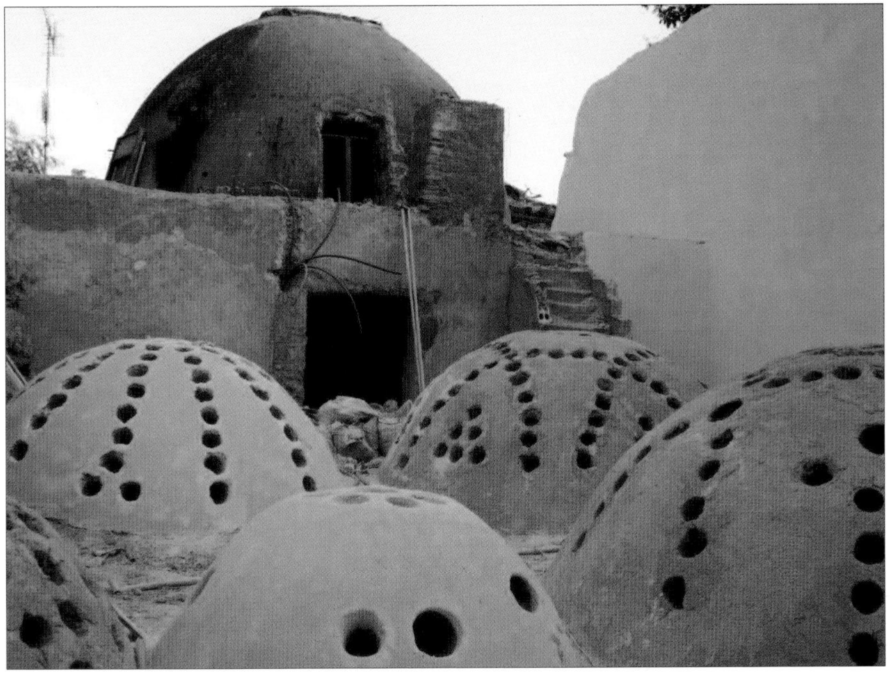

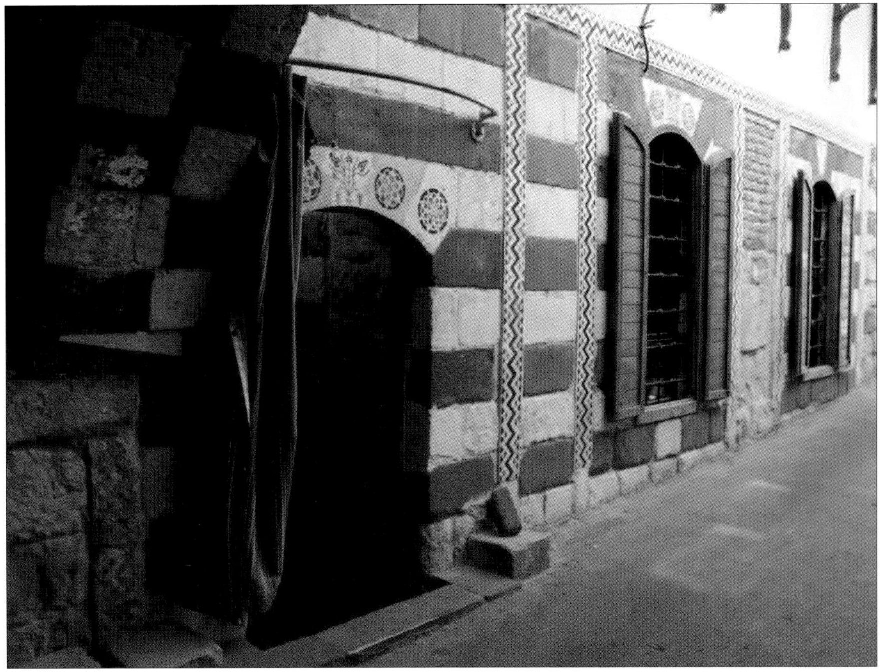

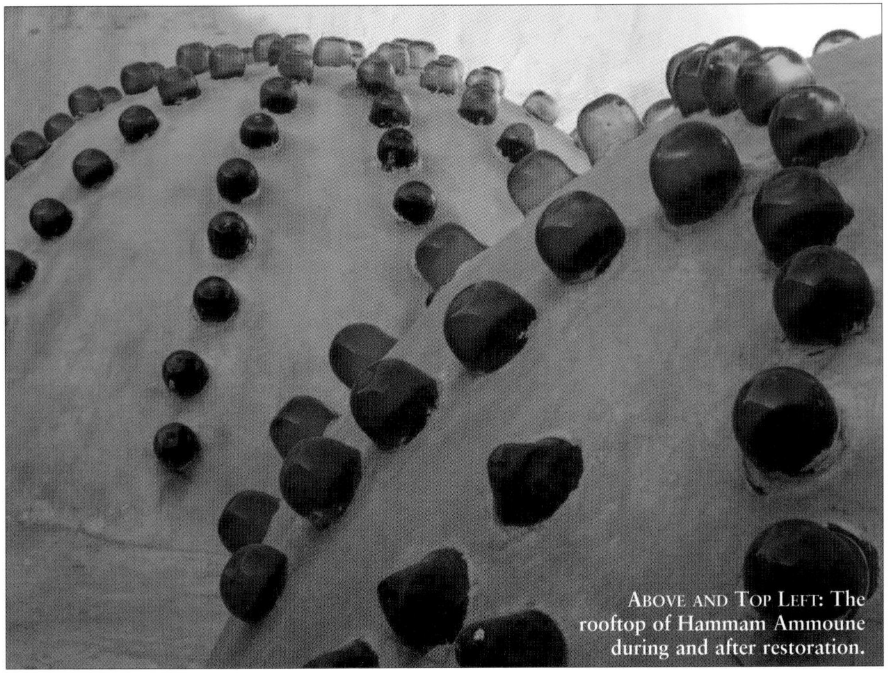

Above and Top Left: The rooftop of Hammam Ammoune during and after restoration.

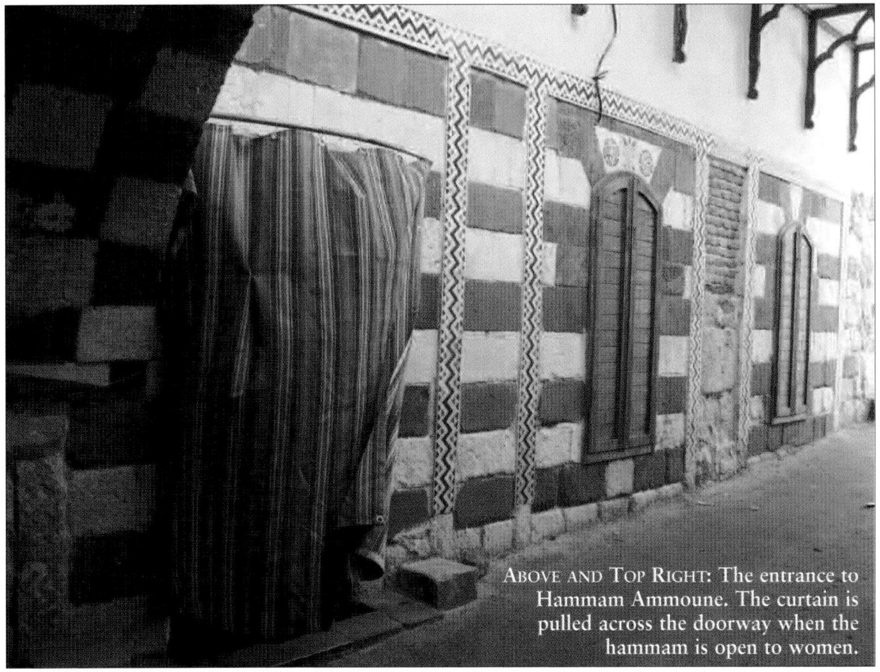

Above and Top Right: The entrance to Hammam Ammoune. The curtain is pulled across the doorway when the hammam is open to women.

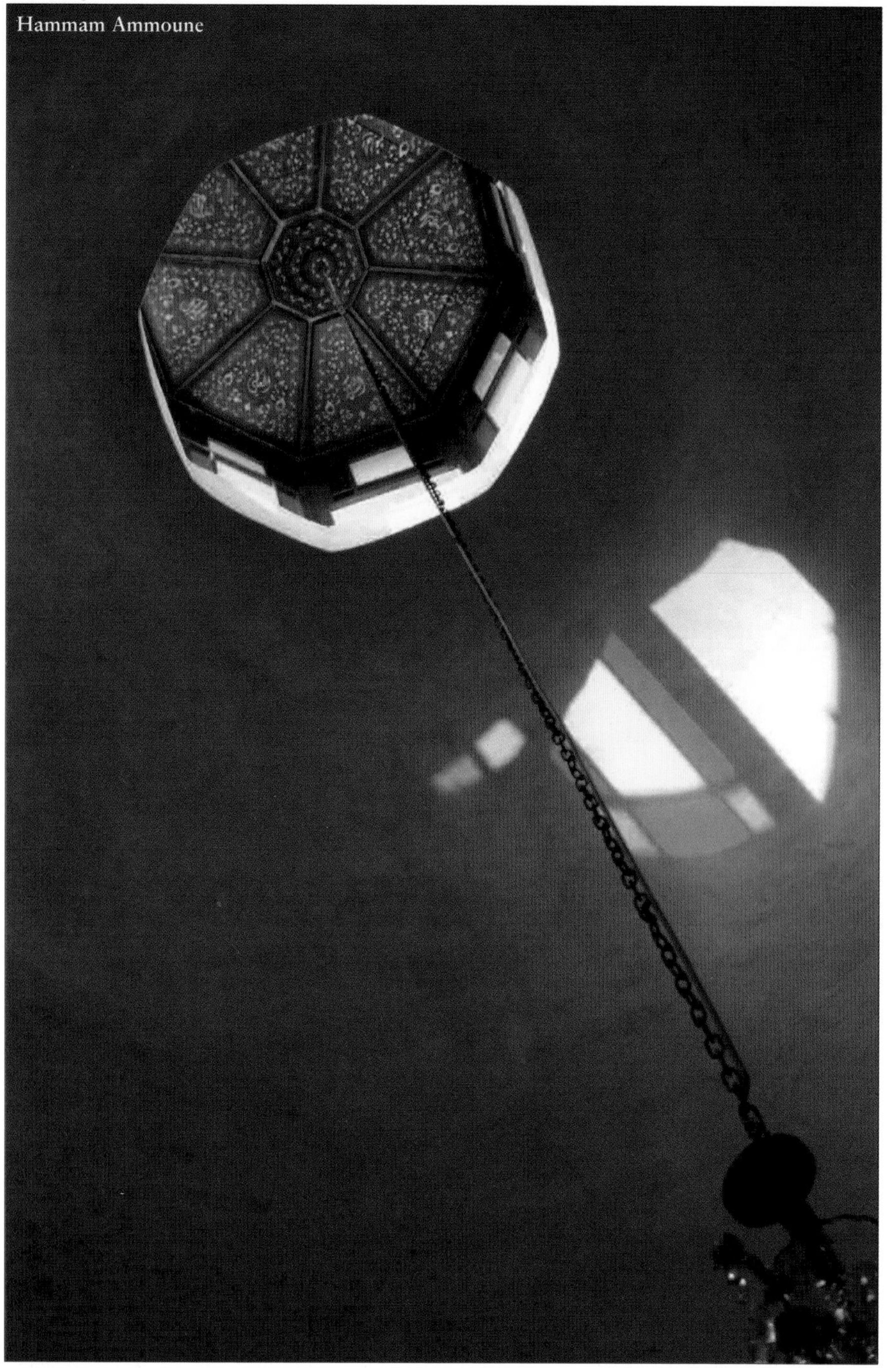
Hammam Ammoune

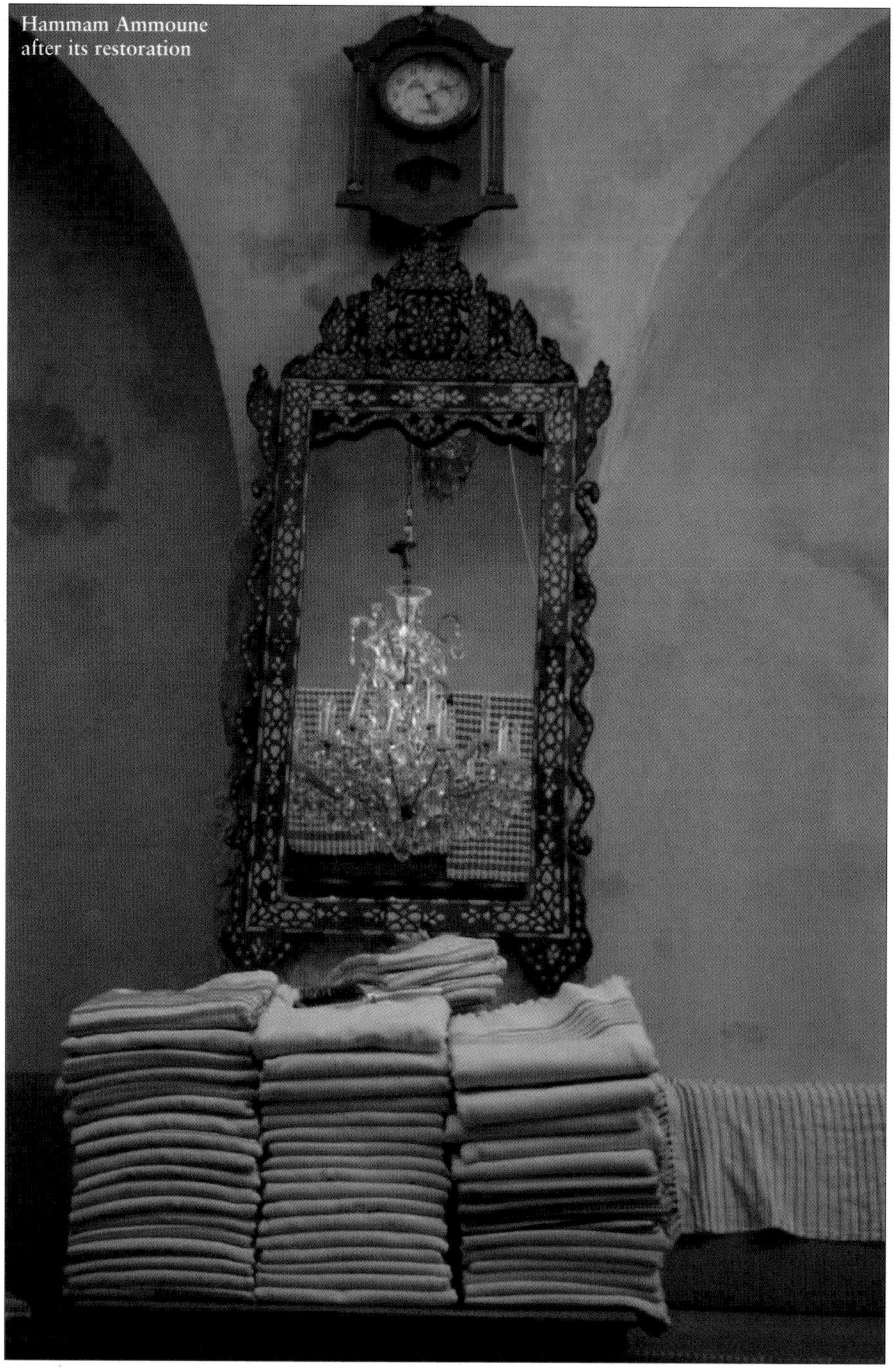
Hammam Ammoune after its restoration

It is great to see it: it's not just a building that is being brought back to life, but the neighbourhood itself. And there is talk that the sad Hammam al-Umari in the decaying Sauruja Lane – near the sheikh's tomb with writing on the wall telling people not to park, as if the sheikh still needed his own private parking space – has changed hands and awaits a new life.

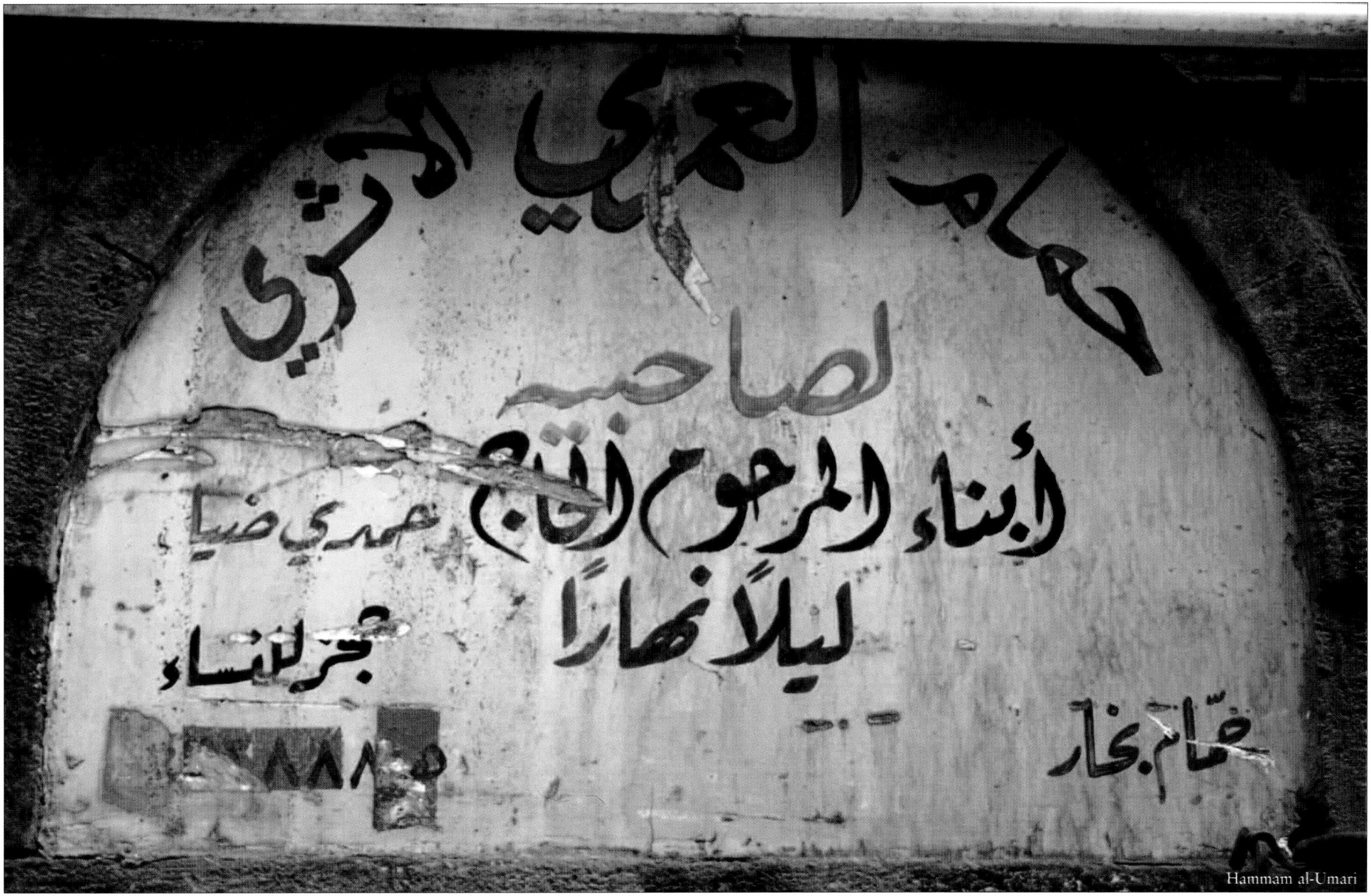

Hammam al-Umari

It seems to me that when I arrived in Damascus the hammams had reached the nadir of their existence. But now, especially for those hammams in the heart of the city, things are on the uptake.

Unveiling the Hammam

The tacky tiles of the *barrani* have been removed; the stone is honeyed in the afternoon light. Through the stained-glass windows the hammam has a warm, Keatsian glow.

A new balcony has been installed, where the masseur pummels flesh. The barber grooms a towel-clad bather before a mirror inlaid with mother-of-pearl.

The fountain reflects discriminating taste, with a brass pot for the charcoal for *nargilehs* perched on its rim. The water does not so much spurt as simmer gently, like a pot on the back burner.

Wooden clogs are lined up for bathers, who consume bottled mineral water after their hammam. The clientele are most definitely the better off, some not without the extensive girth of good living.

At 5.00 p.m. one afternoon the staff were sitting with the *mi'allim,* and urged me to join them in their late lunch. The attendants, thank God, were their unpretentious selves, but they were decked out in tasteful sweatshirts with the name of the hammam. The employees had been branded!

As Sufi rhythms sounded over the speakers, I felt I had received a glimpse of the future. Hammam Milek al Zaher has recently celebrated its first one thousand years; is it in this hammam that a new generation of businessmen will entertain their corporate clients?

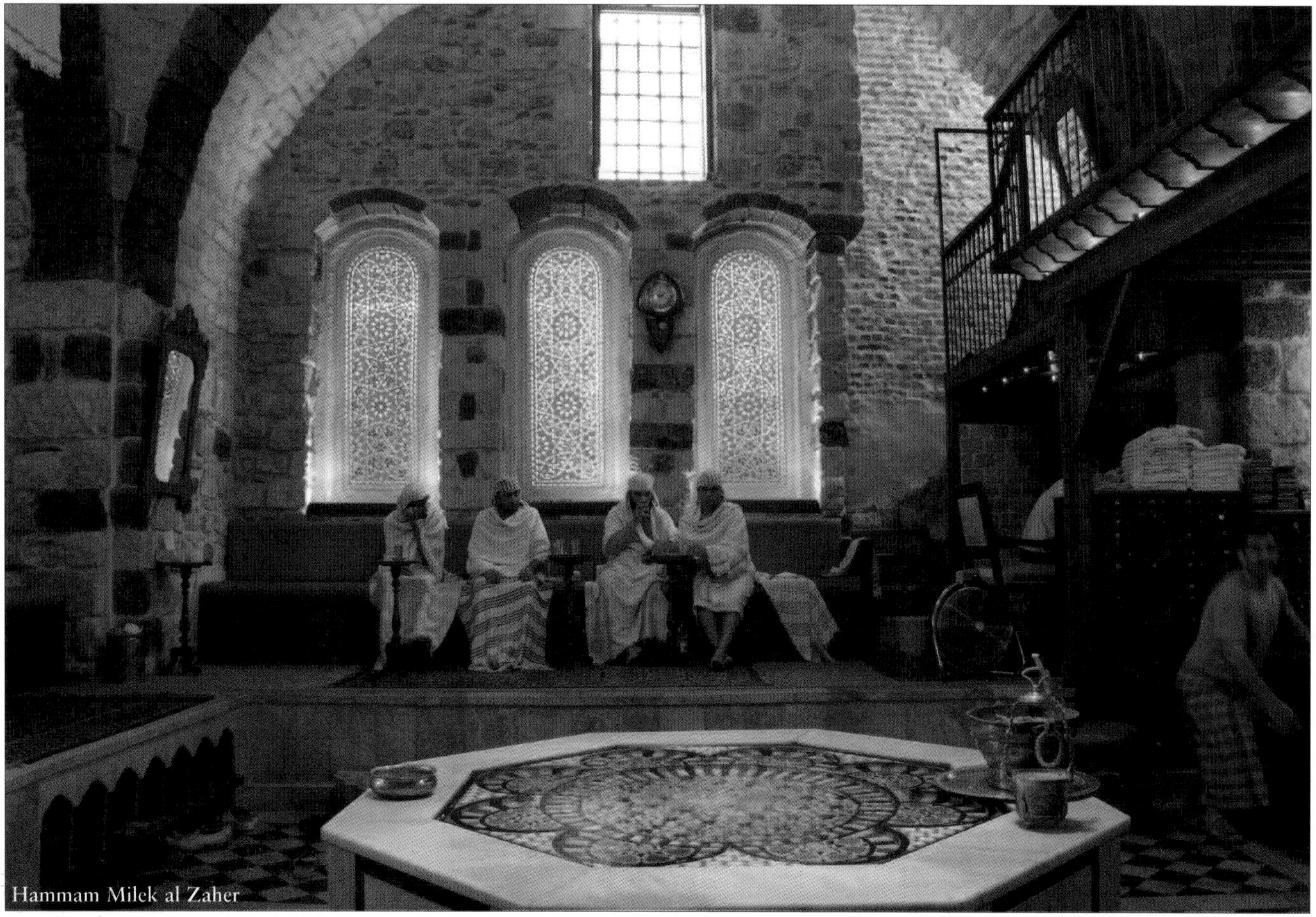
Hammam Milek al Zaher

Hammams Fathi and Tawrizi Revisited

When I was first in Damascus I had found Hammam Fathi semi-derelict. Returning, I found the *sebil* in its façade restored, the inscripton above the hammam doorway renewed with mother of pearl.

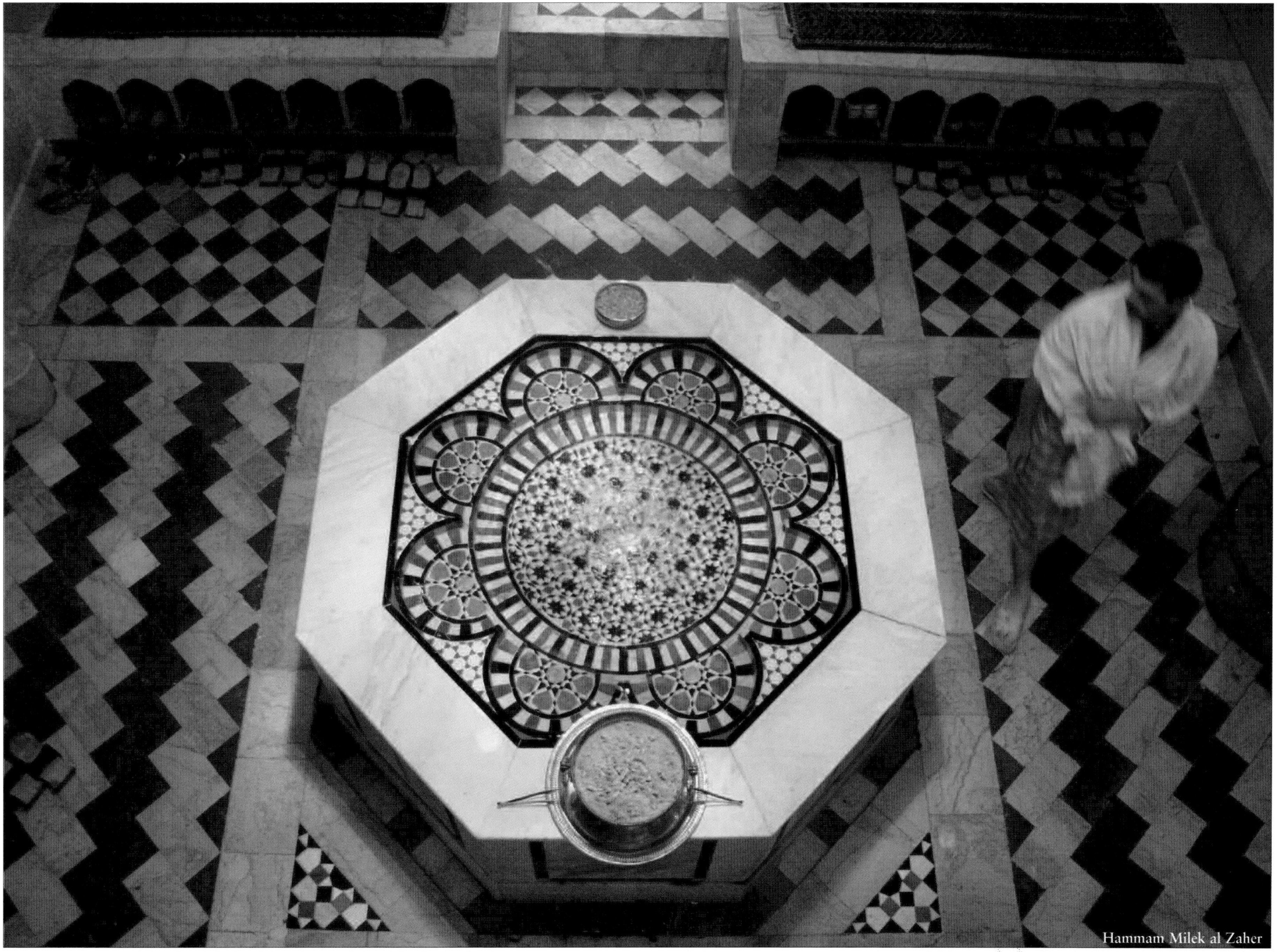
Hammam Milek al Zaher

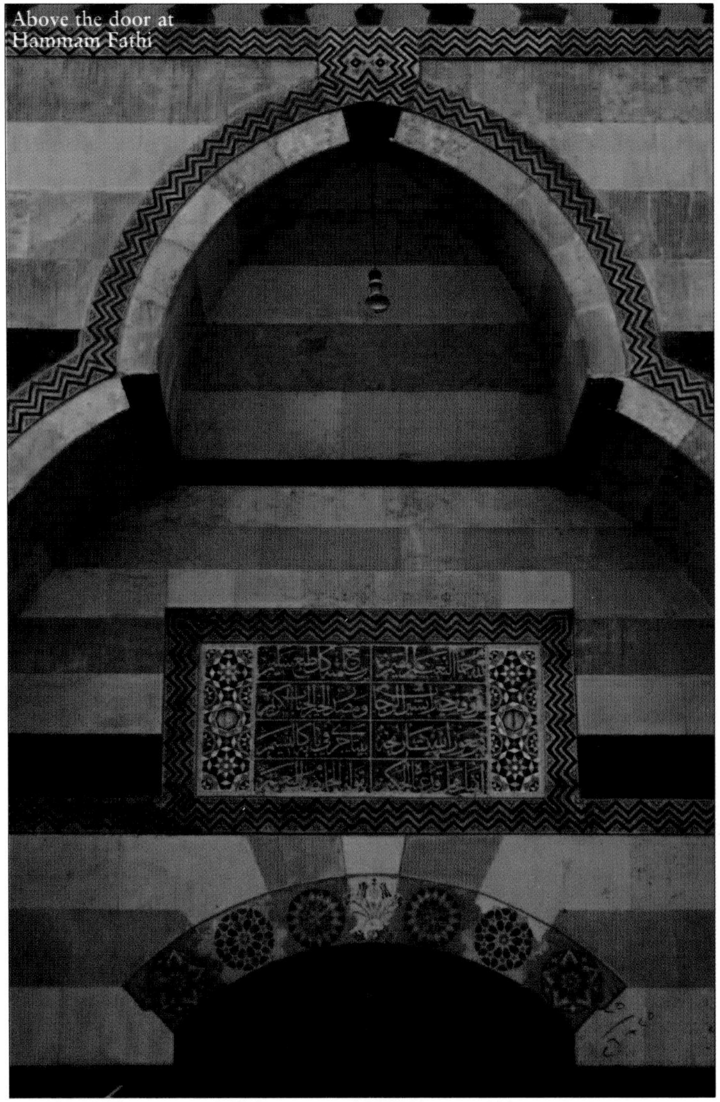
Above the door at Hammam Fathi

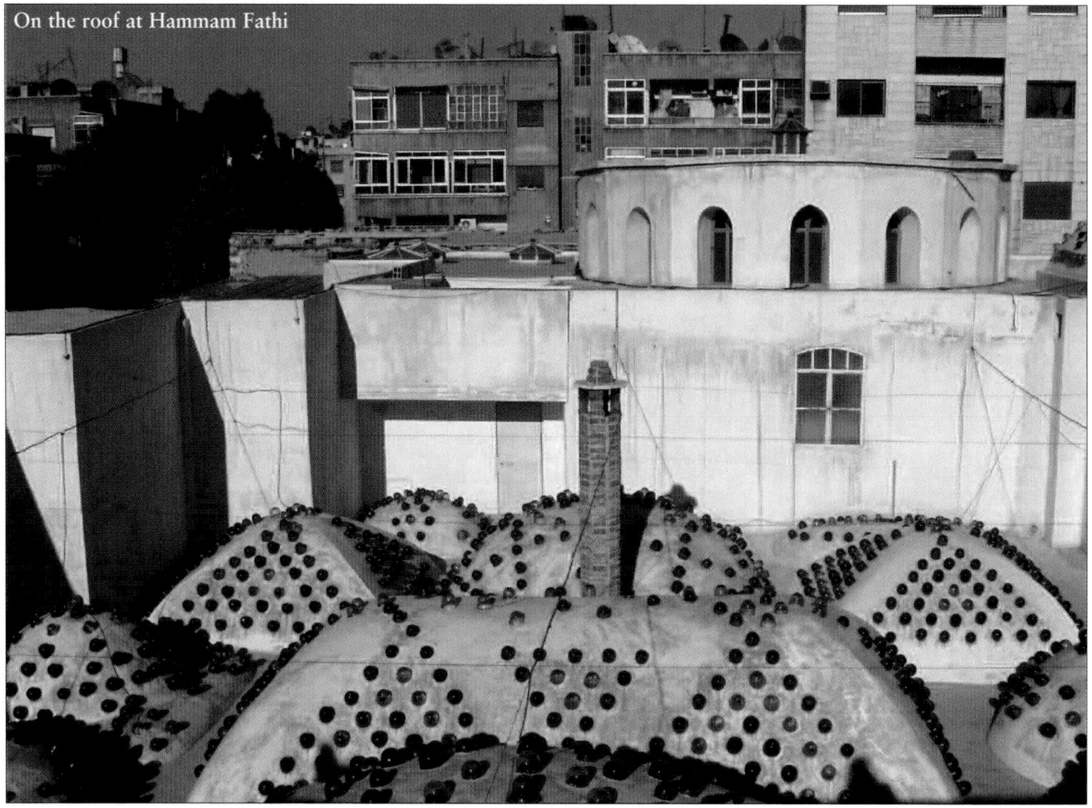
On the roof at Hammam Fathi

Finding a door at the back of the hammam, I knocked. An Iraqi came to the door. Given what was happening in Iraq at the time, in his shoes I would have closed the door on any Westerner's face. However that Iraqi invited me in, and generous with his time, gave me a tour of his labour of love – from the banded stone of the *barrani*, to the light spilling on to the restored walls within. The visitor could sit in the traditional *majlis* area before a fountain. I even had a tour of the multi-domes of the roof, above which was the owner's flat.

His restoration of the hammam was a private project, not a commercial venture;

the hammam would be this Iraqi's Syrian home. I think in some way he envisaged the hammam as functionning as a private cultural centre. And it was not just Hammam Fathi. I was invited to see another hammam he was restoring, not yet quite ready for its opening: another labour of love.

On the walls of the monumental Hammam Tawrizi, the great medallion had been cleaned. A brass door leads into the hammam where the floor was not just being restored but being inlaid with mother of pearl. Within, all was marble and jewelled circles of light. The effect of light filtering through the elephants' eyes of the restored hammam was the most beautiful I had seen anywhere. The icing on the cake would be the pool – not so much a plunge pool as a sky-blue place in which to swim.

Damascus now had its first hammam with a pool. Somehow that Iraqi had managed it – restoring a centuries-old hammam, but incorporating contemporary concerns about hygiene and current tastes in style; bathers would step into a little disinfecting footbath as they entered the *wastani*. There was even talk of a widescreen TV in the *barrani,* but I begged further reflection on that.

After decades of neglect by authorities, hammams were being rescued from oblivion by one individual with a passion for their architecture. It had taken an outsider, an Iraqi, to see the potential of Damascene hammams and begin their restoration.

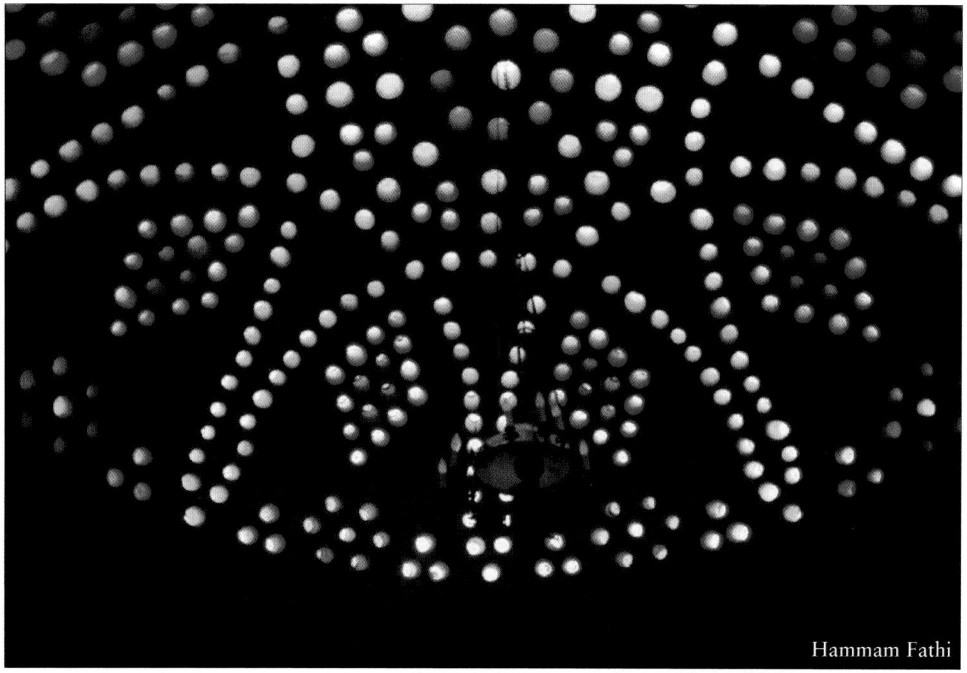

Hammam Fathi

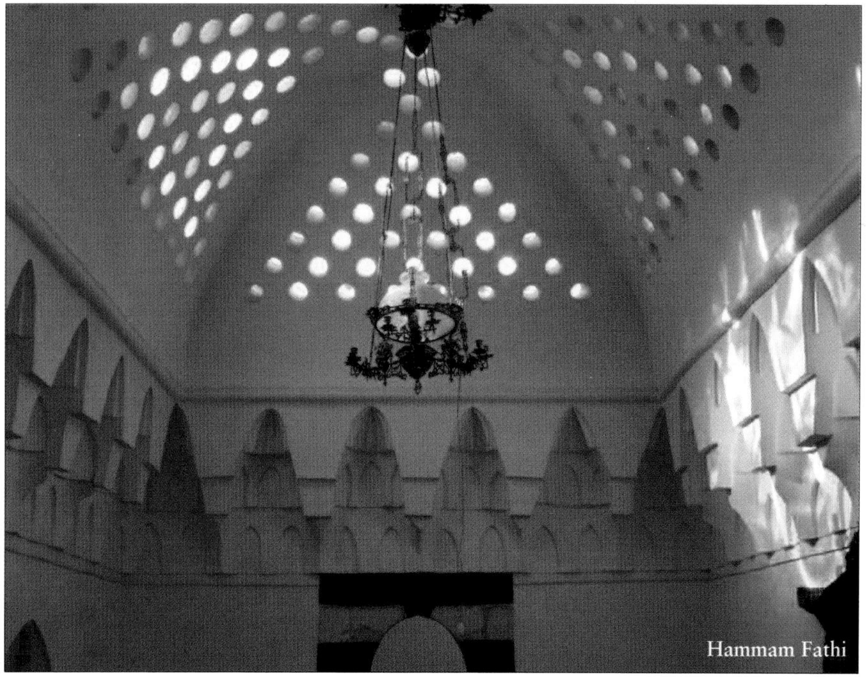

Hammam Fathi

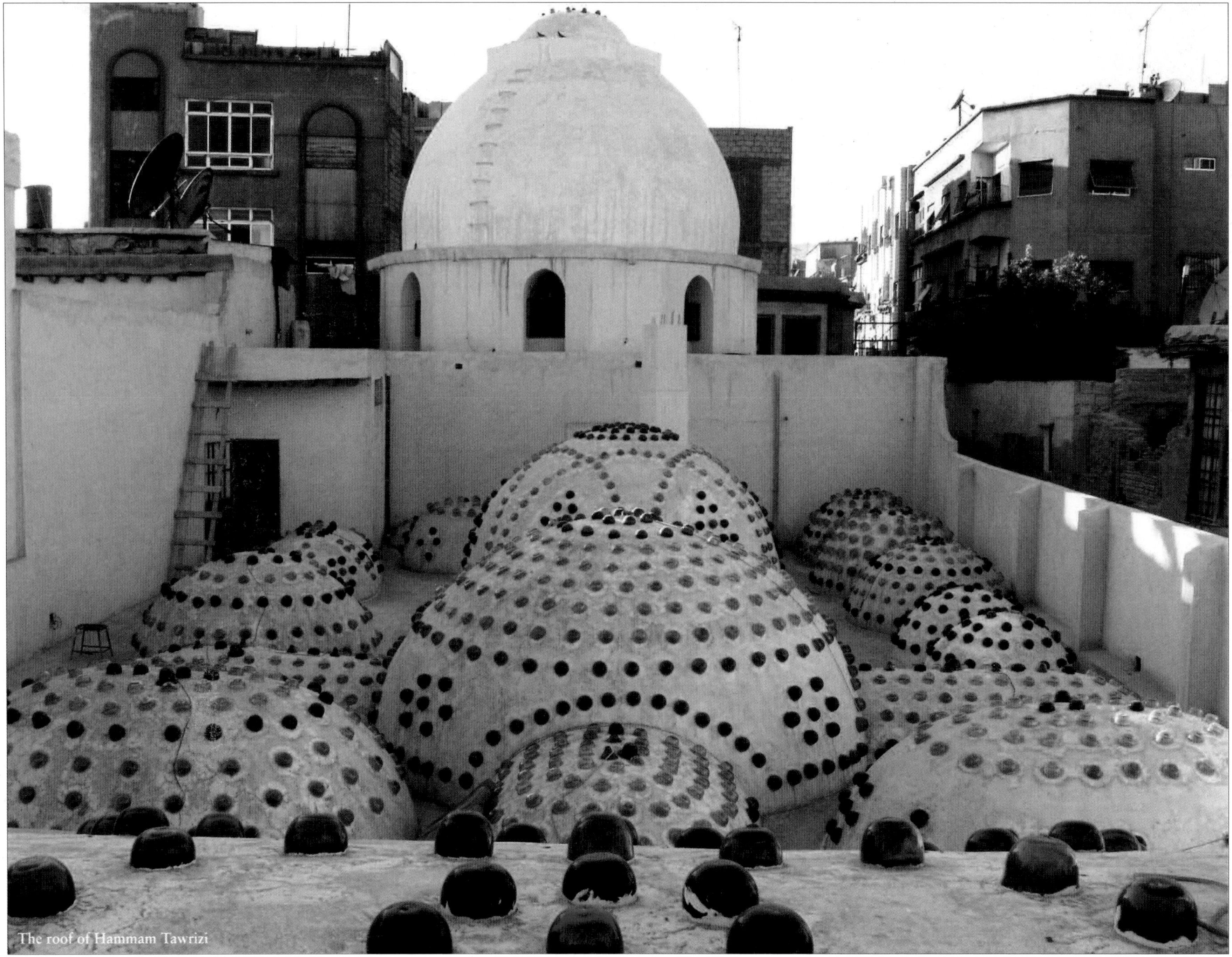
The roof of Hammam Tawrizi

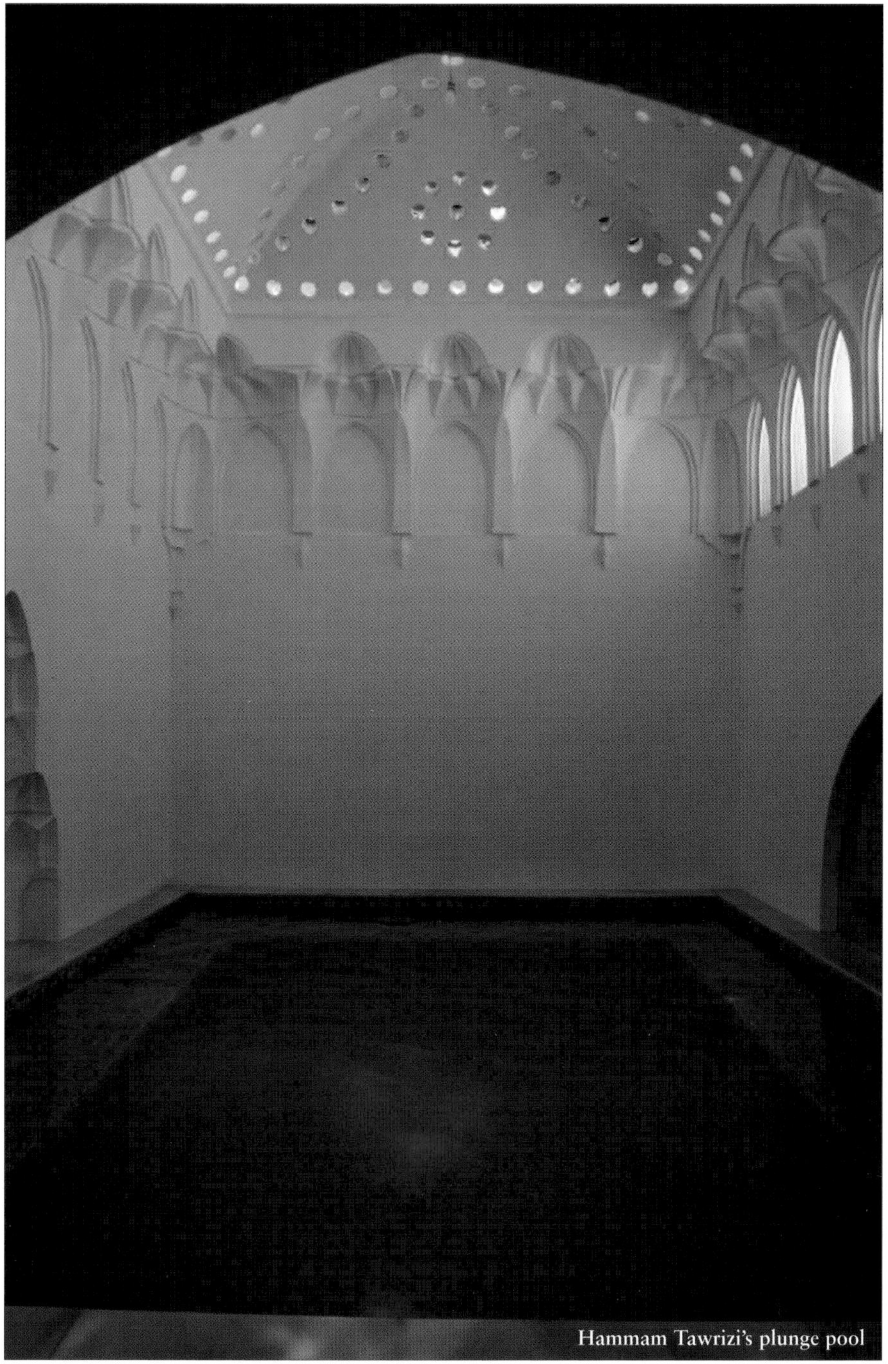

Hammam Tawrizi's plunge pool

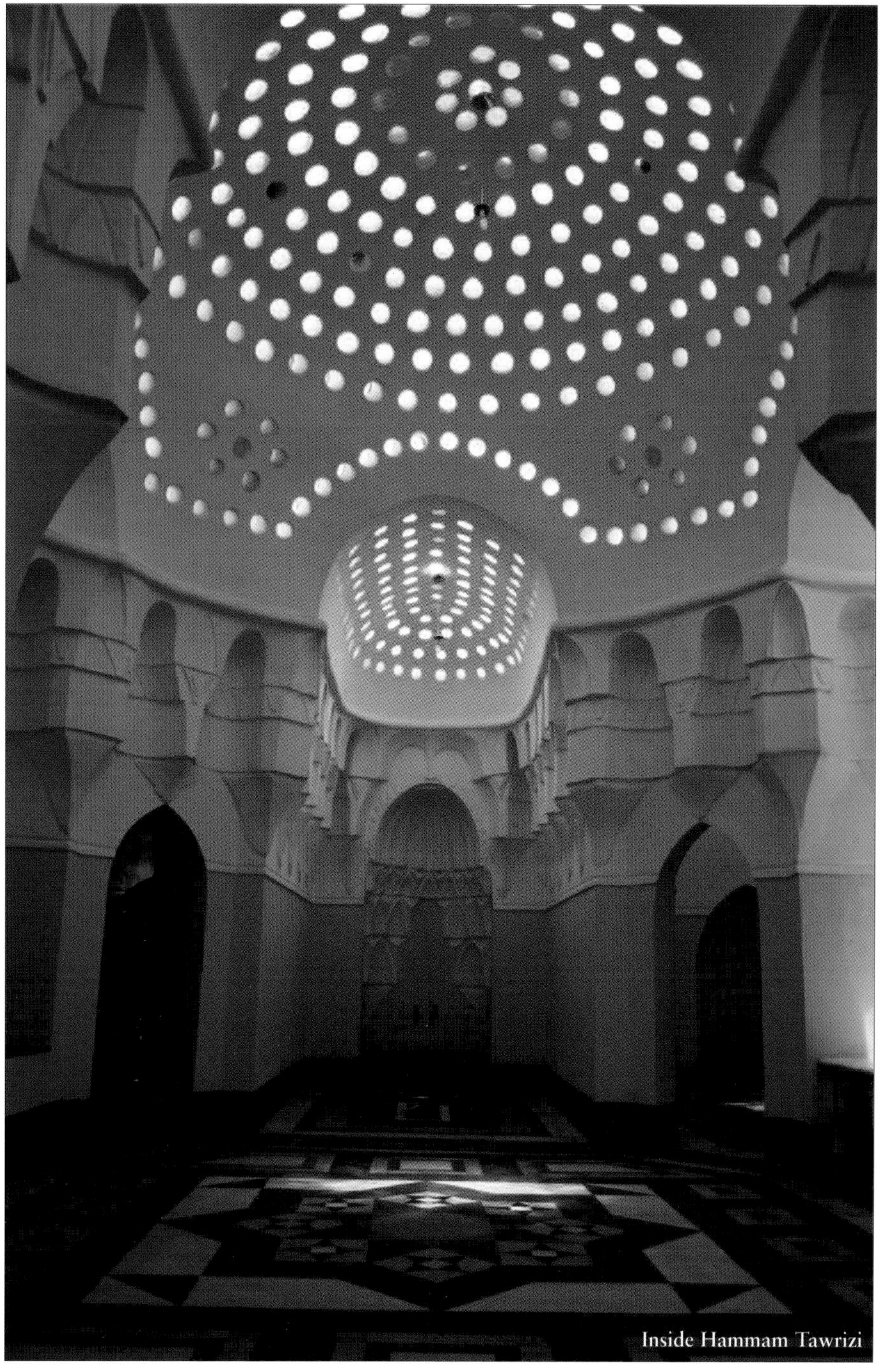

Inside Hammam Tawrizi

Hammam Salihiye Revisited

Up in Aleppo I found that Ibrahim, the *mi'allim* of the Coppersmiths' Hammam, had been to work on the dilapidated Hammam Salihiye. On my first visit I had found a fairly derelict hammam partly used as a workshop. On my return, I found a marbled hammam buzzing with *shebab*.

The commercial instincts that have been to work in Ibrahim's case are reflected in the notice as you enter. Having passed under the doorway with its poetry-inscribed lintel, you find a sign forbidding the kinds of behaviour that have been associated with hammams since Roman days: drinking and gambling. In Arabic the prices are clearly stated: to bathe costs 200 riyals, soap is 15 riyals etc. The translation into English shows considerable creativity: to bathe is 300 riyals, soap costs 50 riyals etc., etc.

With Ibrahim's entrepreneurship it will work. Women hammam by day, children come for the pool, and men hammam by night. He might also get a few tourists: while the women bathe the men will relax over a *nargileh*...

When I bathed that evening the hammam was full of Armenians preparing for New Year celebrations. There were so many bathers the *mukeyyis* could scarcely keep a tally of the number he had done. As the youth of Aleppo milled around the warm *barrani*, Ibrahim seemed not so much a businessman running a hammam as a host throwing a party for the *shebab* of Aleppo.

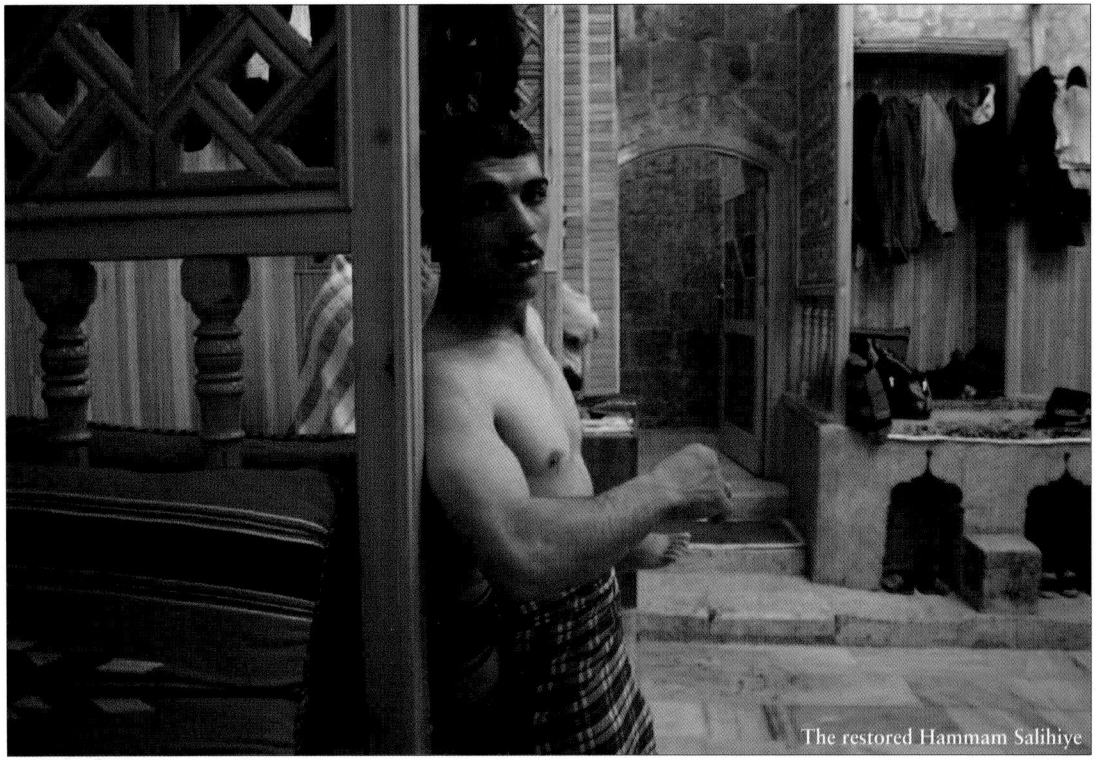

The restored Hammam Salihiye

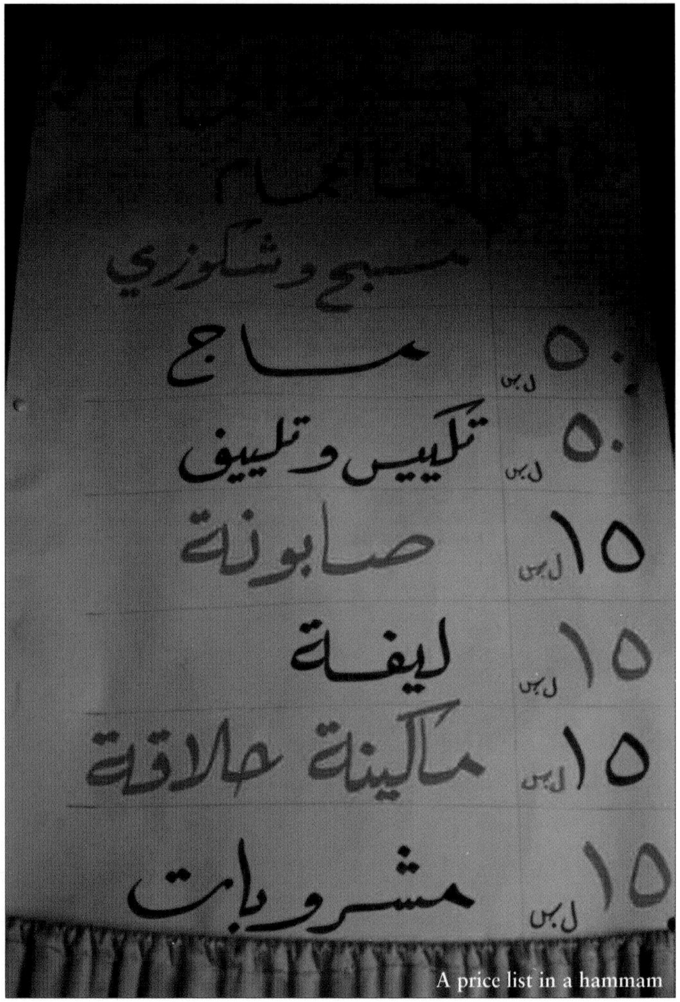

A price list in a hammam

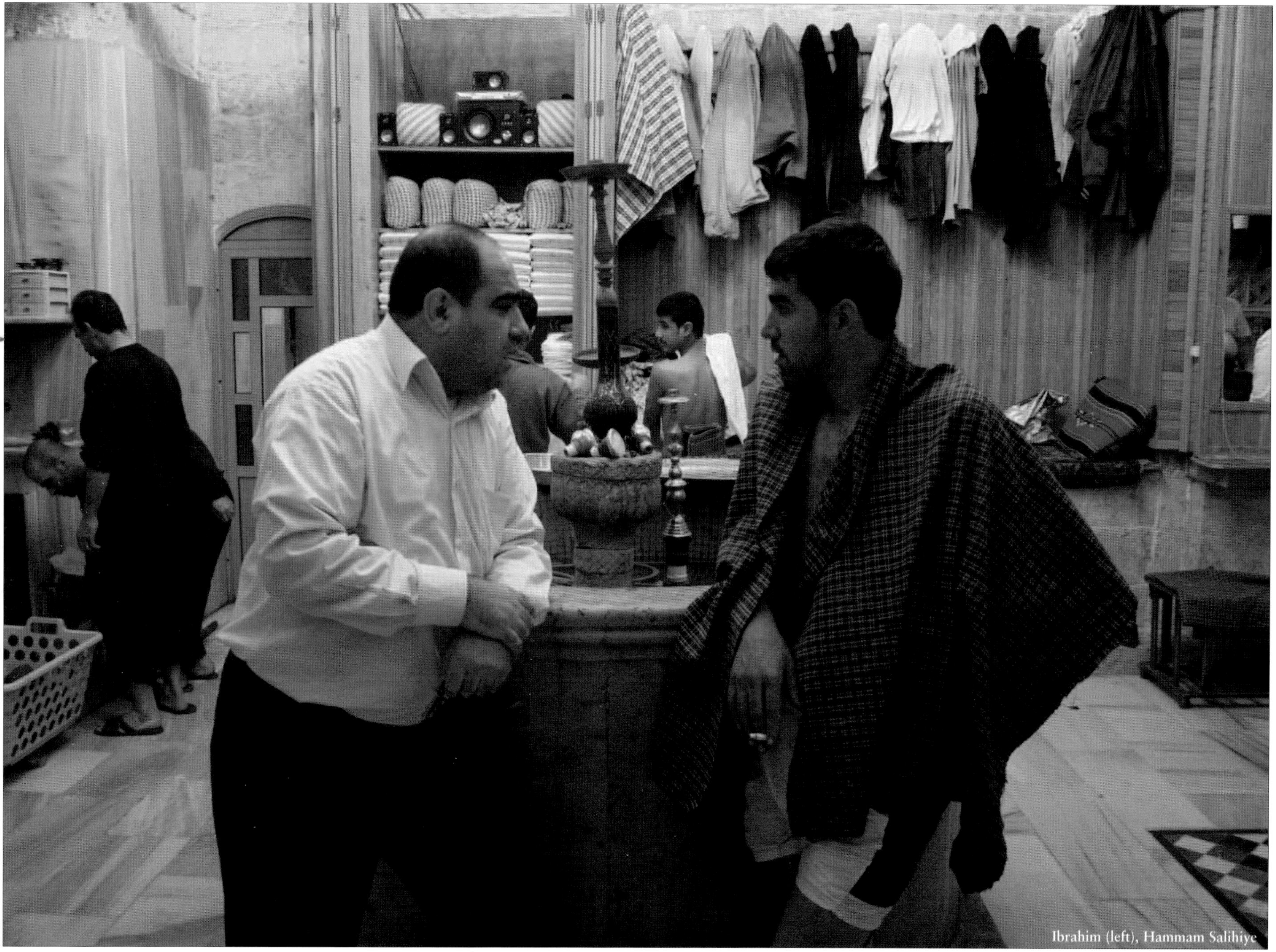
Ibrahim (left), Hammam Salihiye

Ibrahim's next project would be Hammam al-Atiqa. This would be the first hammam with contemporary sofas in the *barrani,* and a coffee bar for serving up drinks. Fortunately, given the traditions of this hammam and popular tastes, plastic plants will also grace the foyer.

One or two individuals in Aleppo have had a huge impact on hammams: doing them up in an appealing way, attracting custom, turning them into going concerns. But the pearl in the crown, the cathedral of hammams under the control of the authorities, the Yalbougha Hammam beneath the citadel, remains closed. *Haram*!

Revival

It is not just the hammams; it is Syria itself. In the heart of Damascus, Suq Midhat Basha once choked with fumes as drivers moved at a snail's pace through the old city. Now it has been tastefully done up, cars have been barred, and the shop fronts stylishly tone in with one another, so that you can walk through the Arab World's City of Culture along a carefully restored Straight Street, but still purchase some dubious herbal cure from the apothecary with lizards and starfish hanging in his booth.

At night the old city buzzes, as Damascenes go down town and savour the heart of the city that they had only recently abandoned, viewing the minarets of the Umayyad Mosque as they dine on garrulous rooftops. Bab Tuma fills with the young and beautiful, stylishly clad, making for the bars and night clubs. In summer, the citadel, once a prison, now rocks to African bands and the audience can quench their thirst with Coca-Cola (how we are blessed!) or nip across to the newly-planted, jasmine-scented gardens by the river.

Who could fault it? Pedestrians now stroll where drivers once inched forward. Ottoman houses that had been condemned to decay fill with the laughter of diners. And it is not just Damascus; you can take the new train up to Aleppo, and find whole neighbourhoods rejuvenated, with cobbled ways leading to restored gateways and immaculate Ottoman courtyards. Beneath the citadel tourists and locals sit beneath the sun umbrellas of the cafés, newly planted palms gracing the entrance to the mosque below its walls. And in Hama builders are again at work near the ruins of the Great Mosque, rebuilding parts of the old city stone by stone, the nearby

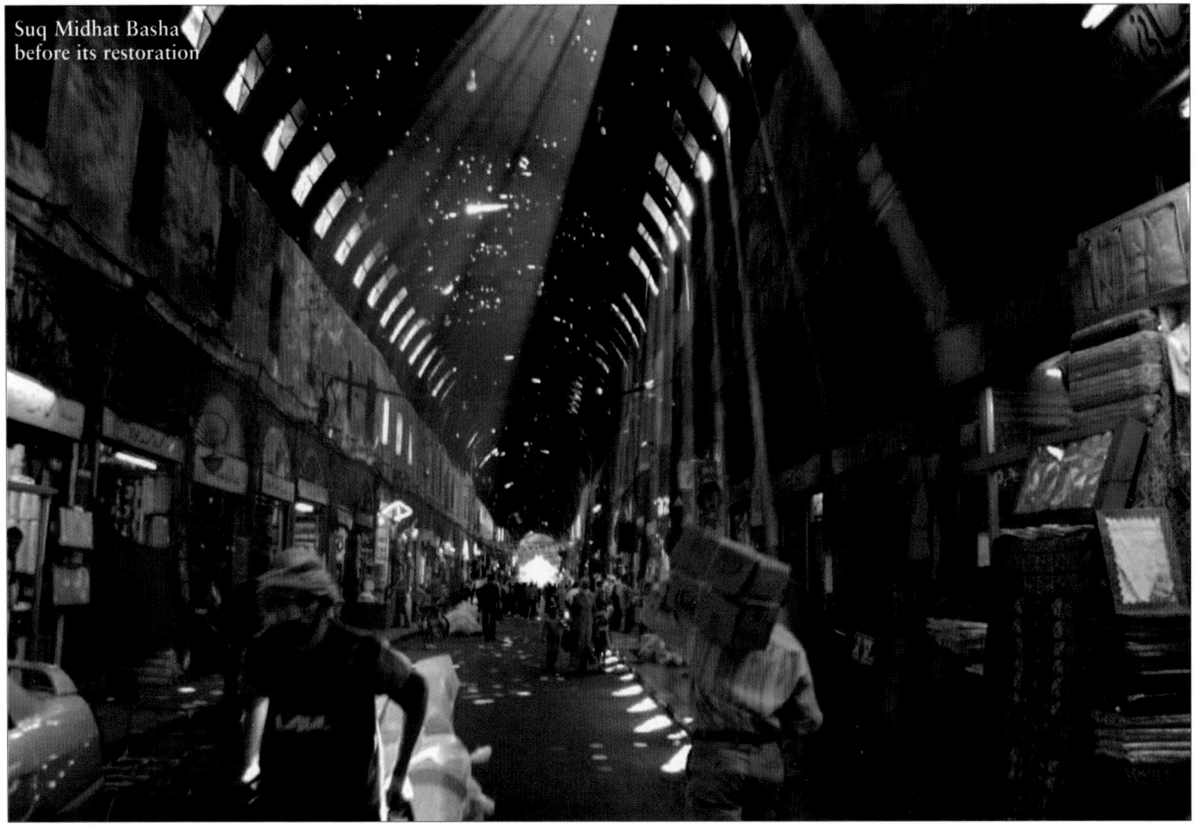

Suq Midhat Basha before its restoration

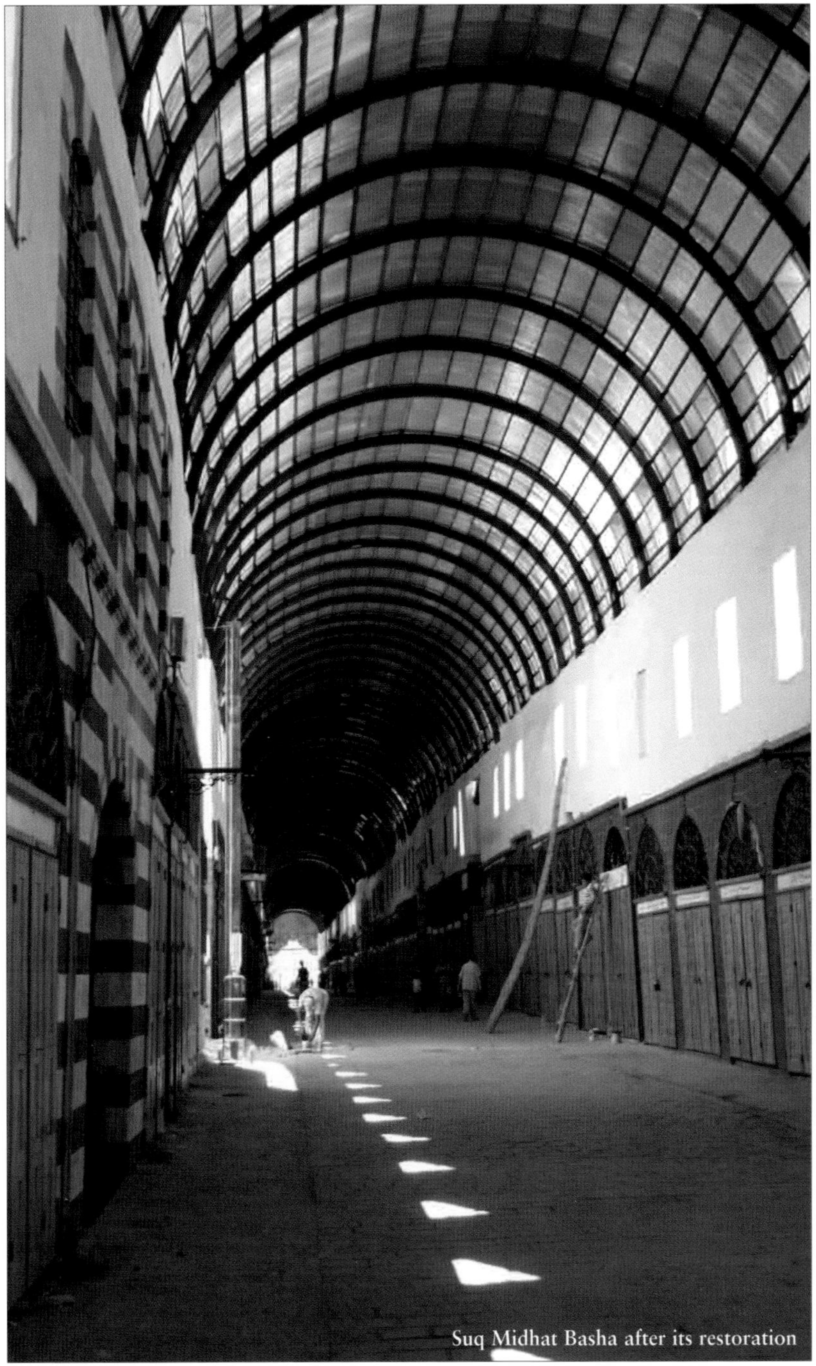
Suq Midhat Basha after its restoration

hammam awaiting its re-opening. Also, by the Orontes, workmen shovel cement and sand within Hammam al Sultan – due to open soon – and near the numbered stones of the old prison, the intimate Hammam Obeisi already delights.

Who could regret such change, such recovery? And yet it would be sad if that natural courtesy of Syrians should become just a commodity for tourism, and the baths merely a destination for tour groups, as in Istanbul. There is a danger too that it might all become too sanitised, although some hammams could most definitely do with more attention to hygiene. It might all become too twee (that antique telephone set by the *mi'allim's* desk for example), as if the UK's National Trust were to take over the hammams of Syria. Will the hammams become accessible only to people like myself: middle-aged, middle-class, and with hints of middle-aged spread?

What is the future of the hammams if they are to undergo a mere gentrification? I

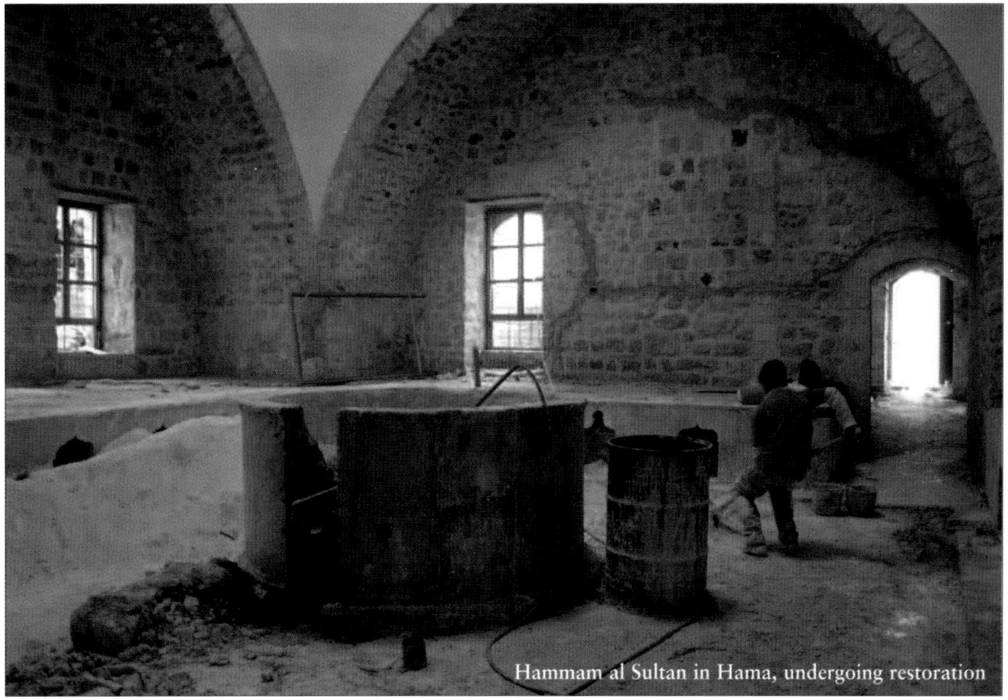
Hammam al Sultan in Hama, undergoing restoration

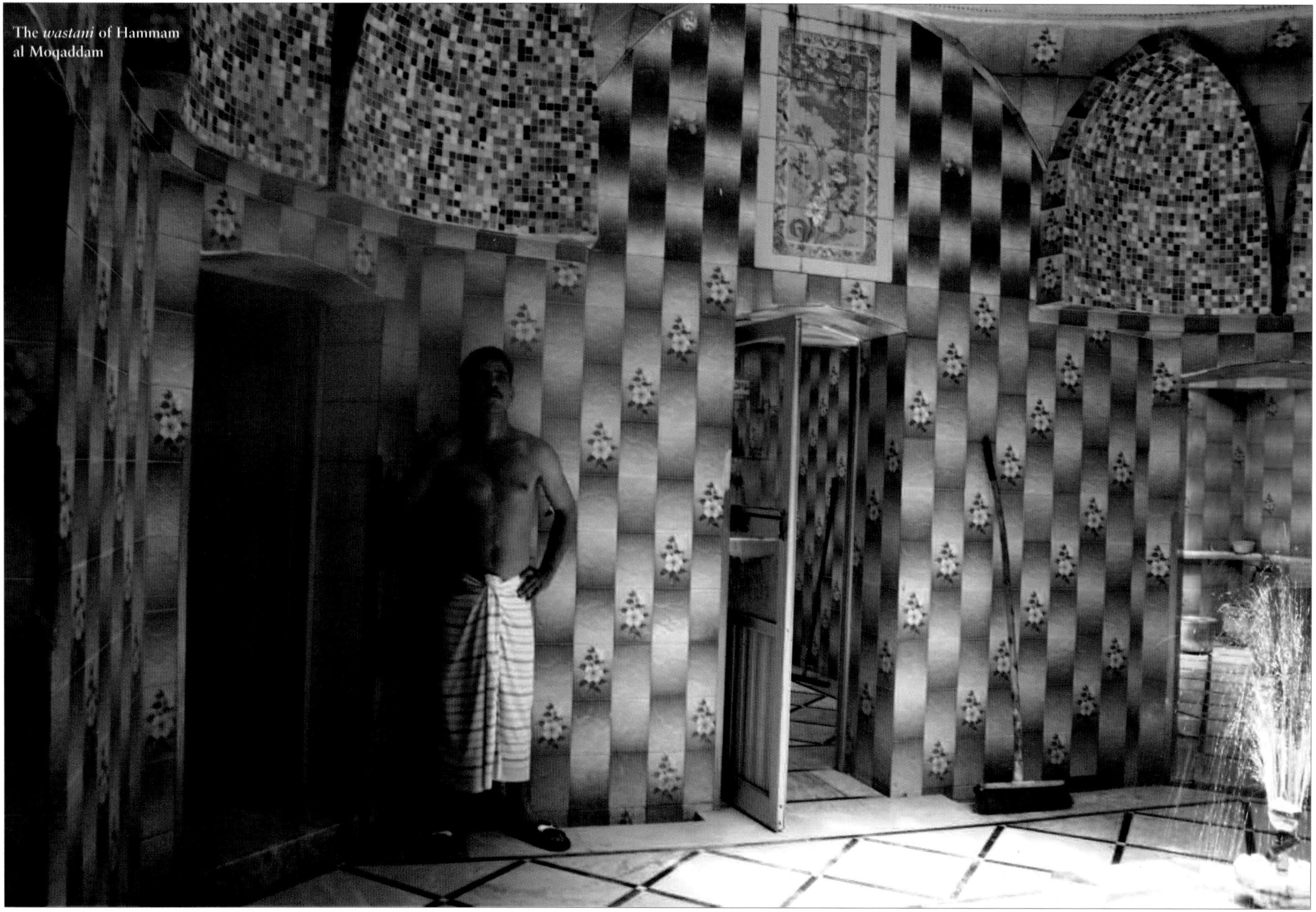

The *wastani* of Hammam al Moqaddam

heard one manager express fears about the impact of narrow lanes on business; where will customers park their four-wheel-drives? It's churlish to fault it – this immaculate restoration, this renaissance – but something in me longs for the old corrugated iron roof of the *suq*, with light spilling on to the rope-makers and belt-makers and sellers of sheep skins, the intense sunlight of summer streaming through rusty holes on to all that vibrant neglect...

I hope to revisit Damascus some day soon, when the heat of summer has eased, and make Hammam al-Moqaddam my first port of call. Hopefully I'll still find its eclectic décor and the history of centuries still veiled, at least for a while longer, by 1970s bathroom tiles.

NOTE

1 Qabbani, Nezar, 'Damascus, What Are You Doing to Me?', translated from the Arabic by Shareah Taleghani.

Epilogue

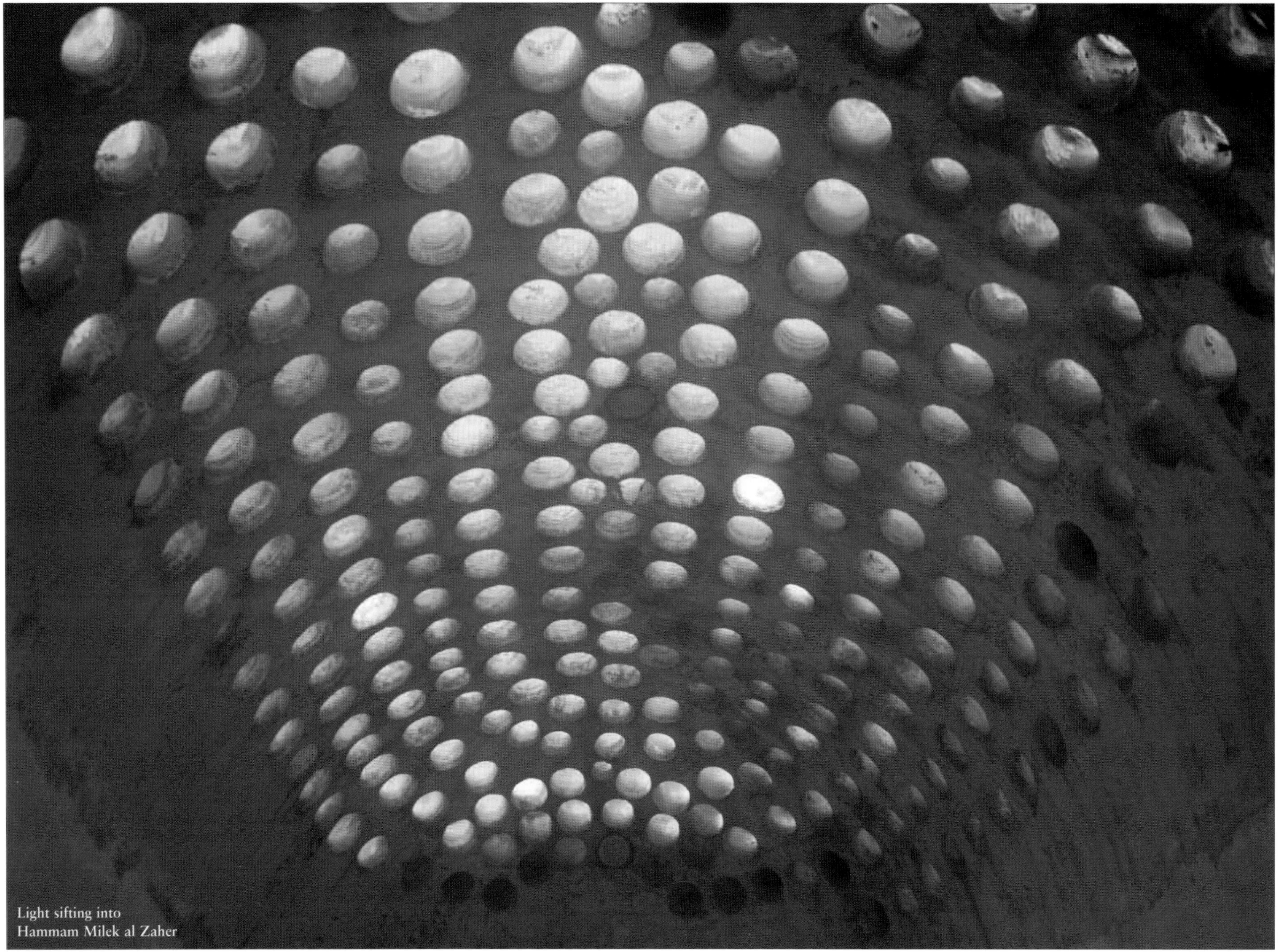

Light sifting into
Hammam Milek al Zaher

I am standing among the ranks of the faithful, in an assembled line beneath the dome, being harangued by the 'imam' for my misdeeds. I know the tones well – not just from the sermon at Friday prayers magnified throughout the neighbourhood, but from growing up in the north of Ireland. The language is different, the religion is different, but the preacher's intonation is essentially the same.

The pulpit is not the delicately carved *minbar* of Aleppo's Umayyad Mosque, ebony inlaid with ivory, but a stone cube on a plain floor beside a font. And the 'imam' is not dressed in splendid robes, but stands half-naked in his *futa*. I am not in a place of worship but in a hammam, one of a congregation of bathers.

Suddenly the 'imam' stops his harangue, and laughs as he raises his arms in supplication, breaking into a traditional song, probably one of Aleppo's own. The city's most famous singer, Sabah Fakhri, went from religious instruction to become a singer of love songs in the Andalusian style, for the expelled Muslims of Spain brought their music back to the Arab world. But just as some Arab singers have gone from the reciting of the Qur'an to the love song, so many a mystic has expressed divine love – or is it love for the divine? – in a song of love.

I have chanced on a work party having their night out in a hammam. I am a stranger to these bathers but they invite me, the foreigner in their midst, to join them for supper.

The floor of the *wastani* has been spread with a plastic cloth as if for a picnic, but we are under the dome of the hammam, not the overarching sky. Nearly twenty men are seated on the floor around dishes of typically Aleppan food. They insist that I join them.

Now I tactlessly decline the *kibbeh neah* (raw meat is a Syrian delicacy) that has been dipped into bread, flat unleavened bread, and offered to my lips. Instead I go for the cooked *kibbeh* with pistachio nuts.

And so I sit among bathers, partaking of the communal meal on the hammam floor.

Index

A
Abdul Hamid (Ottoman Sultan) 128
Aisha (wife of the Prophet) 21
Alawi(s) 26, 30, 68, 99, 109
Alexandria 15
Andalusia 20, 49, 110, 116, 125, 126, 175
Ansariye Mountains 6, 106
Anti-Lebanon mountain range 4, 58, 129
Antioch 8, 31, 56, 129, 131
Antony, Mark 6, 11, 28
Aphamea 6, 7, 8
Arab conquest 15, 58
'Arabi, Mohi al-din Ibn al- 21, 23, 49, 70, 72, 110, 111, 136, 151
Arabian Nights 105, 106, 109
arak 2, 99, 105, 120, 129, 133
Assassins 27, 30
Aybak, Izz al-Din 42, 66
Azarak (in Jordan) 23
Azem Palace (Damascus) 41, 69, 78
Azem Palace (Hama) 69, 75, 77
Azemi, Basheer al- 41, 60

B
Bab al-Faradis 156
Bab al-Faraj 116, 118
Bab al-Hadid 134
Bab al Hara 44
Bab al-Maqam 139
Bab Antakia 34, 128
Bab Tuma 66, 77, 104, 168
Badieh 80, 125
Baghdad 25, 86, 92, 119
Baibars, al-Malik al-Zaher (Mamluk sultan) 31
Barada River 4, 16, 17, 55
Basra 22
Beirut 11, 82, 99, 104
Beit al Deen 58
Bell, Gertrude 16, 25, 37, 40, 60, 75, 77, 109, 114, 119, 164
Bilquis 16
Bosra 9–11
Brue, Alexia 9, 10, 11
Burckhardt, John Lewis 10, 60
Burns, Ross 12, 36, 60, 72, 74, 114
Burton, Richard 84, 88, 104
Byron, Robert 152, 154

C
Cairo 10, 22, 26, 42, 56, 58, 59, 61
Calasseh 56, 142
Chastel Blanc 28
Christ (see also Jesus) 6, 24, 28
Church of Saint John, Damascus 15, 16
Citadel, Aleppo 10, 32, 33, 34, 64, 80, 81, 96, 116, 117, 119, 120, 122, 125, 130, 132, 140, 142, 145, 146, 147, 148, 150, 168
Cleopatra 6, 11
clogs 5, 42, 48, 80, 101, 160
Constantinople (see also Istanbul) 52, 119, 152
Coppersmiths' Khan, Aleppo 11
Coppersmiths' Suq, Aleppo 33
Crusaders 4, 27, 28, 50, 66
Cupping (see *Hijama*)

D
Dalrymple, William 1, 2, 103
Dante 78, 81
Dera'a 9, 99
Derazor 24, 50, 90
derwish, derawish 59, 125, 129
dhibki 34
Dinning, Captain 37, 38, 60, 81, 82, 90, 114
Druze 11, 58, 99

E
Ecochard, Michel 52
Egypt 11, 15, 18, 20, 21, 22, 42, 47, 56, 59, 60, 87, 88, 101, 103, 143

F
Faisal, Prince 21
Farhi, Moris 152, 154
Fathi, al-Daftari 41, 42
Fiji (spring) 17, 94
Flaubert, Gustave 101, 103
futa 22, 70, 80, 92, 95, 103, 120, 125, 128, 131, 175

G
Genet, Jean 47

H
hadith 129
Hadjar, Abdalla 52, 55, 60, 61, 114, 134, 154
Hagia Sophia, Constantinople 152
Hajj 10, 16, 21, 44, 49, 69, 125, 128
Hama 8, 37–39, 69, 75, 77, 84, 85, 104, 168, 169
Hamam (film) 28
Hammam
  Asakakri 17
  Amjak 54
  Ammoune 106, 107, 156, 157, 158
  al-Assadia 84, 85
  al-Atiqa 83, 85, 142, 168
  al Bai'ada 134, 138
  al-Gadi (Aleppo) 139, 140
  al-Gadi (Damascus) 52, 53, 139
  al-Hayateen (Tailors' Hammam) 18, 87
  al-Jadeed (Damascus) 80
  al-Jadid (Tripoli) 69, 70, 76, 77, 152
  al-Jawhari 55
  al-Joseh 42, 48
  al-Malik al-Zaher 5, 22, 77, 87, 88, 102, 103, 156, 160, 161
  al-Mileh 55
  al-Moqaddam 70–74, *83*, 84, 101, 110, 171
  al-Muna 56, *57*

al Naem 15, 91, 120, 122
al-Nahasin 73, 95, 96, 122, 123, 130, 144, 145, 146, 147
al-Obeisi 37, 38
al Saroujeh 54
al Saugheer 57
al-Sukariya (Cairo) 56
al-Sultan, Aleppo 132
al-Sultan, Damascus 53
al-Sultan, Hama 169
al-Umari 53, 159
al-Werd 31, 42–44, 46, 47, 49
al-Zain 64, 66–67
Bab al-Ahmer 80
Bahram Basha 39–40
Bakri 22, 66
Balaban 134–137
Bizdar 136–137
Bizeh 146, 148–150
Cundi (Antioch) 31
Ezzeddin (Damascus) 73, 74, 92, 93, 94
Ezzedeen (Tripoli) 66, 67
Fathi 41, 42, 48, 94
Granada 70, 73, 84, 122, 125–128, 143
Hananu 120–125
Manjak (Bosra) 10
Miliki (Aleppo) 128, 129
Miliki (Damascus) 41
Mustafa Basha 150
Nur al-Din 78, 79, 80, 81, 82, 90, 99, 101, 109, 142
Nuri (Tripoli) 68, 69
Othmania (Hama) 77
Othmania (Homs) 12–14
Qaramaneh 50, 51
Rufai 48, 78, 110, 111
Saddat 127, 128, 144
Salihiye 138, 139, 160, 166, 167
Sheikh Asslan 73, 77, 87, 89
Silsileh 5, 25, 26, 31, 95, 96
Sultan Ibrahim 106, 139, 142
Tawrizi 35, 37, 56, 160, 163–165
Yalbougha 32, 64, 81, 96, 98, 122, 127, 146, 148, 168
Hammam at al-Kahf Castle 30
Hammam in Azem Palace, Damascus 41
Hammam in Beit al Deen, Lebanon 58
Hammam in Beit Ghazaleh, Aleppo 58
Hammam in Saladeen's Castle 30
Hammam on Irwad Island 59, 144
Harvey, Lord 40
Hijama 145
Homs 8, 12,14, 16, 37, 126
Hussein, son of Ali 18, 20

I
Ibn Assakir 52
Ibn Battuta 15, 16, 21, 22, 30, 35, 38, 47, 52, 60
Ibrahim (Prophet) 56, 119
Iraq 22, 31, 84, 114, 162
Irwad Island 59, 144
Irwin, Robert 60, 101, 114, 154
Islam 6, 15, 21, 25, 37, 40, 60, 69, 80, 82, 101, 111, 114, 121, 140
Israel (see Palestine)
Istanbul 28, 34, 35, 42, 111, 129, 148, 154, 169

J
Jerusalem 16, 20, 21, 27
jinn 49, 96, 98, 99, 101, 131, 133
Jobar 18
John the Baptist, shrine of 18, 20
Jordan 10, 11, 84, 101

K
Kahf, Castle of al-Kahf 30
kaif 88
Kayall, M. 17, 25, 41, 42, 48, 53, 60
Kabbane, Nezar 155, 171
Khider, al- 120
kibbeh 49, 78, 175
Kociejowski, Marius 15, 56, 60, 61, 114, 154
Krak des Chevaliers 28, 29
Kuchuk Hanem 103

L
Lane, Edward 22, 60, 114
Lattakia 28, 45, 46, 99, 109, 111, 139
Lawrence, T. E. 9, 20, 24, 28, 30, 37, 103, 116, 164
Lebanon 5, 24, 31, 58, 60, 66, 69, 84, 106

M
Ma'aari, Abu al-Ala 50
Maarrat al-Numan 28
Madrassah 20, 139
Maristan 55
Marqab Castle 28
Mashrabīyah 58
massage 70, 87–88
masseur 72, 87, 88, 160
Massiaf Castle 27
Mejedderah 122
Meunier, Pascal 59, 61
Mohammed, Prophet 141 (see also Prophet, the)
muezzin 40
muqarnas 20

N
Nasimi, Imadaddin 151
nudity 21, 24, 28, 92

O
Occidentalism 104, 105
Omar (Caliph) 10, 15, 16
Orga, Irfan 94, 114, 122, 154
Orientalism 30, 74, 101, 104, 105
Orontes, River 6, 31, 37, 56, 169

P
Palestine 27, 118
Palmyra 8, 90
Paul, Saint 18
Petra 10, 84
pilgrimage 44, 110, 119, 125, 150
Pope, Alexander 40, 41
Prophet, the (see also Mohammed, Prophet) 18, 21, 25, 74, 82, 116, 129, 145

Q
Qadir, 'Abd al- 21
Qasr al Umra 23, 24
Qassioun, Mount 4, 21, 70, 72, 116

R
Russells, Alexander and Patrick 11, 13, 39, 60, 82, 87

S
Said, Edward 101
Saladeen's Castle 28, 30, 46
Salem the First 110, 111
Salih, al- (son of Nur al-Din) 44
Samarkand 36
Sanawbari, al- 129
Saruja 27, 31, 42, 44, 47, 53
Sauvaget, John 17, 52, 55, 60
Sayf al-Daula 148
sebil 33, 41, 70, 160
Selamiyah 9
Serjilla 8, 9
Shajarat al-Durr, Queen 42
Shayzar Castle 6, 28
Simeon, Church of Saint Simeon 131
Simeon the Stylite 119
Sinan (architect) 23, 35, 110
Sinan (Ottoman ruler) 49
Socotra 54
Solomon 16
South Baths, Bosra 9, 10, 11
Stanhope, Lady Hester 30
Sufi 21, 103, 106, 109, 110, 125, 128, 160
Sultan Ibrahim 109, 139
Suq Ahmet Pasha 52
Suq al Hamidiye 74, 86
Suq al tibbin 50
Suq Sinaniye 50
Swift, Jonathan 50
Swimmer, The 2
Synagogue (Jobar) 18

T
Tamerlane 96, 126, 148
Tareq bin Zead 30
Tekkiye Mosque 23
Telmissany, May 56, 61
Thubron, Colin 21, 48, 60, 148
Tripoli (Lebanon) 31, 66, 67, 69, 70, 76, 77, 84, 98, 113, 136, 162, 163

U
Umayyad Mosque, Aleppo 148, 175
Umayyad Mosque, Damascus 4, 8, 6, 15, 16, 18, 19, 20, 21, 24, 25, 27, 33, 40, 42
Umm Quais (Jordan) 11, 12
Usama ibn Munqidh 28

V
Virgin Mary 5, 28

W
wakf 35, 39, 142
Waleed, Khalid Ibn al- 16, 17
Wilde, Oscar 101, 141

Y
Young, Gavin 86, 90, 92, 114

Z
Zechariah 148
Zenobia 8, 90